Frontispiece. The F-105 Thunderchief, better known as the Thud, carried the brunt of the air war in its first years. The F-105D in the foreground (59-1769) in this previously unpublished view wears the natural finish which was quickly replaced by camouflage, as on the Thud in background. (JIM HESTON)

AIR WAR HANOI

Robert F. Dorr

BLANDFORD PRESS
LONDON · NEW YORK · SYDNEY

For Charlie

First published in the UK 1988 by Blandford Press, an imprint of Cassell Publishers Limited, Artillery House, Artillery Row, London SW1P 1RT

Copyright © 1988 Robert F. Dorr

Distributed in the United States by Sterling Publishing Co, Inc, 2 Park Avenue, New York, NY 10016

Distributed in Australia by Capricorn Link (Australia) Pty Ltd, PO Box 665, Lane Cove, NSW 2066

British Library Cataloguing in Publication Data

Dorr, Robert F
 Air war-Hanoi. — (in action)
 1. Vietnamese Conflict, 1961-75 — Aerial
 operations
 I. Title   II. Series
 959.704′348   DS558.8

ISBN 0 7137 1783 1

Typeset by Asco Trade Typesetting Ltd., Hong Kong
Printed in Great Britain by R. J. Acford, Chichester

CONTENTS

ACKNOWLEDGEMENTS

This volume contains thousands of facts. Errors are the sole responsibility of the author. But this history would have been impossible without generous help from many.

This book is dedicated to Captain Charles Blankenship, who did not return from the first Arc Light mission, all honor to his name. I am indebted to editor Michael Burns who believed in this project and who helped to make it possible. Assistance was also received from the Department of State, the United States armed forces, and numerous people who were there.

I especially want to thank Hal Andrews, Robert J. Archer, Paul Auerswald, Colonel Jack Broughton, Robert L. Burns, Philip D. Chinnery, Paul Crickmore, Young Soon Dorr, Lou Drendel, Michael A. France, James W. Freidhoff, Brigadier General Gordon A. Ginsburg, Lieutenant General Gordon M. Graham, Bill Gunston, Colonel Edward Hillding, Marty Isham, Martin Judge, M. J. Kasiuba, Robert L. Lawson, Don Linn, Sam McGowan, David W. Menard, Major General Thomas G. McInerney, Robert C. Mikesh, MSgt James Muelchi, Mike O'Connor, Lindsay Peacock, Jerry Scutts, MSgt Allen K. Stanek, Jim Sullivan, Norman Taylor, 'Deep Throat', Brigadier General Robert F. Titus, Major Joe Viviano, Commander Howard Wheeler, and Nick Williams.

The views expressed in this book are mine and do not necessarily reflect those of the Department of State or of the United States Air Force.

Robert F. Dorr
London, April 1986

PRINCIPAL US OPERATIONS AGAINST NORTH VIETNAM

Gulf of Tonkin	5 August 1964	Son Tay Raid	20 November 1970	FREEDOM TRAIN	6 April 1972– 7 May 1972
FLAMING DART	7 February 1965	LOUISVILLE SLUGGER	February 1971		
FLAMING DART II	11 February 1965	FRACTURE CROSS ALPHA	21–22 March 1971	LINEBACKER	8 May 1972– 23 October 1972
ROLLING THUNDER	2 March 1965– 31 October 1968	PROUD DEEP ALPHA	26–30 December 1971	LINEBACKER II	18–29 December 1972

GLOSSARY

A/A	air-to-air (missiles)
AAA	anti-aircraft artillery
AEW	airborne early warning
ASW	anti-submarine warfare
AWACS	airborne warning and control system
Bear	Nickname for electronic warfare officer (EWO) or back-seat crew member in F–100F, F–105F, F–105G and F–4C Wild Weasel aircraft
BOQ	bachelor officers' quarters
CDIG	Civilian Defense Irregular Guard (South Vietnamese)
CINPAC	Commander in Chief, Pacific Forces
D/F	(radio) direction finding
EWO	electronic warfare officer; see "Bear", above
FLIR	forward-looking infra-red
IFF	identification, friend or foe (sensor)
IO	illuminator operator (in AC–130 Hercules gunship)
IPIR	acronym for timely intelligence report (resulting from reconnaissance flight)
IR	infra-red
JCS	Joint Chiefs of Staff
LRRP	Long-range reconnaissance patrol(s); also 'Lurp'
MiGCAP	MiG combat air patrol
MTI	moving target indicator
NOD	night observation device
NVA	North Vietnamese army, i.e. North Vietnamese regular forces as distinguished from Viet Cong
PACAF	(US Air Force) Pacific Air Forces
POL	petroleum oil lubricant
POW	prisoner of war
recce	reconnaissance
Rescap	Rescue combat air patrol, sometimes used simply to refer to a combat rescue mission
RHAWS	radar homing and warning system
SAR	search and rescue
SARH	semi-active radar homing (missile, such as Sparrow)
TAS	Tactical Airlift Squadron
TAW	Tactical Airlift Wing
TCS	Troop Carrier Squadron (replaced by TAS)
TDY	temporary duty
TFS	Tactical Fighter Squadron
TFW	Tactical Fighter Wing
UHF	ultra high frequency (radio)
USAF	United States Air Force

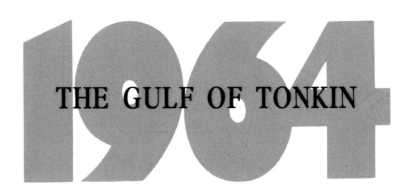

THE GULF OF TONKIN

The war in Vietnam, as Americans usually refer to it, was in fact several wars. In Laos, a three-way civil struggle between rightists, neutralists and the Pathet Lao could not escape American involvement. In South Vietnam, an insurgency by indigenous Viet Cong forces was supported and later dominated by North Vietnam. After 1970, American forces carried out an aerial campaign against the Khmer Rouge in Cambodia. Finally, the United States fought an air war against North Vietnam, which included operations against the infiltration system known as the Ho Chi Minh Trail. The narrative which follows is an attempt to isolate this final conflict—the American air war against North Vietnam—and to describe it in the order it happened. Any history is selective and this history purposely confines itself to American air operations against North Vietnam from 2 August 1964 to 27 January 1973. The tale is told from the US vantage point because an accurate version of Hanoi's side of events remains unavailable.

Long before the first air strikes 'up North', the US had committed itself irreversibly to the Southeast Asia conflict. Even before the inauguration of President John F. Kennedy on 20 January 1961, Americans were involved in opposing the Kong Le and Pathet Lao forces in Laos and in supporting the South Vietnamese regime in Saigon. On 11 December 1961, a batch of US Army CH–21C helicopters became the first American aircraft operational in South Vietnam. C–123B aircraft used for chemical defoliation followed under a program called Ranch Hand, as did T–28D Trojan and B–26 Invader combat aircraft in the Farm Gate program. In fact, a B–26B Invader (44-35703) was shot down on 24 November 1963 which, on the Asian side of the international dateline, was only hours after Kennedy's assassination. Already, there was intense discussion in Washington and Saigon to the effect that the insurgency in South Vietnam could be halted only by conducting air strikes against North Vietnam. The year 1964 arrived with the discussion heating up. It was a time when most Americans were possessed of an almost incredible

innocence. Men in uniform, especially those whose numbers in Vietnam had risen from a few hundred to 5,000 by 1964, were better informed than many and may have seen the prospect of attacking North Vietnam with a degree of realism. But in 1964 even they were possessed of an innocence which brought, with it, a certain charm. None realized what they were getting into.

THE INNOCENTS
In 1964, Americans were still moved by the slain Kennedy's vow to 'pay any price, bear any burden' to defend liberty abroad—which included defending South Vietnam. In 1964, Americans respected their armed forces and trusted their leaders with an easy confidence which the coming war would shatter forever. The draft had been an accepted part of American life since 1940; almost every family sent its young men into uniform and, almost always, the sight of a uniform evoked pride. It was possible to achieve box-office success with a film like *A Gathering of Eagles*, in which all-American boy Rock Hudson wanted nothing more than to build the best B–52 wing in the Air Force. Americans were brave, noble, clean; against foreign aggressors, they would easily prevail. Most of these perceptions would soon be swallowed up in Southeast Asia but, from beginning to end, one basic American principle never wavered: Military men followed orders given by civilian leaders. The warrior's job was to do as the policymaker decided. The military officer accepted with his commission the obligation to take orders from the elected official. Men in high-performance aircraft would be asked to attack targets in North Vietnam, against formidable defenses, often hamstrung by restrictive rules of engagement and by bewildering constraints on which targets could be hit and which could not. Over time, trust and confidence would be eroded, pride in uniform would be endangered, the notion that liberty was being defended would be subjected to serious question and eventually even the draft would become history. But day after day, mission after mission, military men

would continue to fight for goals established not by themselves but by civilians.

Near the beginning of an election campaign where many American voters believed that only his opponent favored it, President Lyndon Johnson tasked the Joint Chiefs of Staff (JCS) with preparing a plan to blunt North Vietnam's infiltration into the south with a bombing campaign. The proposal, approved by the JCS on 17 April 1964, listed 94 of the most important targets in North Vietnam. These included marshalling yards, port facilities, truck parks, petroleum oil lubricant (POL) storage centers and major bridge spans, including the Thanh Hoa Bridge which was nicknamed the 'Dragon's Jaw' and the Paul Doumer Rail and Highway Bridge near Hanoi. The plan was apparently shelved for a time but the notion of employing airpower against the North Vietnamese heartland remained very much in public and private minds.

RF–101Cs IN COMBAT
Though no US aircraft were yet officially flying in combat, the 'Able Mabel' commitment to carry out reconnaissance missions over South Vietnam and Laos had resulted in six McDonnell RF–101C Voodoos being detached to Saigon's Tan Son Nhut Airport. The Voodoos were maintaining a rigorous flight schedule of up to 35 hours a month, a heavy strain for the men of the 45th Tactical Reconnaissance Squadron, placed temporarily under the USAF's headquarters in Saigon, the 2nd Air Division. On 30 April 1964, this hard-pressed reconnaissance force was increased to ten RF–101Cs. Though North Vietnam was 'off limits' for the Voodoos, part of their mission was to acquire photography of infiltration routes from North Vietnam. They shared this job with US Navy RF–8A Crusaders, one of which was shot down over Laos on 6 June. The subsequent loss of another Crusader acting as armed escort for a Laotian reconnaissance flight led on 8 June to a retaliatory strike by eight USAF F–100

Super Sabres against anti-aircraft sites at Xien Khouang, Laos. Crusader and Voodoo reconnaissance pilots were now seeing large numbers of truck convoys moving down the Ho Chi Minh Trail—evidence of a massive increase in North Vietnamese support for the Viet Cong forces in the south.

KC–135 ARRIVAL

With American airpower becoming more deeply involved in Southeast Asia and the possibility of bombing North Vietnam being actively debated, it was apparent that a combat air refuelling capability would be needed. A few, little-publicized refuellings had occurred during the 1950–53 Korean War but in the 1964–73 struggle against North Vietnam, the KC–135 Stratotanker, fuel-carrying cousin of the Boeing 707, would become an ubiquitous and routine sight. On 7 June 1964, the Pentagon's Joint Chiefs of Staff (JCS) ordered the Strategic Air Command (SAC) to move six KC–135s from Andersen AB, Guam, to Clark AB, Philippines, to refuel F–100D strike aircraft operating in Laos. SAC retained control over its tankers throughout the conflict, never surrendering jurisdiction to the 2nd Air Division (later Seventh Air Force) in Saigon.

The KC–135s flew their first combat refuelling mission over southern Laos on 9 June 1964 as part of the Yankee Team Tank-er Task Force, the name being derived from reconnaissance operations then being conducted over Laos. Later, the KC–135 force would be known as Young Tiger and SAC's 4252nd Strategic Wing under Brigadier General Morgan S. Tyler, Jr would despatch 15 tankers to operate from Thailand's Don Muang airfield, which was also the Bangkok international airport. General Tyler was a hard-driving taskmaster who believed that in-flight refuelling could be effective in actual combat operations and who seemed to have clairvoyant knowledge that just such operations would be mounted from Thailand against the North Vietnamese homeland. What he could not know was that over 1964–73, SAC KC–135s would fly 194,687 combat sorties and achieve no fewer than 813,878 individual mid-air refuellings.

ATTACK ON MADDOX

The proximate cause of the air war against North Vietnam was the 'Gulf of Tonkin incident,' the 2 August 1964 attack by North Vietnamese P–4 torpedo boats against the destroyer USS *Maddox* (DD–731). Overlooked at the time was the fact that *Maddox*, although in international waters, was carrying out a 'Desoto Patrol' gathering communications intelligence from Hanoi's military radio nets. The torpedo boats are widely understood to have returned on the night of 4 August when *Maddox* was accompanied by USS *Turner Joy* (DD–951) and a furious sea battle raged for hours. Commander James B. Stockdale, skipper of the 'Screaming Eagles' of fighter squadron VF–51 aboard the carrier USS *Ticonderoga* (CVA–14) was overhead in an F–8E Crusader during the second incident. Stockdale's efforts to acquire a radar vector on the torpedo boats were in vain. The messages he received from the destroyers were frantic and confusing. Stockdale is certain that, on the second occasion, the North Vietnamese boats were a figment of the Americans' imagination. He followed voice instructions from the destroyers, only to find the sea empty where the boats were supposed to be. Nor was there any damage to the destroyers to confirm their attackers' existence. Still, *Ticonderoga* Crusaders plus one A–4 Skyhawk remained overhead until relieved by more Skyhawks from USS *Constellation* (CVA–64) near midnight. At the time, two torpedo boats, the same boats found non-existent by Stockdale, were reported sunk.

It was scarcely noticed that the American destroyers had been on an intelligence-gathering mission perceived by Hanoi as provocative. It mattered very little that only the first of the two torpedo boat attacks was real. The North Vietnamese attack on the destroyers enabled President Johnson to secure

Above: Taken from the American destroyer, this photograph shows one of three North Vietnamese P–4 patrol boats which attacked USS *Maddox* on 2 August 1964, leading to the retaliatory Gulf of Tonkin air strikes three days later. (USN)

Below: The 'Screaming Eagles' of fighter squadron VF–51, flying the F–8E Crusader, were in the Southeast Asia conflict from the beginning, with Commander James B. Stockdale flying an aircraft like that in the foreground (147916) on the Gulf of Tonkin air strikes. NF–102 carried an AIM–9B Sidewinder air-to-air missile above the national insignia on the forward fuselage. (USN VIA PETER B. MERSKY)

Above: First man to fly a combat mission over North Vietnam, Commander James B. Stockdale was skipper of F–8E Crusader squadron VF–51 aboard USS *Ticonderoga* (CVA–14) when the Gulf of Tonkin air strikes were flown on 5 August 1964. More than a decade later, Vice Admiral Stockdale receives from President Ford the Medal of Honor for his conduct as a prisoner of war (POW). (USN)

The US went to war in Southeast Asia with A–26s, T–28s and other propeller-driven warplanes which quickly proved unsuitable against the formidable defenses of North Vietnam. One aircraft which made the grade 'up North' was the Douglas A–1 Skyraider, one of which was lost during the 5 August 1964 Gulf of Tonkin raids. A–1H 139609 of attack squadron VA–176 from USS *Intrepid* (CVS–11) on a combat mission early in the conflict. (USN)

Ensign Everett Alvarez (right) had a future in naval aviation when he received his wings at Kingsville, Texas. Shot down in an A–4 Skyhawk during the 5 August 1964 Gulf of Tonkin air strikes, Alvarez became the first American prisoner of war held in North Vietnam. He remained a POW until March 1973. (USN)

Congress's 7 August passage of the Gulf of Tonkin resolution—a rubber stamp of his decision to carry the war to the North. In the short run, the attack on US vessels on the high seas led Johnson to retaliate. *Ticonderoga* and *Constellation* were ordered to mount strikes against torpedo boat bases, POL facilities and other targets.

Johnson announced the strikes before the carriers had all of their aircraft aloft. Secretary of Defense Robert S. McNamara identified the targets while the strikes were en route. The carriers were about 400 miles (643 km) from their targets and, whether or not McNamara inadvertently helped them, their defenses were ready.

Ticonderoga's carrier air wing CVW–5

launched 34 aircraft including 16 F–8E Crusaders of VF–51 and VF–53 led by Stockdale. Six of the Crusaders attacked torpedo boats at Quang Khe, 60 miles (96 km) north of the 17th Parallel, using Zuni rockets and 20-mm cannon fire to destroy eight P–4 boats and damage 21. Stockdale's force, which included A–4C Skyhawks of VA–55 and VA–56 accompanied by A–1 Skyraiders, assaulted the POL facilities at Vinh. *Constellation*'s strike force included fighter squadrons VF–142 and VF–143, which introduced the F–4B Phantom, flying top cover.

The strikes left plumes of smoke rising thousands of feet into the sky. Clearly, they inflicted damage. But there was a price. AAA (anti-aircraft artillery) damage forced one Crusader to divert to Da Nang, the airfield in South Vietnam closest to the demarcation line which would, in time, become the customary refuge for aircraft suffering battle damage. One A–1 Skyraider (139760) from VA–145 on *Constellation* was shot down and its pilot killed. One *Connie* A–4C Skyhawk (149578) belonging to VA–144 was also

downed and its pilot, Lieutenant Everett J. Alvarez, captured. Alvarez, the first POW (prisoner of war) held in North Vietnam, would be a prisoner for eight years and seven months.

The Gulf of Tonkin raids were soundly condemned by Hanoi and its allies. Hanoi took the position that it was merely giving fraternal support to an uprising in South Vietnam which was, in fact, a local uprising. Washington insisted that the war in the south was caused by infiltration from the North. The truth lay somewhere in between and at this juncture the communist forces in the south, called Viet Cong by everyone else and called the National Liberation Front (NLF) by themselves, really were to a large extent controlled by leaders with local ties. Over time, Hanoi would expand its control over the Viet Cong so that in effect, by attacking North Vietnam, the US created the very aggression from the north which it cited as a

reason for attacking North Vietnam. Furthermore, it took on a new enemy. North Vietnam had its own regular forces, formidable and distinct from the insurgents in the south, and immediately after the Gulf of Tonkin raids, a small number of MiG–17 fighters were brought into North Vietnam from the Soviet Union—the beginning of what would become a powerful air force.

USAF INVOLVEMENT

Although the US Air Force did not participate in the Gulf of Tonkin raids, the incident reversed a long trend towards reduction of the men and aircraft equipping the USAF's Pacific Air Forces (PACAF). Project Clear Water, a long-term program to trim PACAF's fighting strength throughout the region from Hawaii to Southeast Asia, was reversed when the Gulf of Tonkin incident

Southeast Asia jungle passes beneath a formation of Republic F–105D Thunderchiefs, the aircraft soon to be known as the Thud and to carry the brunt of the war 'up North'. In 1964, Thud pilots were not yet in combat but several squadrons served in rotation at bases in Thailand, ready to go. (USAF)

resulted in an accelerated buildup of men and aircraft. On 5 August, B–57s from Clark Field, Philippines, deployed to Bien Hoa AB, South Vietnam. The first combat employment of the Republic F–105D Thunderchief—the Thud—took place on 14 August after 18 F–105Ds of the 36 TFS from Yokota AB, Japan deployed to Korat RTAFB, Thailand. Accompanying this buildup from stateside Tactical Air Command (TAC) assets were three further tactical fighter squadrons, two troop carrier squadrons and six reconnaissance aircraft.

About 70 USAF aircraft were rushed to Southeast Asia in the first phase of this buildup. Composite Strike Force 'One Buck', including six RF–101C Voodoos from Shaw AFB, SC, was sent to reinforce the 'Able Mabel' reconnaissance force at Tan Son Nhut. No fewer than 15 RF–101Cs were operating over Laos and South Vietnam—but not yet up north.

The steadily increasing US presence in South Vietnam and American involvement in the struggle there led to enemy actions which, in turn, heightened discussion in Saigon and Washington about pressing the war to the North on a sustained basis. So far, the Gulf of Tonkin raids had been an *ad hoc* event, but the notion of some kind of greater effort against the North seemed to have an inevitability all its own.

The growing US presence now included no fewer than 47 B–57 Canberra light bombers of the 13th Bomb Squadron under Lt Col. Billy A. McLeod and the 8 TBS under Lt Col. Frederick W. Grindle, Jr, moved from Clark Field in the Philippines to Bien Hoa airfield about 10 miles (1.61 km) north of Saigon. The B–57 commitment at Bien Hoa, more formally called 405th ADVON 1, was an unpopular TDY (temporary duty) posting for airmen who'd been deployed to 'show the flag' but who were still constrained from participating in actual combat. As it turned out, their presence posed a tempting target for the Viet Cong.

On the bloody Hallowe'en night of 31 October / 1 November 1964, the Viet Cong staged a mortar attack on Bien Hoa. In a hellish scene of fiery explosions and carnage, four Americans were killed and 30 wounded. No fewer than five B–57Bs (53-3892, 53-3924, 52-1555, 53-3914 and 53-3894) were destroyed along with an HH–43B helicopter and 13 more bombers were badly damaged.

The B–57 aircraft, its B–57A variant having first flown two decades earlier, on 20 July 1953, was the English Electric Canberra light bomber built under license by Glenn L. Martin in the US, powered by twin Wright J65–W–7 turbojet engines producing 7,220-lb (3 147-kg) thrust. A sample bombload consisted of four 1,000 lb (453 kg) bombs, nine 500 lb (227 kg) bombs, 21 260 lb (118 kg) bombs or two Mark 9 1,500 lb (680 kg) tactical nuclear weapons. Though it had good ordnance-carrying capability, the B–57's range was limited and it lacked air-to-air refuelling capability. It was considered vulnerable to high-density defenses. In the coming months, it would be employed briefly north of the 17th Parallel but would spend most of

In 1964, most of the American soldiers in South Vietnam were Special Forces troopers, like Captain Roger Donlon, here viewing the village of Nan Dang, devastated by Viet Cong attack on 6 July 1964. Donlon was the first American to win the Medal of Honor for valor in Vietnam. The belief that enemy forces were supplied from the North led to air strikes against North Vietnam. (US ARMY)

The B–57 Canberra was an early arrival in Southeast Asia and eventually proved a formidable night intruder, but it did most of its fighting in the South. B–57B Canberra 53-3877, foreground, leads a pair from Bien Hoa on a bomb mission. (USAF)

One of the provocations which led to American bombing of North Vietnam was the 31 October 1964 Viet Cong mortar attack on Bien Hoa airfield which destroyed five B–57B Canberra bombers. Visible here are two burnt-out parking spots where B–57Bs were totally destroyed. (USAF)

Entering service with Military Airlift Command (MAC) on 19 October 1964, the Lockheed C–141A Starlifter was to provide a lifeline, hauling supplies to units in combat against North Vietnam. C–141A (66-154) taxies past RF–101C and EC–47 aircraft at Saigon's Tan Son Nhut Airport. (ROD RICKS)

In 1964, when the 'Triple Nickel' 555 TFS took the F–4C Phantom to Asia, the aircraft still looked like this: gull gray paint topside with white undersides, Tactical Air Command badge on the tail, and 'buzz number' between the national insignia and the words U.S. AIR FORCE. This F–4C Phantom (63-7478), seen in May 1964, had not yet reached the combat zone where Phantoms would shoot down MiGs 13 months later. (ROGER F. BESECKER)

The F–4C Phantom first deployed to the Western Pacific in December 1964 and soon became a mainstay. This previously unpublished view shows an F–4C Phantom (64-686) in its original gull-gray coloring with Sparrow and Sidewinder missiles, flying over Da Nang. This paint scheme did not last long and F–4Cs were soon camouflaged. (JIM HESTON)

15

The Vought F–8 Crusader was the principal US Navy carrier-based fighter at the time of the Gulf of Tonkin raids and throughout much of the war, and was later employed in the land-based role by the US Marine Corps. An F–8D Crusader (147056) belonging to the 'Sundowners' of squadron VF–111 fires a Zuni air-to-ground rocket. (VIA ROBERT F. DORR)

its wartime career relegated to the second leagues in the South.

SAIGON BOMBING

On 24 December 1964, Viet Cong infiltrators struck at the Brink Hotel BOQ (bachelor officers' quarters) in down-town Saigon. A 250 lb (113 kg) plastic explosive killed two US personnel, wounded 71 others and left half of the hotel in a shambles. It was Christmas Eve. Most Americans were still a long way from acknowledging that they were at war and the hotel bombing added fuel to fiery discussions about extending the war to the North on a sustained basis.

Retaining the office to which he succeeded following Kennedy's assassination, Lyndon Johnson had been elected to the presidency the month before with promises to focus heavily on domestic programs and civil rights issues in the US. His unsuccessful opponent, Senator Barry Goldwater, now said openly that it was time to retaliate for events like the Bien Hoa mortar attack and the Saigon hotel bombing by using air power against key targets in North Vietnam.

ENTER THE F–4C

The US Navy's F–4B Phantom had been introduced to battle during the Gulf of Tonkin raids, although it had only a peripheral role.

The US Air Force's F–4C Phantom was introduced to the western Pacific, and moved closer to the combat zone, when a Tactical Air Command rotational squadron, the 555 TFS, arrived at Naha AB, Okinawa in December 1964 to replace an F–102A Delta Dagger unit. The 'triple nickel' squadron would be heard from again. So would the Phantom and within a few months, a second F–4C squadron, the 45 TFS, had taken up temporary station at Ubon, Thailand. This would become the first unit to claim North Vietnamese MiGs.

The Phantom had first flown as the F4H–1 on 27 May 1958. Following lengthy delays in its own TFX (tactical fighter, experimental) program, the USAF reluctantly adopted the Navy design. For years, the Phantom would be seen as the best multi-role fighter and strike aircraft in service, the standard against which all others would be measured. Powered by twin 16,150 lb (7 324 kg) thrust General Electric J79 engines (which emitted telltale smoke, making the Phantom an easy target), the F–4C would eventually join and one day replace the F–105 in carrying the war to Hanoi.

For the moment, however, airmen discovered that the world's best fighter was far from perfect. The Phantom's AIM–7 Sparrow radar-homing missiles had a high rate of malfunction. Some F–4Cs sprang wing tank leaks that had to be resealed after each flight and 85 of them developed cracked ribs on outer wing panels. The Phantom's UHF (ultra-high frequency) radio was located under the rear ejection seat, which had to be removed at the cost of two hours' time even for minor repair. In the Air Force, the F–4C

At the beginning of the conflict, North Vietnam's air defenses were not yet particularly formidable. Here, ground observers are on the watch for US 'air pirate' intruders. Later in the war, they would be backed by an impressive array of MiGs, missiles and anti-aircraft guns. (VIA PHIL CHINNERY)

The Douglas A–1 Skyraider had enormous staying power and could loiter for long periods over a target. This A–1H (139789) belongs to attack squadron VA–115, one of several units based at NAS Lemoore, California, which proceeded to the battle zone on Western Pacific cruises aboard carriers like USS *Kitty Hawk* (CVA–63). (USN)

was still flown by two full-fledged pilots and no one ever said the Phantom was easy to fly. Notwithstanding all of the problems, the F–4C Phantom was the finest fighter in USAF inventory and would remain so for many years. The men of the 45 TFS at Ubon were soon to be blooded in it.

NAVAL BUILDUP

Fortunately for the US, *Ticonderoga* and *Constellation* had been on station during the Gulf of Tonkin incident and had been able to carry out the *ad hoc* air strikes independently, making it unnecessary to rely upon additional forces or upon the permission of another country for airbase or overflight rights. To be

certain that naval forces remained ready if further strikes were needed, the carriers *Ranger* (CVA–61) and *Kearsage* (CVS–33) were assigned to steam toward the Gulf of Tonkin, *Ranger* to provide additional capability and the ASW (anti-submarine warfare), *Kearsage* to guard against possible Chinese submarine activity. It was not the last time the US would think of the Chinese as an enemy in this struggle, although the truth was that Hanoi was far more closely allied with Moscow than with Peking.

There remained an innocence, and a vulnerability, about Americans who had not been involved in a large-scale shooting war since the end of the Korean struggle 12 years earlier. In 1964, few noticed a student upheaval called the Free Speech Movement at

the University of California at Berkeley but it was the first major campus demonstration in the United States and the first of hundreds of protests that would follow when it became clear that once again Americans were going to fight and die in a remote corner of Asia. That sort of clarity would begin to etch itself into the public mind in February 1965.

1965
THE YEAR OF THE BUILDUP

Dissatisfaction with General Khanh's regime in Saigon led to street demonstrations and violence throughout South Vietnam, some of it caused by the Viet Cong. The United States sent a team of officials headed by presidential security advisor McGeorge Bundy to observe the situation and make recommendations.

Returning from his visit on 6 February 1965, Bundy drafted a memo for President Johnson urging a policy of 'sustained reprisal' against the North. Bundy put forth a widely-held view that the war in South Vietnam was being lost and could be turned around only through aerial retaliation against Hanoi. 'The situation in South Vietnam is

---

deteriorating and without new US action, defeat appears inevitable ...'

Bundy's memo was written hours *before* a Viet Cong attack on US military advisors at Pleiku which killed nine and wounded 76— an attack which led US officials in Saigon to seek Acting Prime Minister Nguyen Xuan Oanh's concurrence in a bombing campaign against the North. Bundy recommended 'the development and execution of a policy of *sustained reprisal* [emphasis in original] against North Vietnam—a policy in which air and naval action against the North is justified by and related to the whole Viet Cong campaign of violence and terror in the South.' He was still not seeking a sustained aerial *campaign* against the North but, rather, a policy of conducting air strikes specifically in reprisal against Viet Cong actions. 'We might retaliate against a grenade thrown into a crowded cafe in Saigon but not necessarily to a shot fired into a small shop in the countryside.' Bundy added, however, that 'an "air war" may, in fact be necessary ...' *How* necessary would remain debatable but on 7 February, President Johnson ordered all dependents of US

personnel out of Saigon. Many departed on Pan American flights for San Francisco.

FLAMING DART

In response to the killing of Americans at Pleiku, Johnson authorized a retaliatory air strike against the military barracks and staging area at Dong Hoi, just above the 17th Parallel in North Vietnam. The mission was given the evocative name Flaming Dart I. A very unusual twist, with virtually no military effectiveness but much policy import, was the participation of the South Vietnamese Air Force, its A–1H Skyraiders led by the flamboyant chief of staff, General Nguyen Cao Ky.

The brunt of the strike was borne by 49 aircraft from USS *Coral Sea* (CVA–43) and USS *Hancock* (CVA–19), attacking Dong Hoi, plus 34 aircraft from USS *Ranger* (CVA–61) which ranged inland to the barracks at Vit Thu Lu. *Ranger*'s aircraft, confronting inclement weather, were ineffective but the Dong Hoi strike drew enormous secondary explosions and razed buildings. One A–4E Skyhawk (150075) of attack squadron VA–156 from *Coral Sea* was hit by ground fire. Lieutenant E. A. Dickson limped out to sea in the burning Skyhawk and ejected but was not rescued. The loss of a pilot marred the mood of his squadron mates who wondered now if they had merely escalated into another round of enemy provocation followed by retaliation.

On 10 February, the Viet Cong blew up a hotel being used as a billet for American soldiers at Qui Nhon, killing 23 men. It was still not generally acknowledged that American GIs were in combat but the incident made inevitable another retaliatory strike against North Vietnam. On 11 February, *Coral Sea*, *Hancock* and *Ranger* mounted strikes at a military logistics complex north of the DMZ. This was the mission known as Flaming Dart II. Operating in foul weather, the strike force of 99 aircraft had limited success bombing the Chanh Hoa installation.

An A–4C Skyhawk (149572) of squadron

VA–153 on *Coral Sea* was hit by Triple-A (anti-aircraft artillery, or AAA) but the pilot coaxed his aircraft out to sea, ejected and was rescued. Less lucky was the pilot of an F–8D Crusader (148633) of VF–32 on the same ship, who was shot down and became a POW. At a very early juncture, US naval aviators now knew of the difficulties posed by the northeast monsoon and of the potency of Hanoi's AAA defenses. Ironically, North Vietnam may not at this juncture have had any control over Viet Cong provocations, but Hanoi was determined to defend itself and was quietly asking for Soviet help, including surface-to-air missiles (SAM).

ROLLING THUNDER

With the sole exception of the State Department's George Ball who favored negotiations, virtually everyone in the Johnson administration felt that the Flaming Dart raids were a step in the right direction

The South Vietnamese Air Force was never an important participant in air strikes north of the 17th Parallel, but during the early Flaming Dart missions some of that force's A–1H Skyraiders were led north by the flamboyant Nguyen Cao Ky, who later became Premier. Here, Ky is seen talking to Brig. Gen. Albert W. Schinz in August 1965, as his air arm accepts delivery of four B–57 bombers. (USAF)

and many felt that they were not enough. Most figures in the Johnson administration supported Bundy's recommendations and agreed with the views of State Department counselor Walt Rostow, who advocated a gradual escalation of pressures on North Vietnam until a point was reached where the North Vietnamese decided that a Viet Cong victory was not worth the price. McNamara, Bundy and Rostow each held some version of this opinion. Thus, the policy of attacking North Vietnam only on a retaliatory basis was abandoned and Flaming Dart operations gave way to the sustained air campaign knowh as ROLLING THUNDER.

The F–100 Super Sabre was the first American fighter to fire a Sidewinder missile at a North Vietnamese MiG, but it was never to become a major participant in the war north of the 17th Parallel. This F–100D Super Sabre (54-2281) is depicted on an early operational flight prior to the type's 1965 debut in the conflict against Hanoi. (NAA)

It may be useful for the reader to think of the air war against North Vietnam as consisting of four distinct phases—the ROLLING THUNDER campaign (1965–68), the bombing halt (1968–72), the LINEBACKER campaign (May–October 1972) and the final 'eleven day war' known as LINEBACKER II (17–29 December 1972). Viewed in this manner, ROLLING THUNDER covers the longest, costliest and most painful period of the long struggle.

ROLLING THUNDER, as conceived and begun, had three objectives: to reduce infiltration, to boost South Vietnamese morale and to make it clear to Hanoi that continuation of the insurgency in the South would become increasingly expensive.

In Hanoi, however, ROLLING THUNDER was seen as one more obstacle to overcome in a long struggle to remove foreign influence and unify a divided Vietnam under Vietnamese rule. Ho Chi Minh's followers had removed the Japanese and the French. Now, they would search for a way to withstand the American air assault. They would seek to make the war too expensive, not to Hanoi but to Washington, and in the end they would remove the Americans, too. North Vietnam did not yet fully control the Viet Cong insurgency in the south—it was simplistic to believe that every attack viewed as a provocation, such as the killing of Americans at Pleiku, was ordered directly by Hanoi—but it was going to achieve such control. No official in the North Vietnamese leadership ever saw the American air strikes as evidence that it was time to succumb.

The first USAF participation in ROLLING THUNDER was on 2 March 1965, with B–57s, F–100Ds, and F–105Ds. Of the 150 available at Thai bases, 25 F–105Ds from the 12 TFS and 67 TFS (both part of the 18 TFW) accompanied B–57s to an ammunition depot at Xom Bong, about 35 miles (56 km) above the DMZ (demilitarized zone) and inflicted heavy damage. On this first raid, no fewer than five aircraft were lost to ground fire, two F–100D Super Sabres (55-2857, 56-3150) and three F–105Ds (61-214, 62-4260, 62-4325) and the first USAF pilot, Captain Hayden J. Lockhart, was taken prisoner. Already, illusions that bombing would quickly subdue North Vietnam required further examination.

From the beginning, critics of the sustained campaign against North Vietnam would argue that it didn't really roll and wasn't particularly thunderous. The planning of air strikes was a complex and unwieldy business that began in the Situation Room at the White House where President Johnson retained firm control over what could and could not be attacked. Decisions as routine as

the choice of ordnance for a particular sortie were made at this level, thousands of miles from the fighting. Johnson's decisions were relayed to McNamara, who in turn informed the JCS. Directives were then passed to CINCPAC (commander-in-chief, Pacific forces, in Hawaii) which then fragmented or 'fragged' the various targets among USAF, USN and—on rare instance—South Vietnamese aircraft. The USAF headquarters in Saigon, the 2nd Air Division, made recommendations but could not choose targets. Lt Gen Joseph Moore, who commanded 2nd Air Division, was an accomplished old fighter hand who kept making suggestions for an effective campaign against the North Vietnamese road and rail transportation network, only to find targets approved on what seemed a random and arbitrary basis.

A complicating factor was the expansion of the North Vietnamese air force. Radar-directed AAA guns were a serious enough challenge to the US strike aircraft but they would soon be joined by MiGs and by radar-directed SAMs. The first electronic countermeasures (ECM) capability to be mounted in the conflict was employed on 29 March 1965, when three RF–101C Voodoos, each carrying QRC–160 pods, flew ECM support missions accompanying a ROLLING THUNDER strike force to target. The QRC–160 proved unsatisfactory and was quickly withdrawn from the combat theater, but steps were under way to develop some means of jamming or deceiving the enemy's radar defenses.

DRAGON'S JAW

Included in ROLLING THUNDER objectives was interdiction of the North Vietnamese rail system south of the 20th Parallel, which meant attacking the Thanh Hoa Railroad and Highway Bridge, known as the 'Dragon's Jaw'. The bridge, spanning 540 ft (164.5 m), was 56 ft (17 m) wide and stood about 50 ft (15.2 m) above the river. Other bridges would become as well known, like the Paul Doumer Bridge outside Hanoi which became the brunt of an obscene song by Thud pilots, but the Dragon's Jaw was to stand as a symbol of resistance in the face of American air attacks. Over three years, hundreds of sorties would fail to drop the bridge's span into the river.

The first strike on the bridge was scheduled for 2 April, but because of poor weather and a shortage of tankers the mission was postponed for 24 hours. On 3 April, a strike package was assembled consisting of 79 aircraft: 46 F–105Ds for the actual strike, 21 F–100Ds as escort, two RF–101Cs for pre- and post-strike recce and ten KC–135 tankers.

Strike leader was the slim, gaunt commander of the 'Fighting Cocks' of the 67 TFS / 18 TFW, Lt Col. Robinson Risner. Risner was an ace from the Korean conflict with eight MiG kills to his credit and was one of the most accomplished fighter tacticians in the USAF. He had been uprooted from a comfortable posting on Okinawa, accompanied by his family, when the buildup in Southeast Asia began. Risner wanted to press the fight aggressively, end it quickly, and win.

Risner's aircraft was the Republic F–105D Thunderchief, the Thud. No other aircraft type can be listed as more important during the early part of the 'out-country war'. Designed with an internal bay for the nuclear weapons delivery mission and first flown as the YF–105A a decade earlier (on 22 October 1955), the F–105D variant of the Thud was powered by a Pratt & Whitney J75–P–19W turbojet engine rated at 24,500 lb (11 112 kg) thrust with afterburner, 26,400 lb (11 975 kg) with fuel injection. The long and sleek, mid-wing Thud toted a 20-mm M61A1 Gatling gun and could carry a bombload of around 10,000 lb (4 535 kg) on a long-range strike mission, a typical load being eight 750 lb (340 kg) bombs. This was the payload carried by 30 of the 46 Thuds in Risner's strike force.

The remaining 16 F–105Ds carried pairs of AGM–12B Bullpup air-to-ground missiles and were supposed to launch them at 12,000 ft (3 706 m), a decision which underestimated the enemy's ability to swat down strike aircraft at that height and which placed over-rated confidence, so typically American at that early juncture, in the Bullpup itself. The AGM–12B comprised a 250 lb (113 kg) bomb inside a roll-stabilized airframe with an Aerojet General solid rocket motor, fixed rear wings and nose fins. Radio guidance freed the operator from the need to align the target with his sight, allowing guidance from an offset position. It was a well-designed weapon but nobody had appreciated that the Thanh Hoa Bridge was better, or at least more strongly designed. Flying an F–105D (61-321) with the nickname *Virginia ANG*, Captain Bill Meyerholt watched his Bullpups bounce off the bridge. The improved AGM–12C Bullpup B with its larger 1,000-lb (454-kg) warhead was well received when it began arriving in the combat zone a few months later, its first combat firing taking place in August, but the Bullpup never became one of the more successful weapons of the conflict.

Also involved in Risner's furious first strike on the Dragon's Jaw was the F–100D Super Sabre. Of the 21 F–100Ds in the escort force, seven were assigned to flak suppression, two to weather reconnaissance and four to perform the fighter cover mission which came to be known as MiGCAP (MiG

North Vietnamese AAA crew manning a 37-mm cannon. From the 1965 outset of US bombing, North Vietnam steadily built up its defensive network. (VIA MIKE O'CONNOR)

combat air patrol). The remaining eight F–100Ds were charged with carrying out a RESCAP (rescue combat air patrol) if necessary. Like the flak suppression craft, the RESCAP F–100Ds carried two pods of 19 2.75-inch rockets. It is not clear whether a realistic air rescue effort could have been mounted at this juncture. The scattered Air Rescue Service assets in Southeast Asia included HU–16B Albatross amphibians at Korat and, after June 1965, three HC–54 Skymaster airborne command posts, but the only rescue helicopter in theater was the Kaman HH–43B Huskie, which had been designed for local airbase firefighting. Box-shaped, with twin meshing rotors, the HH–43B and improved HH–43F quickly became known as Pedro, from the radio callsign used by the type. The helicopter was of limited utility any distance from home, especially in heavily fortified North Vietnam.

In any event, notwithstanding Captain Meyerholt's frustration over the way his Bullpups bounced, Lt Col. Risner's first strike against the Thanh Hoa Bridge was carefully executed and carried out. The F–100D escort force from South Vietnam bored almost due north along the coast while the F–105D strike force from Thailand flew northeast for a endezvous which would permit hitting the target at 1400 hours.

Lt Col. Risner led the strike and it was

moments later that he and his wingmen saw their Bullpups exploding but failing to drop the bridge. A further drawback was that since each Bullpup had to be individually guided to its target, an F–105D carrying two Bullpups would have to make a second pass. It would soon be learned that you did not make a second pass on a target where defenses were as intense as at Thanh Hoa. The Bullpup-carrying Thuds were following by F–195Ds carrying bombs which completed the first mission against the bridge by taking out roadway approaches and superstructure—but failing to damage the main span itself.

ROUTE PACKAGES

One F–105D pilot looked at a map of North Vietnam and likened the shape of it to a Colonel Sanders fried chicken drumstick. Names like Xom Bong and Vinh Linh did not roll easily from American tongues, especially in the hyped radio chatter of combat, so to simplify navigation and planning, the country was divided into sections known as Route Packages, or RPs. Pilots talked about RP One or Pak Six. Roman numerals were supposed to be used (Route Package VI) but rarely were.

Moving north from the DMZ at the 17th Parallel, the country was partitioned into

Route Packages One, Two, Three and Four, each consisting of a horizontal slice. The wider region farther north was divided into Route Package Five to the west and Six to the east. It was RP Six which contained the most important targets, the heaviest defenses and the cities of Hanoi and Haiphong.

For the F–105D pilots bearing the brunt of the campaign against the North, Route Package One was a training area. Newly arrived pilots flew ten missions against that area's relatively less intense defenses before earning the right to go into RP Six and, later in the war, to go 'downtown'—to Hanoi.

Originally, there was some thought of dividing the route packages between Air Force and Navy. The US Navy now kept carriers at Dixie Station in the South China Sea for operations in the South and at Yankee Station for strikes against the North. Aircraft from *Hancock* and *Coral Sea* had begun the Navy's participation in ROLLING THUNDER, on 18 March, and began ranging up and down the coast, striking at transportation and supply targets. The first air-to-air engagement was fought on 3 April, when MiG–17s

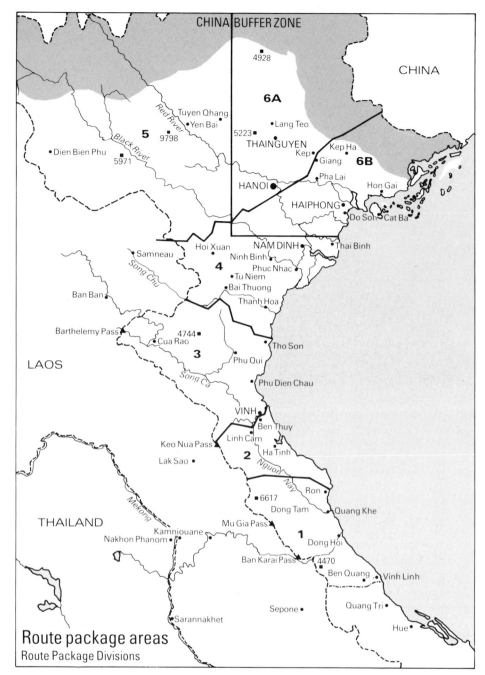

CHINA BUFFER ZONE

CHINA

6A

Tuyen Qhang
Yen Bai
9798

Lang Teo

5223 THAINGUYEN Kep Ha
Kep
Giang 6B

Dien Bien Phu
5971

HANOI
Pha Lai

Hon Gai

HAIPHONG

Do Soh Cat Ba

Samneau
Hoi Xuan
NAM DINH
Thai Binh

Ninh Binh
4
Phuc Nhac
Tu Niem
Bai Thuong

Ban Ban

Thanh Hoa

4744
Barthelemy Pass
Cua Rao
3
Tho Son

Phu Qui

LAOS

Song Ca

Phu Dien Chau

VINH
Ben Thuy
Linh Cam

Keo Nua Pass
Ha Tinh
2
Lak Sao

Nguon Nay

6617
Ron

Dong Tam
Quang Khe

THAILAND
Kamniouane
Nakhon Phanom
Mu Gia Pass
1
Dong Hoi

Ban Karai Pass
4470
Ben Quang
Vinh Linh

Sepone
Quang Tri

Hue

Sarannakhet

Route package areas
Route Package Divisions

Lt Col. Robinson Risner, commander of the 67 TFS, led the 3 April and 4 April 1965 strikes against the Thanh Hoa Bridge. F–105D pilot Risner was shot down twice, became a prisoner the second time, and provided heroic leadership to captured Americans who spent up to eight years in the 'Hanoi Hilton'. Risner later retired as a brigadier general. (USAF)

For ease of planning, US leaders arbitrarily divided North Vietnam into six areas, or Route Packages. The 'hottest' was Route Package Six, which included Hanoi and Haiphong, and was further sub-divided into Route Package 6–A and 6–B

briefly appeared to challenge aircraft from both carriers near Thanh Hoa.

On 4 April 1965, the day Lt Col. Risner's Thud pilots mounted their second strike against the Dragon's Jaw, North Vietnam's air force archieved the first air-to-air kills when two F–105Ds (59-1754; 59-1764) belonging to Zinc flight of the 355 TFW at Takhli were shot down by MiG–17s. The MiG fighters appeared behind the Thuds,

which were laden with ordnance, and blew them out of the sky. It was a sad beginning to an air-to-air war for the Americans, a two-to-nothing score in favor of the enemy.

That same day, Risner narrowly missed being shot down when AAA fire hailed around his Thud. (Later, Risner would be shot down twice, would be captured the second time, and would become a key leader of the POWs' resistance to their captors). One of Risner's 67 TFS/18 TFW aircraft (62-4217) was claimed by ground fire, its pilot, Captain Carlyle S. (Smitty) Harris becoming a POW. Harris would introduce the 'tap code' which enabled POWs to communicate with each other while in solitary confinement, but Harris would not have been shot

down at all had it not been for his need to make that perilous second pass over the target. And he would not have been captured at all had a more effective SAR (search and rescue) capability existed in the combat zone.

The full details of the air actions of 3–4 April are thought not to have been previously published. The following account is from an official document prepared by Brigadier General Robert F. Titus and classified until years afterward (1977), dealing with the air-to-air aspect of the action on those days:

'On [4 April] 1965, USAF F–100D Super Sabres became the first supersonic fighters to launch air-to-air missiles at Soviet-built MiGs. They missed! From that inauspicious beginning emerged a new chapter in the history of aerial combat.

'On the previous day [3 April 1965], in the war's first aerial engagement, a Navy F–8 Crusader had been attacked and damaged by a MiG. As a result, the F–100D crews were expecting enemy fighter activity as they headed north over the Gulf of Tonkin. Their expectations were more than met, and in typical fashion. The MiGs appeared suddenly, without warning. The actions were violent, brief and with tragic results. You remember the headlines ... 2 F–105Ds lost, the crews missing, one MiG–17 probably destroyed. It was an unhappy exchange.

'The events of 4 April occurred simultaneously about 60 miles [96.5 km] apart. The

From the beginning of the ROLLING THUNDER campaign, air-to-air refueling was essential. Here, an F–105D takes on fuel from a KC–135. (VIA JERRY SCUTTS)

first flight of F–100Ds (Green flight) were configured with rockets and 20-mm ammunition, and assigned the task of providing cover for aircrew rescue efforts if needed. They had just taken up their orbit off the coast southeast of the target [the Dragon's Jaw] when they were met head-on by two MiG–17s which immediately wheeled in on the attack. The first MiG pulled in hard behind the lead element; the #2 MiG bent it around on the second element. The F–100Ds took frantic evasion in the flurry of maneuvers which followed. Green 2 succeeded in firing several 20-mm bursts, the last in a vertical dive from 10,000 to 7,000 feet [3 048 to 2 133 m]. Except for a flash on the MiG's right horizontal stabilizer, Green 2 saw nothing to confirm a kill because by now he was totally occupied in recovering from his dive. By exerting a healthy yank on the stick that overstressed his F–100D, he managed to pull out at 'wave top level.' The probable MiG–17 kill was most likely the result of this encounter.

'The other flight of four F–100Ds (Purple flight) carried Sidewinders as well as 20 mm. They were 60 miles [96.5 km] to the north of the first flight, screening the Strike force from the MiGs' most likely avenue of approach. The F–100Ds were headed south in a fighting formation when Purple 2 spotted two MiG–17s 3 miles [4.82 km] out at nine o'clock. The MiGs were moving fast on a quartering course which would take them in front of the F–100Ds from left to right. The MiGs knew where they were going, for five miles ahead in a loose left orbit waiting to be called in on the target was a flight of four bomb-laden F–105Ds. What followed amounted to an end run with the MiGs hitting the Thuds and the alerted F–100Ds accelerating in hot pursuit. Purple lead and 2 saw the first MiG open up with cannon fire. Pieces began coming off the lead F–105D. The #2 MiG maintaining close formation on the lead MiG's right wing, opened fire on the #2 F–105D. Apparently neither of the pilots heard the several warnings transmitted, and were unaware of the MiG's presence until they were hit. The second element of the

The 2.75-in folding fin aircraft rockets (FFAR) being fired by this F–105D were used for a time but proved less effective than ordinary bombs against most targets. (VIA JERRY SCUTTS)

F–105D en route to bomb targets in North Vietnam in 1965. (VIA JERRY SCUTTS)

F–105 formation spotted the MiGs coming out of the haze of about 3,000 feet [914 m] in range. They transmitted warnings as they broke into the attack.

'In the meantime, Purple lead (the F–100 CAP [combat air patrol, or escort]) in afterburner closed on the MiGs but hesitated to fire a Sidewinder because of the proximity of the F–105Ds. By the time he was sure of his target he had closed to 3,000 ft [914 m]. He fired a missile which passed 10 feet [3 m] over the right wing of the lead MiG without detonating. By this time the F–105Ds were in afterburner. Purple lead elected to close for a gun attack rather than fire a second Sidewinder and risk hitting an F–105D. The first missile alerted the MiGs to the presence of the F–100Ds and they pulled up hard into a climb about 20° off vertical. At some time during the encounter Purple 4 fired a Sidewinder without result and seemingly without a target. No further opportunities developed for missile shots, and the maneuverability of the MiG–17s prevented the F–100Ds from

getting an effective gun burst in the wild and hairy acrobatics that followed.

'That day's events signalled a change in US Air Force operating philosophy. The F–100Ds were withdrawn from the CAP (Combat Air Patrol) mission, and shortly F–4C Phantoms arrived from the States. These versatile fighters, each equipped with four AIM–7 Sparrows and four AIM–9 Sidewinders but no gun, assumed the CAP role.'[1]

This official report fails to add that one of the two F–105D pilots to become a fatal casualty in the war's first air-to-air kills succeeded in coaxing his Thud out to the Gulf of Tonkin but died there, almost certainly because no adequate combat rescue facilities yet existed.

The loss of three Thuds on the same day illustrated the need to develop ways of coping with MiGs and to improve the size and scope of available rescue forces. Reflecting the finding that the F–100D Super Sabre was simply not the right platform for close-quarters duelling with the MiG–17, the 45 TFS deployed from MacDill AFB, Florida to Ubon, Thailand in April, the first F–4C Phantom unit to arrive in the combat zone. F–4C pilots were itching to avenge the loss of the two Thuds and the poor showing by the Super Sabres. So far, only the Sidewinder missile had been employed in battle but the

Phantom's other missile, the Sparrow, would see action soon.

ENTER THE SIDEWINDER

The Sidewinder employed with no success by those F–100Ds was developed by a small team of US Navy experts at China Lake, California on a shoestring budget and became not only the most successful air-to-air missile of the Vietnam conflict but nothing less than one of the most influential missiles in all history. Air-to-air missiles carried by US fighters were of two types, the heat-seeking or infra-red (IR) missiles typified by the AIM–9 Sidewinder and the semi-active radar homing (SARH) missiles typified by the AIM–7 Sparrow. The heat-seeking AIM–9 Sidewinder had been employed as early as the Taiwan Straits crisis (in 1958) by Chinese F–86F Sabres and was rapidly becoming standard armament for most USAF and USN fighters, although it did not appear frequently aboard the F–100D. The missile was 113 in (2.87 m) long and had a range of 11 miles (17.7 km). Its infra-red seeker head had to be cooled before it could latch onto a target and be fired, but this was a fairly straightforward and uncumbersome process. Eventually, the Sidewinder would

---

The MiG–17 was the most maneuverable fighter in North Vietnam's inventory and was flown by its top aces. This example, belonging to Cambodia, was evaluated at Phu Cat AB in South Vietnam by US forces. (NORMAN TAYLOR)

score more aerial victories in the conflict than any other weapon, and the majority of the US Navy's air-to-air kills.

Early engagements behind, new complications arose. On 5 April, an RF–8A Crusader reconnaissance aircraft returned to its carrier with the first photographic evidence that North Vietnam was constructing a surface-to-air missile network. As if being inadequately prepared for MiGs and for combat rescue were not discouraging enough, it would now be necessary to cope with an entirely new kind of weapon—the SAM.

CHINESE MiG KILL

Until the advent of ROLLING THUNDER, the North Vietnamese had kept their MiG–17s in safe haven at Chinese bases while despatching additional pilots to the Soviet Union for training and pressing the Soviets to supply more aircraft. Certainly, a request for more advanced MiG–21 fighters must have been a part of Hanoi's shopping list from the beginning. The North Vietnamese air force was in the process of building in size from 36 MiG–15s and MiG–17s at one base, Phuc Yen (in August 1964), to 70 MiG–17s at three airfields. The MiG–17 was dated, scarcely more than an upgrade of the Korean War-

vintage MiG–15, but it was highly maneuverable and, unlike the Americans' Phantom, armed with guns. Early production MiG–17s were powered by the same VK–1 engines as the MiG–15 but the main production aircraft introduced the 7,500 lb (3 400 kg) thrust Klimov VK–1F with a simple afterburner. Capable of 710 mph (1 145 km/h) at 10,000 ft (3 048 m), the MiG–17 was armed with three NR–23 cannons.

When it became clear to North Vietnam's fighter wing tacticians that the arcane rules of engagement for ROLLING THUNDER would not permit strikes on airfields, the MiG–17s were brought in to their bases and put on alert. With the Americans not yet successful in downing a MiG in air-to-air combat, lacking cannons on their principal fighter and hampered by the same rules of engagement which required closing to within visual range before firing, the MiG–17 was going to give a good account of itself in air-to-air action. It had already swatted two Thuds out of the sky, with no losses.

The first air-to-air probable kill of the war, surprisingly, seems not to have involved the North Vietnamese at all and, perhaps, lies outside the scope of this narrative. On 9 April, F–4B Phantoms from *Ranger* battled Chinese MiG–17s near Hainan Island. The Phantom (151403) flown by LTJG Terence

The 'Fighting Falcons' of squadron VF–96 were caught up in the 9 April 1965 air battle with Chinese MiG–17s near Hainan Island. F–4B Phantom 149426 seen here on USS *Enterprise* (CVAN–65) in July 1965 is identical to the F–4B said by the Chinese to have been shot down by a Sparrow missile fired by a wingman. (LIONEL PAUL)

M. Murphy and Ensign Ronald J. Fegan, members of the 'Black Falcons' of squadron VF–96, was credited with a probable MiG–17 shootdown but did not return from the mission. The Chinese promptly reminded everyone that the struggle south of their border was one being waged by the Vietnamese people, not themselves. The Chinese claimed, and other evidence seems to confirm, that Murphy and Fegan were shot down by an AIM–7 Sparrow missile fired by one of their own wingmen! BOTH KIA

ENTER THE SPARROW

Just as the Thanh Hoa bridge strikes had seen the first combat launch of a Sidewinder, the Hainan Island incident had seen the first use of the Sparrow. As noted earlier, US air-to-air missiles were of two types, the heat-seekers like the Sidewinder and radar-guided missiles like the AIM–7 Sparrow. The radar-

25

guided capability was not possessed by the enemy and would have given the Phantom (the only principal US fighter to carry this missile) an enormous advantage if only the rules would have permitted engaging from beyond visual range (BVR). The radar-guided Sparrow was effective at distances up to 28 miles (44 km) and could be employed well in advance of an eye-to-eye sighting of an enemy fighter, if only the rules of engagement would permit. Eventually, Sparrows would account for the bulk of Air Force MiG kills in the conflict. The AIM–7D variant was 144 in (3.66 m) long, introduced a Thiokol pre-packaged liquid rocket motor and had been adopted in 1960 for the F–4 Phantom. All fighter Phantoms could carry four Sparrows in ventral bays beneath the fuselage with target illumination by the fighter's own radar (the inboard wing pylons, where a fifth and sixth Sparrow could be fitted, proved more useful as stations for Sidewinders, bombs and ECM pods). Radar failures and Sparrow malfunctions occurred more often than pilots wanted and the Sparrow was controversial, but it remained a key part of the US arsenal and must be considered, overall, a success.

MARINES LAND

If a single event altered American perceptions of what was happening in Vietnam, it was the landing of two battalions of US Marines at Da Nang on 10 April 1965. The sight of regular troops storming ashore was played on TV screens across the US. For a time, the fiction was put forth that these Marines had been called in solely to guard airfields (and, indeed, they did take this function over from South Vietnamese troops freed for combat), but the truth was apparent. They had arrived for combat. These were the first US ground combat units to be deployed to Vietnam. Marine fighter squadron VMFA–531, the 'Gray Ghosts,' under Lt Col. William C. McGraw, Jr, arrived with its F–4B Phantoms at Da Nang on the same date. The squadron's exec, Major Orie E. Cory, stepped out into the parched tropical heat and promptly labelled the place a 'shithole'. The buildup of airpower was continuing and Marine squadrons VMFA–115 and VMFA–323 were soon to follow. To the Marines would fall many thankless combat missions in the Route Package One area just above the DMZ.

Also on 10 April 1965, the first EF–10B Skyknight arrived to join Marine aviation units at Da Nang. Though the Marine Corps Phantoms and Skyhawks were used primarily for close support missions in the South,

the former venturing North but not very far North, the EF–10Bs of composite squadron VMCJ–1 became yet another aircraft type to be operated over the North. Pilot Lieutenant Frank Littlebury reported that he felt extremely safe inside the EF–10B, which was sturdy and tough. More than 20 years old, with high airframe hours and limited life, the EF–10B initially provided the sole electronic warfare capability for Air Force and Navy missions over the North. Variously nicknamed the Whale or the Drut (the latter term being best appreciated if spelled backwards), the EF–10B escorted the first anti-SAM missions, which came to be known as Iron Hand missions.

C–130 FACT SHEET FLIGHTS

The C–130 Hercules transport, never intended for combat in an area of strong defenses, began journeying to North Vietnam on 14 April 1965 when missions code-named Fact Sheet were begun. The men on these flights took considerable risks to scatter propaganda leaflets aimed at giving readers the 'other' side of the story. The 6315 Operations Group based at Naha AB, Okinawa (which became the 374 TAW two years later) provided the big Hercules transports which operated while on TDY (temporary duty) from Ubon. Sam McGowan, crew member of a 'Herk,' describes the flights which delivered 77 million leaflets and 15,000 'gift kits' by the end of the war:

The 'Gray Ghosts' of Marine squadron VMFA–531 were first to arrive at Da Nang in April 1965. With Army Hawk missiles in the foreground, an F–4B Phantom (151448) of the squadron lands after a combat mission, passing Air Force F–100D Super Sabres which had a brief role fighting MiGs in North Vietnam. (MDC)

'For the loadmasters, the leaflet drops were murder. To begin with, we had to manhandle the boxes from the rear of the airplane to their tie-down position in the cargo compartment. This was hard work in the Pacific sun, especially considering that each box weighed 70 lb [31.7 kg]. After loading, we had to look forward to the drops themselves. The loadmaster wore a parachute, survival vest, pistol, etc., but we also had to wear an oxygen mask which was connected to a central console. The oxygen cord restricted movement. Even though the drops were at 25,000 feet [7 620 m] and above, we perspired heavily. Perspiration would cause the oxygen mask to slide all over the place, and it would also begin to smell, causing nausea. The leaflet drops were relatively not hazardous, since we were above the altitude reached by most ground fire [and not near SAM sites].'[2]

McGowan explains that one squadron, the 35 TCS (later 35 TAS) flew the Fact Sheet mission up to and through 1970. The 'gift kits' dropped on these flights included items such as soap bars, toiletries and transistor radios (set only for Saigon frequencies!) while the leaflets, in Vietnamese, urged Hanoi's populace to end its role in the

The EF-10B Skyknight flew reconnaissance and EW (electronic warfare) missions for the US Marine Corps. Those employed in Southeast Asia, like the Skyknight shown, belonged to the 1st Marine Composite Squadron (VMCJ-1). (USMC)

conflict. These materials, developed by the US Army's 7th Psychological Operations Group at great cost, almost certainly had no particular effect of any kind on the North Vietnamese. Nevertheless, two years after the beginning of the Fact Sheet missions (31 March 1967), a 35 TCS C-130 Hercules was credited with dropping the one-billionth psychological operations leaflet over North Vietnam.

The leaflet operations were the subject of an official report by no less a personage than CINCPAC himself, Admiral U. S. G. Sharp, who saw the C-130 missions as follows:

'The concept was that prior to an air strike

Sgt Sam McGowan, loadmaster of a C-130E Hercules, never expected his big transport to fly in combat conditions over North Vietnam. Beginning in April 1965, the C-130E flew Fact Sheet missions to drop leaflets and 'gift packages' to Ho Chi Minh's citizens. (MCGOWAN)

we would warn the populace, by leaflets or by radio, that certain categories of targets were considered military objectives and that the people should evacuate all targets of the type described.

'[In June 1965] Washington authorities granted to CINCPAC and to the American Ambassador in Saigon the authority to conduct leaflet drops as part of the total air effort. It was intended that the targets for ROLLING THUNDER and the leaflet missions would be complementary. Further, it was directed that the leaflet operations would be expanded to two drops of about two million leaflets each per week.

'Intensified psychological operations were directed and [on 16 July 1965] CINCPAC recommended that leaflet operations be conducted on the major North Vietnamese population centers, to include Hanoi and Haiphong. This was approved by higher authority with the proviso that leaflet aircraft could not penetrate a 40-nautical mile circle [72 km] around either Hanoi or Haiphong. Leaflets for Hanoi and Haiphong were targeted utilizing the wind-drift technique.'[3]

It is very clear that these missions to the region of Hanoi in C-130 transports (not to be confused with armed AC-130 gunships developed later in the war) were among the most dangerous combat missions ever flown in any conflict.

EC-121 DEPLOYMENT

It had become apparent that an airborne early warning (AEW) capability would be needed if US aircraft were to challenge MiGs and still deliver ordnance to their targets. The EC-121D Warning Star, an AEW development of the Lockheed Super Constellation, was to have the task of orbiting off the enemy coast and using radar and other sensors to detect MiGs taking off.

The Air Defense Command deployed its Big Eye EC-121Ds to Southeast Asia in April 1965. The task force flew its first mission in support of ROLLING THUNDER operations on 17 April. Based at Tainan, Taiwan, the EC-121Ds flew their missions out of Tan Son Nhut AB near Saigon. This was the first use of the EC-121D in combat. Later in the war, in March 1967, following a move from Tan Son Nhut to Ubon in February, then to Udorn, the program would be code-named College Eye and the EC-121Ds of the 552nd Airborne Warning and Control Wing would use the radio callsign Disco. Fighter pilots would credit Disco with preventing numerous MiG ambushes. Working in coordination with the Navy's radar picket ship, using the callsign Red Crown, the EC–121D gave strike force commanders a 'real time' picture of what the enemy's air defenses were doing and how to cope with them.

The initial deployment of the Super Constellations, with their huge bulbous radar antenna protruding from their sleek fuselages, was not without its difficulty. Crew of the aircraft could range from 16 to 30 men, depending upon the mission being flown and its intended duration. Tan Son Nhut airbase was growing chock-a-block and its facilities were constantly stretched to the limit, making it difficult to accommodate the EC–121D crews in any degree of comfort. All units on the base, as at many bases in South Vietnam (unlike those in Thailand) shared the problems caused by periodic mortar and sapper attacks, but for the EC–121D crews more mundane comforts like food, lodging and air conditioning were usually inadequate. Because a typical mission could extend up to ten hours in duration, commanders regarded morale as important but, in the early stages, were unable to provide the creature comforts that go with high spirits.

BOMBING HALT #1

With Thailand-based F–105Ds and US Navy aircraft in the Gulf carrying the bulk of the bombing campaign against the North, on 12 May 1965 a new term entered the lexicon of warfare, or, perhaps, of diplomacy—bombing halt. Eventually, the history of the war would involve so many bombing halts that, years later, even a serious effort by US government historians would leave open the question of precisely how many such halts there had been.

The idea was simple enough. Show Hanoi how it feels not to be bombed for a few days (or weeks, or years). In return, Hanoi will become reasonable and aquiesce to an end to the war. The idea was simple, and it was tried repeatedly, and from beginning to end it suffered from one fatal flaw: the North Vietnamese believed that not being bombed was a natural state of affairs, that they had a sovereign right not to be bombed and that they need be expected to make no concessions in exchange. There exists no evidence that Ho Chi Minh, his followers, his successors or the Politburo in Hanoi ever gave any consideration to doing something because the US had ordered a cessation of bombing.

In CINCPAC's official report on the war, the first of its many bombing halts was dealt with in a few words:

'During the bombing suspension initiated in May 1965, information was collected to permit an evaluation of the results of ROLLING THUNDER. On 16 May, CINCPAC suggested to the Joint Chiefs of Staff that further respite for North Vietnam would serve to make future problems more difficult in South Vietnam and Laos. On this basis CINCPAC recommended resumption of ROLLING THUNDER and received authorization from higher authority to resume operations on 18 May 1965.'[4]

Under the resumption, armed reconnaissance and bombing missions were severely limited in size, scope and geographical area, with but one strike being authorized north of 20° North against Quang Suoi Barracks.

A captain flying F–105D fighter-bombers from Takhli recalls arriving just as the brief bombing halt ended.
'Those of us who flew the missions were in a bit of confusion. We had trained hard, worked hard, to become the best in the world at flying the Thud against enemy defenses and carrying our bombs to the target. Suddenly, we had to memorize ROE [rules of engagement]. We had to learn a set of restrictions so complex, so bewildering, that it was almost humanly impossible to avoid making a mistake. You couldn't fly here. You couldn't shoot at this. You couldn't fly there. You couldn't shoot at that. Worse, we were warned, and we believed it, that serious discipline would follow if we broke any of the rules.'[5]

TO RULE THE NIGHT

A key challenge, one for which US tacticians were not fully prepared, was to deny the enemy the night. This was especially important in the campaign to interdict supplies flowing from north to south. Almost everything being carried down the Ho Chi Minh Trail by foot, pedicab, bicycle, truck and convoy was moving during the hours of darkness. Eventually, C–130 Hercules transports, already flying leaflet missions, operated as forward air control (FAC) flare ships, illuminating night targets in Laos while using the callsign Blind Bat and operating over North Vietnam with the callsign Lamplighter. At first, however, strike aircraft including the B–57 Canberra had to carry their own flares.

According to Robert C. Mikesh, the first B–57 night interdiction mission took place a few days before the brief bombing halt, on 21 April 1965. Captain Howard Greene and Captain Fred Huber took two B–57 bombers up to what Mikesh calls 'a vast spiderweb of supply routes leading south from the city of

Vinh,'[6] midway between the 17th Parallel and Hanoi. The B–57s carried eight pods containing seven 2.75-in folding fin aircraft rockets (FFAR), six 500 lb (227 kg) bombs and their own Mark 24 flares. The Bien Hoa-based B–57s went in to attack two bridges near Vinh and were subjected to heavy anti-aircraft fire. Mikesh cites numerous reasons why night strikes of this kind were especially risky: Vertigo frequently resulted from the pilot's lack of visual reference to the horizon, the flares themselves disrupted men's night vision, and maps and terrain-following tools were inadequate or nonexistent. An added problem was that B–57 pilots and navigators began these missions fatigued since they had to sleep in 90°F heat during the day, without air conditioning. Only a few of these missions were flown before an accidental explosion at Bien Hoa on 16 May 1965, not caused by enemy action, destroyed ten B–57s and killed 28 men.

The US Navy's answer to the night interdiction challenge was a new aircraft, the Grumman A–6A Intruder. By 16 May, the 'Sunday Punchers' of attack squadron VA–75 under Commander Michael P. Curphey had finished their stateside workups and were en route to the battle zone aboard USS *Independence* (CVA–62), the first of several carriers traditionally associated with the Atlantic Fleet which would share the burden of the Pacific Fleet's fighting.

14 Jun 65 - LARRY GUARINO - F-105 POW

AIR-TO-AIR KILLS

If the fluke encounter with Chinese MiGs is not counted, the first air-to-air kill of the war occurred on 17 June 1965 as the older carrier USS *Midway* (CVA–41) launched strikes against targets in North Vietnam. Barrier combat air patrol (BARCAP) cover was provided by F–4B Phantoms of the 'Freelancers' of VF–21. In an encounter with MiG–17s, the Phantom at the head of a division (151488) succeeded in downing a MiG with the Sparrow radar-guided missile. A second F–4B Phantom (152219) soon despatched a second MiG–17, evening the overall score in the air war at two kills for each side.

The first MiG killers were Cdr Louis Page and his backseat radar intercept officer (RIO) Lt John C. Smith Jr in the first Phantom and Lt Jack E. D. Batson Jr and his RIO, Lcdr Robert B. Doremus in the second. Naval aviators had long believed, as did their Air Force colleagues, that the Phantom was superior to the MiG–17 in almost every performance regime where a realistic fight could take place, although the absence of a gun on the American aircraft would continue to be frustrating, especially in the Navy which

POW 8/24/65

First American crew to shoot down a North Vietnamese MiG were pilot Cdr Louis C. Page, Jr, and radar intercept officer (RIO) Lt John C. Smith, Jr, of the 'Freelancers' of squadron VF–21. The pair are seen in their F–4B Phantom (151488) on 17 June 1965, the day they shot down a MiG–17 with a Sparrow missile and returned safely to USS *Midway* (CVA–41). (USN)

for further weeks. The men who maintained and flew carrier-based warplanes lived in cramped, noisy, hot conditions with 'round-the-clock' work schedules and almost no free time except for sleep, of which there was never enough. Men in billets near the bow of the carrier were likely to be driven from their bunks by the noise and heat of steam catapults slamming aircraft into the sky. For pilots, studies showed that landing an aircraft on a carrier produced greater stress and tension than 'rolling in' on a heavily-defended target in Route Package Six.

ARC LIGHT

Although not yet a part of the campaign against the North, the entry of the giant B–52 Stratofortress into the conflict was an important milestone. The use of the B–52 had been seriously considered from the beginning of ROLLING THUNDER although, from the beginning, doubts were expressed as to whether the big, slow aircraft could survive 'up North' against MiGs, missiles and AAA. It was decided that B–52 missions would be carried out at first only in the more permissive environment of South Vietnam.

The author believes the introduction of the eight-engine B–52 to be important enough for mention even though operations in the South are outside the scope of this work and not solely because the event killed a schoolmate, Captain Charles Blankenship. Arc Light missions, as the B–52 strikes were code-named, also had implications for the Young Tiger KC–135 refuelling force. As an official history explains:

'Arc Light bombing operations began on 18 June 1965 with a mission which was heralded at the time as a considerable success, although it was marred by the loss of two B–52s, victims of a mid-air collision in the refueling area. There were five refueling tracks, but all at the same altitude; there was a 20 nautical mile [37 km] separation between tracks, but this proved inadequate under the circumstances. As yet there was no provision for [the B–52 bomber] flying a triangular pattern just prior to entering the refueling area to correct timing discrepancies. Thus it was that one bomber cell [a cell being a formation of three aircraft] arrived at the refueling area well ahead of schedule and, on making a turn to use up time gained, [a B–52] aircraft of that cell collided with another [B–52] which was just approaching the area. Corrective measures taken as a result of this accident included: establishing multiple refueling tracks at different altitudes, separating neighboring tracks more widely, instituting timing triangles on the approach and, later, establishing

evaluated under-wing gun pods but never adopted any. Commander Page had enthusiastic remarks about the Sparrow missile, however, as it had enabled him to defeat the MiG in a head-on attack, where the latter could fight only when it closed to within gun range.

On 20 June 1965, a downright bizarre air engagement occurred in which ageing A–1H Skyraider propeller-driven aircraft from *Midway* were covering a rescue mission when

two MiG–17s pounced on them. The bulky but slow Skyraiders kept turning within the faster jets. After five minutes of sweat-drenching maneuver, Lt Clinton B. Johnson and Lt Charles Hartman closed in behind a MiG–17 and shot it down with 20 mm cannon fire, each receiving half credit for the kill. The surviving MiG went scurrying away to escape from an American plane with a paddle-blade propeller up front and a maximum speed of around 390 mph (627 km/h). It was a curious and bittersweet victory.

The naval air war involved a considerable degree of struggle and sacrifice. Carriers put forth to sea for cruises of up to six months' duration. Once in the battle zone, a carrier would spend weeks 'on the line' in the Gulf of Tonkin cycling air strikes, would gain brief respite by retiring to Subic Bay in the Philippines, and would return to the 'line' again

[an] en-route refueling procedure. Also, the Philippine government consented to the re-location of the refueling tracks, somewhat closer to the Philippine Islands. To some extent, however, Arc Light refueling areas had to compete for space with commercial airline routes for the duration of the South-east Asia hostilities and Manila Air Traffic authorities naturally tended to give prefer-ence to the profitable commercial business.'[7]

The Stratofortress introduced into the South was the B–52F variant, distinguished from those employed later in the war by its tall tail fin. The two machines lost in the collision (57-0047, 57-0179) belonged to the 7th Bomb Wing at Andersen AB, Guam. Among the 27 bombers in that first mission, some also came from the 320th Bomb Wing at Andersen. General William C. Westmore-land, commander of US forces in South Viet-nam, was convinced of the effectiveness of using B–52Fs for saturation bombings of Viet Cong base areas but, if an Army general and SAC people (the latter being outside the Saigon chain of command) liked the B–52F, other officers lamented the independence given to SAC:

'The inability of the USAF air commander in Vietnam [commander, 2nd Air Division] to integrate Arc Light operations into the over-all air campaign is a contradiction difficult to accept, impossible to reconcile with USAF doctrine and worst of all has resulted in far less than effective employment of this useful instrument of airpower.'[8]

While B–52F bombers were being flown over the South (and, said some critics, merely destroying a good many trees), SAC decided to improve on the type's maximum bombload of 51 750 lb (340 kg) bombs, 27 carried inter-nally and 24 externally. The entire fleet of B–52D bombers, also distinguished externally by a tall tail fin, was being prepared for the conflict, almost certainly with the notion that the big machines would eventually fight in North Vietnam. A 'Big Belly' modification program was begun in December 1965 to increase the capacity of the B–52D to carry 500 lb (227 kg) bombs from 27 to no fewer than 84 or its capacity to carry 750 lb (340 kg) bombs from 27 to 42 internally. In addition, the B–52D could still carry 24 500 lb (227 kg) or 750 lb (340 kg) bombs externally. The maximum bomb load became about 60,000 lb (27 215 kg). In a seemingly contradictory move, Secretary of Defense McNamara an-nounced that all older Stratofortress variants (B–52C, D, E and F) would be retired within six years (by June 1971). McNamara, also quoted during this period as seeing 'the light at the end of the tunnel' which signified an imminent end to the hostilities in Southeast Asia, was right much of the time, was often quoted when he was not, and in this instance could hardly have been more wrong. It would be more than a year after its announced re-tirement when the B–52D finally reached not merely North Vietnam, but downtown Hanoi.

COMBAT RESCUE DEVELOPMENTS

The need for better ways to rescue downed aircrews in North Vietnam was far from solved as ROLLING THUNDER air strikes con-tinued. Plans were afoot to supplant the limited Kaman HH–43B/F Huskie with a lar-ger and longer-range helicopter, the Sikorsky HH–3E. Two examples of the transport var-iant of the latter machine, the CH–3E, had been borrowed from Tactical Air Command and were being rushed to Nakhon Phanom (or 'Naked Fanny', as Americans called the Thai airbase). A few HC–130 Hercules trans-ports, called King Birds, were becoming available to replace HU–16B Albatross and HC–54 Skymaster flying command posts. Greater loitering capacity by the rescue com-mand ship, coupled with larger and longer-legged rescue helicopters would mean for the first time that a downed pilot had a genuine chance of rescue.

On 23 June 1965, Major Robert Wilson of the Takhli-based 357 TFS/355 TFW was on a combat mission in an F–105D (62-4319) when he was hit by ground fire over south-western North Vietnam. Wilson strained and coaxed, but his crippled Thud refused to gain enough altitude to get over a ridge ahead of him. Wilson ejected, parachuted towards a green jungle canopy and soon found himself hanging upside down in a tree 150 feet (46 m) above a shadowy jungle floor, gasping for breath and swinging from side to side. Wil-son managed to use the inertia of his body to swing into the crotch of a tree, cut himself out of his parachute harness and retrieve the seat pack containing his AN/URC–11 survival radio. This item itself was one of the draw-backs in combat rescue, a more durable and powerful combination voice/beeper radio being badly needed, but, in Wilson's case, the radio was adequate. His signal reached an HC–54 Skymaster command ship which vec-tored a flight of four A–1H Skyraiders from 'Naked Fanny'. The Skyraider pilots, whose aircraft were better known by their callsign Sandy, obtained visual sighting of Major Wilson's parachute canopy and saw no enemy troops in the area. Wisely, they 'backed off' and flew orbit at an anchor point some distance away, so as not to lure North Vietnamese troops to the downed Thud pilot. Should enemy troops intervene anyway, the Sandy pilots were prepared to cover Wilson with 20 mm cannon fire and 500 lb (227 kg) bombs. Theirs was an especially hazardous task, since they might have to fight at treetop level where even a single bullet from an infantryman's rifle was a danger.

For once, the short-legged HH–43B/F helicopter was able to effect a rescue in the enemy's back yard. More than an hour after Major Wilson's bailout, an HH–43 from a forward operating location (FOL) in Laos—guided by radio traffic from HC–54, A–1Hs and Wilson himself—swooped down and, with a major effort by its pararescueman, or PJ, plucked the major from the foliage. With Wilson present, no member of the chopper crew was able to pay for a drink that night at the Naked Fanny officers' club.

Two new aircraft types introduced in July 1965 were each, in its own way, designed to overcome problems faced in trying to bring the war to the North. The Sikorsky CH–3E Jolly Green Giant combat rescue helicopter (to be used as an HH–3E but not yet with that designation) arrived at Naked Fanny on 5 July. On the same day, the 'Sunday Punch-ers' of VA–75 began combat strikes from *Independence* in the Grumman A–6A In-truder medium all-weather attack aircraft.

ENTER THE HH–3E - Jolly

A development of the Sikorsky S–61 which had first flown a half-dozen years earlier, on 11 March 1959, and was widely used by the US Navy as the SH–3A Sea King, the slen-der, 54 ft 9 in (16.69 m) CH–3E was powered by two 1,500 shp (1 119 kW) General Electric T58–GE–5 turboshaft engines. Because of the urgent need for an improved rescue heli-copter in Southeast Asia, CH–3E (transport) craft were quickly being converted to HH–3E (rescue) helicopters with the addition of crew armor, self-sealing fuel tanks, rectractable in-flight refueling probe, rescue hoist with jungle penetrator and 0.5 in (12.7 mm) machine-guns. None of these features was found on the HH–43B/F, so the Jolly Green Giant was expected to be a significant im-provement. With a maximum speed of 166 mph (267 km/h) and a combat radius of 625 miles (1 005 km), the HH–3E could accom-pany an HC–130.

Soon thereafter, the HH–3E proved its mettle. Its job, after all, was to prevent downed airmen from becoming POWs, where they faced torture, interrogation and propaganda exploitation by their North Vietnamese captors. Its US Navy cousin, the SH–3A although designed originally for the anti-submarine warfare role, was soon carrying out the same kind of rescue missions.

ENTER THE A-6A

The Grumman A-6A Intruder medium attack bomber was to prove one of the most versatile and effective weapons of the war, especially in the important job of taking control of the night—but nobody knew this at first. First flown at the beginning of the decade, on 19 April 1960, the A-6A was the result of Korean War experience, where the absence of a truly effective night/all-weather strike aircraft had been a serious impediment. *Independence*, the carrier which took the A-6A into combat, had also been the first to operate the type, in February 1963.

Powered by two 8,500 lb (3856 kg) thrust Pratt & Whitney J52-P-6 turbojets with a side-by-side two-man crew of pilot and bombardier/navigator (BN), the A-6A was equipped with DIANE (Digital Integrated Attack Navigation Equipment), which made it a potent strike aircraft in the humid, stormy weather and night

darkness of Southeast Asia. Up to 18,000 lb (8 165 kg) of bombs could be carried on a typical mission.

The Intruder was not a bargain basement purchase. A multi-million dollar aircraft with the most sophisticated computer systems yet put aboard any warplane, it was to test new ways of fighting—including the notion that an aircraft could locate and strike targets using its own radar, without assistance. The Intruders of VA-75 did this successfully in their first strike on a target just south of Hanoi and the squadron was soon joined by a second Intruder unit, the 'Black Falcons' of VA-85 aboard USS *Kitty Hawk* (CVA-63). *Kitty Hawk*'s Intruders began hitting targets in South and North Vietnam.

The Intruder was also entering service with the US Marine Corps, which would also take the fat-nosed, stalky-wheeled attack aircraft north of the 17th Parallel. Captain Peter Vam Zandt, pilot of an Intruder, was never

The Kaman HH-43B Huskie, nicknamed Pedro in Southeast Asia, was loved by crews but inadequate for combat rescue inside North Vietnam. Designed for local airbase rescue and fire-fighting, the HH-43B with its twin meshing wooden rotors was hopelessly outclassed by enemy defenses on the few occasions when it 'went North'. (KAMAN)

able to get accustomed to the side-by-side seating arrangement but was otherwise very enthusiastic.

'We have an old saying about neither snow nor sleet, nor dead of night delaying us in our appointed rounds. There wasn't any snow in Vietnam, of course, but after a few sorties up north in the A-6A we quickly formed the impression that we could take that airplane anywhere, under any conditions, put bombs on a target the size of a dime, and return safely. We were told that the North Vietnamese mistakenly believed our Intruders to

The Grumman A–6A Intruder was introduced to combat aboard USS *Independence* (CVA–62) in July 1965 and quickly proved effective in radar-guided attacks at night and in bad weather. Soon thereafter, the KA–6D tanker variant added to the Navy's air-refueling capability in Southeast Asia. (USN)

be Air Force B–52 bombers. That, in my opinion, is evidence enough that we were hurting them. On a hot, moonless, rainy night, we could hit them when they least expected it.'[9]

FIRST AIR FORCE MiG

With the 45 TFS on station at Ubon with the F–4C Phantom—a big banner claiming 'First to Fight' dangling in the parched heat at the Thai airbase—it was only a matter of time before the USAF would avenge the air-to-air loss of two Thuds and catch up with the Navy in the MiG-killing business. It happened on 10 July 1965. To return to Colonel Robert Titus' view of the air-to-air contest with the North Vietnamese:

'In the summer of 1965, as 7AF pilots [Titus refers to the 2nd Air Division in Saigon, which did not become the Seventh Air Force until the following year] began to strike targets in the northern industrial regions of

North Vietnam, a regular pattern in the MiG activity was detected. The MiGs would become airborne as the first strike flight entered the area but delay their attacks until the last flights, low on fuel, departed. In order to exploit this observed trend, a mission was planned for 10 July 1965 which was to give AF Phantoms their first kills. A flight of F–4s would follow the last F–105 flight into the target area flying the same speeds, altitudes and flight paths as the [F–105] strike flights, thereby giving the impression to the North Vietnamese radar that they were the last strike formation. They would then proceed to an orbit area and screen the strike force while conducting both a visual and radar search. Prior to takeoff, all missiles were thoroughly checked. The Sidewinder [infrared seeker] heads were checked for tone with flashlights on the ground and again during climbout by sighting on another aircraft. [The tone was the signal in the pilot's earphones telling him that the Sidewinder heat-seeker head had 'acquired' a heat source as a target]. Sparrow tuning was accomplished every 15 minutes while enroute to the target to assure immediate availability.

'The flight reached its orbit point without incident. Their altitude was 22,000 ft (6 705 m), somewhat lower than the usual CAP altitude of 30–38,000 feet [9 144–11 582 m] used at that time. They had almost reached Bingo

fuel, a predetermined minimum level on which a normal return is based, when the lead aircraft picked up a radar contact at 33 miles. He immediately called for a 'loose deuce' formation, a pre-arranged tactic calculated to provide a 7–10 mile [11–16 km] separation between elements [an element being a formation of two aircraft] so that the lead element could make positive identification, break away, and permit the second element to attack head-on with Sparrows.

'Things didn't quite work out that way. Due to their low fuel level the lead element was unable to accelerate in afterburner, so only about 3 miles [5 km] separation had been achieved prior to visual acquisition. Two MiG–17s passed slightly high and to the left, and dropped their tanks as they turned tightly in behind #3 and #4 and opened up with cannon fire. The F–4's went into burner and turned into the MiGs while punching off their drop tanks. The first element went high and out of the engagement. The second element of F–4s which we'll call Blue 3 and 4 [not the actual callsigns used that day] found the MiGs out-turning them but their rapid acceleration in afterburner enabled them to gain separation. Blue 4, initially flying a fighting wing position on 3, opted into a right turn to 'sandwich or split' the MiGs. The MiGs did split, one following Blue 3 and the other Blue 4. Blue 3 executed several reverses and forced the MiG to overshoot. He then rolled off into a 30° dive, gained about five miles separation, and bent back around in a hard turn for a head-on pass. He called for 'boresight' unaware that the radar was out [inoperative] just after his GIB ['guy in back,' or backseater] said, 'Go heat,' meaning prepare to fire a heatseeker Sidewinder missile. [The latter did not require working radar.] The MiG passed very close, head-on, firing but scoring no hits. Blue 3 in a slight left turn to keep the MiG in sight went into a steep (60°) dive to 10,000 feet [3 048 m] and ran his speed up to Mach 1.3. With the MiG about one mile [1.6 km] back, Blue 3 pulled into a high-G barrel roll. The MiG closed and opened fire at about one-half mile [0.8 km] but overshot as the F–4 dished out. That's all she wrote. Blue 3 pumped off four Sidewinders within 10 seconds and the MiG, erupting into a large fireball, entered a cloud. Blue 3 didn't observe his first and last missiles, but the second detonated at or just to the right of the tailpipe, producing the fireball. The third went off to the MiG's right.

'In the meantime, Blue 4 was tearing up the sky in a Mach 1.4 dive to 12,000 feet [3 657 m] followed by a high-G climb to 33,000 [feet, or 11 058 m] from which he came back over the top in a 'sort of Immelmann.' From that vantage point he saw his MiG some 4,000 feet

The all-weather A-6A Intruder was introduced to Southeast Asia by the Marine Corps soon after the Navy. An A-6A (152595) of squadron VMA–(AW)– 242 laden with 500 lb (227 kg) bombs takes off from Da Nang AB in South Vietnam. (USMC)

[1 219 m] below falling off on the left wing in a 90° bank. His radar completely out, Blue 4 attacked with Sidewinders. The first, fired without tone, detonated 4-6 feet [1-1.5 m] from the MiG's left wing tip. He hastily fired a second, also without tone. The third, with a good growl [tone] tracked well and exploded just short of the tailpipe. The MiG emitted dense white smoke, continued down until at 6,000 feet [1 828 m] it was inverted and in a 60° dive. Blue 4, closing rapidly and about to overshoot, rolled inverted, pulled his nose through the MiG, and fired his last [Sidewinder]. By this time he was aware of heavy flak and began to jink his way out of the area. As the flight proceeded outbound they were trailed at 10-15 miles [16-24 km] by a large flight of MiGs. Happily, those jokers failed to attack. I think these fights show us that air battles are violent situations in which confusion reigns supreme. Firing opportunities evolve and vanish in a second. To take advantage of those transitory conditions one must have immediate weapon response.' [10]

Failure of the F-4C Phantom's radar, which negated the advantage not possessed by the enemy in the form of the radar-guided Sparrow missile, was a subject of some frustration and much debate. Lieutenant Kenneth W. Cordier, a squadron mate of the pilots of the 45 TFS on that first MiG-killing

mission, says that radar failures were not frequent enough to be a major problem. Others disagree. The same applies to the missiles themselves, even when the radar was working correctly. 'It's sufficient to say that the missiles were a disappointment. That should come as no real surprise when we consider that not one of our missiles was designed to do the job they were asked to do in Vietnam. Every one of those weapons was designed as an air defense weapon to be used against a large, non-maneuvering target under a GCI [ground-control intercept] situation—that is, canned release parameters.' [11] Adds Lieutenant General Gordon

M. Graham, who was soon to become the second-ranking airman in Vietnam: 'The story of A/A [air-to-air] missiles on fighters is very sad. I battled futilely to do two things for years (and I was not alone by any means)— one, put a modern technology gun or guns internally on a fighter aircraft and, two, equip it with an A/A missile that was designed to shoot down a fighter aircraft, not a bomber. We (the USAF and USN) *still* do not have a missile on a fighter [in 1986] that was designed to shoot another fighter down!' [12]

Other aspects of that 10 July 1965 MiG-killing mission show dramatically just how hard it was to fly up north, shoot down a MiG, and return safely. The two crews, consisting of Captains Kenneth E. Holcombe and Arthur C. Clark and Captains Thomas S. Roberts and Ronald C. Anderson, each were down to a perilously tight fuel situation which would imperil Phantom crews throughout the war. They landed at Udorn, which was closer than their home base at Ubon, with a mere 1,800 lb (820 kg) of fuel left in one F-4C and an absolutely frightening 275 lb (120 kg) in the other, the latter amount being insufficient even for a 'go-around' whilst on landing approach. The 'low fuel' warning light on the F-4C Phantom lights up at 2,000 lb (907 kg) fuel remaining, with a gauging accuracy of

Markings on this USAF F-4C Phantom (63-7656), refueling from a KC-135 en route to North Vietnam in 1965, are identical to those of the 45 TFS aircraft which scored the first Air Force MiG kills on 10 July 1965. This Phantom, however, carries two 550 lb (227 kg) bombs and a strike camera under each of its inboard wing pylons. Absence of camouflage dates the photograph at about July 1965.

The MiG killers. Captain Thomas S. Roberts (second from left) and Captain Kenneth Holcombe (right) were the front-seat F–4C Phantom aircraft commanders when two MiG–17s were shot down on 10 July 1965. Standing in front of an F–4C Phantom (64-0693) at Ubon, Thailand, members of the 45 TFS celebrate the aerial victories. (USAF)

plus/minus 200 lb (90 kg). The Phantom's crews taxied to their temporary parking spots while operating on fumes!

Just as Colonel Titus could not recollect the actual callsigns used on that day, other historians have been unable to confirm the serial numbers of the Phantom airframes which scored those kills. None of the four MiG-killing crew members could be contacted for this history and no record survives with this vital piece of information. Cordier, who might have been a source of that information and who was rather keen for a crack at a MiG himself, happened on that day to be on 'rest and recuperation' leave at the Princess Hotel in Bangkok.

GROUND WAR DEVELOPMENTS

Secretary McNamara revealed what everyone already knew, that the number of American troops fighting in South Vietnam—the *raison d'etre* for the campaign against the North—had now risen to 50,000. American innocence may have been fading, but in mid-1965 it remained possible for many Americans to believe that their superior know-how and fighting prowess would

quickly bring the conflict to a halt. Protest against the US role in the war was beginning to spread, but had not yet reached the scale or intensity that would come later. On those occasions where American infantrymen faced Viet Cong guerrillas, or even the vaunted and very professional North Vietnamese regulars, they acquitted themselves well and almost always won the battle, but this seemed to have no influence on increasing popularity of the Viet Cong. Drug problems and racial conflict within the US forces were also beginning to have an effect but also had not yet reached the size and severity that would come later. Many still believed, despite a body of evidence to the contrary, that ROLLING THUNDER was choking off the flow of supplies to the ground troopers being faced by Americans in the south's rain forests.

On 27 June 1965, the US Army's 173rd Airborne Brigade—after the Marines, among the first 'regular' ground units in the fray—launched a major offensive northeast of Saigon which was widely considered to be successful.

SAM MISSILE THREAT

In part because of Moscow's support for North Vietnam's situation, which significantly exceeded Peking's whether Secretary McNamara realized it or not, it had been evident for some time that the SA–2 *Guideline* SAM was being added to the North's 'triad' of air defense weaponry, namely MiG, SAM and AAA. On 24 July 1965, an F–4C Phantom (63-7599) of the 47 TFS at Ubon (which had by now supplanted the 45 TFS there)

became the first casualty of this new weapon when a SAM blew it out of the sky and damaged another Phantom in its flight. The SAM threat expanded rapidly, with 180 missile firings reported during the year, resulting in the loss of four more USAF aircraft and six USN/USMC aircraft by year's end. An analyst at PACAF where people were afflicted with the contagious American fascination for numbers, concluded that the loss rate to SAMs was 61 per one hundred SAMs. Earlier wars had left no precedent to compare this with, but the figure seemed high and planners were worried—almost as much as pilots.

An enlightening view of how the SAM threat was regarded, and one which was classified at the time, deserves quotation at this juncture even though much of the discussion pertains to events which came in the two following years:

'The number of SAM sites remained fairly constant throughout the campaign, at about one hundred seventy-five to two hundred. I [General Momyer] never considered these numbers a significant indication of the threat since a site could be occupied one day and vacant the next. Regardless of how intense our reconnaissance, it became very difficult to determine how many sites were occupied.

'I assessed the enemy capability as varying from about twenty to thirty active [SAM] battalions, each having four to six launchers. This represented a high of 180 launchers and a low of 80. I believe that his capability was at about 100 ready missiles on launchers at any given time. I estimated his total inventory of missiles to have been about four to five hundred. This would provide him with two hundred missiles at launchers and another two to three hundred in the supply system or in the process of redeployment.

'The SAMs were initially deployed around a thirty to forty mile [48 to 64 km] circle centered on Hanoi with considerable thinning to the east and west. When most of the strikes had to fly under forty-five hundred feet [1 566 m], down Thud Ridge for terrain masking [Thud Ridge was a high karst rangeline which pilots hugged to evade radar detection while en route to target], his tactics were to pick us up as far out as possible and fire all the way into and out of the target. Obviously he was attempting to split the formations so as to open it up for MiG attacks.

'As the war progressed . . . the SAMs were pulled in closer to Hanoi. During strike force ingress, he held his launch until we were close to the target area or just about at the roll-in point, at which point he would first salvo-fire the SAMs and then proceed to launch at individual [aircraft]. This was an excellent

formation broke up for one reason or another when we were in the SAM belt, the missile firing became extremely accurate. Pilots, regardless of the pod, depended upon a visual sighting to make a decision as to whether to remain in pod formation or take evasive action. This is the roughest kind of decision to make. Also one could never be completely sure that the pod was working properly. Most force leaders held the pod formation until it appeared the missile was coming into them at which time a break-down in formation was made.

'We experimented with bombing in pod formation. I finally directed that each bomb run would be an individual attack. The formation was too conducive to spraying which defeated the effort. Even though breaking the

A US assessment of the effectiveness of SAM missiles at different periods during the conflict.

Surface-to-air missile (SAM) installations were a threat to US airmen almost from the beginning of the conflict. As the war dragged on, the enemy became more adept at camouflaging them. This SAM site, actually photographed after the end of the war, is hidden among trees and foliage. (USAF)

tactic, executed at the most vulnerable point in the attack, when the strike force is breaking pod formation [abandoning the effectiveness of ECM pods, which depended on aircraft remaining in tight formation for jamming of the *Fan Song* radar used to guide the SAM] to set up individual runs on the target.

'[ECM] pods had a profound effect in our whole operations. When we finally got this equipment working, it gave us tremendous flexibility to improve our bombing while decreasing losses. We went through much experimentation before arriving at a pod formation which was a compromise between the optimum spacing for ECM effectiveness and attack formation. We finally settled on a spacing of 1,500 feet [457 m] out, 1,500 feet [457 m] back and 500 feet [152 m] up between airplanes. The four ship flight with this spacing was the basic formation. The second flight was 5,000 feet [1 524 m] back and in the same formation. The second section of eight flew a little over 5,000 feet [1 524 m] to the left of the lead flight and in the same formation. This gave the appearance of a sixteen-plane box. Although optimum for SAM defenses [meaning defense from SAMs], it was not the most desirable for MiGs or for the assault.

'There is no doubt that the ECM pods caused the SAMs all kinds of trouble. Many reports filtering through substantiate this proposition. Many times SAMs went ballistic or missed by a few miles. Invariably, if a

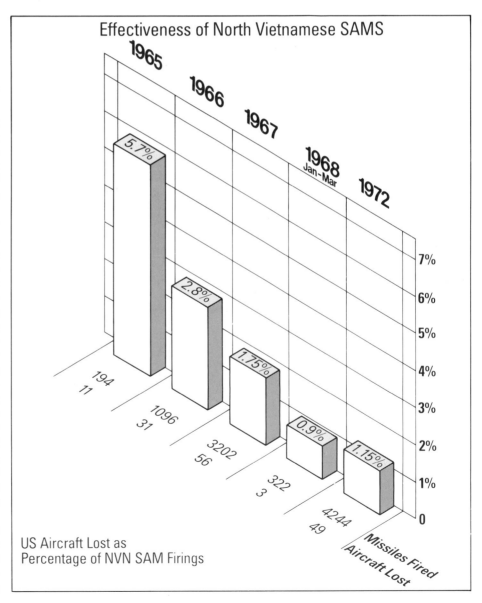

Effectiveness of North Vietnamese SAMS

1965 — 5.7% — 194 / 11
1966 — 2.8% — 1096 / 31
1967 — 1.75% — 3202 / 56
1968 Jan–Mar — 0.9% — 322 / 3
1972 — 1.15% — 4244 / 49

US Aircraft Lost as Percentage of NVN SAM Firings

Missiles Fired / Aircraft Lost

North Vietnamese MiG–17 pilots. Throughout 1965, as the US increased pressure with its ROLLING THUNDER campaign, Hanoi sought to improve its fighter force. (VIA MIKE O'CONNOR)

pod formation may have increased vulnerability it paid off many fold in bombing accuracy . . .

'Those who degrade the missile should recognize that the missile made us more vulnerable to AAA and MiGs. By flying the pod formation, we lost tactical flexibility to maneuver the force. This gave the MiGs a better opportunity to set us up for an attack. When there was a break in the formation, a pilot was forced to go down to the deck to avoid a missile fired at him. This increased his vulnerability to the AAA. It again drives home the lesson that a variety of defense weapons are needed which when blended together give the best tactical posture to the defense force.'

NORTH VIETNAM'S STRATEGY

Ho Chi Minh himself said, and other Hanoi officials repeated, that even if the Americans sent ten times their 50,000 troops into South Vietnam—which, in fact, they eventually did—it would make no difference. While insisting that the Viet Cong were natives of the South rising up against a harsh Saigon regime and that the North's support for them was largely moral support—an assertion which was increasingly inaccurate as Hanoi tightened its hold on the VC leadership and increased its infiltration—the North Viet-

namese leaders also said that if the Americans bombed them forever, they would not succumb. Their own claims for American aircraft shot down were often several dozen times the number actually located in the combat zone. Still, their message was clear. ROLLING THUNDER, Thuds, Phantoms, Crusaders, Skyhawks and brave men flying into battle at almost unprecedented peril, were dropping a good many bombs but failing to influence the course of the war. The 'progressive squeeze' of ROLLING THUNDER was not working.

Secretary McNamara, frequently quoted as saying the war was won when no one else thought so, visited Saigon in July 1965 to get first-hand impressions for President Johnson. McNamara announced further buildup of US forces. In Phase I, he said, the US would 'stop losing the war'. Phase II was the period 'in which we start winning'. Innocence was about to die, yet McNamara lifted none of the restrictions on bombing targets in the North and took no steps to improve fighter pilots' morale, now deteriorating rapidly.

NORTH VIETNAM'S AIRFIELDS

As the air war intensified, the North Vietnamese air force grew. MiG–17s (mistakenly reported by US intelligence as MiG–21s) from Phuc Yen were making limited sweeps south of Thanh Hoa and were now being regarded at the 2nd Air Division in Saigon as a growing threat to control of the air. A further concern was the threat to friendly forces in the South posed by the handful of

Phuc Yen-based Ilyushin Il–28 bombers. Indeed, had the North Vietnamese known how much the Americans fretted about a batch of ancient Il–28s which never numbered more than eight airframes, they might have hurled all of them against the South! The JCS proposed, as it had done earlier, that the taboo on bombing airfields be lifted and that sustained attacks be mounted to neutralize Phuc Yen and render it unusable.

The increasing strength of the North Vietnamese air force was demonstrated on 24 and 25 August 1965 when seven US aircraft and a reconnaissance drone were shot down. General Earl Wheeler, Chairman of the JCS, vigorously sought permission from his boss, McNamara, to attack Phuc Yen. McNamara again refused the request, citing the highly dubious proposition that strikes on North Vietnamese airfields might cause the Chinese to take over the air defense mission in North Vietnam. Again, the Secretary of Defense was overlooking the fact that serious differences existed between Hanoi and Peking. Some leeway was left for a change of this decision at some future time.

THUD MISSION

An especially difficult F–105 mission, illustrating the difficulty of maintaining the ROLLING THUNDER campaign, was mounted on 5 October 1965. Six flights of Thuds, consisting of four aircraft each, from the 23 TFW at Takhli, refuelled from KC–135 tankers and moved towards the Lang Met Bridge, 50 miles (80 km) northeast of Hanoi. Crucial to the flow of supplies from China to North Vietnam (many of which actually originated in the Soviet Union), the bridge spanned the Rong River and was protected by small arms, AAA guns and SAMs. MiGs, too, were an obvious threat.

At Bao Ha on the Red River, the formation dropped down to about 2,000 feet (609 m) and began its run-in on the target. The flights were spaced five minutes apart to assure that only one four-ship flight would be exposed to the target's air defenses at a time. Each Thud was carrying two 3,000 lb (1 377 kg) bombs and carried a 650 US gallon centerline fuel tank.

Captain Richard McKinney, not satisfied that they were low enough, took his four-ship down to a height no greater than 300 feet (91 m). McKinney's earphones were clogged with radio reports of the action as the first flight arrived over the bridge. Yet to arrive, McKinney ordered his wingmen to pickle their fuel tanks and to advance their throttles to full military power. At 600 mph (1 016 km/h) and seven miles (11.2 km) out, they could see the target area, marked by a huge pall of smoke caused by the bomb explosions and AAA fire.

Three miles (4.8 km) out, the flight 'popped up' to gain altitude and begin its dive-bombing run on the bridge. At 7,000 feet (2133 m), Captain McKinney rolled in and lined up his pipper on the bridge. Noticing that the center span was already down in the river, he aimed for one of the bridge approaches.

As puffs of smoke appeared around the Thuds and red and orange tracers filled the air, McKinney flicked the bomb release and felt the aircraft lurch upward as the 6,000 lb (2718 kg) bomb load left its wings. He turned south and rejoined his wingman whose aircraft had been badly riddled by shrapnel. As they started a slow climb for home they heard the beeper signals from survival radios on the ground. Some of their wingmen had been hit and forced to eject.

The mission took three hours and covered 1,350 miles (2172 km). Of the beginning strike force of 24 Thuds, only eight actually returned to Takhli. Three were shot down and the rest had to make diversions to closer airfields because of battle damage. One was so badly damaged that its pilot was awarded the Silver Star for bringing it back in more or less one piece to Da Nang. Once again, as happened so often—this time to men of McKinney's 562 TFS/23 TFW—it was demonstrated that going North in the F-105D aircraft was not an easy task and not for the faint-hearted.

RF-4C ARRIVAL

The RF-4C variant of the Phantom made its debut in Southeast Asia on 30 October 1965 when nine of the reconnaissance aircraft of the 16 TRS from Shaw AFB, South Carolina, arrived at Tan Son Nhut. The squadron began combat operations the following day. The airbase, well-known as Saigon's commercial airfield, would eventually be home for four RF-101C and RF-4C squadrons under the 460 TRW, activated three months later on 2 February 1966 under Colonel Edward H. Taylor. Indeed, at times, the activity at Tan Son Nhut by reconnaissance aircraft would be so intense that commercial operators would complain. Although at the outskirts of Saigon in a built-up area, the airfield was never completely safe, either for airliners or for the RF-4C crews. RF-4C pilot Captain Omni L. Bailes recalls being cautioned, while turning at runway's end for a final check before takeoff to 'watch out for mortar fire.'

Voodoo men did not take to the RF-4C easily. Captain Sam Watson, who arrived with the first RF-4C contingent, wondered why the new reconnaissance aircraft had a back seat. 'Useless as tits on a boar hog,' wrote Watson in his diary. A few days later on a mission, his GIB, or 'guy in back' happened to notice an enemy gun position firing at them and shouted a warning before Watson ever saw it. 'From that moment onward, I praised the RF-4C for giving me a much-wanted extra pair of eyes and a second opinion. That guy in the back seat became more important to me than my mother.'

CAMOUFLAGE

Throughout 1965 and into 1966, aboard *Kitty Hawk* and other carriers, the Navy experimented with a camouflage scheme called vomit green by deck crews. This paintwork appeared at various times on A-4C Skyhawks, F-4G Phantoms, A-6A Intruders and other types. It was part of an experiment, to see whether it mattered, masking the appearance of an aircraft as seen against the jungle. Because there was no enemy air opposition in the south, and because the dark paint scheme caused accidents on carrier decks at night, the experiment was soon abandoned. Navy aircraft returned to their traditional white tops and gray bottoms.

An official history lists 24 November 1965 as the date an Air Force aircraft was first camouflaged in Southeast Asia, a C-130. Air Force aircraft began to appear in the two-tone brown and tan design, with light undersides, often called T.O.114 camouflage in reference to the technical order which prescribed it. Ever since the Korean conflict, it had been conventional wisdom that camouflage was valueless because no paint had been developed which would endure and which would not impede the performance of the aircraft. This was still true. Camouflage on early RF-101C Voodoos, among the first types to be so painted, added as much as 500 lb (226 kg) to the weight of the aircraft. Worse, the paint frequently peeled after only a single sortie. Gradually the quality of paint was improved and its weight reduced, and camouflage was to become the order of the day for the Air Force, not merely in Southeast Asia but for a generation to come.

SKYHAWK MISSION

On 18 November 1965, Commander Eugene E. Tissot, skipper of the 'Golden Dragons' of attack squadron VA-192 strapped into his A-4C Skyhawk aboard USS *Bon Homme Richard* (CVA-31) and went aloft carrying

AGM-12B Bullpup A missiles, with LCDR James W. (Pappy) Morton flying on his wing. The 'bantam bomber' as the Skyhawk was called, first flown (on 22 June 1954) in the form of an XA4D-1 prototype (137812) in another era, was destined to be in the Vietnam fracas from beginning to end, flying in combat long after the aircraft designed to replace it had been introduced, developed and was no longer in production. Tissot's A-4C, the variant of the Skyhawk employed throughout the early period of the conflict, was powered by a 7,700 lb (3235 kg) thrust Wright J65-W-16A engine and carried a 20 mm cannon with 200 rounds. It was a tight squeeze, getting into the cramped and narrow cockpit of the Skyhawk, but the attack aircraft's small size gave it a low radar signature and made it difficult to spot visually. It was, in fact, so small that it was the only American carrier-based warplane without folding wings. Tissot and Morton went up into a pitch-black night, carrying paraflares, and headed towards the port of Quang Khe, south of Vinh.

While Morton dropped a sputtering paraflare, Tissot made a pass over an enemy supply pier and unleashed a Bullpup—the same missile which had been used with dismal lack of success by the Air Force against the Thanh Hoa Bridge. Tissot believed he scored hits but quickly lost interest in the secondary explosions at the pier when North Vietnamese AAA fire riddled his Skyhawk and pieces of debris flew around inside his cockpit.

Tissot headed out to sea with a burning, shuddering aircraft and an inoperable radio. In the darkness, Morton was unaware of the emergency. Tissot had no option but to head towards *Bonnie Dick* and fly anchor orbit in a leftward circle, the distress signal indicating an emergency and an inoperable radio. After a long period of suspense and confusion, Tissot was joined by an F-8 Crusader whose pilot seemed to recognize the problem and who escorted him down towards an approach to the carrier's deck. He thought his problems were solved when he obtained a good visual sighting of the carrier.

They weren't. Struggling with an almost impossible situation, low on fuel, with malfunctioning instruments and the moonless night closing in around him, Commander Tissot made no fewer than four passes at *Bonnie Dick*'s angled deck. The fourth pass looked good to him but, apparently because of a mixup in communication, he was given the visual instruction to bolter, or make a go-around. What was now becoming an interminable ordeal dragged on still farther as another A-4C Skyhawk carrying a 'buddy' refueling pack launched from the carrier and came up intending to refuel Tissot's aircraft.

About to flame out for lack of fuel but joining on the tanker, Tissot received another jolt when the nose cone of his aircraft blew back. It was hinged at the top and simply flipped 180 degrees and stayed there, creating enormous drag, totally blocking Tissot's vision, and leaving Tissot with no way to inform the tanker pilot who had no way to look to the rear.

Tissot disengaged from the attempt to mate on the tanker. He was passing in front of the tanker, its pilot finally seeing the problem, when the nose cone blew off the aircraft with a deafening sound—leaving him with a blunt nose but a lot less drag. Finally, the A-4C tanker pilot, from Tissot's sister squadron the 'Dam Busters' of VA-195, managed to achieve a successful refueling. It was considered safest, now, not to attempt another pass at *Bon Homme Richard*'s pitching deck, so the tanker pilot joined wing on Tissot and led him in a 'divert' to the airfield at Da Nang. One of less than three dozen naval aviators to have made 1,000 carrier landings in his career, Commander (later Rear Admiral) Tissot believes that the night he didn't land on a carrier, but recovered at Da Nang instead, was one of the most harrowing of his life.

Skyhawks were also used very effectively in the Iron Hand mission against SAM sites,

carrying AGM-45A Shrike missiles in this role. A typical load consisted of two Shrikes and two 1,000 lb (454 kg) Mark 83 bombs.

F-100F WILD WEASELS

To counter the SAM threat, the first Wild Weasel aircraft arrived at Korat on 26 November 1965. These were four two-seat F-100F Super Sabres from the 33 TFW at Eglin AFB, Florida, modified so that the back-seat operator had newly-installed RHAWS (radar homing and warning systems) to determine the location of active SAM sites. What had begun as a 90-day evaluation was to become a permanent part of the war—Wild Weasel flights of four aircraft, code-named Iron Hand, carrying out the very demanding and hazardous job of attacking any SAM site which threatened the strike force.

The mission was complex and perilous but highly effective. An Iron Hand formation consisted of four aircraft: two Wild Weasels carrying air-to-ground missiles and two more loaded with conventional bombs or cluster bomb units. The Weasels would eventually carry four AGM-45A Shrike anti-radiation missiles although it was not until much later (18 April 1966) that the first USAF combat firing of a Shrike was accomplished by these F-100Fs. Later, Shrikes were replaced by AGM-78A Standard Arm missiles, having a longer range and a larger warhead. These missiles homed-in on the emissions from the *Fan Song* radars found at SAM sites (although they lacked the 'memory' to continue homing if the enemy simply shut his radar down). Iron Hand missions and tactics

were little-changed throughout the course of the war and their effectiveness was often debated. While it was never clear how many SAM sites they actually destroyed, it was evident that they suppressed SAM defenses to the extent that the missiles could not be fired with nearly as much effectiveness against US aircraft. Another new term was coined, the back-seater of the Wild Weasel being officially an EWO (electronic warfare officer) but, more often, called a Bear.

The men in strike aircraft like Phantoms and Thuds depended on Wild Weasels throughout the war, particularly in heavily-defended areas such as Hanoi and Haiphong. The very high risk associated with the F-100F Wild Weasel mission was proven in short order on 20 December 1965 when Captains John Pitchford and Robert Trier achieved the dubious distinction of being the first Wild Weasel crew shot down. The pair are listed as having been lost in an F-100F (58-1231) of the 6234 TFW, the provisional designation for the unit at Korat. Pitchford was escorting four Thuds when he detected the *Fan Song* radar emissions associated with a SAM site. As he rolled in to make a run on the missile installation, a 37 mm cannon shell exploded in the aft section of his aircraft.

Captain Pitchford found time to fire marking rockets at the SAM installation before turning towards the Gulf of Tonkin some 60 miles (97 km) away. The Thuds expended their own ordnance on the SAM site, then escorted Pitchford in the hope he could go 'feet wet' (get over water) where a rescue would be more likely. It was not to be. His F-100F was disintegrating and sending back ugly black clouds of smoke even as Pitchford managed to gain a few feet of altitude. Pitchford's was one of those classic struggles which should have ended in success but didn't. He actually succeeded in extinguishing his engine fire warning light by reducing power and was on the radio to the Thud flight leader, talking with optimism about how he hoped to coax the Super Sabre to the water. Abruptly, he discovered that he had no hydraulic fluid! This was tantamount to having no aircraft and meant there was no choice but to eject while still feet dry.

Captain Trier ejected first. Pitchford followed. The F-100F blew itself to pieces in mid-air seconds later. Trier was to be listed as MIA (Missing in action), while Pitchford became the first Wild Weasel POW. He faced what can only be called an incredible challenge—preventing the North Vietnamese from torturing him into revealing details of the new anti-SAM operations. As if to avenge the loss of a comrade, eighteen more sorties were mounted in the area where Pitchford had been hit.

The first Wild Weasel aircraft, designed to attack SAM sites, were identical to this two-seat F-100F Super Sabre (56-3803) and suffered their first combat loss on 20 December 1965 when Captains John Pitchford and Robert Trier were shot down over North Vietnam. The two-seat F-100F also served as a 'fast FAC' (forward air control) aircraft in operations above the 17th Parallel. (USAF)

Pitchford P.O.W.

Although it would soldier on as a 'fast FAC' (forward air controller) north of the 17th Parallel, the F-100F Super Sabre was considered too vulnerable for the Wild Weasel role in high-threat areas and was replaced by two-seat F-105Fs from 7 May 1966 and later by F-105Gs and F-4Cs. The '90-day' F-100F Wild Weasels were belatedly withdrawn from Southeast Asia in July 1966 after a much longer stay than had been originally planned.

PRISONERS OF WAR

Although POWs like Alvarez, Stockdale, Risner and Pitchford were severely mistreated by their North Vietnamese captors, their hosts at POW camps like the Hanoi Hilton and the Zoo proved remarkably clumsy at eliciting intelligence information from them. Indeed, the North Vietnamese seemed more interested in forcing from the Americans 'confessions' of 'war crimes' than in obtaining data on the size and capabilities of the American force being employed against them.

One prisoner with a broken leg was denied medical treatment for months until the leg became swollen and gangrenous, yet his captors beat him repeatedly with wooden canes and sought, without success, to coerce him into a 'confession'. American requests for ICRC (International Commission of the Red Cross) access to the prisoners were repeatedly ignored. Some prisoners were tortured mentally rather than physically. The withholding of mail and packages from relatives in the US was a common ruse used against Commander James B. Stockdale, who was also subjected to horrible physical beatings. By not merely resisting this treatment but, in fact, organizing others in their resistance to it, Stockdale earned his Medal of Honor.

If they never managed to ask the right questions to get intelligence data, the North Vietnamese were masters of the propaganda side of the POW situation. While prisoners were tortured, visiting American peace activists were treated like royalty.

Near the end of 1965, bad weather and indecision on both sides brought a period of low activity to the stalemate between American airpower and the North Vietnamese nation. It was probably true, as one airman at Korat wrote to his parents, that an irresistible force had met an immovable object. It was often pointed out that Hanoi was not going to budge, that the resolve of its people would endure relentless bombing, and that the ROLLING THUNDER campaign had failed to cow Ho Chi Minh and his leadership. Even Secretary McNamara acknowledged that the

bombing of targets in North Vietnam had failed to produce clear-cut results. Far less often, far less loudly, it was also said—though not as many listened—that American airmen possessed a resolve of their own, that they continued to fly into the face of heavy air defenses day after day with no sign of relenting, and that not even protests against the war by their own countrymen detracted from the sheer, stubborn courage which caused them to continue the fight. If North Vietnam was solid as concrete in the face of the American attacks, those attacks came on nevertheless with the power and force of a pile driver.

No MiGs were shot down in the second

A nightmarish ordeal in captivity awaited Americans who became prisoners of war. Here, US Air Force Captain Wilbur N. Grubb is given first aid while being guarded by his captors in North Vietnam. (USAF) *Died in Captivity Remains Returned*

half of the year and no important new targets were opened up to the Skyhawks, Thuds and Phantoms that kept flying north each day. Pilots of the Convair F-102A Delta Dagger interceptor, poised to cope with the enemy's Il-28 bomber, never saw an Il-28 at all. Some of them went aloft on night missions, using the infra-red seeker devices on their aircraft to detect hot pinpricks in the jungle,

The Convair F–102A Delta Dagger interceptor came to Southeast Asia to guard against a per- ceived threat by North Vietnam's bomber force of no more than eight Ilyushin Il–28s. Although one F–102A was shot down by a MiG during the war, none ever was credited with an air-to-air kill. (USAF)

and unleashed 2.75 in rockets at Viet Cong campfires.

In a larger sense, the whole arsenal of American airpower was being misused in the same manner as the IR seeker on the F–102A. Even before he arrived in the battle zone to become one of the war's better-known Thud drivers, Colonel Jack Broughton thought it peculiar that F–105s were being used to at- tack strategic targets in the North while B– 52 Stratofortresses were being employed to dump bombs on tactical targets in the South. In 1965, as would remain true decades later, men like Major General Gordon M. Graham considered it unconscionable that no air-to- air missile had been developed for fighter- versus-fighter combat. Almost nobody could figure out why men were sent to fly and

fight in the absence of an organization well- equipped to assure their rescue if shot down behind enemy lines. Above all, there were the frustrating rules of engagement which made it possible to bomb a truck on a highway but not the factory where the trucks were built; to decorate men for valor in combat one day and court-martial them for inadvertently striking forbidden targets the next; to engage a MiG in mid-air but not to attack that MiG on the ground. The problem with the rules of en- gagement, so often cited in every narrative about the war and so essential to its under- standing, lay not merely with a civilian leadership which insisted on making target- ing decisions as far from the war as Washing- ton; even within the military ranks, men were far from able to agree on which targets should be attacked and why. It was almost as if men behind ROLLING THUNDER needed the bad weather, to allow them to pause and reflect.

In November 1965, protests against the US role in the war reached a national scale. In some locations, demonstrations became riots. By year's end, the number of US troops in

South Vietnam was to reach 181,000. It was the making of a quagmire.

ENTERPRISE

Though a general malaise seemed to hang over the conduct of the struggle, the naval air war never slackened. The largest warship afloat, the 75,700 ton, 1,123 ft (342.3 m) USS *Enterprise* (CVAN–65) driven by atomic powerplants which could operate for years without refueling, made an unusual Indian Ocean crossing to arrive 'on the line' in the combat zone on 2 December 1965. The first use of nuclear power in warfare brought A– 4C Skyhawk, F–4B Phantom and RA–5A Vigilante squadrons to the Gulf of Tonkin. The last-named, called Viggie by its crews, was one of the largest warplanes to operate from a ship's deck, having been conceived as a bomber but employed in Vietnam for reconnaissance.

Skipper Captain James L. Holloway III took the ship with its air wing, CVW–9, up to Yankee Station to relieve *Independence*.

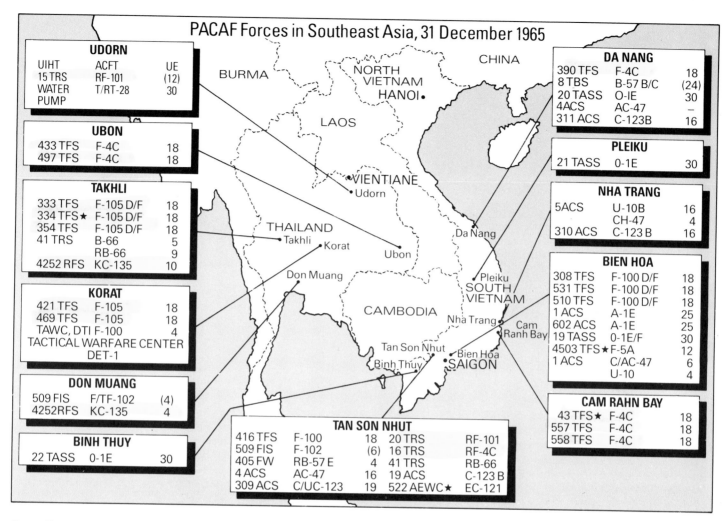

PACAF Forces in Southeast Asia, 31 December 1965

UDORN

UIHT	ACFT	UE
15 TRS	RF-101	(12)
WATER	T/RT-28	30
PUMP		

UBON

433 TFS	F-4C	18
497 TFS	F-4C	18

TAKHLI

333 TFS	F-105 D/F	18
334 TFS ★	F-105 D/F	18
354 TFS	F-105 D/F	18
41 TRS	B-66	5
	RB-66	9
4252 RFS	KC-135	10

KORAT

421 TFS	F-105	18
469 TFS	F-105	18
TAWC, DTI F-100		4
TACTICAL WARFARE CENTER		
DET-1		

DON MUANG

509 FIS	F/TF-102	(4)
4252RFS	KC-135	4

BINH THUY

22 TASS	0-1E	30

DA NANG

390 TFS	F-4C	18
8 TBS	B-57 B/C	(24)
20 TASS	O-IE	30
4ACS	AC-47	–
311 ACS	C-123B	16

PLEIKU

21 TASS	0-1E	30

NHA TRANG

5ACS	U-10B	16
	CH-47	4
310 ACS	C-123 B	16

BIEN HOA

308 TFS	F-100 D/F	18
531 TFS	F-100 D/F	18
510 TFS	F-100 D/F	18
1 ACS	A-1E	25
602 ACS	A-1E	25
19 TASS	0-1E/F	30
4503 TFS ★	F-5A	12
1 ACS	C/AC-47	6
	U-10	4

CAM RAHN BAY

43 TFS ★	F-4C	18
557 TFS	F-4C	18
558 TFS	F-4C	18

TAN SON NHUT

416 TFS	F-100	18	20 TRS	RF-101
509 FIS	F-102	(6)	16 TRS	RF-4C
405 FW	RB-57 E	4	41 TRS	RB-66
4 ACS	AC-47	16	19 ACS	C-123 B
309 ACS	C/UC-123	19	522 AEWC ★	EC-121

BURMA, NORTH VIETNAM, HANOI, CHINA, LAOS, VIENTIANE, Udorn, THAILAND, Takhli, Korat, Ubon, Da Nang, Don Muang, Pleiku, SOUTH VIETNAM, CAMBODIA, Nha Trang, Cam Ranh Bay, Tan Son Nhut, Bien Hoa, Binh Thuy, SAIGON

Soon, *Enterprise*, namesake of a carrier from an earlier era which had fought nobly against Japan, attained a record by launching ~~no fewer than~~ 165 combat sorties in one day.

Approaching year's end, the policymakers authorized a strike on the thermal power plant at Uong Bi, one of the first instances when a hard industrial target was 'allowed' under the rules of engagement. Accompanied by *Ticonderoga* and *Kitty Hawk*, the *Enterprise* launched what came to be known as an Alpha Strike, sending more than 120 aircraft to pulverize the facility 15 miles (23 km) from Haiphong. It was the closest, so far, that air-power had come to the urban centers of Hanoi and Haiphong. The fighter cover flew

the mission unopposed and unscathed but *Enterprise* lost two A–4C Skyhawks (148305, 149521) from squadron VA–76.

BOMBING HALT #2

On Christmas Eve 1965, in what seemed a puzzling contradiction to the Uong Bi air strike, the US suspended operations against North Vietnam in the latest of what was to become an almost endless succession of bombing halts intended to encourage Hanoi's leadership towards negotiations. As would happen frequently when the US attempted to send a signal in this manner, the

US Air Force assets available in Southeast Asia as of 31 December 1965. Many of these units were involved in the air campaign against North Vietnam.

message became completely lost, achieving no apparent purpose and persuading no one of anything. This time, the halt lasted for 37 days. The North Vietnamese simply denounced the halt as a US trick when they finally got around to mentioning it at all. And, of course, Hanoi's General Giap directed that the respite be exploited to rebuild North Vietnam's strength and to speed the infiltration of men and supplies southward.

THE BUILDUP CONTINUES

When it became clear that the bombing halt was not going to sway Hanoi's support for the insurgency in South Vietnam, a meeting was arranged in the middle of the Pacific. President Johnson and South Vietnamese President Thieu and Premier Ky met in Honolulu for a two-day conference beginning on 7 February 1966. Their talks covered political, economic and social aspects of the war and included general agreement that the ROLLING THUNDER campaign against North Vietnam should be continued.

As North Vietnam's SAM network grew, so too did the size and scope of air operations committed against it. The Douglas EB–66C Destroyer EW (electronic warfare) aircraft, which had operated within relatively close range to jam the *Fan Song* radars of SAM sites was suddenly proven vulnerable on 25 February 1966 when an EB–66C (54-0457) of the 41 TRS/460 TRW was shot down by an SA–2. It was the second loss of the very expensive EB–66 airframe in the conflict, one which could hardly be afforded.

Operating relatively close to a major target, the EB–66 could provide effective blocking of acquisition radars. Two pairs of EB–66s, flying in anchor orbit 30 miles (48 km) from a target at its northeast and southwest extremities could provide, in effect, a jamming beam into and out of Hanoi for the Phantom or Thud strike aircraft. At first, it was feasible to position the EB–66s at optimum altitude of 25,000 ft (7 616 m) with F–4 Phantom fighter cover, but the SAM and MiG threat eventually rendered the EB–66 too vulnerable and required its withdrawal to much greater distances, blunting its effectiveness. At a later juncture, on 14 January 1968, an EB–66C (55-0388) of the 41 TEWS/355 TFW was shot down by a flight of two MiGs and the type had to be withdrawn to jamming duties in more permissive areas.

On 2 March 1966, Secretary McNamara announced that US troop strength in South Vietnam was 215,000 and that further troops were scheduled to arrive. These figures never included all of the Navy personnel at sea in the Gulf of Tonkin or the Air Force people flying strikes from bases in Thailand. As an incidental point, but one illustrative of the whole cobweb of confusion surrounding the war, the Thai government would permit its bases used for strikes against targets in North Vietnam but not for missions against tactical targets in the South. Further, Thailand allowed this to happen on the strict condition that no one acknowledge it publicly.

ALBATROSS LOSS

The HU–16B Albatross amphibian had been an important part of the air rescue network in Southeast Asia and had accomplished several dramatic 'saves' under fire of aircrews shot down off the North Vietnamese coast. The success story had begun nine months earlier, on 3 July 1965 when an HU–16B set down in tricky seas to rescue the pilot of an F–105D Thunderchief who had been hit by small-arms fire and had ejected over the Gulf of Tonkin. A two-man Phantom crew had been similarly saved not long thereafter on 24 September 1965 when an Albatross dove through geysers of salt spray kicked up by coastal artillery fire, set down on rough seas and plucked the pair from harm's way.

The Albatross also performed a little-known role as a flying command and control post for rescue operations, two 33 ARRS machines being field-modified with extensive communications gear—a step which hindered flight performance and made crews uncomfortable in the cramped, unpressurized, unheated interiors. Though soon replaced by the HC–54 Skymaster in this latter role, the HU–16B continued to expose itself during rescue missions. The risk to Albatross crews was underscored on 14 March 1966 when a 33 ARRS crew from Korat landed two miles (3.2 km) off the North Vietnamese coast in an attempt to save the downed crew of a 480 TFS/35 TFW F–4C Phantom (64-740). The HU–16B Albatross (51-0071) came under fire from shore batteries and was blown out of the water by mortar blasts. It was the first loss of an Albatross in the conflict.

An incident involving the loss of an SH–3D Sea King helicopter from a carrier in the Gulf of Tonkin gained attention at the same time and, once again, it seemed painfully clear that not enough planning had gone into the preparation and positioning of a rescue force able to operate behind enemy lines.

'HOT' WAR IN THE INTRUDER

In the spring of 1966, the fighting in the North was heating up. There was a gradual but relentless improvement in the size and effectiveness of a defense system which now employed elaborate radar and visual warning networks to coordinate the guns, fighters and missiles which now extracted an increasing toll from the attackers. MiG–17 fighters challenged US strike aircraft more frequently and more tenaciously, and the Soviet Union began supplying newer MiG–21s. MiG tactics still entailed low-risk commitment to battle, making single passes at strike aircraft and scurrying away with minimal contact with escorting fighters. It was precisely this caution which dampened the hopes of fighter pilots itching for a fair contest with the MiG and which precluded further air-to-air victories. Fighter pilots ached to get a shot at a MiG while strike pilots could evade one defensive system, such as the MiG, only to be driven into a position of greater vulnerability to another, such as the missile. MiGs were not particularly successful in shooting down the attackers but did harry and harass, forcing them to abandon run-ins against targets or to jettison bombs prematurely.

The Grumman A–6A Intruder had proven an especially potent addition to the carrier-borne arsenal, but not without cost. The first squadron to employ the Intruder, the previously-cited 'Sunday Punchers' of VA–75 aboard *Independence* lost ~~no fewer than~~ four aircraft and crews before *Indy* completed her cruise and retired from the war zone.

The second Intruder squadron, also already mentioned, the 'Black Falcons' of VA–85 on *Kitty Hawk*, fared little better, suffering the loss of two A–6As in combat and one more in an operational accident early in

their own cruise. The men were paying a steep price for introducing the first fully-integrated computerized all-weather attack and navigation system, an array of black boxes that reduced standard flight instruments and procedures to back-up status. The Intruder, with its complex electronic suite, had run the gamut of skepticism from naval aviation traditionalists, but the heavy-jowled aircraft with its odd bulbous shape was overcoming both doubts and the sheer pain occasioned by the early losses. It was pressing home attacks in driving rain and blackest murk, when no other warplane on ship or land could get aloft. It was, among other things, virtually the only US warplane which could head into battle knowing it would not face the MiG. The A–6A Intruder was in continuous action against North Vietnamese road and rail targets, industrial plants, airfields and ports. This went on day and night, week after week, often in the foulest of weather. Later, it was learned that no other aircraft so impressed the North Vietnamese as a symbol of American persistence, although the North Vietnamese mistakenly believed during some Intruder strikes that they were being bombed by B–52 Stratofortresses! VA–85 took its third combat loss on 17

April 1966 when an A–6A (151974) was crippled by gunfire and limped out to the Gulf of Tonkin where the crew ejected and was rescued. *Kitty Hawk*'s Intruders concentrated on nocturnal interdiction when the weather, which was never really good, became marginal enough to enable other naval aircraft to find the designated targets during the day. This was one area of the world where marginal conditions were, by any comparison, favorable. North Vietnam is consistent with its continuously poor weather during the late winter and early spring, with its surfeit of low stratus, fog and precipitation, and VA–85 often had to be employed in daylight as a pathfinder for Alpha Strikes by Phantoms and Skyhawks. To minimize their exposure to the increasingly numerous SAM batteries, Intruder crews used a high-speed, low-altitude approach to the target, and then a steep climb to altitude before commencing the bombing run. In 'lone wolf' fashion, to further reduce the chance of being detected and tracked by the SAM sites' *Fan Song* radar, the Intruders flew singly or in pairs.

The third US Navy A–6A Intruder squadron to enter the battle area was the 'Tigers' of VA–65, heading into harm's way aboard USS *Constellation* (CVA–64). The A–6A Intruder

Among early Navy fliers to employ the A–6A Intruder were the 'Boomers' of attack squadron VA–165 aboard USS *Ranger* (CVA–61). The all-weather capability of the Intruder, coupled with its ability to locate and stalk a target with its own radar, made it a potent weapon. (USN)

was also introduced into Southeast Asia combat, including some operations over North Vietnam, by the 'Batmen' of US Marine Corps squadron VMA–242. The Marines also brought to Southeast Asia a much-needed augmentation for their EF–10B Skyknight, a new electronic warfare variant of the Intruder, the EA–6A, first operated in the combat zone by the 'Playboys' of squadron VMCJ–2. The Marine squadrons operated from Chu Lai and Da Nang.

CREATION OF SEVENTH AIR FORCE

On 1 April 1966, a major change in US Air Force command structure reflected the growing scale of US involvement in the war. The 2nd Air Division, which had been responsible for USAF operations in Vietnam, was

Soon after the Navy introduced the A–6A Intruder to night and all-weather operations in Southeast Asia, the Marine Corps arranged the debut of the EA–6A electronic warfare (EW) aircraft, intended in part to replace the EF–10B Skyknight. The 'Playboys' (note tail emblem) of squadron VMCJ–2 were first in Southeast Asia with the EA–6A. (USMC)

discontinued and replaced by the Seventh Air Force (referred to correctly with its number designation spelled out, but often abbreviated as 7th Air Force or 7AF), headquartered at Tan Son Nhut airbase near Saigon. By becoming a numbered air force in its own right, the new command was no longer subordinate to Thirteenth Air Force in the Philippines but, rather, reported directly to PACAF headquarters in Hawaii.

Command relationships were to remain cumbersome throughout the war. Seventh Air Force commander Lt Gen. Joseph H. Moore reported to MACV (Military Assistance Command Vietnam) chief, General William Westmoreland, for some purposes and for others to PACAF chief, General Hunter Harris. Moore had control of all USAF aircraft 'in country' but not over Navy aircraft which flew similar missions against the same targets. He had fighter wings at his disposal but never commanded the in-theater KC–135 and B–52 assets which remained under the purview of SAC. Lt Gen. William W. (Spike) Momyer, who replaced Moore as the ranking airman in Saigon on 1 July 1966 said that command and control of the B–52s, which did not even fly over North Vietnam until 11 April 1966, was a continuing problem throughout the war. SAC had a liaison section which functioned in reality, if not on paper, as part of Seventh Air Force headquarters, but this was little help in resolving questions about lines of authority which, at best, remained ambiguous. The targeting situation remained an abomination, to say the least. The Seventh Air Force commander could only 'nominate' targets, the actual approval of any target requiring separate endorsements from PACAF and the JCS, Secretary of Defense McNamara, and not infrequently from President Johnson himself. Quite apart from political restraints, which prevented attacks on North Vietnamese airfields and other tempting targets, numerous opportunities for effective use of airpower were lost simply because, even when a target was approved, by the time the decision was made the military advantage was lost.

General Momyer's views about the situation are an important part of the argument and debate which was to range over ROLLING THUNDER and warrant quotation in detail: '[Our] command structure is more complex than any arrangement we had in World War II. In my judgment, we have gone backwards in our command arrangements. The [mere] fact that the organization works is a tribute to the intelligence and skill of the people in it.'

Speaking later, in the past tense, Momyer felt that a single commander should have been responsible for all air operations, USAF and Navy:

'It seemed to me that the war was perceived as two distinct entities, the war in the north and the war in the south. As a result of this perception, CINCPAC ran the war in the north as the theater commander, while COMUSMACV [General Westmoreland] as a sub-unified commander ran the war in South Vietnam for CINCPAC.

'This was a fundamental fallacy. The war in the north was really inseparable from the war in the south. The same air forces were used for both tasks. The success or failure in the north had a direct impact on the fighting in the south. On the other hand, the fighting in the south was a direct determinent of the stress put on the logistical system. Hence, the decisions for the application of the total forces was inter-related and really couldn't be parceled out.

'There is no doubt the Vietnamese and Thailand problem impacted on the judgments about the organization . . . It was argued that the Thais would not consent to having [US] forces based in their country under a command located in Vietnam. These arguments were magnified out of proportion at least insofar as organizing US forces . . .

'Coordination of air was even more complex. There was no single airman responsible for either air operations in-country or out-of-country. [Eventually] air operations [inside South Vietnam] were placed under single management which made the Deputy Commander for Air MACV [the same person as commander, Seventh Air Force] responsible for the fixed wing and reconnaissance air assets of the Air Force and Marines.

'[It was not General Momyer in Saigon but the commander of PACAF in Hawaii who] was responsible for the USAF air operations in Route Package Five and Six-A. [The PACAF commander] delegated the accomplishment of these operations to the commander of the Seventh Air Force.

'[In order to give the Navy a part of the command structure] CINCPACFLT was given the responsibility for air operations in Route Package Two, Three, Four, and Six-B. He delegated the day-to-day planning and execution of strikes to the Commander 7th Fleet who in turn delegated the accomplishment of the strikes to the Commander, Task Force 77. Short of CINCPAC [in Hawaii], there was no single authority for directing the total war effort. *No commander on the spot where the fighting was taking place had overall authority* [emphasis added].'

General Momyer continues, arguing the need for a single commander of all air operations:

'As Deputy Commander of MACV for Air, I had limited authority since the job was one of coordination. The responsibility for the coordination of air operations with the exception of the internal problem of air support and the control of those missions was beyond [my authority and] the authority of MACV, since CINCPACAF and CINCPACFLT had delegated air operations to their subordinate commands which did not report to MACV.'

Momyer also lamented that, 'SAC B–52 forces operated outside the operational control of either CINCPAC or COMUSMACV.'[14]

It was at about this time that the *New York Times* pointed out that the United States, with less than three million men under arms, now had more generals and admirals than it had had at the height of World

War Two with thirteen million. Admiral Sharp (CINCPAC) and General Harris (PACAF) in Hawaii, General Westmoreland (COMUSMACV) and General Momyer in Saigon (Seventh Air Force) and their numerous subordinates added up to a situation where there were simply too many people in charge. Momyer clearly wanted to command all air assets in Southeast Asia, a situation which would have seemed intolerable to Navy men aboard carriers in the Gulf of Tonkin. The problem was described in somewhat easier language by Momyer's deputy, Major General Gordon M. Graham:

'The necessity and importance of a single air commander for tactical air operations in Southeast Asia is so obvious to those who are employed in the theater that it is difficult to understand how the present command relationships were allowed to generate and continue in being. We learned this lesson in World War II, re-confirmed it in Korea, practiced it religiously in large-scale joint exercises and then proceeded to completely abrogate the principle in Southeast Asia.

'Two air commanders, the commander of Seventh Air Force [Momyer] and the commander of Task Force 77 [Rear Admiral Kent Kreuser] are charged with conducting air operations in North Vietnam. Strikes in Route Packages Two, Three, Four, Five and Six have not followed a coherent plan because integration of USAF and US Navy strike plans is not done. No joint planning and executing agency for air operations exists in Southeast Asia.

'[An] illustration of the fragmentation of command of air operations is the C–130 airlift operation. While these aircraft are under the 'operational control' of Seventh Air Force (just as are Thai-based strike and recce aircraft), here again are continuous problems and less than optimum management of resources occurs. A much more effective operation of the C–130 fleet,'[15] concluded Graham, would be to place all C–130 Hercules aircraft in Southeast Asia under a single command. Later, when the Air Force took over the operation of the C–7A Caribou, which did yeoman service supporting outlying airfields, including many engaged in the war against the North, the same issue would arise.

11 APRIL 1966: B–52s NORTH
As part of the continuing effort to choke the network of supply routes known collectively as the Ho Chi Minh Trail, B–52 Stratofortresses entered North Vietnamese airspace for the first time on 11 April 1966, bombing

By the time B–52 Stratofortress bombers first appeared in North Vietnam's airspace on 11 April 1966, aircraft like this camouflaged B–52D (56-670) had replaced the uncamouflaged B–52F aircraft used initially in the South. (USAF)

Route 15 at the Mu Gia Pass between North Vietnam and Laos, about 65 miles (104 km) south of Vinh. B–52 strikes, known as Arc Light missions, had, as indicated earlier, already been underway in South Vietnam.

At first, the SAC bombers committed to the conflict were B–52F models. Each bomber's maximum payload was 51 750 lb (340 kg) bombs, 27 carried internally and 24 externally. Meanwhile, the entire B–52D fleet was rebuilt for the conflict. The 'Big Belly' modification program was begun to increase the B–52D's capacity to carry 500 lb (227 kg) bombs from 27 to 42 internally. In addition, the B–52D could still carry 24 500 lb (227 kg) or 750 lb (340 kg) bombs externally. The 'Big Belly' B–52D maximum load of 60,000 lb (25 154 kg) was about a 50 per cent improvement over the B–52F.

Normally, two B–52 wings plus augmentee aircraft and crews were maintained at any one time at Andersen AB, Guam, for combat operations in Southeast Asia. While committed to the conflict, these B–52 wings were assigned to the 3rd Air Division's 4133rd Bomb Wing, Provisional, which had been organized a few weeks earlier on 1 February 1966. The first strikes into North Vietnam coincided with the April arrival at Andersen of the 28th and 484th Bomb Wings with the 'Big Belly' B–52D to replace the B–52F as the SAC bomber in the Vietnam conflict.

So far, Stratofortresses were going north only into Route Package One, in the relatively permissive environment at the southern extremity of North Vietnam. For propaganda reasons, Hanoi wanted very much to shoot down a B–52 and claimed to have done so when it had not. B–52s stayed away from high-intensity areas where it could actually happen.

FLYING 'IN THE BARREL'

Two MiG–17s were shot down by F–4C Phantoms of the Ubon-based 'Triple Nickel' squadron, the 555 TFS / 8 TFW, on 23 April 1966—the first air-to-air victories in more than nine months. At about this time, a young pilot sat down and penned his thoughts for those who would follow him into the high risk area where men now faced MiGs, flak and SAMs. Previously classified Secret, the impressions of Captain Edward W. O'Neil, Jr, pilot of an RF–101C Voodoo reconnaissance craft, were made available for the first time for this narrative. O'Neil uses some jargon in creating guidelines for others to follow. He also describes how it feels in the cockpit. He flew 59 combat missions with the 20 TFS / 460 TRW and was left to reflect upon why some men lived and some died.

'I do not believe the people who came back were lucky, but I cannot help thinking some of the people who did not return were unlucky. The atmosphere was hostile but [we were not always threatened by] MiGs. We lost three [RF–101C] crews, very competent crews, each with over 60 missions. We lost them to *something*—if only we knew what.

'My experience and the missions I flew resulted in some flights over all areas of Route Packages Five and Six north of Hanoi. I have never been to the area within 10 miles [1.6 km] of Hanoi, or immediately south of that city. I have never executed a sea entry or escape. I have never seen a MiG. I have done and have seen and have experienced the following. I have been to Kep airfield, the Bac Ninh POL installation, the Thai Nguyen steel works, Yen Bai airfield, Thud Ridge, and throughout and around the valley around these areas many times. I have tried it "high" and I have tried it "in the weeds". I have been hit and have watched them fire at me. I have seen a SAM launched at a flight of Thuds. I have been so scared under fire that I once forgot to turn on my cameras, perhaps because of the fascination of seeing muzzle flashes for the first time. I have tossed and turned in the night, and gagged in the morning when I brushed my teeth. At times I have slept like a child. I have worried about myself

Previously unpublished view of RF–101C Voodoo (66-212) flown by Captain Edward W. O'Neil, Jr, a thoughtful young pilot who wrote a classified report warning others about the dangers of the long-range reconnaissance mission into North Vietnam. During the period after introduction of camouflage but before advent of two-letter tail codes, Voodoos were painted in several different camouflage schemes. (VIA ROBERT F. DORR)

and worried about the mission of others. I have seen men go to God and men go to booze. I have not seen a hero. I have seen a man for what he is, and a war for what it brings.

'[In the RF–101C Voodoo], the single ship concept for reconnaissance in both highly defended and undefended targets is the most profitable employment of aircrews and aircraft and offers the following advantages:

1. Maneuverability, without wingman consideration.
2. High-speed low level terrain masking.
3. Weather penetration [at] any time.
4. Minimum radio transmissions.
5. Maximum speed employment.
6. Minimum enemy target development.
7. [Optimum] use of fuel, i.e., wingman will normally use more fuel than leader.
8. A chance to be alone in a decision and a plan.

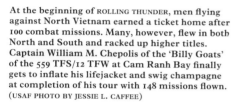

At the beginning of ROLLING THUNDER, men flying against North Vietnam earned a ticket home after 100 combat missions. Many, however, flew in both North and South and racked up higher titles. Captain William M. Chepolis of the 'Billy Goats' of the 559 TFS/12 TFW at Cam Ranh Bay finally gets to inflate his lifejacket and swig champagne at completion of his tour with 148 missions flown. (USAF PHOTO BY JESSIE L. CAFFEE)

The RA–5C Vigilante reconnaissance craft was one of the largest warplanes to operate from shipboard. In short-lived experimental camouflage, an RA–5C (150834) of squadron RVAH–13 taxies on the deck of USS *Kitty Hawk* (CVA–63) off the coast of Vietnam on April 13, 1966. (USN)

'The high threat SAM will always, except in the most unique situation (i.e., movement of a SAM site to previously undefended area in order to surprise launch into known used flight paths) be located in highly defended areas. Therefore, consideration must be given to automatic weapons, 37, 57, 85 and 100 mm, plus the SAM. High altitude flying in a SAM area is out of the question. Although the probability of the enemy launching against a single ship [such as a lone RF–101C on a photo-gathering mission] is much less than their launching against a flight, you *can* expect a launch of up to three SAMs (minimum separation 6 seconds) at any time you fly above treetop level.

'How can you effectively acquire a target in a highly defended, high-threat SAM area? Flying at 4,600 to 8,000 feet [1 491 to 2 432 m], jinking, jinking heavily until you're almost sick, works if you don't have to stay up too long. If you have to be up [moving at high altitude over the target area] longer than two minutes, this method is not satisfactory, and the only way I think you can do it is "in the weeds." By "in the weeds", I don't mean so low that flying becomes more dangerous than the enemy. I mean below the peaks in the mountains and about 50 feet [17 m] in the flatlands. You fly "in the weeds" except over major roads, railroads and rivers. At these points you "pop," jinking, up to at least 4,600 feet [1 491 m], then descend, jinking, back to

"the weeds", and about two minutes before getting into the defenses surrounding your target (always expect defenses around the targets we are presently flying) you hit afterburners, pull the trigger for cameras, and "pop up", jinking and looking. You keep all cameras going, and continue to jink up to altitude for your target.

'During the "pop" you've got to think about missiles, so when you get a launch indication or see a SAM coming at you your best maneuver is *down*. Unfortunately, down means into a high concentration of guns, but the higher you are, the longer the SAM can track you, the less your chances are of ducking it and ending up "in the weeds" or behind a knoll to avoid others. You have to go down, and this does not mean performing a split-S. (A split-S is just long enough in the "roll over" phase to get a hit in your back). It means push the stick forward and keep your eye on the missile. You have to keep seeing it to avoid it. You have to force the SAM into a turn it can't make. Remember, Gs are relative to airspeed and the SAM is going so fast it cannot out-turn you, even in the RF–101C. SAMs can pull about eight Gs, but that is not much of a turn radius when you're going Mach 2.

'Once you have acquired the target it is [time to] get out and get home, keeping out of the hostile areas and "on the deck." Don't go after bonus targets. If you have had your cameras on all the way, from "pop" to back "in the weeds," and you are in a heavily de-

fended area you'll also have a lot of bonus targets without knowing it. You'll also be able to see most of the AAA positions that fired at you—they are easy to spot—their muzzle flashes and smoke are evident on the film. Even the *Fan Song* [radar] pointing at you will be noticeable [on your film]. The mission is fragged [ordered], so fly the frag [follow orders], that is what you are there for.'

Captain O'Neil's narrative turns to getting hit, the principal concern not merely of RF–101C pilots but of every man who flew into North Vietnam:

'Hits must be expected and strangely enough, small arms hits in the aircraft are not usually felt. You will know if a 37-mm [or larger] gets a good hit, and if you are hit, no matter what type of hit, go home! You never know the damage it has caused, and going home is the only answer. Go home as expeditiously as possible and let everyone "on our side" know [by radio] you were hit. It may develop into real trouble.

'Regarding aircraft auxiliary equipment, and the use of same while in a highly defended area, I feel that consideration must be given to the possibility that anything that transmits a signal can be used by the enemy to DF [direction find] your position. The radio, TACAN, radar altimeter and IFF [identification, friend or foe] have to be considered. The TACAN should be turned off. The radar altimeter is useful for the automatic camera function, if used, and transmits only directly down from the aircraft, so I keep it on. The UHF [ultra-high frequency] radio is manually set for SAR [search and rescue] primary and placed on Guard [the international distress frequency], not all the time, but most of the time. The reason: If I want to talk I want everyone to hear me because I'm in trouble. If I'm OK, I don't talk. At other times, I set up the radio to have the strike frequency "tuned in" and listen to the fighters that I know are in the general area. By just listening I can tell how the air action and general defenses are progressing. I always check for callsigns and target locations of strikes going on while I am in the area. It is not SOP [standard operating procedure], but I turn my IFF to "standby"—I don't want hostile interrogation of my set—who knows, maybe they'll think I'm one of them!

RECONNAISSANCE MISSION

'Say, about cameras—have them ready to turn on immediately after you take off. I think the climb check is a good time. You never know when you will overfly something significant, and setting up the cameras might be too late—so, "be prepared," always.

'About flight planning and scheduling. Schedules should be up the day before showing general areas, designated aircrews who will be going the next day. It is not necessary and *not* the best idea to let the crew know the exact target he has tomorrow. If he knows he has a rougher than usual target it affects his

Flying 'in the barrel', as Captain O'Neil put it, meant taking the newly camouflaged RF–101C Voodoo into harm's way. Two RF–101C Voodoos, with 56-0063 in the foreground, pass through Hickam AFB, Hawaii, en route to the combat zone. (USAF)

rest and entire attitude the night before the mission, so I think it is best to let him know the route package he will be in tomorrow [i.e., tell the pilot the general area where he will be heading on the night before] but wait until he picks up the target folder [on the day of the mission] to find out the rest. The schedule, once set, should not be changed under any circumstances short of an emergency. Let the ball fall where it may, but do not change the schedule. If an individual has a rough morning mission and gets a "go," fine. If he gets a "cancel," fine. Then let him have a "piece of cake" but don't put him on another rough target the same day. He is not mentally prepared to 'sweat out' another rough mission. Don't cancel him out completely, either. Make sure he gets an alternate, a "piece of cake."'

BEGINNING A MISSION

Some of RF–101C Voodoo pilot O'Neil's comments at the start of a combat mission apply only to his own, highly specialized aircraft but others apply to the general situation faced by airmen in the spring of 1966. O'Neil's 'nitty gritty' details are the sort of minutia frequently left out of combat narratives.

'The proper time to get your target folder and start the plan, I believe, is three hours before takeoff, not before and not later. I find that laying out the map, and just looking at it, is the best way to start. Have a cup of coffee

and just look. Look at the target. Look at the high-threat SAM sites. Just look. I sometimes just look for one-half hour. I digest the map. I go to the relief map and digest the terrain. I watch others planning. Where are they going, and how are they going in? What escape routes are they using? I watch and ask questions.

'We in recce are individuals, flying single-seat [RF–101C], individual aircraft. We all have ideas, based on self confidence, training, our experience, and the experience of others. When we plan a route, we are all trying to accomplish the same end result. When a recce pilot plans a mission, he alone is responsible for that plan, his life depends on the success of the plan, so *never*, *never volunteer* suggestions on how he should plan his flight. If he *asks* your opinion of his flight plan, tell him it is the best route you have ever seen. If you are asked for information, give it gladly, but do not be critical of anyone else's plan. Confidence in the mission is necessary, and the reasoning behind his plan is not known to you, so look and ask questions but do not volunteer information. The only exception would be something that happened to *you* over an area in his proposed flight.'

Captain O'Neil goes on to emphasize the importance of careful planning. His recommendations square with those of another reconnaissance pilot, Lt Col. Carl Loveland, who feels that eight hours are required to properly plan a three-hour combat mission! Many of O'Neil's comments reflect the pride

felt by RF–101C pilots in flying a very large and very sophisticated aircraft alone. By this stage in the war, the RF–4C Phantom was becoming almost as numerous as the RF–101C and some pilots were already making the transition, but few Voodoo pilots ever felt the same love for the two-man Phantom that they held towards the single-place Voodoo.

That pride in being 'alone, unarmed and unafraid' is reflected in the final paragraph of O'Neil's report, which is testimony to the individualism and bravery of Voodoo pilots. 'What will the flight be like? Well, you won't have MiG cover. Only under ideal conditions will you get a tanker. And ELINT [electronics intelligence] will seldom be around. So you're on your own, fellow, *really* on your own! If you're lucky, you'll not be the last man of the day in the valley. Maybe some strikes will be going on. If they are, then expect some MiGs. But lucky for you most of the [MiG attacks] will be against the Thuds, so maybe you can slip in and out with little trouble. If you have to go in one or two hours after the strike [for post-strike reconnaissance], they'll be waiting for you. They're shooting at you, fellow, and all the training and skill that you have acquired is directed towards this moment. So good luck!'[16]

ENTER THE MiG–21

The origins of the next fighter to be acquired by the North Vietnamese lay in Korean War experience on the side which lost an air-to-air battle, then, by a wide margin. Pilots wanted an air superiority fighter from which all unnecessary equipment would be eliminated, leaving a simple, nimble, lightweight craft designed for the air-to-air role. Limited in range and payload, and not easy to learn to fly, the new fighter—the MiG–21—was far from perfect, but it had a twin-barrel 23 mm GSh–23 cannon at a time when most Phantoms had no guns and it could also carry up to four KA–13 (AA–2) *Atoll* air-to-air missiles, the enemy's closest equivalent to the Sidewinder. Powered by a 16,500 lb (7 500 kg) thrust Tumansky R–25 turbojet with afterburner, the MiG–21 could fly at 1,320 mph (2 125 km/h) or Mach 2 at 36,000 ft (11 000 m). Air-to-air combat in North Vietnam had already proven that speed was not an important attribute when you were trying to outfight a Phantom, but the *Atoll* missiles provided a capability not usually found on the earlier MiG–17 (although neither MiG ever operated with radar-guided missiles like the Sparrow). The MiG–21 was advanced enough to worry US airmen considerably, even if it did not become the favorite mount of the enemy's best fighter pilots. Indeed,

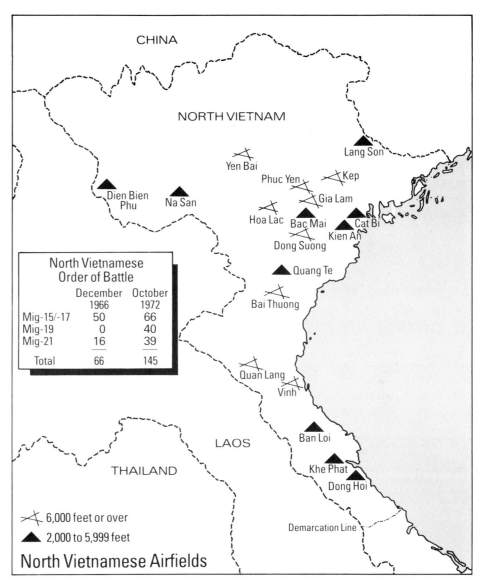

North Vietnamese Order of Battle		
	December 1966	October 1972
Mig-15/-17	50	66
Mig-19	0	40
Mig-21	16	39
Total	66	145

✕ 6,000 feet or over
▲ 2,000 to 5,999 feet

North Vietnamese Airfields

North Vietnamese airfields and jet fighter assets in December 1966 (ROLLING THUNDER) and in October 1972 (LINEBACKER).

North Vietnam's best pilots continued to prefer the older MiG–17, which usually was armed only with guns, because it could outturn almost anything in the sky and because, at close range, the American Phantoms had no weapon with which to counter a gun.

Examined close-up, the MiG–21 is a remarkably crude-looking aircraft and gives the impression of having been put together under lax Third World working conditions by people who do not care if the wings match exactly. Older MiG–21s are held together by relatively crude rivets. A simple device in a nose pitot probe tells the pilot when he is at an angle of attack where the aircraft might depart. The cockpit is narrow and cramped. It would thus be easy indeed to view the MiG–21 with a kind of snobbish disdain, but this would be a mistake. American fighters had the drawback of being too expensive, too complex, and equipped with too many secondary systems which added to weight and reduced performance. The MiG–21 did not.

FIRST MiG–21 KILL

Apparently, the MiG–21 was engaged in battle for the first time on 23 April 1966, which was also the day when USAF fliers shot down two MiG–17s. The MiG–21 was to become a frequent participant in aerial duels. The number delivered to North Vietnam was not significant at first, though it would rapidly grow, but the aircraft seemed to have important political significance as a sign of Soviet support for Hanoi's struggle. By now, groups of MiG–21 pilots were regularly being cycled through Soviet training programs and returning to North Vietnam prepared to fly and fight against the Americans.

On 26 April 1966, Major Paul J. Gilmore (left) and Lieutenant William T. Smith became the first American crew to shoot down a North Vietnamese MiG–21. Gilmore and Smith promptly resurrected a custom from earlier wars by painting a victory star on the splitter plate of their F–4C Phantom. (USAF)

Three days after the first appearance of the type, on 26 April 1966, Major Paul T. Gilmore and Lt William T. Smith, crew of an F–4C Phantom (64-752) of the 480 TFS / 35 TFW, flying from Da Nang, became the first Americans to shoot down a MiG–21. In an air battle near Hanoi, Major Gilmore used an AIM–9 Sidewinder heat-seeking missile to despatch his MiG–21.

With a relatively 'hot' air war now going on—the actual intensity of the fighting was to fluctuate from beginning to end—North Vietnamese leaders continued to scratch their heads and wonder why on earth the Americans were sending brave men to fight in heavily-contested skies while ignoring the opportunity to bomb vital targets. In April 1966, American warplanes still had not attacked Hanoi or Haiphong. There had been extensive discussion about carpet-bombing the two major population centers and even some discussion about how quickly the use of a couple of tactical nuclear weapons might bring the war to a quick end. With significantly greater chance of it actually happening, there had also been discussion about bombing the network of dams and dikes which covered North Vietnam's flooded paddy fields during the growing season. The latter action would have caused major flooding throughout extensive rural areas of the country and would have seriously damaged North Vietnam's road and rail network. On the political level, nuclear weapons, attacks

on cities or bombing of dikes were all ruled out, with leaders in Washington, Honolulu and Saigon continuing to risk their men's lives whilst keeping the conduct of the war on a humane basis. From the purely military standpoint, as would be learned later, attacks on the cities would expose the relatively vulnerable B–52 Stratofortress to SAM missile fire. It remained true in the late spring of 1966 that North Vietnam had not yet shot down a B–52, even if it was not for lack of trying.

Another debate about targeting revolved around North Vietnam's supply of petroleum. The rules of engagement would not permit attacking tankers unloading fuel at Haiphong, and this was not likely to change, but it was thought that strikes against POL (petroleum, oil, lubricant) storage facilities were both justified and directly related to North Vietnam's infiltration of the south. Debate about attacking the POL would continue until it actually happened a couple of months later. Meanwhile, protest against the war intensified and debates on other aspects of the fighting continued.

Secretary McNamara told Congress that the Navy needed to increase its carrier fleet from eleven to fifteen. The carrier which had scored the first MiG kill of the war, USS *Midway* (CVA–43), was undergoing extensive overhaul, and the Navy seemed strapped, everywhere, for needed resources. The practice of despatching some Atlantic Fleet carriers for Pacific cruises in the combat zone ended up being more than a simple sharing of the burden and the risk; it proved necessary and, at times, it depleted carrier forces available elsewhere in the world. A fifteen-carrier fleet would remain a Navy goal for two decades to come, one never achieved. Meanwhile, the nuclear-powered *Enterprise* retired from the battle zone having in six months 'on

the line' flown more than 13,000 combat sorties.

Other serious problems in the late spring of 1966 included serious shortages of everything from personal survival equipment to pilots themselves. The famous 'bomb shortage,' which would recur two years later, left both Air Force and Navy strike groups without sufficient bombs to load their aircraft. A fighter capable of carrying six to eight 750 lb (340 kg) bombs would now fly into North Vietnam with as few as one or two—the risk to its crew being, of course, the same.

While USS *Kitty Hawk* (CVA–63) drew near the close of her spring 1966 combat cruise and was running out of numerous items which could not be resupplied, including bombs, the carrier's experiment of painting half of its aircraft in dark green camouflage was found to be less than successful; indeed, the green was dangerous on a crowded flight deck during the hours of darkness, while gray/white aircraft could be more easily seen. The Navy decided to employ the camouflage scheme no further. Dark-green A–4C Skyhawks, F–4B/G Phantoms, RA–5C Vigilantes and A–6A Intruders were thus a brief and passing sidelight to the war at a time when fighting was intense and losses of aircraft were heavy.

Only twelve F–4G Phantoms were built and the 'Black Lions' of *Kitty Hawk*'s squadron VF–213 operated ten of them, a few of which later ended up in the hands of sister squadron the 'Aardvarks' of VF–114. From

F–4G Phantom (150642) of the 'Black Lions' of VF–213 operating from USS *Kitty Hawk* (CVA–63) in the South China Sea in about April 1966. The short-lived dark green camouflage scheme was dropped after *Kitty Hawk*'s combat cruise. Only 12 F–4G aircraft, equipped with two-way data-link system, were built. (LIONEL PAUL)

the outside, the F-4G appeared little different than the widely-used F-4B. It had come off the St Louis production line, however, with a two-way data link system installed behind the rear cockpit, which could relay information from the carrier concerning mission requirements. The AN/ASW-21 data-link system also allowed the pilot to make a 'hands off' approach to his carrier. Studies were already under way at McDonnell to introduce a simplified, one-way version of the system in a newer model of the Phantom which was not yet ready to arrive in the battle zone, the F-4J. Curiously, the Navy never installed guns on F-4B, F-4G or F-4J at any time during the entire conflict.

The Phantom was proving itself in other ways. Three more MiG-17s fell to Air Force Phantoms in air-to-air combat at the end of April 1966, but so far not a single Phantom had been lost to a MiG. More importantly, Marine Corps aviation was expanding and Marine pilots were taking their Phantoms into Route Package One, the southernmost part of North Vietnam, where they were

cleaning out transportation and logistics targets. The 'Bengals' of squadron VMFA-542 arrived at Da Nang in their brightly-painted F-4B Phantoms, increasing Marine strength which now consisted primarily of Skyhawks at Chu Lai and Phantoms at Da Nang.

The Marines frequently got less credit than they deserved. Because the duration of their missions into Route Package One was often as little as an hour or less, some Marine airmen racked up three or four missions in a day. Unlike their Air Force counterparts, they were given no promise of a trip home after completing 100 missions. They did, however, contribute significantly to denying the enemy the use of daylight hours during the spring of 1966. Increasingly, North Vietnam's General Giap and other leaders had to ignore the fact that their nation bordered on South Vietnam and shift the infiltration away from a straight north-south axis, away from the Marines, away from the impact of repeated US air strikes, and to the more circuitous route followed by the Ho Chi Minh Trail which went through the Mu Gia Pass

and through Laos before reaching South Vietnam.

Edward H. Sergeant was in charge of a group of ground armorers working on Marine F-4B Phantoms during this period and remembers laboring under conditions of danger and sacrifice. A noncommissioned officer, he had the dubious distinction of being Sergeant.

'We would see aircraft of all the services diverting into Da Nang with battle damage, sometimes smoking, sometimes leaving debris falling behind, and we knew they were having one hell of a fight up there. We would send our own F-4B Phantoms off on a mission, watch them head up north with those great engines smoking furiously, and we wouldn't know whether they were going to

The less heavily-defended region of North Vietnam in Route Package One frequently received visits from US Marine Corps F-4B Phantoms like these belonging to the 'Bengals' of VMFA-542 at Da Nang in 1966. (USMC)

come back or not. At times, the anti-aircraft fire up there was just terrible. We also lost a lot of good guys in aircraft accidents simply because, under the stresses and pressures of wartime, it was easier to make mistakes.

'My men lived in Butler buildings [small, metal-frame barracks]. At night, we could hear Charlie [the Viet Cong] out there poking around the defenses at Da Nang, setting off flares and popping at our people with automatic weapons. I think they actually did a lot of shooting just to cause us to lose sleep. A couple of times, there were very serious attacks on the airfield when Charlie used 122-mm rockets or mortars. Those rockets were manufactured in Russia and were coming to Charlie from North Vietnam, and it seemed that with all the guys we were losing, and all the fighting we were doing, we couldn't even prevent those damned rockets from reaching the enemy in the south.'[17]

12 MAY 1966: CHINA PROTESTS

On 12 May 1966, China protested that a Chinese military aircraft was shot down over Yunnan Province by five US fighters. An official US history claims that an F-105D had pursued and shot down a North Vietnamese MiG-17 and inadvertently crossed the border. However, no F-105D kill of any MiG-17 was credited on this date. The only air-to-air kill on 12 May was a MiG-17 shot down by an AIM-9 Sidewinder from an F-4C Phantom (64-660) crewed by Major Wilbur R. Dudley and 1Lt Imants Kringelis of the 390

TFS/35 TFW. Dudley's Phantom, incidentally, would eventually claim three MiGs and survive to remain in service twenty years later.

Still, there were problems with the Phantom's missiles. Missile activity had remained low up to this juncture in the war although, in the previous month, April 1966, in eight engagements 15 Sparrows and 21 Sidewinders were fired for five recorded kills. 'In the summer of 1966 targets in Route Package Six came under daily attack, and air combat activity increased accordingly. The missiles were a disappointment. That should come as no surprise when we consider that not one of our missiles was designed to do the job they were asked to do in Vietnam. Every one of those weapons was designed as an air defense weapon to be employed against a large, nonmaneuvering target . . .'[18]

MOMYER ARRIVES

On 1 July 1966, Lieutenant General William W. (Spike) Momyer replaced Moore as commander of Seventh Air Force in Saigon.

Momyer was a veteran fighter man who had been an ace in World War Two, was regarded as an expert tactician, and could not have failed to experience frustration over the way airpower was being used willy-nilly against North Vietnam, without proper planning and with too many restrictions.

Momyer also had a sense for history. 'He was one of the few senior officers who kept a personal, hand-written diary. Every day after the work was finished he would have a 15-30 minute review with [his deputy] while he wrote notes in his horrible handwriting in his old-fashioned, ledger-type diary. He had been doing this for his entire service career

At Seventh Air Force headquarters in Saigon, this is the team that ran the 1966-67 air war. From left are Major General Gordon M. Graham, Vice Commander; Brigadier General Frank Nichols, Chief of Staff; Lieutenant General William W. (Spike) Momyer, Commander; Brigadier General Don Smith, advisor to the South Vietnamese Air Force, and Brigadier General William (Dingy) Dunham, Deputy for Operations. By remarkable coincidence, all of these men had been air aces in World War Two. (USAF)

Major General Gordon M. Graham became Vice Commander of Seventh Air Force in Saigon on 15 July 1966 and, as such, was the second-ranking Air Force officer in Vietnam. He was also an accomplished pilot of the RF–4C Phantom reconnaissance aircraft, shown here, and flew numerous combat missions. (USAF)

'a real tyrant to work for'. Momyer was demanding, and it is widely understood that he was frustrated about reporting to seniors in PACAF who were bomber men rather than fighter experts like himself.

Two weeks after Momyer settled in at his Saigon headquarters, his deputy arrived in the person of Major General Gordon M. Graham. Another fighter man, Graham had just about done it all. He had been an ace in World War Two. He had commanded a wing of F–84F Thunderstreak aircraft. He had delivered the first operational F–4C Phantom to Tactical Air Command. He had done the test-flying on a new aircraft which would soon be put into the war not by the Air Force, not yet at least, but by the Navy—the Vought A–7 Corsair II. Major General Graham was another accomplished fighter man in a war that seemed to be run by bomber men. He was especially well known for his interest in 'people problems': he cared about the young fighter pilots who were being sent into North Vietnam and he wanted them to succeed.

Graham was incapable of fighting the war from behind a desk. At Tan Son Nhut, he would fly combat missions in RF–4C Phantom recce aircraft of the 16 TRS/460 TRW with Captain Jerry West as his GIB ('guy in back'), or back-seater. The 460 TRW, commanded by Colonel Bob Williams, operated both the RF–101C and RF–4C, and General Graham proved so effective in the latter aircraft that he received a 'recce pilot of the month' award from 16 TRS commander Lt Col. James Schamber. Having a two-star general in the front seat of a Phantom was to prove fatal in the case of Graham's successor, Major General Robert Worley but that, of course, came later.

General Graham liked the RF–4C. 'The RF–4C was a good recce aircraft. It didn't really need two people to do the job but the fact that it came with two made the job easier. The GIB ran the cameras and the INS [inertial navigation system] and radar. The guy up front did the looking and the flying. I was shot up twice fairly thoroughly, both on low-level runs by intense ground fire. Got back OK both times although Jerry [Graham's back-seater] and I left one RF–4C at Korat that was junk [as a result of battle damage]. I got the hook down and took the barrier and we scrambled out. The terrain avoidance radar in the RF–4C was not really reliable enough and accurate enough to do hi-speed, low-level work. Each of us had our own minimums. Mine was 1,500 feet [460 m]. Some went to 1,000 feet [304 m]. The photoflash cartridges, of course, were a neat way to track you and the North Vietnamese gunners were very good at it. Another poor to bad deficiency was the smoke trail the RF–4C and F–4 left at high power settings and low altitude. It took the engine manufacturer years and the Air Force spent a bundle correcting this. The requirements for recce both in and out country [i.e., in South and North Vietnam] were astronomically large. Everyone in the system from the President on down wanted instantaneous photos after every strike up north and every corporal and

and had a two-drawer safe full of these books. He always had a male secretary, a sergeant who had been or was a court reporter. The sergeant was just about the only person who could decipher his handwriting.' In addition to being among the most respected men ever to sit in a fighter cockpit or command a fighter force, General Momyer was also, in the words of the anonymous writer quoted here,

At Tan Son Nhut airbase near Saigon in 1966, after the application of camouflage but before the advent of tailcodes, RF–4C Phantom 65-867 awaits a reconnaissance mission. Major General Gordon M. Graham, vice commander of Seventh Air Force, often flew this aircraft. (USAF)

RF-4C Phantom (66-438) making a turn during a reconnaissance flight in Southeast Asia. (USAF)

grunt worked miles of photos in South Vietnam every hour on the hour.'[19]

SPECIAL OPERATIONS

When the US Air Force first went into Southeast Asia, many of its elite, special-warfare units were called Air Commando squadrons or wings, continuing a tradition from World War Two. Many special operations fell under the 14th Air Commando Wing (later Special Operations Wing), which had been organized at Nha Trang airbase in South Vietnam early in the year, on 8 March 1966, and which later moved on 1 October 1969 to Phan Rang, finally being de-activated only at a much later stage in the conflict, 1 September 1971. Commanded at the outset by Colonel Robert F. Jones and charged with coordinating all USAF special operations throughout Southeast Asia, the wing performed a number of functions in the south which lie outside the scope of this history. A question unlikely to be answered fully even by future historians is, how much did the wing do up north?

One highly unconventional operation was

known as Project Duck Hook and brought six specially-equipped C-123 Provider transport aircraft to Nha Trang. The purpose of Duck Hook was to conduct low-level drops and pick-ups at night. Exactly what were they doing? An official history devotes less than one of its 899 pages to Duck Hook and provides the informative assertion that, 'Penetrations of the north were not frequent.'[20] Duck Hook was apparently intended to support long range reconnaissance teams (LRRP, commonly known as Lurps) and civilian irregular defense group (CDIG) units, these being respectively the American and South Vietnamese elite ground units which fought behind enemy lines and which are widely reported to have carried out some special operations inside North Vietnam. The official history on the subject states only that a 'reinforcement/resupply mission' to North Vietnam was the first C-123 Duck Hook mission to be carried out, and that a total of eighteen missions into North Vietnam was carried out over the next couple of years by the special C-123 aircraft, which inserted teams and extracted them deep in the enemy's heartland. It is unclear whether Duck Hook made use of the skyhook surface-to-air recovery system under which a man on the ground could send up a gas balloon connected to a special harness around his body; a cable would literally snatch him off

the ground and haul him up into the aircraft. The skyhook system is usually associated not with the C-123 but with the C-130 and is perhaps best remembered for its use in snatching a North Vietnamese officer in the John Wayne film *The Green Berets*.

Did the Green Berets themselves journey into North Vietnam, perhaps carried there by the CH-3C helicopter, C-123 Provider, or C-130 Hercules aircraft of the Air Commandos? Philip D. Chinnery, a researcher on the war, recalls Operation Kit-Kat under which US Army Special Forces troopers went into North Vietnam on reconnaissance missions. 'They were intelligence gathering. They had orders not to kill anybody or sabotage anything.'[21] Other accounts indicate that feasibility studies were made, at least, of using skyhook to extract elite troopers, John Wayne-style, although it is clear that the skyhook system was never actually employed on a real mission. Sam McGowan, the C-130 Hercules crew member quoted earlier in this history, says, 'I know without question that some of the Special Operations transports [C-123s and C-130s] were flying into North Vietnam and I have heard very convincing stories that some of them were *landing up there.*'[22]

Other special operations, including those involving B-26K Invader bombers at Nakhon Phanom ('Naked Fanny') come later in this chronology. In the spring of 1966, however, one of the squadrons under the 14th Air Commando Wing, the 20th Helicopter Squadron (later 20th Special Operations Squadron) was up to its ears (or rotors) in elite-force operations which may have extended north of the 17th Parallel. The 20th Squadron, which was later to suffer inordinately heavy losses fighting in the south, operated two separate elements. A detachment of CH-3C helicopters, the 'cargo' equivalent of the Jolly Green Giant rescue craft which eventually numbered fourteen airframes, operated from Naked Fanny and on a regular basis, as the official history confirms, penetrated North Vietnam. Known as Pony Express, the 20th squadron's CH-3C helicopter group made at least eight of 37 planned missions into North Vietnam, apparently to drop or extract elite reconnaissance troops. Penetration missions were ordinarily screened by strike aircraft and sometimes included refuelling stops in Laos. Resupply deliveries could be parachuted, free-dropped,

The RF-4C was well-liked but it could come to grief. Here, RF-4C Phantom 65-882, hit by a SAM missile on 12 August 1967, falls in flames over North Vietnam. Miraculously, the crew ejected safely. (MDC)

or lowered by cable. Most unsuccessful missions were the result of not making contact with the ground teams. As with the C–123 crews, the CH–3C people found that it was not an easy situation, attempting to hug the terrain going into North Vietnam in total darkness. Many missions were purposely scheduled when moonlight was available.[23]

A second such squadron, the 21st, eventually arrived in the combat zone with its own more powerful CH–3E helicopters and absorbed all of the special-operations CH–3 assets in Southeast Asia. (These should not be confused with HH–3E helicopters employed solely for air rescue). The 20th squadron continued, however, to operate its other element, the only Air Force unit to fly the ubiquitous UH–1 Huey helicopter.

The UH–1 part of the 20 SOS was known as the Green Hornets, a callsign devised by Captain William Tankersly, who survived 113 combat missions only to die later in a civil

air crash in the US. Initially situated at Tuy Hoa and later moved to Nha Trang, where a lovely coastal area devoid of population permitted easy test-firing of ordnance, the 20 SOS initially flew Bell UH–1F Iroquois (Huey) helicopters which had been bought years earlier to support intercontinental ballistic missile sites belonging to the Strategic Air Command in the US. Huey addicts will recognize Major Joe Viviano's comment that the UH–1F 'had the Army B model fuselage but the GE engine configured for the H model.' The unit later operated the UH–1P, which Viviano says was 'similar to the UH–1F but with [ordnance] hardpoints added, avionics improved, and armored seats.'[24] Like their US Army counterparts in the south, these Hueys were flown in two different missions—as slicks to carry troops and as gunships to provide fire support. Major Viviano will not say that these helicopters flew into North Vietnam. He also will not say that they did not.

In the slick role, the aircraft carried two pilots, a crewchief and a gunner, plus two door-mounted 7.62 mm (0.3 in) M60 machine-guns, later replaced by GAU–2 miniguns. The craft carried rope ladders and a 'McGuire rig' consisting of a seat, ropes and hoisting apparatus designed to pull men up from the ground. In the gunship role, the

aircraft carried the same crew (the crewchief also served as a second gunner), two cannisters each containing seven 2.75 in rockets and two GAU–2 miniguns mounted on sponsons with up to 4,000 rounds. Much of the work done by these special operations USAF Hueys, the Green Hornets, was within southern borders and thus outside the scope of this history. This included work in the major ground battle known as Junction City and frequent search and destroy operations, including one called Operation Oregon which came later, in May 1967. The Green Hornets are of interest here, however, only because they are generally understood to have dropped and extracted elite troopers not merely behind Viet Cong lines in the south but in North Vietnam as well.

The Hueys belonging to the Green Hornets were devoid of serial numbers or national insignia but carried a silhouette of a hornet on the tail boom. Lt Col. Philip D. Stinson, one of the Huey pilots, remembers that the men often lived in Special Forces camps where they parked their helicopters 'out in the dirt', shared a common latrine, lived in wooden buildings at best and tents at worst, and flew in conditions where they were surrounded by red dust ('like talcum powder') in the dry season and red mud when it was wet.[25] One of Stinson's fellow UH–1F pilots in the 20th squadron, Lt James P. Fleming, later became one of only twelve Air Force personnel to receive the Medal of Honor in the Southeast Asia conflict, for a Huey helicopter mission which occurred in the south.

The official history states that, 'The UH-1s assigned to the 20th Squadron lacked the necessary range and altitude capabilities and were therefore not used for missions against North Vietnam.'[26]

It is perhaps worth mentioning that no aircraft type of the Southeast Asia war was better known than the UH-1, the vast majority of which were of course operated by the US Army and used to transform the struggle in the south into a Helicopter War. The UH-1 was also used by the US Navy for various missions in the south, including riverine operations, and may have participated in special missions elsewhere.

JUNE 1966: WIDER WAR

Although the F-8E Crusader had been in the fight from the start, its first chance to prevail over a MiG came on 12 June 1966. Commander Harold L. Marr, a veteran Crusader airman and skipper of the 'Checkmates' of squadron VF-211 from *Hancock* found him-

self in trouble while escorting an F-4 Sky-hawk force. Four MiG-17s engaged Marr's Crusader formation. Commander Marr turned into the MiGs, fired a Sidewinder which missed and unleashed a second missile which blew apart a MiG-17. The persistent Marr then kept after the North Vietnamese with 20 mm fire and a second pair of Side-winders. His F-8E aircraft (150924) is cred-

While airmen fought in North Vietnam, American soldiers faced heavy action in the South and were often brought into the fray by the most ubiquitous aircraft type of the war, the Bell UH-1 Iroquois, or Huey. This UH-1B is dropping American soldiers on a combat mission. Air Force UH-1F and UH-1P aircraft were used for special operations. (US ARMY)

ited with bagging one certain MiG and one probable, both with AIM-9D Sidewinders. These were the first US Navy air-to-air victories in a full year.

LtJg Phillip V. Vampatella, who had been in the air with Marr that day, repeated the feat on 21 June when he used an AIM-9D Sidewinder to dispose of a MiG-17 that challenged his Crusader. As it happened, Vampatella was flying the same aircraft that his skipper had flown during the earlier engagement, so that the F-8E (150924) had now single-handedly achieved two certain kills plus the probable. The Crusader had been a potent fighter-bomber in the hands of Navy and Marine pilots and now it was proving a first-rate dogfighter.

In a major move which widened the war and brought it home to the enemy's urban centers for the first time, North Vietnam's POL facilities near Hanoi and Haiphong were removed from the restricted target list and were struck by air on 29 June 1966, almost simultaneously with a major press

At Nha Trang airbase in South Vietnam, members of the UH-1F Huey-equipped 20th Special Operations, Squadron display a North Vietnamese flag they obtained in a combat action. Two decades later, it remained unclear whether these UH-1F helicopters operated inside North Vietnam. (MAJOR ED VIVIANO)

conference by Secretary McNamara announcing the event. (The technique of 'war by announcement' would have its critics from beginning to end). The attacks four miles (six kilometers) from Hanoi were carried out mostly by F-105Ds, with one Thud being lost to AAA. Excellent results were claimed, but lessons were only being learned and General Momyer observed that the absence of ECM pods on some aircraft and RHAWS gear on others was simply intolerable in a high-threat region. 'These early missions were planned in great detail and with less freedom of action for the strike forces because of the initial uncertainty about how best to operate within a SAM environment with acceptable losses.'[27] North Vietnam being sliced like a pie as far as Air Force and Navy jurisdictions were concerned, virtually identical POL facilities near Haiphong were attacked by A-4C Skyhawks and F-4B Phantoms from *Ranger*. Miraculously, not a single Navy aircraft was lost in the action, which involved a TOT (time over target) of only seven minutes for the entire Alpha Strike force. McNamara stated that the decision to carry the war 'downtown'—Petula Clark's hit song had never been intended that way, but was used by pilots to refer to Hanoi—was based on North Vietnam's refusal to relent in its support for, and infiltration into, the south. The campaign against POL supplies was to continue and air action against the two major cities would soon cease to be unusual.

Three more MiG-17s and two MiG-21s were shot down by Air Force and Navy aircrews in June and July. It was abundantly clear that the North Vietnamese expected their opponents to return to Hanoi and were girding-up for a long struggle.

INCREASED NVN DEFENSES

On 5 August 1966, two years after the Gulf of Tonkin incident, Seventh Air Force people in Saigon put together their estimate of the tremendous increases in North Vietnam's defenses. The number of radars had increased from 24 to 271; the number of AAA guns of all calibers from 500 to 4,400; the number of SAMs from zero to 20-25 battalions, and the number of MiGs from a half-dozen to 65. Further deliveries were under way of the *Fire Can* radar unit associated with radar-directed

AAA guns, of SAM equipment including its *Fan Song* radar and of the Soviet-built MiGs. The numbers all pointed to an obvious conclusion—that two years of warfare north of the 17th Parallel had only strengthened the communists' resolve.

The pattern was set. Bitter American airmen who saw themselves being given confusing and contradictory instructions blamed the enemy's build up on the way policymakers had hamstrung warriors. An official history attributes the buildup to 'US policies such as buffer zones, sanctuaries, bombing halts, and the concept of gradually [rather than quickly] increasing pressure.' The grim verdict: 'The US provided Hanoi both the incentive and the time to bolster air defenses, and suffered accordingly.'

Did any of this make sense at all? Many of the pilots, especially those who flew F-105s from Takhli and Korat, were very experienced and very dedicated men who simply could not understand being asked to perform an incredibly dangerous task when it seemed to have behind it neither a sensible plan nor the will of the American people. An extremist's view of these men, coming from the same domestic Americans who had viewed Rock Hudson on film screens with such innocence two years earlier, was that they were callously dropping napalm on children. In fact, many were graduates of US military academies, representing an officer corps which has been widely regarded as among the world's best. Most enjoyed flying; few enjoyed war. Most were glad enough to roll in on a target, center it in a gunsight, and unloose 20 mm fire or rockets at what they understood to be an enemy intent on killing them, but most also wanted to go home to their families. A few could not hack combat missions, grounded themselves, or had to be grounded by senior officers—no shame, con-

sidering that theirs was an almost incredibly risky job. A few, like Korean War ace Major James Kasler whose exploits were written up in *Time* magazine, fought the war with such aggressiveness that a shootdown and eventual captivity was inevitable. (The magazine seemed to be a jinx. F-105 pilot Risner had appeared on its cover a short time before his shootdown and capture. F-105 pilot Kasler was featured in a *Time* story only days before his shootdown and capture. With the pair also sharing the attribute of being aces from Korea, the coincidence was almost uncanny, especially since almost no other fighter pilots ever appeared in *Time*.)

Kasler down 8/8/66

U-TAPAO OPENS

On 10 August 1966, the newly-built airbase at U-Tapao, Thailand, designed to accommodate KC-135s and B-52s, became operational. Like all airfields in Thailand, it was officially a Thai base (and in this instance a Thai *naval* base), but it had been built with American effort and expense. Construction of the cantonment area at U-Tapao had commenced only a few months earlier, 15 April 1966, with an additional US$44 million allocated for the base. An 11,500 ft (3 090 m) runway, the longest in Southeast Asia, was completed in record speed on 4 July 1966. U-Tapao was not especially busy when it first opened but its future importance to the war effort would be enormous. Bed-down of SAC B-52s at U-Tapao did not actually take place until a year later, April 1967, but their arrival would place targets within three hours, rather than the twelve-hour flight required from Guam.

Living conditions at bases in Southeast Asia varied considerably, with some men in tents, others in stucco, air-conditioned bil-

lets. In general, everything came to war with the American warrior—the PX (post exchange), commissary and club, local TV and radio stations, movie theaters, and so many other amenities that fewer than one man in every ten were actually participating in combat. Later on, at Cam Ranh Bay, F-4C Phantom pilots would live in corrugated metal trailers which sometimes had air-conditioning and sometimes did not. Few ever enjoyed genuine comfort and the weather was a constant irritant—dry heat, wet heat, thunderstorms.

ENLISTED TROOPS

Although few of them were actually on board the warplanes which penetrated North Vietnam, enormous risks were taken by almost all of the enlisted men who maintained, worked on, spit-shined and sometimes cried over the Thuds, Phantoms, Skyhawks and Crusaders that waged the war. Aboard a carrier at sea, it was not uncommon for an enlisted armorer or electronics technician to work eighteen hours, catch a few hours of sleep and begin the cycle over again. At Takhli and Korat, the men maintaining F-105 Thunderchiefs worked all night in hot, high-pressure conditions so that pilots could fly the Thuds all day.

Sergeant Rod Ricks arrived at Tan Son Nhut to begin his brief tour as a 'photo fixer', maintaining the reconnaissance package on the RF-101C Voodoo, only to find that he was in nearly as much danger as the pilot of the craft. Ricks served with the 460 AEMS (aircraft and engine maintenance squadron), part of the 460 TRW under Colonel Robert G. Williams.

'My job involved repairing the photo systems on both the RF-101C and the RF-4C. We worked 12-hour shifts at odd hours to provide in-depth photographs of the progression [sic] of the enemy. Parts for the cameras were hard to come by. Many times we had to cannibalize parts in order for a bird to fly. Working conditions were not so bad because sensitive film and electronics had to be kept air-conditioned. We were not safe from the enemy, however. Many times, our shop was riddled with shrapnel from the famous 122-mm Russian rockets [fired by Viet Cong forces in the Saigon area]. In fact, a buddy of mine was killed early one morning

Living conditions at US airbases in Southeast Asia ranged from uncomfortable to abominable. F-4C Phantom fighter pilots of the 12 TFW at Cam Ranh Bay were billeted in these relatively accommodating, corrugated metal trailers, replete with air-conditioning units that worked some of the time. (USAF)

The hardest-working men in Southeast Asia were the enlisted airmen aboard Navy carriers and at USAF bases, like these men at Korat working at night on an F-105D (66-4423) to prepare the mighty Thud for a day mission against Hanoi. Note bombs hanging from aircraft centreline. (VIA JERRY SCUTTS)

as he exited our shop during a rocket attack. He had pulled [finished] his time in the Air Force and was back over there as a civilian tech rep.

'Our living quarters with the 460 TRW at Tan Son Nhut were certainly better than tents but they weren't the Waldorf, either. They afforded little protection except from the elements (rain and mosquitoes). The food was not too bad except for powdered eggs and milk. VD [venereal disease] was very predominate among the homesick GIs. Many guys received Dear John letters [a letter from a girl friend breaking off a relationship], as did I.'

It was difficult enough laboring on, and managing others who labored on, delicate and cantankerous aircraft radar dishes, cluttered and entangled hydraulics lines, and bomb and rocket shackles and fuses. The whole paraphernalia associated with preparing an aircraft for combat was fraught with difficulty and danger, as an A-1H Skyraider worker aboard a carrier learned when an air-

craft propeller chopped off his arm. Indeed, it was extraordinary how seldom bombs and rockets went off by accident at airbases and on carriers. With all these difficulties, incredibly, there existed the added annoyance that even something as easily understood as camouflage was a source of constant difficulty for the men working on Air Force fighters. T.O.114, the order specifying tan, brown and green camouflage with light undersides, was clear enough. But the amount, quality and texture of available paint varied from one base to another, so that a Thud from the 388 TFW at Korat was not the same color as a Thud from the 355 TFW at Takhli. Colonel Dave Roeder, who flew from Korat, says that, 'even within a single squadron of a single wing, the airplanes were so many different colors that we didn't need tail numbers to tell them apart'.[29] Some of this would never be put right. Enlisted men had to repaint some aircraft after almost every mission. Throughout the war, some F-4C Phantoms were 'greener' while others were 'browner'. Captain William J. Swendner of the 480 TFS/35 TFW at Da Nang who shot down a MiG-21 during this period (on 14 July 1966) flew an F-4C Phantom (63-7489) whose camouflage had peeled so badly that the original, precamouflage paint scheme was showing through from beneath, including the words U. S. AIR FORCE painted across a gull gray

fuselage—all in all, on the basis of its colors, perhaps the ugliest single aircraft of the entire war. Over time, a better quality of paint became available and a better degree of standardization was achieved, but even before camouflage was perfected an irreversible trend had been set. By the summer of 1966, natural metal was 'out,' camouflage was 'in,' and Air Force combat aircraft would never be silvery in color again. This was to be their last major change before the introduction of two-letter tailcodes (which the Navy had used since the 1940s), known as tactical unit identifiers.

RF-4Cs AT UBON

With the formation of the 432 TRW at Ubon, Thailand on 18 September 1966, the Air Force's tactical reconnaissance assets were neatly divided among two wings, the 460 TRW at Tan Son Nhut for Vietnam and the 432 TRW for Thailand. With Colonel Robert W. Schick as its first commander, the 432 TRW was always something of a wrongly-named unit. Throughout much of the war it was primarily a fighter wing, operating fighter variants of the Phantom, with never more than a single squadron of the reconnaissance RF-4C. The 'reconnaissance' title in the wing's designation is thought to be in part a

gesture towards Thai sensibilities. The government of Thailand fully supported US combat operations up North but was always anxious to make the whole business sound as reasonable as it could.

FIRST F-4 LOSS TO MiG

In fact, it was Colonel Schick's wing which suffered a grave indignity—the first loss of an Air Force Phantom in air-to-air combat. On 21 September 1966, three MiG-17s teamed up to shoot down an F-4C Phantom (63-7642) of the wing's 433 TFS, which was temporarily on detachment to the 8 TFW. It was the very first time an Air Force Phantom had been shot down and a harbinger of the enemy's continuing efforts to improve his own fighter force.

ECM PODS

A late-year assessment in 1966 failed to yield any proof that the original purpose of the war against North Vietnam was any closer to attainment, but it was abundantly clear that the war was becoming more sophisticated. Although early ECM pods introduced briefly with the RF-101C Voodoo almost two years earlier had been a resounding failure, im-

proved ECM pods became available in September 1966 and F-105Ds of the 355 TFW at Takhli, now commanded by Colonel Robert R. Scott, tested these new tools of electronic warfare in action against SAMs and radar-controlled gun defenses. Heading into battle, it was customary for an F-105D flight leader to order his wingmen, 'clean 'em up, green 'em up, and turn on your music.' This meant, clean your cockpit of any loose objects to prepare for action, turn on your armament switches (from red to green) and switch on your ECM pod. This 'music', of course, was barrage jamming intended to foul the enemy's radar reception. The pod introduced at this time, designated ALQ-71, was not yet the final word in this very new field of electronic warfare, but it was reported by Thud pilots to be a significant improvement over the unsuccessful pods tried earlier.

At the end of the previous month, on 18 August 1966, Major Kenneth T. Blank of the 34 TFS/388 TFW at Korat had employed 20 mm gunfire from his F-105D to shoot down a MiG-17 deep in North Vietnamese airspace. On the same day as the first Phantom shootdown, 21 September 1966, yet another Thud victory was scored. 1Lt Fred A. Wilson, Jr of the 333 TFS/355 TFW at Takhli, flying another F-105D, also scored a cannon-kill against a MiG-17. The same day, 1Lt Karl W. Richter of the 421 TFS/388

Introduction of camouflage to a previously all-silver Air Force produced some interesting twists. This F-105D Thunderchief (59-1749) wears a 'reverse' camouflage pattern—that is, the areas which would normally be dark are light, and vice-versa. By mid-1966, camouflage was standard for the Air Force and two-letter tailcodes were about to introduce the next change in the outward appearance of its warplanes. (VIA JERRY SCUTTS)

TFW at Korat also claimed a MiG-17. These victories took place amid fast and furious actions which included heavy bomb strikes by Air Force and Navy aircraft. Richter, although very junior, was one of the most respected of Thud pilots. He was a graduate of the Air Force Academy at Colorado Springs, was universally respected as a tough and very aggressive fighter pilot and seemed to have a bright future—the kind of man who would kill MiGs in his twenties, command a fighter wing in his thirties and be Chief of Staff in his forties. But the fortunes of war were not to allow Karl Richter to come home alive. He was to ignore the opportunity to go home after 100 combat missions over North Vietnam, complete nearly 200 and die of injuries sustained while ejecting over the North—die, that is, aboard the rescue helicopter carrying him home.

Men like Scott, Blank, Wilson and Richter were uncommon heroes in an unusual war. In

ELLA RAINES

In September 1966, there existed no job on earth more dangerous than driving the F–105D, the Thud, into North Vietnam. At the time, most looked like this one (62-4364), their natural metal replaced by camouflage but two-letter tailcodes not yet applied. This photograph, taken at Takhli, shows Colonel Jack Broughton, deputy of the 355 TFW, taxiing out on a mission. (VIA JERRY SCUTTS)

September 1966, there was no line of employment on this planet more dangerous than flying the F–105 Thunderchief into North Vietnam. One method of assembling numbers proved, beyond doubt, that it was statistically impossible for any pilot to complete 100 missions. Despite its toughness and survivability, the Thud was to suffer proportionately the greatest losses of any American aircraft type ever flown in any war, at any time, anywhere.

ENTER ROBIN OLDS

On 30 September 1966, command of the F–4C Phantom wing at Ubon, the 8 TFW or 'Wolfpack,' passed from Colonel Joseph G. Wilson to Colonel Robin Olds. Wearing a handlebar mustache throughout much of his tour, exuding a particular image of roughness and ruggedness, Olds was very simply the best-loved and most able fighter wing commander of the war, a leader whose men would follow him into the pits of hell if it meant a crack at North Vietnam's MiG pilots. Olds

had been an all-American tackle at West Point, had toted up $24\frac{1}{2}$ aerial victories in Europe during World War Two and had married a film actress. He had missed out on the Korean conflict despite repeated requests for combat duty there and he was not going to miss out again.

One of Olds' early tasks was to commit his resources to night operations against the Ho Chi Minh Trail. The Phantoms of the 497 TFS, part of the 8 TFW, drew this task. As recalled by Lieutenant Myron L. Donald, who later was shot down and became a POW, 'the 497th was primarily a night truck-hunting squadron that flew over Laos and Route Package One in the southern part of North Vietnam. Usually, we had no assigned targets at the time of takeoff. We checked with the [C–130 Hercules] Airborne Combat Control Center (ABCCC) that would assign us an area. The lead aircraft carried flares, CBUs [cluster bomb units], and bombs. Lead would usually attack in the dark if he saw truck lights, or would drop flares in a likely area. Two would be in trail far enough back so that he could be over the area as the flares lit. The number two aircraft usually had CBUs, rockets and bombs. Both had guns [centerline pods, introduced a few months after Olds' arrival]. Once we were on a target, we would fly a racetrack pattern over the target until we were out of ordnance or fuel.

'We flew out and back in radar trail and usually never saw each other during a mission.

'Missions lasted from one hour to one and a half hours.

'The night missions were flown from 50–100 feet [15–20 m]. With a little experience, it was possible to work under a 500-foot [161 m] overcast at night without flares.

'The F-4s carried two pilots. The command pilot would turn off all his cockpit lights so that he could see outside better. On all but the blackest of nights, flares were unnecessary.

'The back-seat pilot kept his eyes on the instruments and instantly took control of the aircraft if everything didn't look just right. Without instruments, the front seat pilot would occasionally become disoriented. Therefore, once in an attack pattern, the back seat pilot couldn't take his eyes off the instruments and watch the attack. At those low altitudes and high speeds, the F–4 could hit the ground in less than a second.

'About 50 night missions were necessary to become really proficient at truck-hunting. [To have the same crew] flying both day and night missions does not work.

'Prior to my arrival at Ubon, the [North] Vietnamese had been moving in large convoys.'

The enemy's infiltration down the supply network known as the Ho Chi Minh Trail had, at the beginning, amounted to nothing more than thousands of men carrying small items, like mortar shells, on their backs or on bicycles. By 30 September 1966, this had grown to the point where North Vietnam was

2/23/68

simply sending trucks full of supplies down the roadways. The efforts of Robin Olds' fighter pilots and of the other men flying at night under difficult conditions was to make it far more difficult for the North Vietnamese to move in convoy.

'When they were moving in large convoys, once the first and last vehicles were stopped the convoy could be destroyed at will. The 497 TFS was very effective while the Vietnamese were using convoys.

'[Eventually] the Vietnamese were moving supplies in single trucks or groups of two and three. Truck hunting became very difficult and, I must say, quite ineffective.'[30]

This last observation seems to be one sign that the aerial campaign at night was, in fact, having an impact on the supply of Viet Cong forces in the south.

Also on Robin Olds' team with the 8 TFW or 'Wolfpack' at Ubon was Colonel Vermont Garrison, an old fighter hand who had been an ace in Korea with eight MiG kills, and

Colonel Daniel (Chappie) James, a dedicated and aggressive fighter man who was one of the Air Force's early black aviators. In a word-play on the names of comic-book characters, the deputy commander for operations and the wing commander, when they flew together, were known as Blackman and Robin. Another fighter pilot says, 'That Chappie James guy had the best attitude toward the race thing I've ever seen.' When he was a young second lieutenant, eager to fly his P–51 Mustang against the *Luftwaffe*, Chappie James was assigned to an all-black squadron, standard practice before President Truman integrated the armed forces in 1951. Chappie James fought for civil rights and he fought his country's enemies from fighter cockpits. With Robin Olds, Vermont Garrison and Chappie James directing the Wolfpack against North Vietnam, dramatic events were about to take place.

But it was a junior officer, Captain John B. Stone, who put into motion the events that

would make the Wolfpack the prime MiG killers of the period. Stone remembered a ruse which had worked, once before— disguising F–4C Phantoms on their ingress into North Vietnam so that they resembled bomb-laden and vulnerable F–105 Thunderchiefs. Stone wanted to try this again on a larger scale. With Secretary McNamara's rules of engagement making an assault on enemy airfields impossible, this seemed the only way to score an effective blow against Hanoi's MiG force. Reportedly, Stone suggested the idea directly to Colonel Olds. Young captains do not usually tell senior colonels what to do. In this instance, Olds is

Commander Dick Bellinger of the 'Superheats' of VF–162 aboard USS *Oriskany* (CVA–34) was the first Navy pilot to shoot down a MiG–21. In Front of his F–8E Crusader, Bellinger describes the MiG–21 victory in fighter pilot language. (VIA PHILIP D. CHINNERY)

reported to have replied, 'I was thinking of that myself. We'll try to talk them into letting us do it.'

The Wolfpack was in the war to stay.

CRUSADER VERSUS MiG-21

On 9 October 1966, the US Navy scored its first victory over the MiG-21 and racked up another kill for the prop-driven Skyraider, these being the 24th and 25th aerial victories of the war. Commander Richard (Dick) Bellinger, skipper of the 'Super-heats' of VF-162 aboard USS *Oriskany* (CVA-34), an aircraft carrier soon to become victim of a fatal fire, had been shot down himself five months earlier, on 17 July, when a MiG-17 hit him with cannon fire and sent him limping out to sea where his F-8E Crusader (150300) was too badly damaged to take on fuel from a tanker and he had to eject. Bellinger's chance to get even came as he went aloft in another F-8E Crusader (149159) leading the air cover for an Alpha Strike from USS *Intrepid* CVS-11. Bellinger and his division of Crusaders were directed towards approaching MiGs by a Grumman E-1 Tracer, the Navy's first airborne warning and control (AWACS) aircraft.

Beginning at wavecap level, Bellinger led his flight over the beach and up to meet the MiGs at 3,000 feet (900 m). He chose a MiG-21, engaged it in a close maneuvering contest, and unleashed two AIM-9D Sidewinder missiles. Bellinger leveled off to see his MiG-21 splattered across a rice paddy below him.

On the same day, LtJg William T. Patton of VA-176 from *Intrepid* shot down a MiG-17 with 20 mm fire while flying an A-1H Skyraider (137543). The big prop plane had prevailed again.

McNAMARA, JOHNSON VISIT

On 10-14 October 1966, the Secretary of Defense visited South Vietnam for a first-hand look at US bases and installations. Because men were being asked to fly dangerous missions without being given the authority to bomb important targets, because of the kind of reasoning which permitted destroying a MiG on the ground but not in the air, some airmen had begun to remark upon Robert Strange McNamara's middle name. In fact, the architect of ROLLING THUNDER and the most influential decisionmaker on targeting and other issues was now beginning to experience doubt for the first time. On an earlier occasion, McNamara had seen 'the light at the end of the tunnel,' the first glim-

mer of hope that the long struggle in Southeast Asia would see its way through to success. Now, though he shared his views with few, McNamara was beginning to wonder if the tunnel was endless. Air Force Chief of Staff Curtis Le May, typical of the SAC bomber men who ran a war where the risks were taken by fighter pilots, had said that the US would 'bomb the bastards back into the stone age', although the rules of engagement had never permitted a serious attempt at any such thing. Ho Chi Minh's premier, Pham Van Dong, had said that, 'Each time we withstand an American bomb, we win a victory.' McNamara looked at bases, talked to people, formed conclusions. But in his heart, for the first time, he was beginning to wonder if success was within reach. If it was not, he would have to decide whether to continue restrictive rules of engagement, permit more bombing, or pull out entirely.

Soon after McNamara's fact-finding expedition, President Johnson made a 17-day, seven-nation Asian tour which included a stopover at Cam Ranh Bay airbase. Johnson pinned a few decorations on a few airmen, looked around the gigantic airfield which had been constructed from out of nothing but marshland, and left. The President had begun his term with a strong interest in civil rights and domestic issues and had not wanted to be distracted by a war in Asia. He was often given too little credit for his honesty, decency and compassion while receiving the fullest recognition for his undeniable talent as a consummate politician. Johnson had been looking for ways to begin negotiations with Hanoi through secret channels and had been rebuffed at every attempt. Some Americans wanted the war ended, period, and reduced their demand to two words, 'Out now!' Other Americans wanted permission to attack those MiGs on the ground and to bomb Hanoi itself, feeling that the quickest way to end the bloodshed was to defeat the enemy. Johnson wanted the problem to go away and did not seem to know how to make it do so.

At Cam Ranh Bay, Johnson asserted that 'the most important weapons in Vietnam are patience and unity'. A fighter pilot wrote to the President to assert that the most important weapons were the 750 lb (340 kg) bombs he was not permitted to drop on the enemy's MiG airfields.

ORISKANY FIRE

Carrier operations in the Gulf of Tonkin were essentially so routine that they received far less attention than they deserved, at least until something went wrong. On 26 October 1966, something did. The inadvertent explo-

sion of a magnesium flare ignited a fire aboard the ageing USS *Oriskany* (CVA-34), killing 44 sailors and injuring 38. One A-4E Skyhawk (151075) was destroyed and had to be dumped over the side. The disaster at sea sent *Oriskany* limping back towards the US west coast for repairs.

On the same date as the *Oriskany* fire, an Air Force report from Headquarters Saigon made note of continuing problems in supporting the force of F-4 Phantoms deployed to fight the war. The secret report noted that 208 F-4C and RF-4C aircraft were now operating from five locations, these being Tan Son Nhut (460 TRW), Cam Ranh Bay (12 TFW), Da Nang (366 TFW), Udorn (432 TRW) and Ubon (8 TFW). The average monthly flying hours per aircraft had tripled since assignment to Southeast Asia. For those aircraft located in South Vietnam, the figure had risen from 23 to 65 hours per month.

Supply and support problems were compounded by conversion of the supply system to a Univac 1050 computer. Air Force supply people, the report found, were not sufficiently trained in 1050 operations. Various items, like cabin cooling turbines, were not being scheduled for replacement at the right times. The report optimistically predicted a 'get well date' seven months hence, June 1967.

SLAR FOR THE RF-4C

On 15 November 1966, a secret report for Major General Gordon Graham prepared at Seventh Air Force headquarters in Saigon addressed the difficulties in introducing the AN/APQ-102A side-looking airborne radar (SLAR) to the RF-4C Phantom fleet in the combat zone. Reconnaissance had an almost unbelievably high priority in Southeast Asia, with everybody from local commanders to President Johnson demanding more and better reconnaissance work over North Vietnamese targets, so the AN/APQ-102A unit was considered very important.

'SLAR and Infrared (IR) intelligence collection sensors replace and augment optical sensors [cameras] under certain circumstances. At the present time, of the thirty-five RF-4Cs at Tan Son Nhut and the twenty RF-4Cs at Udorn, twenty-seven have SLAR equipment and all have IR sensors. Five additional aircraft equipped with SLAR and IR are programmed for this theater in the near future.

'SLAR (AN/APQ-102A) has not been used successfully to date, primarily because of equipment deficiencies and incomplete knowledge of its capabilities and limitations.

'SLAR can detect a variety of targets under day or night conditions, and can penetrate haze, smoke, and most clouds. It is claimed that it can record targets such as convoys on open sections of road, trains, airstrips and support facilities, parked aircraft, bridges, boats, and missile sites. Its high-resolution mapping mode can be used in conjunction with its moving-target indicator (ATI) mode to clearly show moving vehicles against a high-resolution background. The minimum speed at which moving vehicles can be detected and recorded is a direct function of the altitude, speed, and angle between direction of aircraft and vehicle movement, with targets moving at 90° to the aircraft flight path giving the best returns. The SLAR offset capability allows it to cover targets as much as 30 miles [46 km] to one side of the flight path, providing the aircraft safe separation from defended target areas. Optimum altitude for SLAR flights in the RF-4C is 30,000 to 35,000 feet [10 000 to 12 000 m], although lower altitudes at times provide better shadows on some targets to improve interpretation potential.'

Reading no farther, Seventh Air Force planners might have concluded that SLAR would solve many of the deficiencies in ROLLING THUNDER reconnaissance operations.

'Unfortunately, SLAR has many limitations, chief of which is its fixed scale of 1/400,000. This is far too small a scale to provide good interpretations, and special skills and techniques must be developed by the interpreters in order to properly exploit the product. Two fixes have been proposed for changing the scale to 1/200,000, but both appear to be too costly for implementation at this time. [Furthermore], SLAR cannot separate targets closer together than 50 feet [17 m], penetrate foliage or water, or detect targets under trees or similar cover.'

While Brigadier General Jammie M. Philpott and others labored to get SLAR into use, cameras on the RF-4C were augmented by the most proven recce tool of all—the eyeball.

TAILCODES AND BLACK FRIDAY

By 2 December 1966, most Air Force fighters in Southeast Asia were beginning to wear tailcodes, the two-letter 'tactical unit identifiers' which were supposed to help tell the observer what squadron the aircraft came from. Lieutenant Kenneth Cordier, mentioned earlier in this narrative and back in Southeast Asia for his second tour, unaware that he would soon be a POW, remembers

seeing the letters XC painted on the tail of a Phantom and thinking, 'Gee, I thought that stood for cross-country.' In fact, XC happened to be the tailcode assigned arbitrarily to the 557 TFS/12 TFW at Cam Ranh Bay, the Phantom outfit from which Ken Cordier was about to make a one-way journey to the Hanoi Hilton. The intention at the time was for all aircraft in a single squadron to have the same two-letter code, the first letter of which would apply to all aircraft in the wing. Thus, the Thuds at Takhli belonging to the 355 TFW wore codes like RE (44 TFS/355 TFW), RK (333 TFS/355 TFW), RM (354 TFS/355 TFW) and so on. In a major change to be introduced years later (in 1972), all aircraft in the same wing would wear the same two-letter code, with no distinctions for individual squadrons.

At Da Nang, the 'Gunfighters' of the 366 TFW under Colonel Allan P. Rankin read the directives (the tailcodes were supposed to be 45.7 cm wide for each letter and 60.9 cm high) but regarded the purpose of the whole thing very differently. Although most of the Air Force did not fly with 'hard' crews anyway, Rankin's F-4C people frequently did, and wanted to use the tailcodes to be able to identify individual crews visually while in combat—a purpose for which they had never been intended. The squadrons of the 366 TFW thus became the first and only squadrons in the Air Force which, for a brief period of time at least, had individual tailcodes for each *aircraft*. As Brigadier General Robert F. Titus, a lieutenant colonel at the time, describes it:

'F-4C s/n 820 [64-820] was my airplane with AT on the tail. I convinced the wing CO [Rankin] that we needed individual tail markings and that was because of an experience I had had shortly prior. The idea was so that

you could identify who was up there without getting in too close to check the small black tail numbers and compromise your electronic jamming pattern in the process (all this after becoming separated in the combat area). I suggested that the 389 TFS be the A squadron, the 390th the B and the 480th the C. On my bird, the T was for Titus, hence AT. Bob Janca was AJ. Sandy Vandenberg, the 390th CO was BV, etc.' Frederick C. (Boots) Blesse, a Korean War ace and another well-known fighter pilot among the Da Nang crowd, was in the 390 TFS and flew an F-4C Phantom, nicknamed *The Blue Max* with tailcode BB. 'Today each wing has two tail letters and every plane in the wing has the same letters. What this accomplishes eludes me.'[32]

It was not for nothing that Rankin's men at Da Nang, Robin Olds' men at Ubon and a host of naval aviators aboard carriers at sea were scheming and plotting to take on the North Vietnamese air force. The triple-threat defense system of SAMs, MiGs and Triple-A had caused too many losses and confounded the ROLLING THUNDER campaign more than anyone was prepared to accept. Some men were talking about a North Vietnamese fighter wing commander, Colonel Tomb, who was supposed to be as good a pilot as Robin Olds. That was probably a muddled version of some intelligence report. The North Vietnamese had been flying fight-

handwritten annotations present
DAVID REHMANN

ers since 1964, while Olds had been flying them since 1944. Tomb is not even a name in the Vietnamese language. The fact remained, the North Vietnamese *were* getting better, and their defenses were taking a heavier toll. It was not uncommon for two or three Air Force and Navy aircraft to be lost on a single day. This situation was simply unacceptable.

And the situation got worse. Black Friday, 2 December 1966, was perhaps the worst day in the war up to that point.

Ken Cordier woke up that morning at Da Nang in the full knowledge that he was at the height of his profession. To be an Air Force officer flying the F–4C Phantom in combat against targets in Route Package Six was just about the highest achievement a man could attain. Walking out to his aircraft on an earlier mission, he had remarked to his GIB, 'We're on top, the very top.' Ken did not know that he was to become a guest of the North Vietnamese for seven years.

It was a day when there was heavy activity up North and the risks were high. The campaign against POL facilities, begun a few months earlier, was continuing. Early in the morning, F–105D Thunderchiefs from Brigadier General William S. Chairsell's 388 TFW at Korat and F–4C Phantoms of Rankin's 366 TFW at Da Nang were charged with attacking POL facilities near Phuc Yen, which was also the enemy's best-known MiG base. F–4C Phantoms from Ken Cordier's 12 TFW out of Cam Ranh Bay were tasked with flying cover to keep a sharp eye on those MiGs. These air strikes, as had so many before them, inflicted severe damage on the chosen targets at a time when prohibited targets remained unscathed and the North Vietnamese leadership showed no sign of bending. The cost, on Black Friday, was *eight* American aircraft and crews lost in combat.

The first was an F–4C Phantom (64-663) of the 389 TFS/366 TFW which suffered a fatal near-miss detonation from a SAM. With the aircraft on fire, both crew members ejected and became prisoners. One survived the ordeal. The other died in captivity.

Victim number two was also one of Rankin's Da Nang-based birds with the individualistic tailcodes, an F–4C Phantom (64-653) of the 480 TFS/366 TFW which was flying fighter cover when it, too, was hit by a SAM. The crew ejected. Both became POWs, illustrating again the difficulty of any hope of rescue in a high-density area, and survived captivity to be released at war's end.

In the late morning, a Thud striking Phuc Yen was also claimed by one of the dozens of SAMs flinging through the air. The F–105D went in and its pilot was killed.

At about the same time, victim number four was an RF–4C Phantom, apparently from the 460 TRW at Tan Son Nhut, which was hit by gunfire while trying to gain photo coverage of the Phuc Yen strikes (without the benefit of SLAR, which still had not been used successfully in combat but soon would be). The RF–4C Phantom (65-829) almost made it to the coast and the crew ejected, but only one of the pair survived captivity.

A Navy F–4B Phantom (151014) from the 'Black Knights' of VF–154 from USS *Coral Sea* (CVA–43) was also shot down that day. Victims six and seven were both A–4C Skyhawks from the same carrier. Then it was Ken Cordier's turn. Being at the height of his profession was about to have less reward for Ken than he had hoped.

Ken was at the controls of an F–4C Phantom (63-7608) of the 559 TFS/12 TFW with the newly-adorned XC tailcode (later changed to XT) which had caused him so much initial puzzlement. His is an excellent source for pinpointing the time by which these codes had appeared, because Ken knows he was using them, and he could not have seen them a day, a week or a year later. Ken Cordier was last into the battle area, escorting an EB–66C electronic warfare aircraft on a jamming mission, when more SAMs began to heave violently through the air around him. The Americans' electronic systems were beginning to damage the enemy's effectiveness with the surface-to-air weapon, but Hanoi's response was simply to fire larger numbers of the SAMs with less accuracy and to prove that numbers did make a difference. Soviet Premier Kosygin had said openly that the USSR would supply Hanoi with all the SAMs it wanted. While orbiting near Phuc Yen in support of the EB–66C mission, Ken's Phantom was struck by yet another SAM. The blast from the missile caused a fire in the cockpit and burned both crew members severely. Ken ordered an ejection and, as usual in Phantoms, his backseater Captain Bob Lane went out of the aircraft first. Both men were captured immediately.

SAMs, MiGs and Triple-A were causing too many problems for the strike forces and the rules of engagement prevented the logical reaction—bombing them into oblivion. Some other solution had to be found and the man to find it was in command of Ubon's Wolfpack, Colonel Robin Olds.

Said Major General Gordon Graham: 'Robin Olds is the most courageous fighter pilot I know. He took on some chores in Southeast Asia which no one else would have done and he personally headed some missions which were almost suicidal.' [33]

Olds was to get his chance at Colonel Tomb's MiG force, but it was not to come until the arrival of the new year. At the end of 1966, the old year looked very bleak for American airpower in many respects.

SAPPER ATTACKS

It is often forgotten that, unlike in previous wars, the Americans in Vietnam fought from bases which were constantly under threat. RF–4C Phantom pilots of the 460 TRW flying from Tan Son Nhut, in the capital of the country they were defending, 'stepped on the gas' to make unusually rapid, high-angle take-offs because of the danger of being hit by Viet Cong mortar or rocket attacks. The enemy was constantly prowling around the perimeters of the airfields. A lesser but persistent danger existed at the Thai airbases, where an insurgency was brewing although it never reached the scale of the Viet Cong's fighting force.

The Americans repeatedly confirmed that the Viet Cong were reconnoitering their bases. An especially vicious attack on Tan Son Nhut took place on 4 December 1966, and the US Air Force Security Police found their own weapons wanting. Sentry dog handlers reported it almost impossible to operate the M16A1 infantry rifle (rapidly becoming the standard ground combat rifle with the Army and Marine Corps but originally developed by the Air Force) while also attempting to handle their guard dogs. It was suggested that the sling be attached to the top rather than the underside of the rifle. This would let the handler sling the weapon from his left shoulder and carry it in a firing position on his right side. Another criticism was that the M16A1 was too long for easy handling in the airbase defense mission, a problem solved by the manufacturer, Colt, when it produced a modified M16A1 with an 11.5-inch barrel, telescoping stock and sturdier flash hider (a devise attached to the muzzle and designed to conceal the muzzle flash). This version eventually evolved into the GAU–5A/A submachine-gun.

Prisoners taken after the sapper raid which destroyed several US aircraft told of a two-month prestrike reconnnaissance of the base by a seven-man team. It seemed likely that some of the enemy's information about the airbase came from sources on the base itself, a constant problem in a war where the enemy was a part of the population. The enemy's intelligence was rated as good on the munitions storage area at the base but poor on the runway and aircraft parking aprons. The Viet Cong successfully identified a point to infiltrate Tan Son Nhut's perimeter and cut three wire fences without being detected. They also correctly assessed infiltration cover afforded by excavation work, fixed the posi-

<comment>handwritten annotations in margins: "2 CRB" on left, "CRB" on left margin</comment>

CAPT M.L. MOORBERG, 34TFS - KIA

tions of aircraft parking areas and traced out routes for undetected access to three munitions bunkers.

Still, the enemy somehow failed to assess correctly the sentry dog units spotted around the base and nine of them were killed by airmen using M16A1 rifles during the attack. The Viet Cong had, however, made a point of which the Americans were never unaware: There were no front lines, no rear areas.

FIRST ATOLL LOSS

The first USAF loss of an aircraft to the AA-2 Atoll missile carried by the MiG-21 occurred on 14 December 1966 when an F-105D was shot down near Hanoi. The pilot ejected safely and was rescued. Air-to-air missiles, associated with the MiG-21 but not usually employed by the MiG-17, had been introduced into combat six months earlier on 7 July 1966, without result.

Just when it was succeeding with a missile remarkably similar to the US Sidewinder, North Vietnam managed to lose two ancient biplanes. Two Antonov An-2 biplanes were shot down by US Navy fighters on 20 December 1966. These were the 29th and 30th confirmed air-to-air kills of the war and followed six Air Force MiG kills in the final months of the year. F-4B Phantom (153022) of the 'Black Lions' of VF-213 piloted by Lt H. Dennis Wisely and F-4B Phantom (153019) of sister squadron the 'Aardvarks' of VF-114, both from the deck of USS *Kitty Hawk* (CVA-63) claimed the fabric-covered biplanes by downing them with AIM-7E missiles. LtJg David L. Jordan and Ens David Nichols were the back-seat radar intercept officers (RIOs).

SALISBURY TO HANOI

Near the end of 1966, the *New York Times* finally received permission to send its distinguished assistant managing editor, Harrison Salisbury, to Hanoi. Until now, the only American citizens permitted to visit North Vietnam had been those clearly identified with the anti-war movement or, at least, sympathetic to it. For several years, the Hanoi leadership had resisted efforts by legitimate journalists to gain entry. Salisbury was the first. He was a veteran of the Asian scene and an expert on Asian communism. His credentials as an impartial observer and respected journalist were beyond reproach.

Salisbury's findings verified that the ROLLING THUNDER campaign was inflicting some serious damage on North Vietnam but was not reducing the enemy's will to fight.

Salisbury found that, as in all past wars and in spite of President Johnson's assertions to the contrary, there was no way to avoid having bombs fall on civilian as well as military targets. The North Vietnamese made a point of showing him a civilian hospital at Dong Hoi which had taken direct hits from US bombs. Salisbury concluded that the Soviets would continue to support North Vietnam, but with a measured degree of caution rather than with any and all weapons Hanoi might request.

The men flying the ROLLING THUNDER missions were facing danger and dying, and success seemed to elude them.

BOMBING HALT #3

In the now-established tradition of bombing halts, which were supposed to send some kind of signal to Hanoi but only confused everybody, the US declared a Christmas cease-fire over 24–26 December 1966 and repeated the occasion for New Year's, 31 December–2 January. While the communists were largely ignoring the cease-fire, a Saigon analyst toted up losses for the year. USAF losses in Southeast Asia came to 379 aircraft in 1966. Again, the erstwhile Thud was the aircraft type which suffered the most punishing losses, no fewer than 126 airframes having become casualties, of which 111 were in North Vietnam. Four of these were downed by SAMs, three by MiGs and the remainder by ground AAA fire, which sometimes claimed its victims while they were seeking to elude the other two threats.

Other losses included 56 F-4 Phantoms (42 in combat), 26 F-100s (presumably all in South Vietnam) and 41 A-1 Skyraiders. Similar figures for the Navy were not made available on an annual basis. Always masters of statistics, the Americans concluded that between 1 July 1965 and 31 December 1966, the North Vietnamese had fired 1,219 SAM missiles against US aircraft, causing 18 losses or a loss rate of 1.47 per 100 missiles. Whatever it was, it was too much. Since a Thud pilot was *still* statistically unlikely to finish his 100 missions unscathed, the 'low' kill ratio for the SAM would have offered precious little comfort even if the numbers had been believable, which they were not. Not that Hanoi's figures were credible either, not when Hanoi claimed to have downed 6,000 American aircraft or at least ten times the number actually participating in the fight. The numbers game up North was similar to the body count situation down South where, in the absence of visible front-lines and terrain to conquer, US forces reported their success based upon the number of enemy bodies located after a battle. These numbers were usually presented at the 'Five O'Clock Follies,' as the MACV briefing for journalists had become known, and were believed by no one, not even the unfortunate officer giving the briefing. At one point, the US forces claimed to have killed more Viet Cong combatants than could have existed if half the men of fighting age were on the other side and all had become deceased. To counter the charade in Saigon, the officials in Hanoi often released figures on the numbers of innocent farmers, workers and civilians slain by the American air pirates. Reporter Stanley Karnow, as entitled as anyone else to use numbers and at least as authoritative in doing so, says that by this time the Americans had inflicted $300 million damage against North Vietnam but at the cost of some 700 aircraft valued at $900 million.[34] Karnow has better credentials than the author of this work, but his dollar figures are almost certainly too low while his figures for aircraft losses are beyond dispute too high.

With 1966 drawing to a close and yet another brief bombing halt in effect, the war had changed Americans forever. The innocence and confidence that had sent them into Asia to achieve a quick victory over a second-rate foreign enemy now belonged to the past. President Johnson, who had taken office on a crest of popular support because of the tragic circumstances behind the loss of his predecessor, and who had won re-election in his own right by one of the widest margins in any election in history, had suddenly become an unpopular president at the helm of a foreign war that no one quite wanted or understood. The SAC bomber men who were running a war being fought by non-SAC fighter pilots *still* wanted to bomb Hanoi back into the stone age—the idea of an aerial campaign against North Vietnam's dikes was being resurrected in Pentagon options papers, as was the notion of an outright carpet-bombing of the cities—while the fighter pilots risking their lives wanted fewer restrictions and simpler rules. The fighter pilots did not understand why Thuds were bombing heavy targets in the North and Stratofortresses were bombing rice paddies in the South. They could not understand why they could fight a MiG in the air but not bomb it on the ground. They wanted to go in and clean out Phuc Yen. They also knew, by now, that they were the first Americans ever to fight an armed conflict without the full support of their own countrymen. It was a situation which could only have seemed incredible and, had it been fiction rather than fact, no one would have believed it for a moment. To the men in fighter cockpits, at least, there was some relief in sight—to be provided by Colonel Olds and Operation BOLO. But a long slog lay ahead.

1967

REAL ROLLING THUNDER

On the final day of what would have been an American bombing halt, North Vietnamese MiG–21 pilots were hurled aloft for a radar-guided intercept of what seemed certainly to be a strike force of slow, vulnerable, bomb-laden Thuds. The MiG pilots must have thought they had easy pickings. Instead, after a battle ensued, seven of the MiG–21s had been blasted out of the sky with no loss to the

Colonel Robin Olds spray-paints a MiG kill on the splitter vane of F–4C Phantom (63-7668). Lieutenant General Gordon Graham: 'My candidate for the most courageous and dedicated man in the Southeast Asia operations is Robin Olds. As commander of the 8 TFW, he demonstrated by personal leadership the greatest courage and professional dedication you could ask for.' Olds was credited with four MiG kills. (USAF)

Americans. In a magnificent ruse, the Wolf-pack of Colonel Robin Olds' Ubon-based 8 TFW had ingressed North Vietnam with the same speed, altitude and ECM characteristics as a vulnerable Thud strike force—but actually flying heavily-armed F–4C Phantoms. Operation BOLO had dealt a sudden and dramatic blow to the North Vietnamese air force, with no losses. Historian Michael A. France, who has studied the battle extensively, picks up the story of the 2 January 1967 action:

'The strike force consisted of 56 F–4C Phantoms drawn from the 8 TFW at Ubon and the 366 TFW at Da Nang. These were divided into 14 flights of four aircraft in each flight. Aircraft from the 366 TFW covered the east side of North Vietnam while aircraft from the 8 TFW covered the west side. Of

these 14 flights only three actually made contact with North Vietnamese MiG aircraft. These three flights were all from the 8 TFW and in fact were the [wing's] first flights into North Vietnam. It seems that the action that did occur was fast and furious. A MiG–21 was engaged by Olds 01 [callsign for F–4C Phantom (63-7680) flown by Colonel Robin Olds and 1Lt Charles C. Clifton] which let fly two AIM–7E Sparrows and a single AIM–9B Sidewinder, all of which missed. There then followed two successful encounters by Olds 02 [the F–4C Phantom (63-7589) crewed by Lt Ralph F Wetterhahn and Lt Jerry K. Sharp] and Olds 04 [the F–4C (63-7683) flown by Captain Walter S. Radeker III and Lt James E. Murray III], both of which shot down MiG–21s, before Olds 01 came back and got his MiG. In the end, a total of 28 air-to-air missiles were fired, 16 of which missed for a number of reasons. The total effort spent to down seven MiGs with one [more] claimed as a probable was a total of 96 aircraft. In addition to the Phantoms, there were:

'F–104C. 4 flights. 16 aircraft drawn from the 435 TFS based at Nakhon Phanom.

'F–105D/F. 6 flights, 24 aircraft. Unit not known. These provided Iron Hand [SAM suppression] cover.

'EB–66. [Probably four EB–66E aircraft].

'F–4C. Possibly 4 aircraft. Unit unknown. To provide cover for the EB–66. That is in addition to the Phantoms already mentioned.

'RC–121. Radar surveillance.

'KC–135. Tankers.

'To return to the Phantoms, contrary to details published Operation BOLO was originally thought up by junior officers at Ubon and not the big deals in Hawaii. I believe that Captain John B. Stone was the original guiding light. I do not know what part Colonel Olds played in the plan's conception. [It was considerable.] The plan was for a good-sized force of missile-armed Phantoms to simulate a bombing raid into North Vietnam normally made by heavily-laden F–105s. The reason for this deception was that the North Vietnamese pilots were well aware of the differences between the bombers and the fighters and they would not normally take on the escorts but planned their missions to hit the bombers only. Being controlled from the ground, they were frequently vectored into favorable intercept positions that made them difficult to get at. Added to that, the restrictions on hitting them on the ground meant that they were going to be a serious threat to the strike forces heading North. If they could be lured into the air to hit what they thought was a bomber force that was in fact a fighter force then the resulting action would do much to reduce that threat.

'F–105 aircraft were now carrying ECM pods on missions North. If the Phantoms were to appear on enemy radars as a force of F–105s, they would have to have the same ECM gear. It seems that the only place such a pod could be fitted on the F–4C in those days was to the right outer wing pylon normally used to carry the wing fuel tank. Apparently, it was something to do with the wiring. Anyway, despite the obvious weight distribution problems that arose, the outer pylon is where the ECM pods went. Any flight control difficulties existed only so long as the left wing tank was carried. As these were dumped prior to any combat, the problems were of limited duration. I believe that this was the first time these pods were used by Phantoms in Southeast Asia and I also believe that Phantoms were subsequently modified to carry the pod on the right wing inner pylon. Colonel Olds flew a low-level raid into North Vietnam on a later date [30 March 1967], flying F–4C 64-829 with an ECM pod on the right outer pylon so any mods must have taken [longer] to complete.'[35]

Colonel Daniel C. (Chappie) James failed to score a MiG–21 kill that day, or ever, though he was in the midst of the fight. Other MiG–21 killers were Ford 02, the F–4C Phantom (63-7710) flown by Captain Everett T. Raspberry, Jr and Lt Robert W. Weston; Rambler 01, the F–4C (64-720) flown by Captain John B. Stone and Lt Clifton F. Dunnegan, Jr.; Rambler 02 (63-692), crewed by Lt Lawrence Glynn and Lt Lawrence Cary; and Rambler 04 (64-838), flown by Major Philip P. Combies and Lt Lee R. Dutton. There must have been an enormous celebration at Ubon that day. Seven MiGs in one day was to stand for several years as a record and was perceived as a smashing blow against the North Vietnamese air force, including the legendary Colonel Tomb—if, indeed, Colonel Tomb existed. Only much later would US analysts question the use of such great expense to claim seven MiG–21s. Four days later, two more Wolfpack crews in F–4C

Phantoms claimed two more MiG–21s, making it seem that 1967 was going to be a great year in air-to-air action for the Americans. Why, incredible as it seemed, someone might actually down five MiGs and become an ace.

TARGETING PROPOSALS

Among military men who were watching US aircraft losses increase and seeing North Vietnam's defense network grow, a brief success here and there offered little comfort. Brave men were risking their lives and facing death or capture without sharply-defined purpose and with no way of measuring success. On 10 January 1967, CINCPAC Admiral U. S. G. Sharp proposed a stepped-up air campaign which would restore a sense of purpose by assaulting six elements of the North Vietnamese infrastructure: electric power, war industries, transportation, POL facilities, garrison installations and the air defense network. Sharp wanted an integrated approach to bombing and destroying targets in these six basic areas, rather than the arbitrary and random targeting now being allowed. But despite an occasional success—Operation BOLO being one—decision-makers were still not ready for a sensibly orchestrated campaign to take the North out of the war. Sharp was listened to, but not completely. Some new targets were opened up to US airstrikes, but a 30 mile (48.2 km) *cordon sanitaire* still existed around Hanoi itself and the minor changes made in targeting policy were still piecemeal in nature.

In his annual State of the Union speech, also on 10 January 1967, President Johnson continued to assert that the US would prod Hanoi into a settlement by increasing the pressure. 'Our pressures must be sustained until [North Vietnam] realizes that the war [it] started is costing more than [it] can ever gain. I know of no strategy more likely to attain that end than the strategy of accumulating slowly, but inexorably, every kind of material resource.' Johnson also counseled patience. The number of US troops inside South Vietnam had now risen to 385,000, a massive military operation in the south known as CEDAR FALLS was achieving mixed results and patience was not available in large measure—not to the American public, which now resisted the war even more strongly, and not to American airmen who wanted to be unfettered and unleashed.

According to General Momyer, by the time of Johnson's address, the ROLLING THUNDER campaign had three purposes:

Colonel Daniel (Chappie) James was vice commander of the 8th Tactical Fighter Wing, the 'Wolfpack', and a key figure in Operation Bolo which resulted in seven MiG–21s being shot down in one day. This half of the pair of 'Blackman and Robin' (Wing Commander Robin Olds) wore a black panther on his helmet. (USAF)

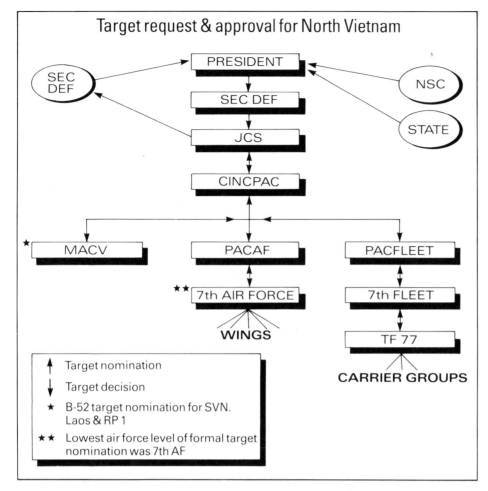

Target request & approval for North Vietnam

PRESIDENT

SEC DEF

NSC

SEC DEF

STATE

JCS

CINCPAC

★ MACV

PACAF

PACFLEET

★★ 7th AIR FORCE

7th FLEET

WINGS

TF 77

CARRIER GROUPS

↑ Target nomination

↓ Target decision

★ B-52 target nomination for SVN. Laos & RP 1

★★ Lowest air force level of formal target nomination was 7th AF

The system for requesting targets in North Vietnam started with the Seventh Air Force fighter wings and the Task Force 77 carrier groups in the battle zone and went all the way to the President (during the ROLLING THUNDER campaign of 1965–67). The system was unwieldy and opportunities to achieve surprise against attractive targets were often missed.

Reduce the flow and increase the cost of infiltration; raise the morale of the South Vietnamese (those on the US side, that is), and convince the North that it must pay a very high price, in the North, for its aggression in the South. It was a familiar litany. Almost nobody believed it any more. An F–105D Thunderchief pilot at Takhli wrote home that morale had slumped to its lowest point. 'My pal Jim was shot down the day before yesterday and nobody got a beeper or a parachute [his bailout could not be confirmed]. Now, there's an empty bunk next to mine. Tomorrow, maybe it will be me. And no one will tell us why.' The writer was killed in combat before the letter reached his parents.

AIR-TO-AIR WAR

1967 was to be a year of air-to-air fighting over the North of unprecedented intensity. It was also to be the year of the Thud, which continued to carry most of the bombs and would also now perform its share of the MiG killing. The air-to-air fighting was to prove the mettle of the Navy's F–8 Crusader at the very time that single seat, supersonic fighter was being more widely supplanted by the F–

4B Phantom. It was also to be the year when a few 'attractive' targets would be opened up to US warplanes, albeit on an almost unpredictable and incomprehensible basis.

Reflecting upon his mandate to counter North Vietnam's growing MiG force, Seventh Air Force commander General Momyer made use of his penchant for writing by recording a few impressions:

'I looked at the counter air battle as a continuing campaign that would never be completed because of the sanctuary in China [not, in fact, employed much any longer by the North Vietnamese] and the unlimited production ability of the USSR to replace [North Vietnamese aircraft] losses. The only real limitation was one of how many aircraft the Russians were willing to make available.

'The best we could hope to achieve was to take a high toll of the North Vietnamese Air Force so that pilot training and replacement would become a problem. Rate of replacements, however, could be controlled by the Vietnamese by their willingness to engage. If they wanted to hold attrition rates down, they could move their fighters out of the conflict until our raids were finished. If they did this, my fundamental purpose was achieved since I wanted to get the strike forces into target

without the MiGs interfering. The real damage to the North Vietnamese fighting ability came from the targets we were trying to knock out with the fighter-bombers and not the insignificant attrition we could inflict in air-to-air engagements.

'In Korea, we had proved fairly conclusively that air-to-air fighting is not the way to knock out an enemy air force. In the first place, the enemy can evade combat if he elects. In the second place, the amount of engagement is limited by the time of engagements. Thirdly, the number of aircraft knocked down per engagement is small. Thus, the way to knock the air force out is to get it on the ground when it is concentrated and vulnerable to attack. While our attacks on North Vietnamese airfields forced the enemy to keep most of his air in sanctuaries in China, thereby reducing his flexibility, we were never able to neutralize, let alone destroy his air. His sanctuaries, his ability to replace aircraft promptly from external sources, and his capability to repair airfield damage all quickly militated against our counter air efforts. In addition, the weather and force limitations further compounded my problems by making it impossible to sustain the frequency of counter air strikes necessary to succeed.

'The air defense problem for the [North] Vietnamese was relatively simple. They had a small area to defend, our choice of penetration routes to the target was limited, and they had information on the strike forces from two hundred miles [320 km] out. Conversely, the same reasons that made the North Vietnam problem simple, made our air attack problems very tough.

AAA

'[Long before the beginning of 1967], there were some seven thousand guns of all caliber in North Vietnam. About thirty-five hundred of these were located in Route Package Five, Six-A and Six-B. At the time I increased the tempo of operations against the northeast railroad and the Thai Nguyen line, the AAA was deployed along the main marshalling yards. Since we were not cleared for targets within 30 miles [48 km] of Hanoi, except on case by case release, the tactical disposition of the guns was proper.

North Vietnamese anti-aircraft artillery crew firing at US aircraft attacking targets in Route Package Six. By 1967, Hanoi had built up an exceedingly formidable array of anti-aircraft weaponry. (VIA MIKE O'CONNOR)

'As the war moved into 1967 and the target system was expanded, the guns were concentrated around these more sensitive targets. The defenses around the [Paul] Doumer Bridge, Hanoi car and repair shop, Thai Nguyen steel mill, Viet Tri thermal power plant, and many others became exceedingly dense. By this concentration of fire, the Vietnamese could employ more barrage fire which was the tactic they used toward the end of 1967.

'Important targets were relatively few and were concentrated in a small area. Our choice of routes in and out were [sic] very restricted. Therefore, the enemy's problem in determining ingress paths was simple. He had more than 200 fire control radars which provided ample redundancy to cover penetration approaches. While I feel we enjoyed some ECM success, we were never able to block out AAA radar to the extent some people seemed to think we were. Usually we encountered a combination of guns ranging from 100-mm to 37/57-mm types. The 37/57 continued, throughout my tour, to constitute the most lethal weapon. These guns are at their best in the 4500–7500 foot [1370–2290 m] altitude range and were brought to bear in mass as strike aircraft were in this altitude regime during pullout from diving runs. About 65% of our losses were due to AAA.' Most reports place the percentage even higher.

Momyer's views on the SAM missile have already been noted. 'Our loss rate to SAMs is not a true measure of their effectiveness. In 1967, the rate was about one aircraft loss for fifty-five missiles fired. This eventually went up to a hundred missiles fired for a single aircraft loss. This war demonstrated that high performance aircraft can operate in a surface-to-air missile environment. It requires alert tactics and organic ECM. Although the EB–66s are very valuable, pods on fighters did the main job of blocking the *Fan Songs* [the radars associated with SAM sites]. In a sophisticated defense environment, ECM must be organic to the strike aircraft.' Here, Momyer is saying that a separate ECM mission, as performed by EB–66C and EB–66E electronic warfare platforms and F–105F and F–105G Wild Weasels, cannot substitute for the strike force carrying its own ECM capability. 'I believe the pod is still the best way to handle it. We may have to give up a bomb to carry it, but it gives the needed flexibility at small sacrifice.' ...

'As the war progressed, the North Vietnamese air defense system continued to improve. Only when we started into the targets within the ten-mile [16-km] circle [around Hanoi] were there signs of a breakdown. Outside of this circle they were very adroit in passing targets to either AAA, SAMs or fighters. In most cases, the direction of the air battle was handled by sound tacticians. Usually the SAMs and AAA handled all targets which started into the Hanoi area. The fighters held off until the force started to egress.'

While General Momyer was trying to run the Air Force's part of the war, the MiG–17 and MiG–21 pilots of North Vietnam's air arm were becoming more numerous, although their actual performance was inconsistent. It appeared that some of the MiG pilots were significantly more capable than others. This could be explained to an extent by the strong suspicion that some Russian and North Korean fighter pilots were participating in the fray but, even then, it remained evident that some North Vietnamese pilots were significantly better than other North Vietnamese pilots. It was not a matter of different units performing differently: those stationed at Kep seemed to be both good and bad, as did those stationed at Phuc Yen. No clear explanation for the disparity emerged, but it did become clear that the better and more aggressive enemy pilots, including the mysterious Colonel Tomb, preferred the MiG–17 to the MiG–21. Though the MiG–17 was older, slower, and usually not armed with IR air-to-air missiles, it was a far more nimble dogfighter and seemed to be far more responsive to a pilot's touch on the controls.

The MiG–21 remained a potent element in the North Vietnamese arsenal. New pilots traveling from Vietnam to training bases in the Soviet Union often seemed to begin on the MiG–21 without flying the MiG–17 at all. The Soviets acknowledged that they were training North Vietnamese pilots, but emphasized the defensive nature of the pilots' mission—guarding their homeland against the gathering waves of Yankee air pirates.

AMATEUR EMISSARIES

The question would recur so often: would the bombing persuade Hanoi to halt its infiltration of the south and negotiate a settlement? Except for Harrison Salisbury, almost no Americans who could be rated as impartial had visited North Vietnam to ask. In January 1967, William Baggs and Harry Ashmore—private newspapermen affiliated with the Center for the Study of Democratic Institutions, a California think tank—not merely followed Salisbury's footsteps to Hanoi but, further, met directly with Ho Chi Minh. North Vietnam's elder statesman, the single figure who could fire imaginations throughout the country, who had fought to rid the country of foreigners since his battles with its Japanese occupiers, Ho has long since ceased encumbering the helm of day-to-day management of his government—but he remained the personification of his nation and its will. Baggs and Ashmore, who were respected figures but were amateur diplomats, their journey endorsed neither by the State Department nor by President Johnson, took it upon themselves to bring a message from Ho. Ho Chi Minh had strongly suggested to them that any outstanding problems could be resolved if the US would halt its continuing troop buildup and if the bombing of North Vietnam were halted.

Even though the proportion of the US

North Vietnamese pilots being trained in the Soviet Union, like these, often went straight into the MiG-21 without flying the MiG-17 at all. The aircraft in the foreground, seen at a training base in the Soviet Union, bears an inscription describing it as a 'Training Vehicle'. (COURTESY PHILIP D. CHINNERY)

population which opposed the war had grown significantly, visits to Hanoi were frowned upon by many Americans. Among them, President Johnson not merely frowned but, according to one insider, cursed. A career Foreign Service officer at the State Department's headquarters in Foggy Bottom wrote a memo asking whether salaries would continue to be paid to diplomats in an era when too many private persons, lacking credentials, seemed to be attempting to manage diplomacy on their own. Johnson, in fact, used an informal channel to let Ho Chi Minh know that, if anything, he would not only not halt the bombing, he might increase it. Other Americans would travel to Hanoi, Americans ranging in diversity from former Attorney General Ramsey Clark to folk singer Joan Baez, but none achieved significant results,

via amateur diplomacy or any other method, and none won the endearment of US Air Force and US Navy pilots who continued flying into MiGs, missiles and Triple-A.

PACAF COMMAND CHANGE

On 1 February 1967, command of US Air Force units in the Pacific (PACAF) passed from General Hunter Harris, Jr, to General John D. Ryan, a bomber man who had spent most of his career in SAC. Harris's background was largely in bombers too, but he seemed to have gained the respect of fighter pilots in a way that Ryan was unable to do. Back in Washington, the most famous bomber man in the service's history, LeMay had long since been replaced as Chief of Staff of the Air Force by General John P. McConnell, a bomber man like LeMay, although his background was more broadly-based. McConnell was widely respected and did not utter unhelpful homilies such as the threat to bomb Hanoi back into the stone age. But it remained true that, in the perception of some at least, SAC-trained bomber generals

were running an Air Force which was caught in the midst of a fighter war. Things were 'arse-backwards'. F-105s and other fighters, as has been noted, were assaulting strategic targets in the North while B-52s were unleashing their bombs on rain forest and paddy fields in the south.

Fighter men believed, rightly or wrongly, that General Ryan from his perch in Hawaii would be especially stringent in applying the rules of engagement. Some criticized Ryan for not fully understanding the tactical problems faced by men in fighter cockpits. An extreme view, perhaps an unfair one, from the hardly impartial Colonel Jack Broughton, DCO of the 355 TFW at Takhli and veteran of 102 combat missions over North Vietnam, was scarcely flattering to the PACAF chief. '[General Ryan] is an extremely forceful person and has chosen to dictate the tactics of strike fighter attacks in the North down to airspeeds, formations, and altitudes from his position [in Hawaii] as CINCPACAF. He leans heavily on his SAC bomber background and his World War Two experience.' Broughton, who later wrote a book called *Thud Ridge,* felt this was a mistake. 'Many of us who had extensive fighter missions in the Hanoi-Haiphong complex and several of our general officer supervisors did not concur in this standardization and considered [Ryan's] dictated tactics unsound.'[37]

NAVY CARRIER STRIKES

In many respects, the US Navy was spared the sort of internecine warfare which went on inside the ranks of Air Force leaders at this point in the conflict. The important distinction in the Navy lay not between fighter and bomber men (the Navy's brief attempts to compete with SAC via such outlandish means as the carrier-based P2V-3C Neptune being past history) but lay, instead, between aviators and sailors. Fortunately for the men who flew from carrier decks, virtually everyone in the Navy's chain of command, from the CAG (Carrier Air Wing commander, still abbreviated after the carrier air *groups* of an earlier era) to CINCPAC himself, was either an aviator or had personal experience with Navy, carrier-based operations.

The Navy approached some problems differently than the Air Force. With combat

rescue, for example, the Air Force relied upon assembling a massive force of tankers, EW aircraft, fighter cover, Sandy strike ships and helicopters before 'going in' to attempt to extract a survivor. The Navy's view of combat rescue was that speed was everything. Whether or not it could be adequately protected, the helicopter had to be gotten to the scene of the downed airman as quickly as possible. The Sikorsky SH–3A Sea King of Helicopter Anti-Submarine Squadron HS–6 was the most effective Navy chopper for the rescue role, the Kaman UH–2B Seasprite being considered too short-legged and vulnerable.

In early 1967, squadron HS–2 appeared in the battle zone aboard the destroyer USS *Hornet* with 21 SH–3As, some of which had been modified for rescue duties. Although no serious threat from submarines materialized during patrols off the North Vietnam coast, one SH–3A was soon lost in an ASW (anti-submarine warfare) exercise. Two further SH–3As were lost shortly afterward in accidents. Finally, as the year progressed, a rescue attempt on 18 July 1967 was marred when a gunner aboard an SH–3A was killed after intense ground fire prevented an attempted rescue. A day later, yet another SH–3A was attempting a rescue of the same downed aircrew when it was riddled with gunfire and downed with the loss of all four crew members. It was an incredible and tragic cruise for one of the several Navy helicopter squadrons which contributed significantly to both the ASW and the rescue effort.

One 'success story' which won recognition for many naval aviators involved was the KA–6D, the aerial refueling tanker version of the Grumman A–6 Intruder attack aircraft. For reasons which no Pentagon policy-

Colonel Jack M. Broughton, author of a postwar memorium entitled *Thud Ridge*, was one of the unsung heroes of the campaign against North Vietnam. Vice Commander of the 355 TFW at Takhli, Broughton was a product of West Point, a natural leader, and an aggressive fighter. He was credited with a 'probable' MiG kill and completed 102 missions in the Thud. Broughton was also court-martialed for destroying gun camera film of an inadvertent firing on a Soviet freighter in Haiphong harbor—an illustration of the conflicting demands placed upon men in fighter cockpits. (BROUGHTON)

Seemingly 'minor' damage to one of Col Jack Broughton's 355 TFW Thuds, in a photograph which was classified SECRET at the time. 'This is a good example of how small-arms or automatic weapons can knock a supersonic fighter down: hits are at the base of the vertical fin probing for hydraulic control or engine fuel lines.' (USAF, VIA BROUGHTON)

Thud, camouflaged, with bombs, before tailcodes. Colonel Jack Broughton: 'We found that we could load her down so she could barely get out of the chocks, yet that huge burner would deliver the brute force to hurl her into the air from a jungle airfield on a hot, sweltering day. We found that we could hold the force together while staggering inbound through thunderstorms that arched high above 50,000 feet [15 240 m] and through rain that reduced the guy on your wingtip to a single red or green Christmas tree light ...' (REPUBLIC, VIA BROUGHTON)

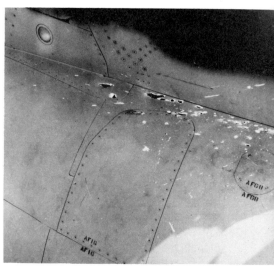

Although the A-7 Corsair was introduced to battle in 1967, the A-4 Skyhawk—which it had been designed to replace—would continue the fight against North Vietnam through to the end. The Skyhawk was important not only to naval aviators flying near Hanoi, but to Marine Corps pilots who sometimes fought in the lower reaches of North Vietnam. A-4E 151080 of attack squadron VMA-121 seen at Chu Lai, South Vietnam. (USMC)

maker can enunciate with any assurance of historical accuracy, the Air Force and Navy have always used different refueling systems, the Air Force relying on the 'flying boom' method whereby a KC-135 'plugs into' its recipient while the Navy employs the British-developed 'probe and drogue' method. Today, there is significant interchange between the two systems, but in early 1967 there was not. The Navy's principal tanker had been the KA-3B Skywarrior but it was quickly becoming clear that the KA-6D Intruder was far less trouble-prone, less expensive to operate, and more flexible for the missions being flown—although it retained one drawback of all Navy tankers in that its crew could not look directly back at the receiver aircraft. The KA-6D had required relatively little modification from the A-6A (and later A-6E) attack aircraft (though tanker and attack missions were not interchangeable in the same air-

frame). It was also considered a pleasure to fly.

It seemed to have become tradition, though it was not necessarily part of the ever-present rules of engagement, that while the area around Hanoi belonged to the Air Force (at least most of the time, up to this point), the area around Haiphong was the Navy's province. Here, questions about targeting arose again. President Johnson's tough attitude toward Ho Chi Minh, the continuing growth of the North Vietnamese defense systems and the ever-present lure of targets in Haiphong itself caused some Navy captains and admirals to come at loggerheads. One Navy commander wanted to 'go in and clean the whole place out'. Permission was not yet forthcoming.

Like their Air Force counterparts, particularly those at Takhli, Navy men made suggestions which were based on solid professional experience—and were ignored. The decisions as to which targets to hit and when to hit them continued to seem, aboard ship as on land, too arbitrary to convey any clear message to Ho Chi Minh.

BOMBING HALT #5
No previous cease-fire or bombing halt had produced any result, including the paired

bombing halts over the Christmas and New Year's period celebrated by Americans and by the Roman Catholic majority of Vietnamese, but a truce was declared in recognition of the Vietnamese new year, known as Tet, to last for four days. During the 8–12 February 1967 truce, reconnaissance flights identified more than 1,500 trucks along Route 15 heading south and the evidence that the enemy was using the truce period to supply forces in South Vietnam seemed almost overwhelming.

Halt or no halt, the continuing problems with air-to-air missiles were being subjected to scrutiny and corrective measures. A US Navy instruction dated 8 February and issued to carriers and carrier air wings in the combat theater pointed out problems in the 'storage, handling and maintenance' of AIM-7 Sparrow and AIM-9 Sidewinders and tasked armament officers to conduct a study to determine whether these problems were related to undocumented but persistent reports of missile failures. No one had carried out a statistical study to show that the Navy's missiles were not working as well as they should but all pilots believed it. Commander James McBride, an A-4C Skyhawk pilot aboard USS *Shangri-la*, recalls speculating on whether Crusaders and Phantoms would be able to help him out if needed. 'None of us had firm

information, but it was clear that there were worries about the reliability and effectiveness of the air-to-air missiles.'

AIR FORCE MISSILES

The continuing concern of the USAF over the effectiveness of its missiles was exacerbated when an F–105 Thunderchief came back to its base with an AIM–9 Sparrow firmly embedded in its burnt, twisted tail section. Had the Thud, which survived only by an apparent miracle, been hit by an American missile because of some error in the missile's design? Or was the more likely explanation—pilot error—the cause of a Thunderchief nearly being shot down by a Phantom? In other incidents, US airmen *did* mistake friendly aircraft for MiGs and zap them with Sparrows or Sidewinders. One American pilot was reputed, perhaps partly in jest, to have shot down as many Phantoms as MiGs! At least one POW in Hanoi came back from imprisonment with persuasive evidence that he had been shot down by a wingman.

Though the radar-guided AIM–7 Sparrow gave US fighters a head-on fighting capability not enjoyed by the MiG, pilots continued to have doubts about its reliability after frequent MiG encounters when the air-to-air missile failed to fire or track properly. Charging Sparrow, a program begun four months earlier in November 1966 and concluded after some delay on 23 February 1967, had required that every F–4C Phantom in inventory launch a Sparrow against an aerial target. Results indicated that only two-thirds of the F–4C force could successfully launch an AIM–7 and that only 80 per cent of the missiles met functional requirements.

THAI/US ANNOUNCEMENT

On 9 March 1967, Thailand's Prime Minister Thanom Kitti-kachorn announced what everyone had known for two years—that US

F–4J Phantom (155761) of the 'Pukin Dogs' of VF–143 takes on fuel in mid-flight from a KA–6D Intruder (151824) of the 'Lancers' of VA–196, both flying from the deck of USS *Enterprise* (CVAN–65). Introduction of the KA–6D was one of the quiet and little-noticed 'success stories' which improved the Navy's ability to refuel its strike aircraft heading into North Vietnam. (USN)

aircraft based in Thailand were bombing targets in North Vietnam. On 13 March, he announced something else that everyone knew already, namely that the new base at U-Tapao would be used to support B–52 Stratofortress operations. On paper at least, these installations belonged to Kittikachorn's sovereign government, although the reality was that nearly every man and every aircraft on each airfield was American. Udorn, Ubon and others were called Royal Thai Air Force Bases (RTAFB), although it was difficult to find anyone at a higher level than the cook or shoeshine boy who possessed Thai nationality. U-Tapao, for reasons known to no one,

An 'on again, off again' target in a war where the logic behind target selection was understood by no one, the Thai Nguyen iron and steel works was attacked for the first time on 10 March 1967 and again (photograph) on 23 April. Smoke is shown coming from the complex's water supply facility which controls the plant's water cooling system (top). The blast furnace area, damaged on previous raids, can be seen between bomb explosions. (USAF)

was called a Royal Thai Naval Base although, despite its proximity to a bay, it was better known for B–52s than for boats. What the Prime Minister did not announce was that, as in Vietnam, the American bases had given birth to 'boom towns' consisting of bars, beerhalls, brothels and an inexpensive, exotic world of entertainment for the US military men. The term 'boom town' has been coined by University of Kansas anthropologist Felix Moos, himself a former Air Force pilot, to describe the villages where an American military presence creates an unusual and unique

sub-culture, having little in common with the culture of the country where it is located.

Abundant alcohol and easy sex were the principal entertainments in these backwater bastions of the war against North Vietnam. The typical B–52 or F–105 pilot was less likely to partake of either than the enlisted man or NCO who maintained his aircraft. The pilot was likely to be more mature, more settled in life, married and less impressed by the easy availability of women and drink. Further, no one wanted the clap, the American term for gonorrhoea, while at risk of becoming a prisoner of war. A routine medical ailment, easily cured with antibiotics, might be fatal to an air crewman in North Vietnamese captivity. So there existed little linkage between prostitutes and pilots, between bottle and throttle.

U-Tapao veteran Lee Duckett remembers that Americans at the B–52 base patronized a 'boom town' called New Land, where black airmen drank and caroused in an establish-

ment called the King of Soul and other members of Duckett's squadron hung around the Yellow Balloon. 'The mama-san at the Yellow Balloon had a group of girls who were for rent.' No one associated with the terrible risks posed by MiGs, SAMs and Triple-A can deny that the svelte and sultry Thai girls at places like the Balloon, perhaps even more than their sisters at bases in Vietnam, were alluring and adept. For fifty *baht*, about five dollars, expert sexual performance could be readily rented.

Following upon the Prime Minister's announcement, a swarm of journalists descended on the 355 TFW's base at Takhli when it was opened to them for the first time on 17 March.

STEEL PLANT BOMBED

In another shift of targeting policy, F–105 Thunderchiefs and F–4 Phantoms attacked

the Thai Nguyen iron and steel works for the first time in March 1967. Previously 'off limits' like many lucrative targets in the North, the Thai Nguyen works were the only ones in Southeast Asia which made bridge sections, barges and POL drums. Several strikes on the steel works came over a period of a couple of weeks.

In one of his more daring exploits, MiG killer Colonel Robin Olds, commander of the 8 TFW's Wolfpack, led a low-level assault against Thai Nguyen in an F–4C Phantom (64-829) flying at about 500 knots (800 km/h) with full bombload at an altitude of ten feet (3 m). This must surely have been one of the missions General Graham had in mind when he used the word 'suicidal', meaning not that Olds was reckless but that he was a man of almost incomparable courage and leadership. It can be supposed that the workers at Thai Nguyen never knew what hit them. The steel and iron works, however, was never subjected to bombing which was regular enough and steady enough to have a significant effect on its output.

General Eugene Tighe, who was on the targeting staff at Seventh Air Force, is reported to have argued that the USAF ought to be bombing Thai Nguyen 'every day until it's nothing but flatland'. If so, he was over-ruled, though he later became director of the US Defense Intelligence Agency (DIA).

F–105 ACHIEVEMENTS

On 10 March 1967, Captain Max C. Brestel of the Takhli-based 354 TFS/355 TFW became the first double MiG killer of the war when he shot down two MiG–17s with 20 mm cannon fire. Using the callsign Kangaroo 03, Captain Brestel was flying an F–105D Thunderchief (62-4284). By coincidence, the same Thud airframe later received credit for a third MiG–17 kill on 27 October 1967 at the hands of Captain Gene I. Basel.

Brestel's achievement occurred during a period of exceedingly heavy fighting, a period when courageous F–105 pilots fought against overwhelming odds while, at the same time, remaining hamstrung by restrictions on targets, sanctuaries and stringent rules of engagement. On the same day that Brestel shot down two MiGs, Captain Merlyn H. Deth-

A–4E Skyhawk from the 'Golden Dragons' of VA–192, the squadron to which Lcdr Michael J. Estocin belonged when he won the Medal of Honor for attacks on SAM sites in April 1967. Estocin, who was killed in the action for which the award was made, was the only fixed-wing naval aviator to win the Medal of Honor in Southeast Asia. (VIA LOU DRENDEL)

Previously unpublished view of the personal mount of the great fighter wing commander of an era, Colonel Robin Olds' 64-829. Olds flew 64-829 in his low-level mission against the Thai Nguyen steel works and scored two of his four MiG kills in it. By the time of this 1968 photograph, 64-829 had been transferred from Olds' 8 TFW at Ubon to the 12 TFW at Cam Ranh Bay and was wearing the XC tailcode. (RICHARD KAMM)

lefsen of the 355 TFW went into North Vietnam as number three in a flight of F–105F Wild Weasels on an Iron Hand, or SAM suppression, mission. Using the callsign Lincoln 03, Captain Dethlefsen took his F–105F (63-8354) against SAM sites in the vicinity of Thai Nguyen despite unusually heavy MiG and SAM opposition. Dethlefsen shook off persistent firing passes from MiG–21s without jettisoning his ordnance, and continued to press an unusually courageous attack on SAM sites while under heavy fire. Dethlefsen became the first airman to receive the highest

Lcdr Michael J. Estocin was the A–4E Skyhawk pilot from USS *Ticonderoga* who earned the Medal of Honor for his missions against SAM sites in North Vietnam. (USN)

American award for valor, the Medal of Honor, for action against North Vietnam. Only eight USAF people received the decoration (two for conduct as prisoners of war, along with the Navy's Stockdale) and it was a measure of the intensity of the fighting in March/April 1967 that two fighter pilots earned the Medal of Honor during Iron Hand missions—Major Leo K. Thorsness of the 355 TFW in an F–105F (63-8301) on 19 April and Navy Lcdr Michael J. Estocin of the 'Golden Dragons' of attack squadron VA-192 from USS *Ticonderoga* in an A–4E Skyhawk on 20 and 26 April. Thorsness and Estocin both carried out valiant Shrike attacks on SAM sites and Thorsness, whose callsign was Kingfish 01, also shot down a MiG–17. F–105F Wild Weasel pilots at least had their second man in the back seat, the EWO (electronic warfare officer) or Bear, to help search for the *Fan Songs* used by SAM sites and to assist generally, but the A–4E pilot had to do it all by himself.

Thorsness was shot down a few days later and became a prisoner of war after a series of ghastly mistakes in communication prevented what should have been an easy rescue. With Colonel Jack Broughton and others circling overhead, enemy defenses were effectively suppressed and a helicopter pick-up was possible, but no one ordered in the choppers in time. Estocin was first listed as missing, then as KIA (killed in action) following his failure to return from his 26 April mission. His fate, and the agony of his family, typified one of the war's dilemmas: for

several years, while considered missing, Estocin was promoted to commander, then captain (men in POW camps also were promoted regularly). Eventually, it was learned that he had, in fact, died on 26 April while a lieutenant commander.

BATTLE DAMAGE ASSESSMENT (BDA)

At Seventh Air Force in Saigon, Lt Gen. William W. Momyer continued to feel himself 'under the gun' because of the serious difficulties in obtaining timely, accurate photo reconnaissance which would provide battle damage assessment (BDA) information for planners. Too often, the brave efforts of RC–101C Voodoo and RF–4C Phantom pilots were failing to bring home the results. Taking the unusual step of sending a 'Specat/Air Force Eyes Only' message to PACAF commander General Ryan in Hawaii (a document declassified only on 31 December 1975), Spike Momyer lamented the difficulties:

'I share your [Ryan's] concern over recent failure to obtain timely BDA [battle damage assessment] of 7AF [Seventh Air Force] strike targets. As stated in [an earlier message], weather continues to be the major factor preventing us from getting the photographic coverage we all desire. Target weather has prevented acquisition in most instances, and en route weather has caused a number of aborts short of the target. Too, the fighters can frequently bomb through three-eights or four-eights cloud coverage which precludes acceptable BDA photography.

'As a result of the heavy reconnaissance losses we sustained in November/December 1966 and January 1967 (three RF–101Cs and six RF–4Cs), I closely examined our reconnaissance tactics in high threat areas with the Udorn wing commander [Colonel Robert W. Schick, 432 TRW] and my staff. As a result of that examination, I established a policy that normal post-strike BDA photography would be accomplished not earlier than two hours after a strike and that a minimum daytime target altitude of 12,000 feet [3 700 m] would apply. If less than two hours of useable daylight remains after an afternoon strike, photography is scheduled for the following day unless the target is of the utmost importance. In the three months that this policy has been in effect, our losses have been less than one-fourth of the November, December, January rate. I am briefed daily on all reconnaissance missions, including alternate targets, into high threat areas at our 1700 [hours] planning conference, and authorize any deviations from our tactics and policy at that time.

'In the case of [two particular targets], the last fighter was off the target at approximately 0850Z [hours]. [One target] was not scheduled for night BDA because the target is 4,400 feet by 8,000 feet [1 300 by 2 400 m] with the only logical axis of approach being along the 8,000-foot [2 400-m] side. Enemy knowledge of our optimum photo height (3,500 ft [1 100 m]), low night cloud ceilings, and ever increasing enemy defenses have forced us to fly lower than 3,500 feet [1 100 m] in Route Package Six-A and a large percentage of our night work is being flown at 2,000 feet [608 m] or less. At this altitude, the lateral coverage is approximately 2,500 feet to 2,700 feet [775 to 810 m]. [One target] was studied for night BDA. However, a difficult radar-run-in, coupled with the size of this target, would almost certainly have resulted in only partial target coverage. Under these circumstances, and considering the night weather encountered in Route Package Six-A in recent weeks, it was decided to schedule [this target] for BDA coverage on the following day rather than expose a crew at night on a target that undoubtedly would require back-up coverage the following day.

'. . . I believe a review of the overall photo interpretation intelligence reports system for PACAF and 7AF is in order. Briefly, the mission flow follows the guidance given by DIA, CINCPAC, and CINCPACAF. This flow is as follows: After recovery, the mission is processed on a priority basis. This also applies to the interpretation and reporting of fragged [assigned] objectives. Because the mission was executed against a primary and alternate objective, they are, as a matter of priority, reported immediately (IPIR). [The IPIR was the Intelligence Photo Interpretation Report distributed to end-users when photo analysis had been completed.] The mission film is then put back into production for all required prints, dupe negatives and positives for higher headquarters. The time required for this function is dictated by the amount of original film exposed and the products required, which varies with each mission.'[38] Momyer's report goes on to discuss the difficulties in producing IPIRs on a timely basis and disseminating them to the various subordinate commands who needed them. A post-strike photo report of a North Vietnamese truck park was not much use to the F–4C pilots preparing to attack the same target again, unless the photography and the accompanying IPIR report could reach them in time. The main theme of Momyer's message, though, was that he was having difficulty getting battle damage assessment reports into the hands of his superiors on a timely basis. Not said, but strongly implied, was that this was one problem a field com-

mander would not have to worry about, were he given more authority to choose his own targets. More than two years after the onset of ROLLING THUNDER, Spike Momyer still could not select a target on his own authority without going through the cumbersome chain of command which seemed to impede and impair the prosecution of the war at every step.

One method of disseminating IPIRs in the field created a new role for the USAF's version of the twin-engine Cessna 310, which had been purchased for light transport, utility and 'hack' duties as the U–3B (having been designated L–27 prior to 1962). About a dozen U–3Bs, in their factory blue/white paint scheme which earned them the nickname 'Blue Canoe', were located at Tan Son Nhut where they were flown by 460 TRW and Seventh Air Force officers. A little-known role of the Cessna was to airdrop intelligence reports to field commanders. Many of these reports undoubtedly involved targets in the South which posed a more pressing danger to infantrymen than did targets in the North, but the U–3B was used to distribute reports about both, and thus belongs in this narrative. 'In any typical day, I might fly as much as eight to ten hours and log five or six missions,' says Colonel Omni L. Bailes, Jr, who was an RF–101C Voodoo pilot but, while at Tan Son Nhut, flew the Blue Canoe. 'Sometimes it was a real challenge, figuring out how to get through the thunderstorms, find the friendlies instead of the enemy out in

the jungle, and sometimes landing on strips of mud out in the field. I find flying the RF–101C or the F–4 Phantom much easier in many ways.'

The principal purpose of the Cessna U–3B was to disseminate the 460 TRW's intelligence 'product,' the IPIR, to local forces in the field. Colonel Bailes recalls: 'The U–3B aircraft were modified on the starboard side, in the rear seat area, with an eight-inch pipe (approximate size) and pin.' When the pin was pulled, clearing the passage, a container could be dropped through the pipe from an altitude of 50 feet [14 m] to friendly troops on the ground. The pilot simply pulled the pin and ejected the container. 'These contained photographic pictures, film and IPIRs which we could deliver to friendlies without landing the U–3B.'[39] The Cessna U–3B was also used for various supply and hack duties, often under fire (indeed, as noted earlier, anyone taking off from Tan Son Nhut could come under mortar or rocket fire at any time) and Colonel Bailes logged a total of 133 missions in this little-publicized aircraft type.

THUD BATTLES

The period which began on 10 March 1967 with Brestel's twin MiG kills was a springtime of unusually vicious fighting, especially for the men in F–105 Thunderchiefs operating from Takhli and Korat. While facing greater risk each day, Thud pilots saw their

Though it never flew a mission over North Vietnam, the Cessna U–3B Administrator, better known as the 'Blue Canoe', performed a vital function in disseminating the IPIRs, these being the intelligence reports based on RF–101C Voodoo and RF–4C Phantom photo reconnaissance. U–3B 60-6073 is seen on the ground at Tan Son Nhut airbase, where the 460 TRW and Seventh Air Force were headquartered. (NICHOLAS M. WILLIAMS)

friends killed, captured, or cut down to size by the very nation they served—criticized, denied promotion, and in some cases actually court-martialed for violating rules of engagement so complex that it was almost impossible to memorize them all. On 26 March, Colonel Robert R. Scott, the commander of the 355 TFW at Takhli, was flying a Thud with the callsign Leech 01 when he tangled with a MiG–17 and shot it down with 20 mm gunfire. A MiG kill was a crowning achievement, but Scott—a virtuoso fighter pilot and respected commander—spent far too much of his time trying to sort out the problems posed by the chain of command and the rules of engagement.

On 19 April, in a furious battle, no fewer than four Thud pilots claimed MiG–17s in air-to-air action. The two-seat F–105F Wild Weasel crew of Major Leo K. Thorsness and Captain Harold E. Johnson, flying an F–105F (63-8301), callsign Kingfish 01, claimed a MiG–17 as an incidental part of the already-mentioned sortie against SAM sites which earned Thorsness the Medal of Honor.

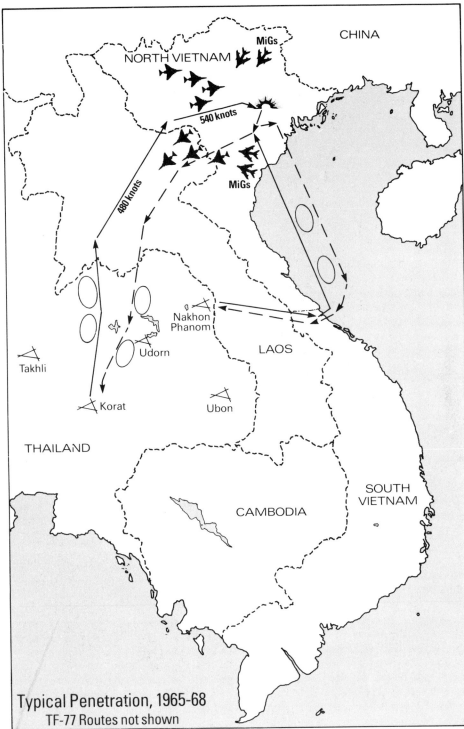

Map labels:

CHINA

MiGs

NORTH VIETNAM

540 knots

480 knots

MiGs

Nakhon Phanom

Udorn

Takhli

Korat

Ubon

LAOS

THAILAND

CAMBODIA

SOUTH VIETNAM

Typical Penetration, 1965-68
TF-77 Routes not shown

Korat, and aboard carriers at sea, fighter pilots fumed and cursed over the bizarre vagaries of a war which had them taking so much risk for so little gain. A naval aviator aboard USS *Kitty Hawk* (CVA–63) wrote a letter to Secretary of Defense McNamara pleading, courteously, for the chance to strike more lucrative targets—such as airfields—if so much risk had to be taken. What the aviator did not know was that McNamara, for the first time in years, was beginning to doubt the effectiveness of continued bombing of an essentially agrarian society. The Navy pilot had the wrong man. So often criticized for not bombing enough, McNamara's thoughts now lay in the direction of not bombing at all.

With a Cultural Revolution going on in China and with North Vietnam being more closely aligned to the Soviet Union in any event, it continued to be difficult to find a solution which did not involve bombing. For any American public official to talk directly to the North Vietnamese would undermine US support for the South. Various indirect methods of communicating with the ageing Ho Chi Minh and his Premier Pham Van Dong had failed to produce any hope of a North Vietnamese gesture which would permit an end to the bombing. In early 1967, Soviet Premier Kosygin visited British Prime Minister Harold Wilson and went away believing from his discussions that some settlement could be found in Vietnam. A Harvard professor, Henry Kissinger, who was not especially well-known to the public at large and not particularly liked in the democratic administration, found a personal acquaintance of Ho Chi Minh's and sent the acquaintance to Hanoi for talks. Ho was too ill to speak of substantive issues and Pham Van Dong had decided that the bombing would have to stop before any gesture of conciliation could be made. President Johnson, now in one of his toughest moods and certainly in a tougher frame of mind than McNamara at this point, had decided that a gesture of conciliation would have to be made before the bombing could stop. Moreover, Johnson was prepared to 'open up' to US airmen targets they had been previously denied—including airfields.

While backstage efforts were underway to achieve some form of communication between Washington and Hanoi without undermining American goals, Navy and Air Force airmen continued to press the war to the enemy. On 23 April, Da Nang-based Major Robert D. Anderson of the 389

Major Jack W. Hunt, another 355 TFW pilot, downed a MiG–17 which flying an F–105D (58-1168), callsign Nitro 01 and making use of the Thud's 20 mm cannon. Captain William E. Eskew, also from the Takhli-based 355 TFW, used 20 mm fire to down a MiG–17 while flying an F–105D with the callsign Panda 01. Finally, Major Frederick G. Tolman of the same base and same wing claimed a MiG–17 with 20 mm fire. Ironically, Tolman, who also earned high respect from his wingmen as a skilled and courageous

fighter pilot, was one of three men later court-martialled for destroying gun camera film of an inadvertent firing upon the Soviet supply vessel *Turkestan* in Haiphong harbor.

19 April was a fast, furious day in other respects. An attempt to rescue a downed fighter crew went sorely awry when an A–1E Skyraider, attempting to cover a helicopter pick-up, was shot down by a MiG.

Four MiG kills in one day should have been cause for celebration, but the losses were too heavy. In the billets at Takhli and

TFS / 366 TFW went into North Vietnam at the controls of an F–4C Phantom (64-776), callsign Chicago 03. Under the unique tail-code system in use only at Da Nang and described earlier, Anderson's Phantom was coded AK. Captain Fred D. Kjer was his back-seater. The men became involved in a fray with a MiG–21 force and, from a considerable distance, successfully used an AIM–7E–2 Sparrow missile to blast a MiG–21 out of the sky. This was the 47th air-to-air kill of the war.

Aboard *Kitty Hawk* in the Gulf of Tonkin, the 'Aardvarks' of squadron VF–114 were getting ready to add to the total.

FIRST AIRFIELD ATTACK

The Pentagon brass continued to want a fiercer bombing campaign while Secretary McNamara continued to have doubts. It is thought that a personal decision by President Johnson, supported by the JCS, CINCPAC and field commanders, led to a momentous decision which, for a time at least, loosened the rules of engagement. Embittered pilots and frustrated field commanders, long denied the chance to attack the MiG airfields, gained their first relief from the longstanding

On 24 April 1967, some North Vietnamese airfields were opened up to attack by Air Force and Navy jets. But the most vital part of North Vietnam's war effort was still to be found in its principal cities of Hanoi and Haiphong. This April 1967 Navy reconnaissance photograph is a pre-strike assessment of the Haiphong thermal power plant at the west side of the port city. (USN)

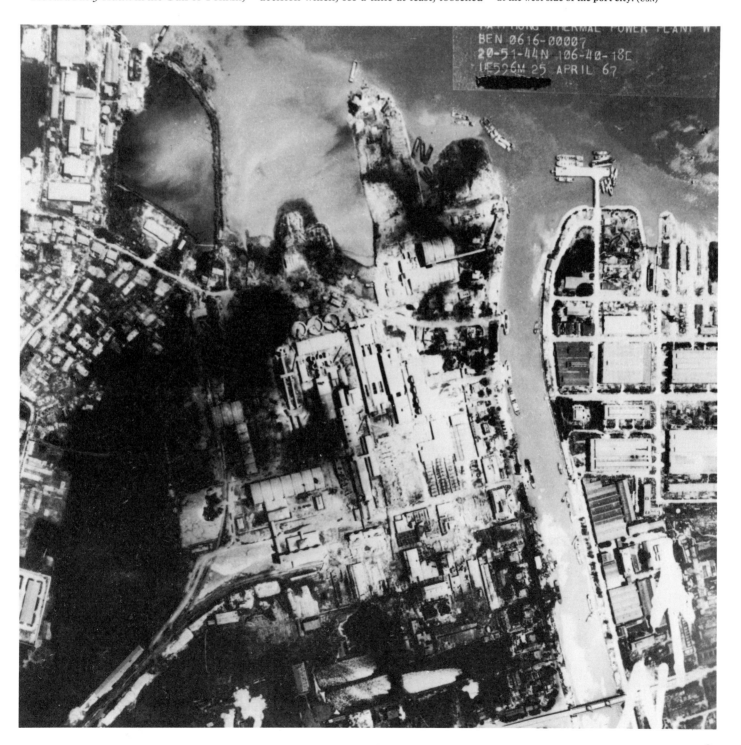

prohibition on 24 April 1967, amid very intense fighting, especially by F-105 squadrons. The main airfield, Phuc Yen, would not be authorized as a target until much later (October 1967), and Gia Lam (which was also Hanoi's civilian airfield) was spared attack throughout the war because US policymakers decided to permit transport aircraft from China, the Soviet Union and the International Control Commission to have safe access to North Vietnam, even though Gia Lam remained an active MiG base.

But the absolute taboo on attacking airbases was reconsidered not only for political reasons but because the enemy was continuing an ambitious buildup which increased his number of jet-capable airfields from nine to fifteen. Expansion and improvements were underway at Kep and Phuc Yen while a new Hoa Loc airfield was being completed in the western part of the country.

A rather limp argument for not attacking the airfields, but one that some officers made repeatedly, was that US aircraft losses would exceed the damage inflicted on the enemy. Strike forces were already penetrating the areas where the airfields were located and no action by the enemy could make losses greater than they already were over targets in the area.

Relief came when eight F-105Ds attacked Hoa Loc on 24 April and 14 MiGs were reported destroyed on the ground. Throughout the 1965–68 ROLLING THUNDER campaign, authorization for intermittent attacks on airfields would remain the exception rather than the rule. When exceptions were made, neither pilots nor commanders seemed to know why they were permitted to hit a MiG base one day but not another.

24 April was also a day of heavy fighting for the Navy airmen who waged war in the eastern extremity of Route Package Six and whose job was, perhaps, the riskiest of all. The 'Aardvarks' Lt Charles E. (Ev) Southwick went into battle in the front seat of an F-4B Phantom (153000) and managed to prevail over a MiG-17 using a Sidewinder, scoring the war's 48th MiG kill. His back-seater was Ens James W. Laing. A squadron mate, Lt H. Dennis Wisely (who, as noted earlier, had shot down an Antonov An-2 on 20 December 1966) maneuvered a second F-4B Phantom (153037) to the point where he was able to rack up MiG kill number 49, using an AIM-9B Sidewinder. Southwick, however, had begun to have problems. He had actually been hit by AAA over Kep *before* downing his MiG and had continued through the battle nursing an aircraft suffering from indeterminate damage. He was able to fly the F-4B Phantom eastward, and so to go feet wet (get out over water), before it became abundantly

clear that 153000 had fought its last battle. The AAA damage made it impossible for Southwick to transfer fuel, and therefore impossible to get back to *Kitty Hawk*. He and Laing ejected and were rescued almost immediately by the dedicated Navy helicopter crews whose contribution was often too easily overlooked.

24 April was also the day when a MiG-17 claimed an A-4C Skyhawk in air-to-air combat. This ignominious event occurred when a *Bonnie Dick* A-4C (147799) of VA-76 was limping home from one of the many air battles raging in Route Package Six when a plucky MiG-17 pilot decided to follow it. It is thought that Lt Ira H. Levy was the pilot of the hapless A-4C, although the record is not completely clear. The MiG-17 managed to make a single firing pass before its presence was noted by MiGCAP aircraft. The North Vietnamese pilot got off a burst of cannon fire and the A-4C took hits immediately. A minor maneuvering contest seems to have followed, but it was only moments until the crippled A-4C, smoking, rolled over and dived into the sea—taking the pilot with it.

The men of the 'Spirits' of VA-76 aboard USS *Bon Homme Richard* (CVA-31) would have liked to avenge this loss, although at the time no one could conceive of it happening the other way around—i.e., a Skyhawk downing a MiG. As usual, the naval aviators had forgotten Clarke's Law which, roughly paraphrased, goes something like this: If you say it can't be done, you're probably wrong; if you say it might be possible, you'll turn out to be right. No one had heard of Theodore R. Schwartz yet—and for the moment the squadron simply had to sit back and suffer the latest of no fewer than eleven Skyhawk combat losses in the first four months of the year.

On 26 April, the 50th MiG to be claimed in aerial combat went down before an F-4C (64-797) piloted by Major Rolland W. Moore, Jr and Lt James F. Sears of the Da Nang-based 389 TFS/366 TFW. It was small comfort. Setbacks continued to be more noticeable than gains.

26 April was also the day when F-105F Wild Weasel pilot Major Leo Thorsness, who had already earned the Medal of Honor, was shot down with his back-seater, Captain Harold Johnson. As has been noticed, the pair should have been rescued. The 355 TFW had a force of Thuds over the area, including one flown by the wing DCO, Colonel Jack Broughton, and the enemy's defenses were suppressed. Thorsness and Johnson were to spent six years as prisoners of war because of a mistake on the part of someone who failed to bring in the helicopters soon enough. Broughton, holder of the Air Force Cross and soon to be nominated

for his second—ironically—joined the trio of men court-martialled for destroying gun camera film of an apparent firing on the Soviet freighter *Turkestan* and, at the height of his career, just short of his goal of flying 105 combat missions in the F-105, was removed from Takhli. Broughton was eventually fined a hundred dollars for breaking the incomprehensible rules of engagement—or, more correctly, for destroying film which showed it happening—but the damage to his career and his life cannot be calculated.

Men like Thorsness, captured by the North Vietnamese and used as propaganda pawns, were evidence enough that there existed a significant difference between the two sides in the Vietnam war. Prisoners were beaten, denied medical treatment, tortured. Many were placed in solitary confinement. Commander Stockdale's wife wrote to him regularly only to learn later that the North Vietnamese withheld her letters from the prisoner. Captain Cordier was tortured by being forced to bend down on his knees and maintain an almost impossible position while being beaten with wooden canes. Though the American side was to be accused of committing crimes (and did so, in the case of the My Lai massacre, where American soldiers shot innocent civilians), the evidence abounded that most Americans fought the war with decency and with respect for the lives and welfare of the innocent. More than once, a Thud pilot was killed by missiles, MiGs or Triple-A solely because he refused to dump his ordnance in a civilian area.

The treatment of POWs was beyond the inhumane. Thud pilot Major James Kasler, a Korean War ace, had an infected leg which bloated to elephantine proportions—and went without medical treatment not merely for months, but for years. The very few POWs who were trotted out at public press conferences had usually been tortured into doing so. At one such conference, Stockdale blinked a message in Morse code with his eyes, saying to the world that the press conference was a fake and that the POWs were being badly mistreated.

From about mid-1967 onward, any resolution of the conflict would have to involve a release of all the POWs and an accounting for all of the missing. The former would end up, in a future day, as the only issue left. The latter would never be accomplished.

SKYHAWK VERSUS MiG

Perhaps the most bizarre MiG kill of the conflict, the 55th, occurred on 1 May 1967 when Lcdr Theodore R. Schwartz of the 'Spirits' of attack squadron VA-76 launched

This North Vietnamese photograph supposedly shows a Vietnamese MiG pilot (at left) talking to an American prisoner of war. In fact, American POWs, who were badly mistreated, never met enemy pilots and were usually questioned by people who knew little or nothing about military aviation. (COURTESY PHILIP D. CHINNERY)

from the old wooden deck of *Bon Homme Richard* thinking that he was going to expend ordnance on ground targets—which he did. Schwartz joined the heightened air activity taking place around North Vietnamese airfields during this period and, like so many others, found himself in a battle where SAMs, MiGs and Triple-A were wreaking havoc all around him. Intending to make a mess of the end of Kep's runway with ordnance from his A–4C Skyhawk (148609), Schwartz was astounded to see a MiG–17 in the pattern, either unaware of him or under the mistaken impression that he was another MiG. Schwartz unleashed a barrage of Zuni rockets—intended for air-to-ground work, totally unguided, and never meant for air combat—and watched them blow the MiG to bits.

It must have seemed sweet, sweet revenge for the VA–76 Skyhawk with Ira Levy on board that had been claimed by a MiG a week earlier. Indeed, for months afterward, not merely 148609 but *several* 'Spirits' Skyhawks would be noted with the red silhouette of a MiG–17 painted on them. As much as two years later, when the squadron had been transferred to *Independence* and to the Atlantic Fleet, at least two of its Skyhawks (148578, 149645) carried MiG kill markings to celebrate Schwartz's victory.

MOMYER BRIEFS McNAMARA

On 8 July 1967, Secretary of Defense Robert S. McNamara visited South Vietnam for the first time in a full nine months. He received a secret briefing from Seventh Air Force commander Lt Gen. William W. Momyer in Saigon. The general's assessment was devoted largely to the war in the south but Momyer could also report a few developments in the campaign north of the 17th Parallel. One was the closely-guarded plan to use F–100 Super Sabres as forward air controllers, or 'fast FACs', in the Route Package One area of southern North Vietnam. Commando Sabre, the use of the two-seat F–100F in the Misty FAC role, had commenced a fortnight earlier on 28 June. These aircraft would be concentrated in one squadron at Phu Cat. Said Momyer: 'By multiple refuellings, while using FAC-trained pilots, I hope to achieve a visual reconnaissance and forward air control capability throughout the entire RP 1 area during the daylight hours.

This will degrade [the enemy's] ability to effectively supply his forces.'

Momyer provided a wealth of statistics, including the fact that 6,852 anti-aircraft guns were now arrayed against him in North Vietnam. Somehow, he knew that air strikes had denied the enemy precisely 34,498 short tons of supplies in the past year. He knew that 22,935 feet (6 990 m) of railroad track had been destroyed. All such numbers, and Momyer had extensive figures on 'North Vietnam throughput denial', meaning destruction of supplies, must be questioned in retrospect. But the introduction of the F–100F Fast FAC was an important development, introducing a new way of visually finding targets and pinpointing them for strike aircraft. For more than two years to come, Hanoi's intelligence would never succeed in learning the purpose of the F–100Fs which prowled the lower area of the country, nor link them to the precision-guided strikes which followed their appearance.

Other aspects of McNamara's visit to the battle zone seem, in retrospect, ambiguous. The Defense Secretary clearly sought to display a mood of confidence, but he was no longer in the practice of making predictions about when the war would end, or how many casualties would be required to end it.

Even at this late date, with the price of the conflict growing both in terms of battlefield casualties and domestic opposition, American leaders still were incapable of imagining a defeat, or an end to the regime in Saigon which seemed too much a part of accepted geography. Even in secret intelligence briefings, McNamara appears to have received no hint that a massive enemy offensive lay only a few months away. Even then, when the word Tet would no longer be foreign to American ears, the administration never really believed that the war could be lost or that the government in Saigon could cease to exist. All of the arguments were over the question of how many men, and what resources, were needed to end or win the conflict. The United States had never lost a war and losing was not discussed as a possibility.

AIR-TO-AIR COMBAT

Throughout the spring and into the summer of 1967, air-to-air action between US and North Vietnamese fighters continued at a heightened pace. In a period of two days, six MiG–17s were claimed by F–105D pilots. Five more MiG–17 kills by Air Force F–4C Phantoms followed. Then it was the Navy's turn, with the next four aerial victories, again all MiG–17s, being achieved by F–8 Crusaders from USS *Bon Homme Richard*. As the

Unpublished view of F–4C Phantom 64-820, flown by Lt Col. Robert F. Titus of the 389 TFS/366 TFW at Da Nang. Not quite visible to the naked eye in this photograph are three MiG kills painted on the nose beneath the windscreen. Although Titus scored three kills with the three available systems—20 mm cannon, Sparrow and Sidewinder—none of the victories was actually achieved in this airframe. (VIA GEORGE W. PENNICK)

fighting went on, more Air Force kills followed. The crew of Lt Col. Robert F. Titus and 1 Lt Milan Zimer, flying an F–4C Phantom of the 389 TFS/366 TFW out of Da Nang, scored an achievement that no one would ever match: they racked up three MiG–17 kills, using all three systems available to the Phantom—gun, Sparrow and Sidewinder. The centerline-mounted SUU–16/A gun pod carrying an M61A1 cannon had been introduced during this period and gave Air Force Phantoms something the MiGs had had all along—the capability for gunfighting at close range.

All three of Titus' kills were MiG–21s, and he had the greatest respect for the Soviet-built fighter. He also felt that he and his fellow Seventh Air Force pilots were developing ways to combat the MiG–21:

'[Beginning in] August 1967 fewer MiG–21s directed by better-trained radar controllers achieved greatly improved results through high-speed hit-and-run attacks against trailing or isolated flights. They not only set up for an ideal missile launch position, they also had the speed for an immediate disengagement. If they arrived undetected—which was frequently the case, especially when they had cloud cover—it was difficult if not impossible for the CAP [combat air patrol] to accelerate and successfully launch missiles. [By early 1968] the controllers were able simultaneously to coordinate low and high attacks with mixed forces of MiG–17 and MiG–21s and at greater distances from Hanoi.'

Titus goes on to discuss 'the type formations and fighter missions that Seventh Air Force aircraft flew. Initially, the F–105 strike formations were flights of four separated by several minutes from the next succeeding flight and running in at low altitudes and high speeds hoping to achieve surprise. Intense ground fire soon drove us to higher altitudes but ultimately the SAMs forced a compromise to a band of altitudes from roughly 7,000 to 16,000 feet [2 133 to 4 877 m]. As ECM gear became available the advantages of large formations and mass jamming became evident.

'The MiGs helped to drive the character of the formation so that the F–4 escort could provide complete coverage of the force. The F–4s attempted to screen the force from MiG attacks particularly during the dive bomb runs and also to act as a covering defense during force egress. Eventually the F–4s served in an escort role by joining with the strike aircraft miles short of the target and remaining with them until out of MiG range on the withdrawal.

'While the term MiGCAP came to be used to denote any role of the F–4s in primary defense of the strike force, it is a misnomer CAP (Combat Air Patrol) or as the Navy prefers BARCAP, short for barrier CAP, more properly denotes a blocking force separating the target from its fighter defenders. In contrast, *Escort* [emphasis in original] implies just that—a protective force that stays with the strike formation. A sweep is another type of counter-air mission, a swing around the enemy air bases or areas known to be patrolled by enemy fighters. We employed all of these means to maintain air superiority.'[40]

Colonel Robin Olds racked up his second, third and eventually fourth air-to-air kills during this period of intense fighting. At the time, Olds did not receive full credit, nor did other Phantom crew members. The custom at the time, amid the ROLLING THUNDER campaign, was to award *half* a credit to *each* member of a Phantom crew for a MiG defeated in air-to-air action. This made sense in many respects but it was not good for morale, especially for front-seat pilots and most

particularly for men with the dedication and fighting spirit of Robin Olds. To turn the equation around backwards, Thud pilot Max Brestel was credited with two kills because his crew (of one) had shot down two MiGs, while Olds was credited with two kills because his crew (of two) had shot down four. Even this is a simplification, because Olds did not always fly with the same back-seater. Anyway, later in the conflict it was decided to award full credit to both men in the Phantom. Many of Olds' wingmen feel that he should have become an ace and that only restrictions and bureaucracy prevented him from attaining the magic fifth kill that would accord unofficial but coveted ace status.

RYAN'S RAIDERS

The bad weather over North Vietnam, especially in the rainy season at the beginning of the year, was a constant source of frustration. By August 1967, the Air Force was taking steps to be able to operate in the Hanoi-Haiphong region in bad weather and at night. In the same period, debate continued over how targets were being chosen and why some targets were not being bombed. PACAF chief General John D. Ryan was enmeshed in both issues. Whether the civilians who dictated policy allowed his men to attack lucrative targets or not, Ryan wanted a capability to fight in bad weather. It was a source of special embarrassment that, at this time, such a capability was possessed only by the A–6A Intruder being operated by the Navy and Marine Corps.

In Washington, Senator John Stennis held Preparedness Sub-committee hearings to investigate whether men like Ryan and Momyer were being shackled by 'unskilled civilian amateurs' who selected targets. In a gesture widely interpreted as a response to Stennis rather than a real change in warfighting policy, President Johnson on 9 August eased some restrictions to allow US aircraft to strike previously prohibited targets within the city limits of Hanoi and Haiphong. Meanwhile, a parade of top-ranking officers appeared under the kleig lights in front of Stennis and other lawmakers to proclaim that the United States was squandering men and aircraft on an ill-advised and poorly-planned bombing campaign. Some of the generals and admirals wanted to invade North Vietnam, an idea which was especially appealing because, up North, there was no problem of distinguishing friend from foe. All, including Admiral Sharp, saw an absolute necessity to expand the air war and allow strikes on better targets. One general told Stennis' inquiry that his men were shackled, his hands were tied, and that nobody really understood or supported targeting policy.

With new targets under attack for the first time, the MiGs came up. On 10 August, Navy F–4B Phantom crews shot two of them down. Meanwhile, Navy, Marine and Air Force people kept trying to devise new ways to deliver bombs accurately in a region which sometimes went for weeks without a clear day.

Lt Col. James McInerney was one of three brothers, the offspring of the kind of family which quietly and without fanfare sends its young men through the long gray line at West Point and produces a disproportionate share of a nation's warriors, casualties and heroes. One McInerney brother had died in Vietnam. Two others were aloft on 11 August 1967, taking the war to targets which Lyndon Johnson had opened up for the first time.

Jim McInerney had been associated with the Wild Weasel (anti-SAM) mission since the early days in Super Sabres, back when Captains Pitchford and Trier had been shot down in an F–100F. McInerney commanded the 44 TFS at Korat, a part of the 18 TFW, which in time was absorbed by the 13 TFS which he also commanded, flying the F–105F on the Wild Weasel mission. Four months earlier, he and his aircrews had begun flying night and adverse-weather missions under the most difficult circumstances, performing the same function as the Navy's A–6A Intruder.

The new mission had been mandated by General Ryan. McInerney's bad-weather strike function was given the name Commando Nail but his outfit quickly became known as 'Ryan's Raiders'. The 'Raiders' nocturnal sorties were made in F–105Fs equipped with modified radar scopes giving expanded presentation and sharper target definition of enemy radar pulses. Seeking their targets at low level over enemy territory at night was no easy task, but 'Ryan's Raiders' helped take the pressure off the daytime strikes and considerable success was achieved against North Vietnamese ground installations of all kinds. The literature of the period has created the impression that 'Ryan's Raiders' were carrying out the Wild Weasel mission. In fact, while they were the same men and the same aircraft which had performed the Weasel job, the 'Raiders' delivered ordnance against an encyclopedic variety of targets and were not, in any sense, dedicated to the campaign against SAM sites.

On 11 August 1967, in daylight, Lt Col. McInerney's men and machines were part of the force that went against the Paul Doumer Bridge. Lt Col. McInerney and his backseater, Captain Fred Shannon, *did* fly a Wild Weasel mission on this date. The pair earned

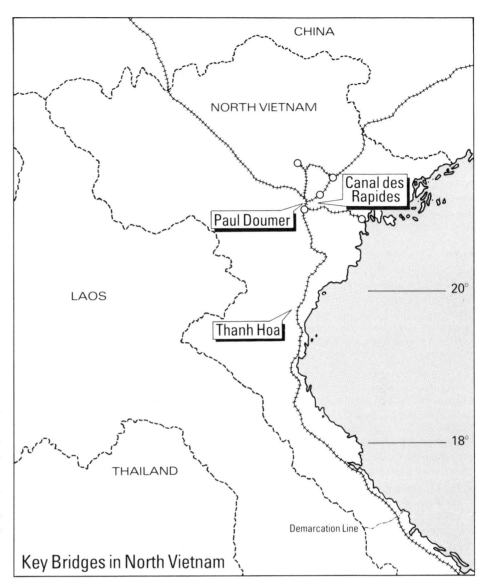

Key Bridges in North Vietnam

Location of the three principal bridges in North Vietnam, which were targets for US aircraft during the 1965–68 ROLLING THUNDER and 1972 LINEBACKER campaigns.

the Air Force Cross, the second highest award for valor, for leading a Wild Weasel strike that destroyed six SAM sites and damaged four others. It was to be a shining achievement of McInerney's that on both Weasel and 'Ryans Raiders' missions, he never lost a man who flew with him.

The Paul Doumer Bridge was, of course, one of the targets which US airmen most wanted to attack. Named for the French Governor-General of Indochina who built the nation's railway system at the end of the previous century, the bridge was on the outskirts of Hanoi. It was readily visible on most missions in the region and thus seemed to stand out, as if mocking the men who wanted to bomb it but could not. With 19 spans crossing the Red River not far from the industrial area around Gia Lam airfield, the bridge was 5,532 ft (1 686 m) long and 38 ft (12 m) wide. Its length became 8,467 ft (2 580 m) when approach viaducts were counted. It was by far the longest bridge in North

Vietnam and a vital transportation link, although its direct link to the infiltration of the South was questionable.

On 11 August 1967, the first attack on the bridge was mounted by 26 F–105Ds, each carrying one 3,000 lb (1 360 kg) bomb, swarming down on the bridge in three waves. Each wave of Thuds was escorted by four F–4C Phantoms in the MiGCAP role, four more for flak suppression, and four F–105F Wild Weasels to suppress SAM sites. The strike force's Thuds climbed from treetop height to 13,000 feet (3 965 m), dived at a 45-degree angle, dropped their bombs, lowered air brakes, and pulled out. The use of a single heavy bomb by each Thud might have been more effective if some means of attaining precision accuracy had been attained, but *that* goal lay ahead. 'The necessity to improve visual weapons delivery accuracy [is great]. We are now delivering iron bombs with a fixed sight from a $2.5 million vehicle instead of a ... World War I aircraft—remarkable progress in 49 years.'[41] Still, the number two Thud in the strike force released its bomb after diving to 7,000 feet (2 135 m), scoring a direct hit that dropped one span of the bridge into the water.

A couple of weeks earlier, the F-4D Phantom had been introduced to Route Package Six when 16 F-105Ds from Korat and eight F-4Ds from Ubon made a strike on a rail yard near Kep. The F-4D variant marked an effort by the Air Force to adapt further a Navy fighter design for its own needs and for precision bombing with a new dive-toss method of dropping ordnance. Captain Thomas G. McInerney, Jim's brother, already a veteran of one tour of duty in Vietnam, had helped to develop ordnance and tactics for the F-4D model at Eglin AFB, Florida, and had come to Ubon with the first F-4Ds. It was widely understood that another squadron was scheduled to be first to receive the F-4D, but Colonel Robin Olds pulled strings and had the new aircraft assigned to the 555 TFS, the 'Triple Nickel' squadron which was part of his 8 TFW, or 'Wolfpack'.

Tom McInerney's recollection is that the F-4D Phantom played a critical role in the 11 August 1967 strikes on the Paul Doumer Bridge. Lt Col. Jesse Allen, the 'Triple Nickel' skipper, led a mixed force of F-4Cs and F-4Ds which put the finishing touches on the long highway and rail bridge, completing the job that had been begun by Thuds. The 'dive-toss' mode employed by the F-4D which permitted greater accuracy and earlier bomb-release from greater height turned out to be an enormous improvement.

McInerney remembers F-4D Phantom pilots using their automated bomb-release mechanism to drop ordnance at 8,000 feet (2 432 m), while F-4C Phantom pilots had to drop their bombs manually at 6,500 feet (1 981 m), increasing their exposure to AAA fire. Only one F-4C Phantom is listed as having been lost in combat that day, but McInerney, Allen and others remember that the North Vietnamese AAA fire was furious.[42]

Carrier-based Navy aircraft also played a full role in the strikes on various targets in the Hanoi and Haiphong region which had been rendered possible by Johnson's decision to open-up targets. F-4Bs from *Constellation* were especially active, but suffered no losses.

At the Paul Doumer Bridge, one railroad and two highway spans were destroyed. The bridge was to be essentially out of service for seven weeks, until it was hit again, but the

innovative North Vietnamese quickly found ways to ford the river, getting both vehicles and rail cars across via barge. Later strikes temporarily dissuaded the North Vietnamese from their inventive efforts to replace broken spans and, instead, prodded them to build an adjacent pontoon structure. Unlike the Dragon's Jaw at Thanh Hoa which could not be severed, the Paul Doumer Bridge was temporarily neutralized.

The 11 August 1967 air strikes took place in a setting where the enemy's MiG opposition remained difficult to measure and evaluate. Many US airmen believed that the North Vietnamese had not recovered from Operation *Bolo* eight months earlier, for although the absolute number of MiGs destroyed in that operation (seven) may not have seemed high, it represented an enormous proportion of the MiGs the enemy could get into the air at any one time. It remained true, and unavoidable, that missiles, MiGs and AAA complemented each other and made the Americans' job more difficult.

Ensign Francis B. Newman, an F-4B Phantom pilot with the 'Ghostriders' of VF-142 aboard *Constellation*, recalls a different kind of MiG pilot than the kind reported by most Americans during this period—an aggressive, hard-hitting enemy flier who began the dogfight on his own terms, stayed in the fight, and refused to give up or back out. Newman and his wingman were bounced by a pair of MiG-21s and struggled with them inconclusively for more than five minutes, seemingly an eternity in an air combat situation where fuel is devoured rapidly. The Americans were unable to add to the total score of 90 MiGs destroyed by this point in the war, and the North Vietnamese were also unable to seize the advantage. It was a hard-fought battle which resulted in no success for either side.

WALLEYE OPERATIONAL

On 24 August 1967, direct hits were observed in the first USAF operational use of the AGM-62A Walleye. The TV-guided missiles were first employed by F-4D Phantoms. A follow-up mission two days later resulted in destruction of a bridge, dropping the two center spans with the first Walleye used. On this mission, because the first firings were so successful, two F-4D Phantoms returned to base with their ordnance unexpended. A total of 22 of the expensive Walleye weapons was used by USAF aircraft during the year. The Navy employed its own variant of the Walleye with the A-4E Skyhawk.

Like many of the munitions employed in the conflict, Walleye had been developed ear-

lier and was steadily improved over time by its manufacturer, Martin Marietta. With an 825 lb (374 kg) warhead based on the Mark 84 bomb, the 13 ft 3 in (4.04 m) Walleye II variant was used very successfully by F-4Ds and A-4Es, and later by Navy A-7 Corsair II aircraft which could launch them at targets from ranges as great as 35 miles (56 km).

GEORGE DAY'S ORDEAL

On 26 August 1967, an F-100F Super Sabre (56-3954) of the 416 TFS/37 TFW at Phu Cat AB, South Vietnam was shot down over the North. It was the beginning of an almost unspeakable ordeal for the front-seat pilot of the F-100F, Major George E. (Bud) Day, who was quickly taken prisoner and was determined to prevent his North Vietnamese captors from knowing that the F-100F was being used in the Fast FAC mission.

When he ejected, Bud Day's arm was broken in three places and his left knee was badly sprained. Denied proper medical treatment, interrogated, tortured, Major Day not only refused to divulge any information, but actually lulled his captors into allowing him to escape. Day got loose in the jungle and trekked south toward the demilitarized zone, dodging enemy patrols and surviving on a diet of berries and uncooked frogs. Day succeeded in crossing the Ben Hai River which separates North from South Vietnam.

For 12 days, at times delirious, Major Day evaded capture. His normal weight of 170 lb shrank to a mere 100 lb. At one point, Major Day was within eyesight of two US Marine Corps helicopters on the ground but, before he could reach them, saw them lift away into the air. Finally, he was recaptured, beaten, tortured. At one time he was bound by a rope under his armpits and suspended from a ceiling beam while an interrogator ordered his wrist broken, seeking to learn about the F-100F Fast FAC mission. Day, who eventually promoted to colonel, was to remain a prisoner of war until the end of the conflict. He was, in fact, quickly transported to Hanoi, cancelling out his success as the only man to escape from North Vietnam to the South. Colonel George E. Day continued to resist his captors, withheld critical information from them, and became one of three POWs to be awarded the Medal of Honor for conduct while in captivity.

HH-53B ARRIVAL

The Sikorsky HH-53B Super Jolly Green Giant helicopter arrived in Southeast Asia on 8 September 1967. Rescue squadrons had pre-

viously had to 'make do' with the Kaman HH–43B Huskie, alias Pedro, which was a fine machine for local airfield fire-fighting and rescue but which had never been intended for combat rescue, and with the HH–3E Jolly Green Giant, which had been very successful rescuing downed airmen in North Vietnam but existed only in limited numbers. An earlier variant of the new helicopter, the CH–53A, had been in service with the Marine Corps in South Vietnam virtually from the time the Marines landed. The HH–53B, soon to be joined by the HH–53C, was to become the principal USAF tool of air rescue behind enemy lines.

The US Navy continued to rely on the Sikorsky SH–3A, and later the SH–3G Sea King, which operated from the decks of a variety of ships, and the Kaman UH–2A/B Seasprite, soon joined by the HH–3H, operating from destroyers in the Gulf of Tonkin. Most of the Navy's helicopter rescue efforts took place feet wet—that is, no attempt was made to pick up a downed airman unless he had gotten out over the sea—but there were dramatic exceptions. Throughout the war, the helicopter pilots and crews who went into harm's way to rescue their buddies rarely received the full credit they earned and warranted.

AC–130 SPECTRE GUNSHIP

27 September 1967 marked the first combat mission of the C–130 Hercules transport modified to serve as a fixed-wing gunship, a role in which it would eventually be nicknamed Spectre.

Already being used for flare-drop missions in North Vietnam using the callsign Lamplighter, the C–130 was the logical airframe to prove out gunship theory (flying an airplane in a pylon turn to aim side-mounted guns at a fixed position on the ground) which had been understood for years but was never seriously tried until Vietnam. The gun-armed FC–47 Gooney Bird, later called the AC–47 Spooky, was the first fixed-wing gunship and was remarkably successful in hosing down Viet Cong insurgents as they mounted night attacks on installations in the South. Captain Ronald W. Terry, who had done much of the combat flying in the early AC–47, was one of several junior officers who persuaded the Air Force to modify a C–130A transport (54-1626) into a gunship.

Terry's first machine was converted at Wright-Patterson AFB, Ohio. Although the progenitor of a Spectre force to follow, it did not, itself, receive the 'AC' for 'attack' designation. Terry's C–130A was equipped with four 7.62 mm General Electric GAU–2/A minigun modules and four 20 mm General Electric M61A1 Vulcan cannons. To assist the gunship crew in locating and lining up on its target, the C–130A was also equipped with a night observation device (NOD), or Starlite Scope, an infra-red sensor, a target-tracking computer and a 20-kW searchlight. Terry and his C–130A made the journey to Southeast Asia and, on their first combat mission,

The Air Force HH–53B/C helicopter was introduced to Southeast Asia in September 1967 and quickly became vital to combat rescue operations. Here, HH–53C (68-10360) of the 37 ARRS at Da Nang has temporarily moved to Phu Cat AB, South Vietnam on 7 July 1971 to avoid an approaching typhoon at its home base. (NORMAN TAYLOR)

blunted a Viet Cong assault on a firebase in South Vietnam. Terry's new-style attack aircraft was first employed in the conflict against the North only weeks later, on 9 November 1967, when his C–130A flew a successful night mission against the Ho Chi Minh Trail, destroying a six-truck convoy.

The Air Force quickly commissioned E-Systems Inc. of Greenville, Texas, to convert several more airframes to AC–130A standard. These fixed-wing gunships retained the armament on Terry's prototype but introduced Texas Instruments AN/AAD–4 forward-looking infra-red (FLIR) sensors, a new fire-control computer and a moving target indicator (MTI) radar. The FLIR package enabled the crew to observe trucks and other targets on a monitor, in effect removing the benefit of darkness upon which the North Vietnamese supply effort depended. These AC–130A gunships were to join the 16th Special Operations Squadron at Ubon in 1969, while even further modifications continued to produce an improved AC–130.

Few of the innovations during this long and tortured war were as readily adopted or as free from growing pains as the AC–130 gunship. No aircraft used against North Vietnam called for greater ability or courage on the part of its crew. AC-130 pilots and crew members routinely faced every defense the North Vietnamese could muster in the rural regions where the Ho Chi Minh Trail snaked southward. Their night combat mission was exceedingly destructive to the enemy at relatively low cost to the US Air Force. It was also about as dangerous as any job that could be undertaken in the air war against North Vietnam.

STRATEGIC RECONNAISSANCE

On 27 September 1967, the first operational RC-135M recce mission was flown by the newly-established 82nd Strategic Reconnaissance Squadron at Kadena AB, Okinawa. The strategic reconnaissance mission, which remained under the jurisdiction of SAC, was very much a vital part of the war effort against North Vietnam. The reconnaissance version of the Boeing Stratotanker, although little-publicized and only recently described in detail in a SAC history, was crucial to these operations, especially since replacing the RB-47 Stratojet in the combat theater at the beginning of the year. SAC has now released some details on the RC-135M mission, known by the code name Combat Apple.

A Combat Apple flight consisted of flying 12-hour orbits over the Gulf of Tonkin, and later over Laos, collecting electronic intelligence with special attention to picking up indications of *Fan Song* radar signals. If correctly identified, this intelligence made it possible to pinpoint and plant strikes against North Vietnam's ever-growing SAM network. Some 50-odd Combat Apple missions were flown per month at first, a figure which soon settled to a more relaxed 30.

Other strategic reconnaissance operations by variants of the RC-135 and by A-12 and SR-71 platforms, added to the knowledge available to commanders based on the more familiar tactical recce flights by RF-101Cs and RF-4Cs. RC-135 aircraft operated by SAC continued to operate through the end of the conflict on various missions which shed light on Hanoi's capabilities and intentions.

NAVY SEARCH AND RESCUE

Navy carriers at Yankee Station continued to pound targets in North Vietnam as the intensity of fighting remained high and MiG activity was constant. At the end of September 1967, the warships committed to the battle were the carriers *Oriskany* and *Coral Sea*, and USS *Intrepid* (CVS-11), an anti-submarine carrier but with A-4B Skyhawks embarked in the attack role. Naval aviators

operating from carrier decks paid a heavy price for the high risks of their profession, a point illustrated in October when no fewer than 11 A-4 Skyhawks were lost in battle in a single month. Navy men were gradually realizing that their much-needed combat search and rescue function could not be performed solely by anti-submarine warfare (ASW) helicopter squadrons, and that the mission really was best conducted by a unit with the equipment and training to snatch up survivors in the face of increasingly tough enemy defenses. Helicopter Combat Support Squadron Seven (HC-7) had been formed for this very purpose at NAS Atsugi, Japan, with Commander Lloyd Parthemer as its skipper. HC-7 quickly acquired responsibility for the UH-2A Seasprite helicopters operating from search and rescue (SAR) surface vessels off the Vietnamese coast.

On 3 October 1967, the squadron flew its first combat mission and Seasprite pilot Lt Tim Melecosky performed spectacularly. Melecosky's UH-2A Seasprite was already aloft, alerted by the loss of an Air Force

On 3 October 1967, a dramatic rescue was made by the crew of a UH-2A Seasprite helicopter. Shown here is a more advanced HH-2C Seasprite (151335) of squadron HC-7, wearing toned-down camouflage for the Southeast Asia rescue mission. (HARRY GANN, VIA TAILHOOK PHOTO SERVICE)

aircraft, when the helicopter was diverted towards Haiphong harbor. An A–4B Skyhawk (142114) from *Intrepid* had been hit by gunfire and the pilot had ejected and landed in the water only 60 yards (55 m) from a moored, light-gray merchant vessel. The Skyhawk had belonged to the 'War Eagles' of VSF–1, a curious unit in the history of naval aviation—technically an anti-submarine squadron although, in fact, the Skyhawk was never equipped for, or assigned to, the ASW function. That day, the Skyhawk pilot had been on a typical strike mission.

While other A–4 Skyhawks orbited overhead in the RESCAP role, Lt Melecosky brought his UH–2A Seasprite into Haiphong a breath-taking *five feet (1.5 m)* above the wavecaps. Melecosky was literally dodging gunfire by needling his way between merchant vessels, knowing that the enemy would not bring guns to bear on the freighters. Melecosky spotted the Skyhawk pilot bobbing from a raft and igniting flares. He brought the Seasprite overhead, hovered, and, in keeping with standard practice, dropped a rescueman. After struggling for a moment in the shallow mud bottom between freighters and raft, the rescueman got himself and the Skyhawk pilot attached to the rescue line and the pair were hoisted aboard. Lt Melecosky, at considerable risk, had pulled off the first combat rescue by a Navy squadron created solely for that purpose.

Only a day later, Melecosky's Seasprite was shot down on another rescue mission and he had to be saved himself. The Navy soon realized that the lightly-armed, single-engine UH–2A and UH–2B variants of the Seasprite were highly vulnerable in places like Haiphong and that twin engines and heavier armament were sorely needed. The UH–2C, powered by twin T58 gas turbine engines, soon arrived in the combat theater, appearing first aboard USS *Kitty Hawk* (CVA–63) with the second rescue squadron operating in the battle zone, HC–1. However, the Navy ordered six examples of the HH–2C Seasprite which, with twin engines, General Electric 0.3 in (7.62 mm) miniguns and other improvements, were more appropriate for the combat rescue role.

The SH–3A Sea King helicopter, assigned to ASW squadrons but used in the rescue role, was soon supplanted by the HH–3A variant designed for the combat rescue role and armed accordingly. Sikorsky produced one HH–3A conversion and nine knockdown kits which made it possible to bring SH–3A airframes to HH–3A standard. The Sea King's primary mission continued to be ASW, however, and given the absence of any serious threat from submarines, its contribution to the conflict remained unsung.

KC–135 COMBAT LIGHTNING

By October 1967, two basic KC–135 tankers with AN/ARC–89 equipment installed were operating from U-Tapao as airborne relay platforms to support the USAF command and control system in Southeast Asia. These were joined by two EC–135L airborne command posts from SAC's Post-Attack Command Control System (PACSS). Three additional KC–135s eventually brought to seven the number of airframes employed in the relay mission, which carried the code name Combat Lightning.

D MODEL PHANTOM

The first air-to-air kill for the F–4D Phantom was scored on 24 October 1967. Major William L. Kirk of the 433 TFS/8 TFW flying with the Wolfpack from Ubon used the externally-mounted 20 mm cannon pod to shoot down a MiG–21. Kirk's backseater, 1Lt Theodore R. Bongartz, shared credit for the war's 93rd MiG kill.

The air-to-air situation heated up further two days later, when three MiG–17s and one MiG–21 were shot down by Navy and Air Force fliers. Included in the day's tally was the first kill to be scored by the AIM–4D Falcon missile, which had been introduced concurrently with the F–4D. Captain Larry D. Cobb and Captain Alan A. Lavoy of the 555 TFS/8 TFW were the Wolfpack crew who claimed a MiG–17 with the Falcon.

None of the missiles employed by US aircraft had been designed for fighter-versus-fighter combat but, of the three major types employed, the AIM–4 Falcon proved least suitable. As Thomas McInerney recalls, 'the Falcon required all sorts of fancy-setting-up and had to be cooled before firing'. All infra-red missiles, including the AIM–9 Sidewinder, required cooling before their heat-seeker heads would work, but the arrangement with the Falcon was more cumbersome than most. Most airmen supported Colonel Robin Olds when he trashed the AIM–4 Falcon and ordered AIM–9 Sidewinders installed on the F–4D Phantom, even though the variant had not been designed for the Sidewinder.

A Thud pilot and a Navy F–4B crew downed two more MiGs at the end of the month, bringing the war's total to 99.

If a time and place had to be chosen when combat missions were at the height of danger for the men involved, the statistics showed that North Vietnam in October 1967 was the choice. Airmen remained certain they were fulfilling the demands of their profession but, because of protest at home, few believed with

any surety that they enjoyed the full support of their countrymen. In October, a massive demonstration against the war was held at the Pentagon, where protesters faced armed troops with bayonets. Playwright Arthur Miller and author Norman Mailer were among celebrities who participated in the huge outpouring of anti-war sentiment and Mailer later wrote a best-selling book about it.

Also in October, EC–121 Warning Star operations were centralized at Korat to provide better common maintenance and more economical logistical support. The EC–121Ds of the College Eye Task force relocated to Korat from Udorn to join the sole Rivet Top EC–121K and the newly-assigned EC–121R radio relay aircraft. The latter was simply another of the many means of improving communications throughout Southeast Asia. The EC–121R variant of the Super Constellation, however, lacked the now-familiar 'hump' found on the early-warning aircraft where their radars were located.

The decision at the end of October to permit strikes on Phuc Yen airfield was another of those 'on again, off again' measures which gave conflicting signals to everyone involved. The official line was that the ROLLING THUNDER campaign was methodically destroying the North Vietnamese supply and transportation network, and the time had come for stronger action against the MiG threat at Phuc Yen. Like all targeting decisions during the period, it was made without any clear reason why it could not have been made earlier or later. A three-day effort against Phuc Yen and Cat Bi resulted in 20 MiGs being damaged or destroyed on the ground but, at the same time, a new threat developed from North Vietnam's SAM installations. Optical tracking devices had been installed at SAM sites, seriously downgrading the effectiveness of the ECM pod which had become so important to the integrity of a strike mission.

A few MiGs destroyed, improved SAM capability . . . The battle seemed to continue, leaving in its wake milestones that were confusing and ambiguous. In the wake of the Pentagon protest, Senator Eugene McCarthy from Minnesota was preparing to do what few American politicians would dare—seek to wrest the presidential nomination from a White House incumbent of his own party. McCarthy would seize on the popular feeling, particularly among young people, against the war. The coming of an election year at a time of anti-war protest caused some to speculate that if McCarthy could challenge Lyndon Johnson's presidency, another member of Johnson's party might do so even more effectively—Robert F. Kennedy.

Although Phuc Yen was one of North Vietnam's principal MiG bases from the beginning of the conflict, US aircraft were not allowed to bomb it until October 1967, and then only briefly. This overhead photograph of two MiG–17 fighters parked at Phuc Yen was taken a year earlier. (USAF)

RADAR BOMBING

Throughout the war, efforts were made to find improved ways of radar bombing from high altitude, a method which would keep US aircraft out of range of most North Vietnamese defensive weapons. Flights of strike aircraft were led to their targets by a pathfinder aircraft, usually an EB–66E Destroyer or an F–4D Phantom equipped with long-range navigation (LORAN) gear. Using a radar 'fix' on a target established in part by the pathfinder, in part by a Sky Spot or other powerful radar on the ground in the South, the strike aircraft would release their bombs from as high as 30,000 feet (9 144 m). The precision and accuracy of this kind of bombing was open to question. As General Momyer put it:

'When we started the radar bombing program, some thought we could sustain the offensive throughout the bad weather months. It was never possible. The nature of the targets was beyond the capability of the radar systems. The magnitude of the enemy defenses made it prohibitive to fly above an overcast. We found from bitter experience that formations above an overcast in a heavy SAM environment [were] not tactically feasible regardless of the effectiveness of the ECM. There was so much redundancy in the enemy radar system, supplementary data gave accurate position, speed and altitude of the strike force. By the time the pilots saw the missiles coming through the overcast, it was almost too late for evasive action . . .'[43]

On 9 November 1967, Captain Lance P. Sijan was flying one of these high-altitude radar bombing missions. At the controls of an F–4C Phantom (64-781) of the 480 TFS/366 TFW, Captain Sijan was brought down not by enemy gunfire but by a fuse malfunction which caused his bombs to detonate—a malfunction which happened far too often, in all types of aircraft, Air Force and Navy. Although Captain Sijan ejected over Laos, as many airmen did, his story is very much a part of the war against North Vietnam.

Surrounded by North Vietnamese troops in the hostile Laotian rain forest, Captain Sijan eluded his pursuers for no less than six weeks, surviving on moisture from forest leaves, berries and frogs. During his six-week evasion effort, he suffered severe lacerations, serious injuries to his left leg and right hand, a concussion and horrendous loss of weight. At one point, a C–130 Hercules on a Lamplighter flare-drop mission succeeded in bringing in an HH–3E helicopter; the HH–3E was within a few feet, lowering its hoist, when Sijan realized that it was about to be bracketed by North Vietnamese guns. Using his survival radio, he ordered the helicopter away. When he was inevitably captured, the weakened Captain Sijan quickly overpowered a guard and escaped. He was recaptured within hours. The North Vietnamese tortured him and kept him confined alone. He was then taken to a village to begin the arduous journey to downtown Hanoi.

Other American POWs observed Captain Sijan's resistance to enemy pressures during the long and punishing truck ride to Hanoi. This ended with Captain Sijan being taken to the Hoa Lo prison camp, known to Americans as Vegas. Here, he continued to resist under harsh treatment. His condition was made worse by the inadequate living conditions, poor food and lack of clothing and medical treatment. Shortly after arrival in Hanoi on 18 January 1968, Captain Sijan contracted pneumonia. Because he would have been literally drowned by the fluid in his air passages, he was unable to lie down. For more than three days, he struggled to keep his ravaged body in a standing position. He was still resisting when the North Vietnamese took him from his cell. Later, they reported that he had died.

Captain Sijan is the third American POW to be awarded the Medal of Honor for 'conspicuous gallantry and intrepidity at the risk of life above and beyond the call of duty' while in captivity in North Vietnam. Unlike Jim Stockdale and Bud Day who survived the POW ordeal, Captain Sijan's award was made posthumously.

Even when the fuses on their bombs worked correctly, men like Sijan were taking enormous risk for something which remained an elusive goal. General Momyer noted that successful high-altitude radar bombing remained 'more a requirement than a reality'. He did not seem optimistic that radar bombing would become effective under any circumstances: 'With tactical targets of the nature one finds in [the North Vietnamese] transportation system, visual conditions are manda-

tory for target acquisition and attack. We spent many hours trying to develop a radar attack capability organic to the F–105 and F–4. All of these efforts led to the conclusion that we could only work against area targets which had very good radar features. Nevertheless, if we could consider such attacks as harassment, they serve a very decided purpose of keeping pressure on the enemy. I believe our all-weather capability should be directed to the objective of harassment and not destruction per se.

'[Ours] is not a suitable radar system for a heavily-defended environment such as the one in Route Package Six. In order to get target coverage, it is necessary to employ a formation. Formation flying made us extremely vulnerable to barrage fire from AAA and SAMs. Furthermore, the last part of the bomb run, about thirty miles [48.2 km] into the target, had to be straight and level. This made the force even more vulnerable to ground fire and MiGs. On 18 November 1967 we lost two [F–105D] aircraft over Phuc Yen trying to execute [a radar bombing] attack over a solid overcast. This experience coupled with other missions conclusively demonstrated that [our radar] bombing was not tactically sound for such a defense environment.'[24]

Momyer was later to indicate that despite 'Ryan's Raiders' and despite the radar-bombing attempts, there was really no good way for Air Force aircraft to bomb North Vietnam during the months of bad weather—which meant the early months of the year. If they did not say so, Air Force pilots apparently felt a degree of envy for the Navy with its A–6A Intruder, the only genuine all-weather system capable of operating inside North Vietnam even during the very worst season.

The A–7A Corsair II was introduced to combat on 4 December 1967 by the 'Argonauts' of VA–147 under Commander James C. Hill. This example (153228) was still in the Pacific with the 'Ravens' of VA–93 a decade later and is seen on approach to NAF Atsugi, Japan, in May 1976. (HIDEKI NAGAKUBO)

ENTER THE A–7A

4 December 1967 marked the introduction into combat of the A–7A Corsair II, the carrier-based light attack aircraft intended as an A–4 Skyhawk replacement and created by a Vought design team under J. Russell Clark. The 'Argonauts' of attack squadron VA–147 under Commander James C. Hill arrived in the combat zone aboard USS *Ranger* (CVA–61) and included a cadre of Air Force officers assigned to test the A–7A in battle in anticipation of their Service purchasing the aircraft.

Hill's squadron flew its first strikes against bridge and highway targets around Vinh. On 17 December, A–4s, A–6s and A–7s from *Ranger* assaulted the Hai Duong rail and highway bridge complex between Haiphong and Hanoi. Hill evaded a SAM just in time to spot MiGs circling and eyeing him from a distance. Perhaps because the A–7A carried Sidewinders and possessed air-to-air capability, the MiGs did not engage. Hill and his fellow pilots, including Air Force Major Charles W. McClarren, concluded that the A–7A was a highly effective attack craft, although it had a nasty tendency to suck up catapult steam and suffer compressor failure. On 22 December, one A–7A (153239) was lost, but it was the only loss on the type's first combat cruise.

The A–7A had made its first flight at Dallas two years earlier on 27 September 1965 with Vought's chief test pilot, John W. Konrad, at the controls. It was thus the first major war-

Commander James C. Hill, skipper of the 'Argonauts' of VA-147, brings A-7A Corsair II 153219 towards landing aboard USS *Ranger* (CVA-61) in January 1968, only a month after the A-7A was introduced to combat. (USN VIA M. J. KASIUBA)

On 17 December 1967, Captain Doyle D. Baker became the first US Marine Corps officer to receive credit for shooting down a MiG. Baker was serving an exchange tour with the Air Force's 13 TFS / 432 TFW and was at the controls of an F-4D Phantom (66-7709), nicknamed *AWOL* (absent without leave), with lLt John D. Ryan, Jr, in the back seat. Baker is said to have 'singed the tail feathers' of a MiG-17 with fire from his cannon pod before employing an AIM-4D Falcon missile for the final kill.

Two days later, the crew of an F-105F of the 357 TFS / 355 TFW at Takhli, Captain Philip M. Drew and Major William Wheeler, shot down a MiG-17 with 20 mm fire. The pair were flying the same two-seat Wild Weasel (63-8301) in which Major Leo Thorsness had earlier won the Medal of Honor. On the same day, 19 December, a pair of two-man crews in an F-105F and an F-4D shared credit for a MiG-17 which the two American fighters hounded down with 20 mm cannon fire. The 105th air-to-air kill of the war was also the last for the F-105 and the last for the F-105F.

At the end of 1967, opposition to the war at home was growing, confidence in President Johnson's policy was at a low, and the ROLLING THUNDER bombing campaign, now nearly two years old, had failed to disrupt the North Vietnamese transportation network or prevent infiltration of the south. The United States had committed a massive ground force to the fight in South Vietnam, now numbering nearly 400,000 troops and soon to peak above the half-million mark. Few Americans could view the conflict any longer with innocence, fewer still with enthusiasm. It seems remarkable that brave men fought on, shored up by the support of comrades and by their profession, if not by their nation. An official PACAF history sums up the year in two sentences: 'Although the enemy failed to win any major battles in 1967, he demonstrated a willingness to accept the situation and continue to attack, harass and terrorize. He was not beaten, and the war would continue until one side or the other grew tired and opted to quit.'[45]

plane to take to the skies after the start of the ROLLING THUNDER campaign. Powered by a 11,350 lb (5 150 kg) thrust non-afterburning Pratt & Whitney TF30-P-6 turbofan (or, in the view of many, *under* powered), the A-7A could carry a 20,000 lb (9 100 kg) bombload and also carried two Sidewinders on the fuselage sides and two Mark 12 internally-mounted 20 mm cannons with 680 rounds. Navy pilots soon found that its considerable combat radius of 715 miles (1 150 km) enabled the snub-nosed, swept-wing Corsair II to range over North Vietnam, hounding and

harassing the enemy, searching out targets of opportunity and loitering overhead for extended periods when a RESCAP (rescue mission) was necessary.

The venerable Thud, the Air Force's F-105, remained at the end of 1967 the principal means employed to carry bombs into North Vietnam. The extent of commitment by the F-105 and the men who flew it was reflected in official, year-end figures which showed that in 1967 the USAF lost 421 aircraft in Southeast Asia, 334 of them to hostile action and 87 to operational causes. As in previous years, the F-105 continued to suffer the greatest losses, with 113 lost in the year to all causes for a loss rate of 2.86. The increasing use of the F-4 Phantom was reflected by rising losses. In 1967, 95 F-4s (plus 23 RF-4Cs) were lost for a rate of 0.99. Three F-4s and 17 F-105s were claimed by SAMs, while MiGs shot down nine F-4s and 11 F-105s.

THUNDER'S END

The American election year began. For a period in January 1968, it appeared that American attention might shift from Southeast Asia to the very different, sub-zero climate of the Korean peninsula when the seizure of the US spy ship *Pueblo* and a raid on Seoul by North Korean commandos threatened to open a new, major conflict thousands of miles from the war already in progress. The US rapidly reinforced its tactical air units in South Korea at the very time when its men and machines were most needed in Vietnam. The Korean diversion was brief. By the end of January, attention once more focused on Vietnam where the word Tet became part of the American vocabulary and sharply altered perceptions of the war and its price.

It had been apparent for months that Viet Cong forces in South Vietnam had secret instructions to prepare for a major offensive. Some communist guerrillas were told that Ho Chi Minh was in deteriorating health and that an assault had to be mounted to achieve total victory while Ho still lived. In a world where events are shaped by what people believe from broadcasts, Tet was a triumph for the Viet Cong and the North Vietnamese precisely and exclusively because it was perceived by American television viewers as a triumph. The fact that communist forces were soundly defeated in battle did not become well known until much later and, therefore, did not really matter. All this, of course, came at the end of January.

BOMBING HALT #6

At the start of the New Year, once again a cessation of bombing was announced for the holidays. The News Year's Truce had begun on Christmas Eve and was supposed to last until 3 January.

As usual, the North Vietnamese used the respite to increase the flow of military supplies and the United States spent the time analyzing its limited, inconsistent air campaign. The North Vietnamese were setting up for the siege of the Marine base at Khe Sanh later in the month, an event outside the scope of

this narrative which was to end in Hanoi's failure to recreate another Dien Bien Phu. A brilliantly conceived and directed interservice operation was mounted to supply and eventually relieve the Marine defenders of the tiny bastion, much of the airpower available in Southeast Asia being melded into a radar/computer-controlled pattern of operations known as Combat Skyspot. Khe Sanh, of course, came on the heels of Tet and this, again, was at the end of January.

At the outset of the month, Navy and Air Force pilots ranging into North Vietnam found little changed in the familiar pattern of threat and counter-threat. There are reports of a severe bombing shortage and some airmen may have flown exceedingly dangerous missions only to deliver very small loads of ordnance. Nothing else was new and as usual the men engaged in the battle sought ways to cope with North Vietnam's defenses. Some men wanted the chance to attack anti-aircraft artillery positions and some wanted to be effective against SAM sites but throughout the hundreds of pilots flying fighters in Southeast Asia one goal outshone all the others: Every man wanted to get a MiG.

On 3 January 1968, Major Bernard J. Bogoslofski of the Wolfpack was over North Vietnam in an F–4D Phantom (66-7748) of Ubon's 433 TFS/8 TFW. He was carrying a gun pod beneath the fuselage and Captain Richard L. Huskey in the back seat when he became involved in a furious tangle with a MiG–17. Major Bogoslofski disposed of the North Vietnamese fighter with 20 mm cannon fire. Two weeks later, another Ubon-based Phantom crew despatched another MiG–17 with an AIM–4D Falcon missile.

ANTONOV ATTACK

An exceedingly rare incursion by the North Vietnamese air force occurred on 12 January 1968 when two Antonov An–2 biplanes attacked the government outpost at Phou Pha Thi, Laos. Details on the attack—carried out in support of ground forces—are sketchy, shedding little light on the incident.

Although Hanoi maintained special forces designed to mount paramilitary operations using the mostly-fabric biplane (which was almost impervious to radar), the chance to deliver ordnance, drop paratroops or land elite forces was never really exploited. It is not even clear what kind of ordnance was used in the one-of-a-kind Laos attack or why the biplanes were employed on that occasion.

A big machine with a 59 ft 8 in (18.18 m) wingspan, powered by a 1,000 hp (746 kW) Shvetsov ASh–62R radial engine driving a 'paddle blade' variable pitch propeller, the ugly and ungainly An–2 was in fact conceived for agricultural duties but could drop up to a dozen armed men. North Vietnam had about 40 of these flying museum pieces, though the number had been reduced by two earlier in the war when, on 20 December 1966, two Navy F–4B Phantom crews happened upon a pair of the slow Antonovs, stalked them with AIM–7E Sparrow missiles and blew them out of the sky. Of the 197 North Vietnamese aircraft shot down during the conflict, these were the only ones with propellers up front.

RF–4C VERSUS MiG

On 13 January 1968, Lt Col. Clark Taylor of the 432 TRW became one of the few recce pilots in the RF–4C Phantom to scrape with a MiG at close range and survive. The Tet offensive might be brewing, but the war remained very much an individual experience for men in cockpits. Luckily, reconnaissance aircrews did not usually find enemy interceptors to be a hazard over North Vietnam. The greatest danger remained unchanged, namely the anti-aircraft system, incorporating radar, observers, SAMs and all calibers of AAA.

Many RF–4C Phantom missions were at night and consisted of single-aircraft sorties. During the day, for missions north of the Red River, RF–4Cs generally flew in pairs. Earlier in the war, Phantoms usually had flown CAP for the reconnaissance aircraft but this practice was eventually discontinued.

Lt Col. Taylor's brush with a MiG was too

close for comfort. 'We were going to Yen Bai on the Red River. My back-seater was Major Wayne Porter and we were flying aircraft 65-847. I was flying wingman to the wing commander [Colonel Victor N. Cabas].'

Their speed approaching the notorious MiG airfield at Yen Bai was about 500 knots (820 km/h). They were on the deck. Taylor decided to pop up to about 4,000 feet (1 219 m) above the hills, to start their target run.

'We'd been getting some 37 mm and 57 mm AAA and some 85 mm stuff as well. Very black puffs, that 85. It was all radar-controlled and they knew just when to stop firing if the MiGs were coming in. Those gunners on the 85s, if they hit your altitude and got you once ahead and once behind, they'd just walk the stuff up to you and you were finished. They were really great gunners, in fact both optically and by radar.'

The two RF–4Cs snapped their target in the midst of the flak barrage and their full attention was focused on the task, leaving the rear unguarded for crucial seconds.

'I felt a nice thump. Nothing violent. I looked back and there was a MiG, high and wide and working in on the old man. We were pretty tight together, line abreast about 40–50 yards [36–45 m] apart. So I called a 110 break and [Colonel Cabas] broke right. We had a fire light on the left engine and I said, "Wayne, I think we've been hit," and he said, "Yes, we have . . ."'

The standard technique for an RF–4C caught in a tight situation was a head-on pass at the attacking enemy aircraft. In instances of adequate warning time, the RF–4C had enough power to escape MiG–17s and MiG–21s. Without the warning, a head-on dash past the interceptor was a good alternative and gave the enemy pilot little opportunity to sight and fire.

RF–4C pilots were warned, however, never to 'mix' with MiGs in the hope that they could get out of a spot through sheer maneuverability. It just wouldn't work. Speed was the essential factor and, combined with the defensive systems incorporated within the aircraft, it was supposed to give an RF–4C the upper hand, enabling a rapid escape to be made.

The Phantom went into afterburner and made a dive for the deck, with Major Porter screwing his neck back to watch for the MiG. 'We were about 200 feet [60 m] off the ground and I was north of the Red and a bit worried about the MiG and our fuel state. I went on burner with one engine across the Red and then pulled out of the burner when we were well into the green.' It was unlikely the MiG had followed this far, with the RF–4C's high speed at low level. It was more likely that Lt Col. Taylor had evaded the interceptor in his

rapid dive to the deck. 'But I couldn't put the fire out and I still worried about the MiG. Still, we would have to go up to save fuel. So we climbed to about 12,000 feet [3 657 m], making turns to check our six o'clock.'

Taylor got on the radio to see if any fighters in the area could help him. There were none. Worse, there were no tankers.

'But there didn't seem to be any problems so I thought the fire light was just a system malfunction. I homed on the Tacan at the Laos border, then we got across and I pulled out my two bady-bottles full of water and drank them. It's not until you're safe that you know how thirsty you are. I had those two bady-bottles full, and needed every drop.

'We landed with half flaps at Udorn. We had no brake chute because, as it turned out, the connection had been severed. We had 600 pounds of fuel left. That's not even enough for a go-around in the pattern. There was a three-foot (1 m) hole in the left inboard trailing edge flap. We never learned whether the damage had been caused by the flak or the MiG.' [46]

Lt Col. Taylor was just happy that he had gotten safely home in the battered RF–4C. The notion of using the RF–4C's high speed to elude the MiG was made a part of the training syllabus with the 363 TRW at Shaw AFB, South Carolina, where aircrew trained before deploying to the battle zone.

TET OFFENSIVE

Beginning 30 January 1968, the Viet Cong supported in some locations by North Vietnamese regular forces launched their all-out offensive which took the war into the cities of South Vietnam and into the living rooms of millions of Americans. The assault came on Tet, eve of the lunar new year, when they had promised a cease-fire. At least 180,000 men were committed in the sudden, surprise attacks which included fighting at several locations inside Saigon, an attack on the American Embassy and the brutal capture and pillage of the old imperial city of Hue. An elite group of nineteen sappers fought their way into the Embassy chancery and wreaked havoc until the following day when the last of them was killed by a pistol-armed official on an upper floor. In Hue, hundreds of innocent civilians were slaughtered and heaped into mass graves. The communists appeared, at first, to be inflicting stunning casualties and they succeeded in disrupting much of the

---

Many of those who fought up North never got to see it at all, but to those who did, the city of Saigon was unforgettable. It had been called the 'Paris of the Orient', and while the American presence changed this image, the South Vietnamese capital remained an interesting and exciting city to everyone who saw it. (NORMAN TAYLOR)

transportation and communications which made South Vietnam function. For days, life everywhere in the country was disrupted as battles raged.

Tet was a turning point on the home front. Americans glued to TV sets saw fighting inside their own ambassador's office. They saw the much-publicized footage of a Saigon police official using a pistol to execute a Viet Cong prisoner. They perceived that the communists were winning. To many, the win was occurring over a repugnant and disreputable ally. When Lyndon Johnson precipitously called the Tet offensive a defeat for the communists before he had any way to know, many became *certain* the communists were winning.

Tet has been called an attack, a retreat, a victory, a defeat. Most Western analysts and historians now agree that the evidence available shows that the Tet offensive was a devastating military and political defeat for the North Vietnamese and the Viet Cong. In their attempt to ignite a general uprising against the South Vietnamese government, the Viet Cong, with the assistance of North Vietnamese regulars, had clearly aspired to capture the provincial capitals of South Vietnam.

Errors by Hanoi in communication and coordination resulted in large enemy elements attacking a day before the other elements began their attacks. This fundamental military error alerted the South Vietnamese

Though it was little publicized, the Cessna O–1 Bird Dog (foreground) and O–2 Skymaster served as forward air controllers, or FACs, not merely in South Vietnam but in the adjoining regions of the North. The 20th Tactical Air Support Squadron at Da Nang flew these aircraft, seen here over the Vietnamese coastline. (USAF VIA ROBERT C. MIKESH)

and Americans who during the offensive killed 39,000 enemy troops and captured 7,000 during which time 318 Americans and 661 South Vietnamese were killed. This military action effectively eliminated the Viet Cong as a fighting force and, thereafter, most Viet Cong cadres in the South were really North Vietnamese soldiers posing as southerners.

It was a suicidal effort that failed not only militarily but, in the short run at least, politically. Boasting to the Western press and anti-war critics for years of their popular support, the Vietnamese communists found, to their utter astonishment, that the South Vietnamese people allied to the Saigon government had fought vigorously against the attacking communist troops.

Unfortunately, in a world where perceptions matter as much as reality, a defeat on the battlefield may have become a victory solely because it was seen as one. Disagreeing sharply with Johnson, before the dust had settled and the facts were in, the Western press and particularly the American television media, pronounced Tet a devastating defeat for Allied forces.

It cannot be emphasized too strongly that during Tet, though they lost the battle, the communists may have won the war. The harsh truth was that Hanoi was willing to accept 39,000 fatalities while Washington found it difficult to cope with 318 added to the nearly ten thousand already lost in the conflict. More importantly, it bears repeating, Tet was a communist victory because it was perceived as a communist victory. Television viewers in their American homes, knowing their husbands and sons were dying, perceived that no progress had been made towards South Vietnam being able to defend itself and, worse, that South Vietnam did not *deserve* to defend itself or enjoy US support. They resented spending blood and treasure supporting a Saigon regime which could be so easily disrupted. The strongest opponents of what was considered to be Johnson's war, among them McCarthy and Kennedy, found sympathy among countless Americans who just wanted to get the hell out. The few remaining Americans who wanted to stay, fight and win had their views represented by the front-runner of the other party, Richard M. Nixon.

Tet was also a victory for North Vietnam in a strange but important way that has already been alluded to. For years, the US had insisted that the insurgency in the South was the work of an outsider, namely North Vietnam. Before Tet, this was untrue. The Viet Cong had been formed, motivated and driven by southerners, admittedly communists but *not* puppets of Hanoi; indeed, these men

often differed sharply with Hanoi's policy. After Tet, the Viet Cong command apparatus simply ceased to exist. Control over the communist insurgency in South Vietnam was finally, indisputably, in the hands of Hanoi. 'Aggression from the North,' manufactured by the US as its reason for being in the conflict, was no longer a fiction. The reason had become reality.

Tet was followed by the 71-day communist siege of the US Marine outpost at Khe Sanh, which was resupplied by intrepid C–123 and C–130 crews and protected by B–52 Arc Light missions. Outside the scope of this report on the war against the North, Khe Sanh simply was another American victory which was treated in the press and in public perceptions as a defeat. Meanwhile, the ROLLING THUNDER campaign against targets in North Vietnam continued and men and aircraft maintained their ongoing contest against SAMs, MiGs and Triple-A.

THE 'SLOW MOVERS'

While the role of 'fast FAC' jet fighters has been described, it should also be said that the 'slow movers,' forward air controllers in prop-driven Cessna O–1 and O–2 aircraft, were exceedingly active in the lower regions of North Vietnam, namely Route Packages One and Two. In these zones, it had been determined that the Cessnas could perform an important role snooping out, identifying and marking targets for the faster jets. Anywhere farther north than Route Package Two, the defense environment was too sophisticated and too intense. Even in RP One

The Cessna O–2A as forward air controller. O–2A 67-21308 of the Da Nang-based 20th Tactical Air Support Squadron heads into the lower reaches of North Vietnam carrying smoke rockets. These FAC aircraft pinpointed targets for faster jet fighters. (USAF VIA ROBERT C. MIKESH)

The Cessna O–2B as psychological warfare aircraft. Unpublished view of camouflaged O–2B 67-21450 of the 9th Special Operations Squadron, based at Nha Trang. The aircraft depicted was employed to drop leaflets. Others were used to broadcast messages to the enemy via loudspeaker. It remains unclear whether these 9 SOS aircraft operated in North Vietnam. (JIM HESTON)

and RP Two, things were bad enough. Men of the 20 TASS from Da Nang faced heavy flak and, as Colonel Robert C. Peck pointed out in a letter to *Air Force* magazine, even had some SAMs fired at them about 100 nautical miles (180 km) north of the DMZ.

The Cessna O-1, which had begun life as the L-19, was a simple and straightforward lightplane. Those in Vietnam were the O-1F and O-1G variants, powered by 213 hp (159 kW) Continental O-470-11 pistol engine and capable of 130 mph (209 km/h). They were rigged to carry small rocket projectiles to mark ground targets for the very fast jet fighters which, without such help, could easily overshoot. The larger Cessna O-2 was an 'off the shelf' purchase of the pusher/puller Cessna 337 Super Skymaster powered by two 210 hp (157 kW) Continental IO-360 air-cooled engines. With a maximum speed of 200 mph (332 km/h), it was capable of loitering for a respectable period in the target area. A total of 501 O-2A models was delivered to the USAF. A version equipped for psychological warfare entered service as the O-2B, 31 of these being delivered. On FAC missions, the O-2 had four underwing pylons to carry flares, smoke rockets and such light ordnance as a 7.62 mm (0.3 in) machine-gun pack. It was never really intended that these aircraft would unleash firepower on North Vietnamese ground installations. The enterprising FAC who installed an M60 machine-gun in the cabin of his cramped O-1F may have been overdoing things, a bit much.

It was no easy job, heading across the DMZ at the Ben Hai River, or the 17th Parallel, and heading into North Vietnam to pick out and identify targets. The pilot of the FAC aircraft was very much alone, very much reliant upon his own resources. When he located a target, he was expected to expose himself to enemy gunfire, partly for the purpose of learning more about the target and of determining the best way that it could be attacked. No one really expected the FAC to hit the mark when he fired smoke rockets at the target but, by placing the rockets *around* a target, he could pass accurate instructions ('about 200 yards uphill from the smoke') to jet fighter pilots. Most of the FACs were jet fighter pilots themselves, some resented being relegated to small, prop-driven flivvers, and many exhibited great courage. Although they did it in South Vietnam, and thus do not belong in this narrative, it should be noted that two FACS, Captain Hilliard A. Wilbanks and Captain Steven L. Bennett, were among the twelve USAF people who earned the Medal of Honor in the Southeast Asia conflict.

It remains unclear whether the Cessna O-2B, used for psychological operations by the 9 SOS at Nha Trang, ever flew into North Vietnam. The O-2B was equipped to drop propaganda leaflets, a job which—as has already been noted—was performed over the North on a grander scale by the C-130 Hercules. Some O-2Bs were fitted with loudspeakers to convey voice messages to enemy troops on the ground. It seems likely that the leaflet mission, if not the loudspeaker work, was performed over the North at some stage.

To return to the forward air controllers, Captain James B. Tierney of the 20 TASS remembers being hit by more than a dozen small-caliber rounds while flying on O-2A over North Vietnam in February 1968. One bullet actually took away Tierney's thumb, leaving him with no other injury. With most of his controls barely useable, Tierney somehow coaxed his battered Cessna to a safe landing at Da Nang.

AIR-TO-AIR ACTION

The struggle continued between the American fighter pilot and the North Vietnamese MiG driver. 3 February 1968 saw the only occasion in the entire war when an F-102A Delta Dagger was shot down by a MiG, apparently a MiG-21. The F-102A (56-1166) of the 509 FIS/405 TFW appears to have been on a night sortie when downed. This ended up being a decidedly one-sided contest, for no F-102A pilot ever got a chance to claim a MiG kill.

On 5 February 1968, Captain Robert G. Hill of the 13 TFS/432 TRW at Udorn shot down a MiG-21 using an AIM-4D Falcon missile while at the controls of an F-4D Phantom (66-8714). 1Lt Bruce V. Huneke was Hill's back-seater. The next day, Captain Robert H. Boles of the Ubon-based 433 TFS/8 TFW repeated the feat, with an AIM-7E Sparrow missile this time, but also flying an F-4D Phantom (66-8688) with 1Lt Robert B. Battista in the back seat. Two further MiG kills by F-4D pilots occurred later in the month but, although it did not seem apparent, these would be the last Air Force kills for more than four years.

The Navy still had a few encounters with MiGs waiting just ahead. During this period, almost equal numbers of F-8 Crusaders were competing with F-4B Phantoms for the chance to bat down the enemy's jet fighters. F-8 Crusader pilots were an especially proud lot who considered theirs the only real fighter being employed in the conflict. They were to have a few more chances in the final months of the ROLLING THUNDER campaign.

AC-130 HERCULES GUNSHIP

On 22 February 1968, the original C-130A Hercules gunship (54-1426) returned to Southeast Asia after having been withdrawn following its initial deployment. Now, serious effort began to use the giant, four-engine aircraft for night missions against the Ho Chi Minh Trail and other supply routes from the North. The 16th Special Operations Squadron at Ubon, placed nominally under command of the 8 TFW's Wolfpack, was activated to mount gunship operations. The arrival of a further seven AC-130s was scheduled for the remainder of the year.

As noted, the newer machines retained the armament of the prototype tested in combat earlier by Captain Ronald R. Terry but introduced forward-looking infra red (FLIR) sensors which permitted the crew to observe North Vietnamese trucks and other targets on a monitor, removing the benefit of dark-

In a serious moment, Colonel Ivan Dethman prepares to lead the force of six F-111A strike aircraft being taken to Southeast Asia in March 1968. During this departure briefing at Nellis AFB, Nevada, Col. Dethman could not have known that the first three combat missions flown by the F-111A would result in the aircraft being lost. (USAF, VIA BILL GUNSTON)

The F-111A aircraft of the 428 TFS being introduced to the combat zone for the first time are seen arriving to join the fray. Given their baptism of fire in Operation Combat Lancer in March 1968, these F-111As almost immediately began falling from the sky with little help from the North Vietnamese. (USAF)

ness upon which the North Vietnamese supply effort depended. Soon after the 16 SOS became settled in its risky night missions, often functioning together with the F-4D Phantom in a hunter/killer team, further modifications and developments to the basic AC-130 gunship were decided upon, under a program known as SURPRISE PACKAGE. It remained in the future, but men were already talking about fitting the AC-130 with *howitzers* which would be some of the largest-bore weapons ever carried aloft by any combat aircraft.

F-111A DEPLOYMENT

One of the more controversial additions to the air effort against North Vietnam came on 17 March 1968 when six General Dynamics F-111A aircraft were introduced to Southeast Asia in Operation COMBAT LANCER. The F-111A had resulted from a USAF specification for a TFX, or tactical fighter experimental, which Secretary McNamara had originally hoped would prove suitable for both Navy and Air Force use. A swing-wing brute of a long-range strike fighter powered by two 25,100 lb (11 385 kg) thrust Pratt & Whitney TF30 turbofans, the F-111A, first

flown 21 December 1964, had sophisticated low-level terrain-following equipment which seemed to make it ideal for pinpoint navigation on solo missions to sensitive targets around Hanoi. The F-111A reached operational readiness with the 474 Tactical Fighter Wing at Nellis AFB, Nevada under Colonel Frederick C. Blesse, the same well-known fighter commander who had earlier introduced the gun pod to combat on the Phantom. The initial force of six F-111A aircraft was brought over to Southeast Asia by cigar-smoking, tire-kicking Colonel Ivan H. Dethman of the wing's 429 TFS—and quickly ran into serious trouble.

In its first combat test, on 25 March, a camouflaged F-111A (66-0022) laden with two ALQ-87 jamming pods and 24 500 lb (227 kg) Marks 82 bombs lifted off from the aircraft's new home in Takhli, headed towards a target in North Vietnam and vanished forever. A second F-111A was lost almost immediately, on 30 March, and, following a brief suspension of operations with the type, a third was lost on a solo mission to the North on 22 April.

Eventually, 51 successful combat missions were flown by Colonel Dethman's F-111A people, their aircraft now receiving the unofficial nickname Aardvark because of its drooping nose. At the time, the F-111A operations were widely portrayed in the US press as a total failure though, in fact, the aircraft was exceedingly effective in the low-level, solo strike role. Just how effective was explained by Captain Melvin Pobre, an F-111A pilot, who recalls a mission to the outskirts of Hanoi where: 'We were at an altitude of 250 ft

[76.2 m] moving at Mach .87 in a region of odd-shaped peaks and ridges and we were in clouds and haze for the final 14 minutes of our run-in to target but our bombs landed right where we wanted them ...'

Notwithstanding this enthusiasm, plus the fact that the F-111A provided the all-weather capability so long sought by General Momyer and others, the aircraft were soon removed from Southeast Asia and did not return until some four years hence. Only after the war was over would it become clear that abrupt tailplane failure caused by fatigue at a welding fault—not enemy action—threw the F-111A into an uncontrollable maneuver and that this had caused the first three losses. Although the F-111A had been a subject of controversy during its development and had had a terrible beginning in the combat zone, it was to prove in the end an exceedingly well-designed war machine with great potential and a long service life ahead.

STANDARD ARM MISSILE

For the continuing campaign against missile sites, the Navy and Air Force needed an anti-radiation missile (ARM) offering a larger warhead and longer range than the Shrike,

The AGM-78A Mod 0 Standard ARM missile was introduced to the combat zone in March 1968, aboard F-105F Wild Weasel aircraft, to improve capabilities against North Vietnam's SAM installations. Here, a Standard ARM has just been fired from a US fighter over Southeast Asia. (VIA PHILIP D. CHINNERY)

which was producing indifferent results. The Pomona Division of General Dynamics came up with the Standard ARM, or AGM–78A Mod 0 which was introduced to combat aboard the F–105F Wild Weasel in March 1968. This variant of the Standard ARM was equipped with the seeker head employed by the Shrike but was soon replaced by the AGM–78B production version with Mark-

son broad-band seeker, identified with the later F–105G.

Powered by an Aerojet Mk 27 Mod 4 rocket motor, the AGM–78B was 180 in (4.57 m) long with a body diameter of 13.5 in (343 mm), and a rear fin span of 43 in (1.09 m). At launch, the Standard ARM weighed about 1,400 lb (635 kg).

The Standard ARM provided greater standoff capability, enabling an F–105F to attack SAM sites from greater distance. Like the Shrike, the missile was unable to continue homing on *Fan Song* radars after they had been shut down, so the result was often that the Wild Weasels put the SAM installations out of action without actually hitting or destroying them.

Tactics were evolved to make most effective use of the Standard ARM and capability

to fire the missile was to be added to A–4E Skyhawk and A–7B Corsair II aircraft. Improved versions of the Standard ARM would remain very much in service no less than two decades later.

THE WAR AT HOME

Richard M. Nixon, not in public office and with no visible power base, continued in March 1968 to make slow but relentless progress toward attaining the nomination of the opposition Republican Party. Traditionally more conservative than the more numerous Democrats, the Republicans were not yet moved by those in their ranks who opposed the US role in Southeast Asia. They were,

Secretary of Defense Robert S. McNamara was a key architect of the ROLLING THUNDER campaign against North Vietnam. Here, he is seen at Tan Son Nhut Airbase near Saigon in 1964 with General Maxwell Taylor, Ambassador Henry Cabot Lodge, and Vietnamese officials. By the time he left office in July 1968, McNamara was said to be discouraged and disillusioned about the air war against North Vietnam. (USAF)

however, exceedingly interested in foreign policy and Nixon's credentials were impressive. He had even been photographed pointing a finger in challenge at the Soviet leader, Khruschev.

There were widespread rumors that General Westmoreland, the American field commander in Vietnam, wanted 200,000 more American troops in addition to the half-million already committed. In fact, General Earl Wheeler, chairman of the JCS, and Westmoreland wanted only about half that number but the ceaseless demand for more troops, like the body counts from which enemy casualty figures were derived, were no longer credible. Critics were referring to the Saigon commander as 'General Waste More Men', and Westmoreland was constantly a target of abuse in the rhetoric of the anti-war movement.

In the New Hampshire primary, upstart Senator Eugene McCarthy came within a hair's breadth of defeating President Johnson in the first test of election-year voter sentiment. Among 500,000 ballots for Democratic

candidates, McCarthy received a mere 300 fewer than Johnson in an extraordinary near-upset of an incumbent. McCarthy had the support of anti-war young people; his was sometimes called the children's crusade. McCarthy still did not have any realistic hope of unseating the President, but another anti-war challenger did. Three days after McCarthy's remarkable showing, promising to restore a lost legacy, Robert F. Kennedy declared his candidacy.

Robert S. McNamara has never talked in later years about his attitude toward the Vietnam conflict when he stepped down as Secretary of Defense. After having shaped Vietnam policy for two presidents, McNamara was visibly discouraged and dis-illusioned. McNamara was particularly concerned that the ROLLING THUNDER campaign had failed to sever North Vietnam's supply and transportation network. According to reporter Stanley Karnow, McNamara was on the verge of a nervous breakdown.

Clark Clifford, who replaced McNamara, was a respected Washington figure but was

Perhaps the most dramatic surprise of the Vietnam war was President Lyndon Johnson's 31 March 1968 annoucement that he would not seek re-election. Johnson also imposed a bombing halt which ended the ROLLING THUNDER campaign later that year. On an earlier, happier occasion, in short sleeves, Johnson rides a Jeep while reviewing troops at Cam Ranh Bay Airbase. Standing beside him is General William Westmoreland. (USAF)

better known as a lobbyist than as a military expert; he certainly was not an authority on the use of airpower. Clifford did not clean house. Many key positions remained unchanged. General Joseph McConnell remained as Air Force Chief of Staff, General John D. Ryan as commander, PACAF, and Admiral U. S. G. Sharp as CINCPAC. General Westmoreland remained in Saigon, as did the Seventh Air Force commander, General Momyer. Changes would come in a few months, in July, but by then many Americans would regard the flagging Johnson administration as a lame duck government.

In a surprise announcement early in the

election year's activities, on 31 March 1968, President Johnson revealed his decision not to seek re-election. At the same time, he announced a bombing halt which, he felt, would resolve the American dilemma in Vietnam by prodding Hanoi towards negotiations. Always shrewd on domestic affairs, Johnson had correctly seen that he was unlikely to win an election campaign, anyway, because of the growing opposition to the war and demands for a total withdrawal of US troops.

Johnson was wrong about the bombing halt, however. He was making a misguided gesture of good faith, the sort of conciliatory step which he frequently employed in domestic politics, at the very time when the cumulative effect of three years of ROLLING THUNDER air operations was finally beginning to damage the North Vietnamese infrastructure. It was the restraints on the use of airpower which had prevented ROLLING THUNDER from being a complete success. Removing those restraints and increasing the air strikes might have ended the war on Washington's terms. Johnson was, in short, giving the North Vietnamese a chance to rebuild.

Johnson announced a cessation of bombing north of the 20th Parallel, effective 1 April 1968, and this was moved down to the 19th Parallel on 4 April. Though he obviously hoped that Hanoi would reciprocate with a gesture of its own, even an official history from the period says that North Vietnam interpreted Johnson's action as a sign of a weakening in US resolve and used the bombing halt for restoration and reconstruction to reinforce its air defenses and to move more material and troops to the south.

Prior to Johnson's surprise announcement, the ROLLING THUNDER campaign in the first three months of 1968 had been seriously hampered by the northeast monsoon. The early months of the year were the time of worst weather and during all three months, conditions were even worse than predicted. In the northern Route Packages, there was only an average of three days per month on which visual strikes could be carried out. The weather during February was the poorest experienced during any month since the start of the ROLLING THUNDER campaign.

Bombing operations against North Vietnam continued with the principal aim of isolating the harbor at Haiphong from the rest of the country to prevent the distribution within the country of material being imported. This concerted campaign against lines of communication around Haiphong forced the North Vietnamese to adopt extraordinary efforts to maintain a flow of material over existing lines. Distribution problems for Hanoi were further aggravated by the arrival

of a near-record number of foreign ships in Haiphong in January and again in March, when over 40 ships arrived each month for off-loading. The port of Hon Gai was used in February as an off-loading point for a Soviet and a British ship, probably in an effort to reduce the pressure on Haiphong. This port normally served the nearby coal-mining area and did not contribute significantly to the flow of imports into the country.

Expansion of the road transportation net continued as North Vietnam sought to gain greater flexibility by the addition of bypasses and the construction of entirely new road regiments. The strikes were having an effect on the flow of supplies, beyond doubt.

It was because of this effect that military men fumed in private over the 31 March decision by President Johnson to stop all bombing north of the 20th Parallel. As the air commander on the scene in Saigon, General Momyer had his own views:

'The halting of the bombing was to test the sincerity of the North Vietnamese to sit down and talk about stopping the war. As the commander on the spot for air operations, I was opposed to any stopping of the bombing. We knew from all previous stand-downs the North Vietnamese had taken advantage of these periods to move all the supplies they could into South Vietnam. We had seen this happen at Christmas and at Tet.

'I took the position that if the bombing was to be halted to test the sincerity of the North Vietnamese to negotiate, the month of April was the latest it could be done with the least adverse effect on our forces. The reason I said this was because of only four days of predicted good weather over the Hanoi delta in April. As it turned out, there were six days. Thus, one couldn't say whether our bombing operations would be adversely affected. I further stated that come 1 May, if the North

Vietnamese had not reached substantive agreements about a cessation of the war, we should resume the bombing with no restraints on targets. I put 1 May as the date because this was the transition period from the northeast to the southwest monsoon, and operational weather would start to appear with increasing frequency.

'When asked what I thought would happen with a limitation on the bombing I stated the following: the anti-aircraft defenses in the southern Route Packages would increase significantly; more SAMs would be deployed as close to the DMZ as they could get them; MiGs would begin to challenge us as far south as the DMZ; the radar and GCI system would be filled out from Bai Thuong south; airfields at Bai Thuong, Vinh, and possibly Dong Hoi, would become operational; large quantities of supplies would be moved through the lines of communication; supply dumps would shift to the Bai Thuong area since this would shorten the line; marshalling yards, bridges, power plants and other destroyed facilities would be repaired at a feverish pace; finally, I thought the enemy would consider this suspension a sign of weakness and would exploit it by an increased military effort. All of these things happened.'

BOMBING HALT #7

The 1 April 1968 measure by President Johnson, cleansing the skies north of the 20th

It may have been a bombing halt, proclaimed by President Johnson, but reconnaissance missions over North Vietnam continued, most of them flown by RF–101C aircraft. This camouflaged RF–101C Voodoo (56-215) was passing through Hickam AFB, Hawaii, en route to the Vietnam combat zone in April 1968. (NICHOLAS M. WILLIAMS)

On 10 April 1968, prop-driven Skyraider aircraft of the US Navy flew in combat for the last time, although the type remained in service with the US and South Vietnamese Air Forces. Aircraft carrier deck scenes, like this view of an A–1E aboard USS *Oriskany* (CVA–34), were no longer a part of the air war against North Vietnam. (USN)

Parallel, stopped bombing attacks over the principal populated and food-producing areas of North Vietnam except in the area north of the Demilitarized Zone where enemy actions were seen as directly threatening US and South Vietnamese forces in South Vietnam. Because of this limitation on ROLLING THUNDER, primary strike emphasis was now directed against truck parks, storage areas and military complexes. Armed reconnaissance strikes were directed against logistic vehicles and interdiction points along the main lines of communication.

Of course, the bombing limitation did not affect operations in Laos. Although flights in Laos are not properly part of this narrative, it should be pointed out that until this time, airmen frequently flew missions into Laos one day, and into North Vietnam the next, receiving credit only for the latter.

President Johnson's decision amounted to an end of the 1965–68 ROLLING THUNDER campaign against North Vietnam, although the real end would not come until months later (1 October 1968) when the bombline would be brought down to the 17th Parallel and all of North Vietnam would become 'off limits' for US combat aircraft.

EXIT THE SKYRAIDER

The US Navy's final combat loss of an A–1H Skyraider had occurred just weeks before

Johnson's speech. On 24 February 1968, an A–1H (134499) belonging to the 'First of the Fleet', as squadron VA–25 called itself, somehow managed to take enemy fire and go down at sea whilst on a ferry flight from *Coral Sea* (CVA–43) to Cubi Point in the Philippines.

The diversity of the Skyraider was legend. So it was a historic moment on 10 April 1968 when another A–1H belonging to VA–25 made an arrested landing on *Coral Sea*, completing the final combat mission by a Navy Skyraider. The aircraft type would continue to fight in USAF and South Vietnamese colors, but the Navy's carrier-based attack force would be all-jet from now on.

Reconnaissance missions verified that North Vietnam was able to repair and improve its supply and transportation network virtually from the moment the bombing stopped north of the 20th Parallel. The roads between Hanoi, Haiphong and Hon Gai were improved and maintained. Bridges between Hanoi and Haiphong were repaired and traffic began to flow smoothly during day and night hours. Rolling stock inventories in Hanoi and Haiphong appeared to be on the increase.

Off-loaded cargo at Haiphong was not being stacked but was being loaded directly onto trucks which immediately departed the wharf area. Photographs indicated extensive storage throughout the port area but stockpiles did not remain static, suggesting that cargo flowed unrestricted. The labor supply

at the docks was reported adequate and efficient and morale was reported as high.

Once the presence of US aircraft over the northern portion of the country was stopped, North Vietnam took maximum advantage of the freedom of action by increasing training activities and all elements of the air defense system. Moves were afoot to locate SAM sites farther south, in the Route Package One area.

The situation must have been especially frustrating to the kin of pilots and airmen who continued, after 1 April 1968, not merely to fly but to die. Aircraft losses continued unabated while strikes were concentrated in the southern regions of the country. It was some relief not having to fly into Hanoi and Haiphong, but a man could still become a casualty, even while bombing a truck park.

Because of the bad weather and the partial bombing halt, no MiG kills were scored in March and April. On 9 May 1968, a Navy F–4B Phantom with an Air Force exchange officer in the front seat scored a probable kill of a MiG–17, apparently in a very southerly location. Major John P. Hofferman was flying with the 'Fighting Falcons' of VF–96,

A–1H Skyraiders 135324 and 137523 of VA–25, the squadron which flew the final combat mission in this prop-driven attack aircraft in April 1968. Supplied by Robert L. Lawson of *The Hook*, journal of the Tailhook Association, this photograph taken on board USS *Midway* (CVA–41) emphasizes the folding wings and deck maneuverability of the Skyraider. (USN VIA LAWSON)

operating from the deck of the nuclear-powered USS *Enterprise* (CVN–65). His aircraft was an F–4B Phantom (153036) using the squadron's radio callsign Showtime, and his weapon was the AIM–7E Sparrow missile. LtJg Frank A. Schumaker was the radar intercept officer in the Phantom's back seat.

With the bombline now moved down to the 19th Parallel, air strikes were being flown only in Route Packages One and Two, and a southerly portion of Route Package Three.

North Vietnam's jet fighter force was thus provided with sanctuary. There were no jet-capable airfields within reach of Air Force and Navy strike aircraft which were actually being used by the North Vietnamese. The MiGs could sit in their revetments, safe from assault.

Communist efforts to move the MiG force farther south were half-hearted and until the end of ROLLING THUNDER the North Vietnamese never succeeded in their goal of shooting down a B–52. On 23 May 1968, a force of MiGs did venture down into Route Package Two and the offshore area nearby. One MiG–21 was downed by a Talos surface-to-air missile fired from a US Navy vessel in the Gulf of Tonkin. Later in the year, Navy Crusaders would add to their laurels with new MiG kills, but the presidential bombing halt had effectively ended the air-to-air war.

MORE CORSAIR SQUADRONS

Though the war against North Vietnam was now of very limited scope, air strikes continued. Two new squadrons employing the A–7A Corsair II attack aircraft arrived in Southeast Asia and began launching strikes on 31 May 1968, operating from USS *America* (CVA–66), an Atlantic Fleet carrier taking its turn in the combat zone. The 'Marauders' of VA–82 under Commander John E. Jones and the 'Sidewinders' of VA–86 under Commander Jack E. Russ went into action against a barracks complex, a supply depot and truck parks.

The newly-arrived squadrons suffered their first casualty when Lt Ken W. Fields' A–7A Corsair II (153255) was hit by ground fire just north of the DMZ. Fields ejected. He parachuted into thickly vegetated terrain

The 'Sidewinders' of squadron VA–86 were the third unit to go into combat in the A–7A Corsair, in 1968. Later, the same squadron flew in operations against North Vietnam using the A–7C variant of the Corsair II, shown here. (LTV)

The A–7A variant of the Corsair II was soon followed into action by the A–7B variant, shown here, which had an improved TF30 engine but was still regarded as underpowered. One squadron which flew machines like this A–7B (154468) was the 'Barn Owls' of VA–215, with Commander James Crummer as skipper. (DUANE A. KASULKA)

swarming with North Vietnamese regular troops. The Navy flier had the use of his survival radio and was able to talk to other Corsair pilots overhead as he scrambled away from the enemy troops. An HH–3E Jolly Green helicopter piloted by Major Lewis Yuhas succeeded in locating Fields and plucked him out after a marathon 39 hours on the ground. During the same mission,

another A–7A from Ken's squadron (153258) suffered fuel starvation and its pilot ejected safely near the carrier.

Lt Benjamin Short wrote into his diary that half of his squadron's A–7A pilots were flying night missions while the other half slept. A typical bombload consisted of 12 500 lb (227 kg) Mark 81 bombs fitted on multiple ejector racks at outboard wing stations one

and eight on the A–7A. Short was carrying this payload when he located a concrete bridge on Route One, about 300 to 400 feet (91 to 121 m) long. Being somewhat new to the low-level attack business, Short decided to dump his entire bombload on the bridge. He made his run-in and cut across the bridge at a slight angle, putting eight or nine of the bombs on the bridge. As he pulled off, he rolled up on a wingtip after getting his nose well above the horizon to observe the hits. There was a lot of smoke and fire but after the smoke blew away Short was astonished to see no sign of damage to the bridge!

On another occasion, Short spotted a small brush fire going on the ground near a canal.

Anything north of the bombline belonged to the enemy, so he decided to drop a couple of bombs on the fire. His hit was long, but he got a secondary explosion and got a fire going. He dropped the rest of his ordnance on the fire and saw some secondary explosions. In jest, Short told himself that some North Vietnamese barge driver let his rice-cooking fire get away from him, and Short's A–7A came along and spoiled the whole evening. The fire was still burning when the next flight of A–7As crossed the beach an hour and a half later. The next flight dropped its ordnance on the fire as well.

Men like Ben Short were discovering that the A–7A, with its low gaping nose air intake,

had a way of ingesting steam from the carrier's catapults and then stalling out. Steam-induced compressor stalls were the cause of several A–7A losses, and the design of the new attack aircraft was not really perfected until much later when the A–7E variant, with a different TF41 turbofan engine, entered service.

ENTER THE F–4J

Also aboard *America* with Ben Short's Corsairs were two fighter squadrons employing the new F–4J variant of the Phantom. The F–4J had made its first flight two years earlier on 27 May 1966 and had been designed with higher gross landing weight and lower approach speed to permit for more flexible carrier operations. The 'Tarsiers' of VF–33 and the 'Diamondbacks' of VF–102, although traditionally located on the east coast, had been chosen to take the F–4J into battle.

In the F–4J the Navy had not elected to add an internal gun, even though the Air Force was doing exactly this with its upcoming F–4E. The F–4J was equipped with APQ–59 radar with a 32 inch (81 cm) dish and AWG–10 pulse-doppler fire control system, permitting the detection and tracking of low and high altitude targets. The F–4J also incorporated space provisions for the AN/ASW–25A datalink landing system originally introduced on the Navy F–4G. The J model also had improved TACAN and an upgraded AN/AJB–7 bombing system as well as APR–32 radar homing and early warning system (RHAWS). The new variant was powered by two 17,900 lb (8 120 kg) thrust General Electric J79–GE–19 engines with afterburners. Approach speed was reduced from 137 to 125 knots (253 km/h to 231 km/h) with the installation of drooped flaps. As will soon be demonstrated, although it was to prove an effective bomber as well as a MiG killer, the F–4J would actually begin its Southeast Asia

The 'Tarsiers' of VF–33, traditionally an east coast/Atlantic Fleet squadron, were first in combat with the F–4J variant of the Phantom. Here, F–4J Phantom 155544 of the squadron leads two mates in a low-level flyover above the deck of USS *Independence* (CVA–62). (USN VIA M. J. KASIUBA)

combat career by figuring peripherally in a
rescue story.

SMART BOMBS

The 'smart' bomb, one of the most dramatic
technical advances of the entire conflict, arrived just when the bombing halt deprived it
of the chance to inflict more than token pun-
ishment. The Wolfpack 8 TFW at Ubon
under Colonel Robert V. Spencer made the
first use of a Paveway laser-guided bomb
(LGB) in combat near the end of May 1968.
Only five LGBs were employed in May, but
the results were excellent. The F–4D Phantom, unlike the earlier F–4C, was equipped
from the start to carry the new precision-
guided ordnance while modified F–4Ds
equipped with laser illuminators were used to
designate targets for the strikes.

The 'Pave' family of target-illumination
devices, developed and controlled by the
USAF's Systems Command, sent to Vietnam
for prolonged evaluation, began with the

bulky Pave Sword laser designator carried in
a long cylindrical tube under the F–4D fuselage, an arrangement which caused serious
drag-producing and weight and balance problems. The next generation of laser desig-
nators, Pave Knife, was in a drooped wing
pod in the F–4D and was followed by the
smaller, more effective Pave Spike pod which
could be accommodated in the Sparrow bay
of a Phantom. In practice, laser designator F–
4Ds created a 'basket' or inverted cone of
space over a target: if laser-bomber Phantoms dropped their LGBs within this 'basket', the bombs were almost certain to be
dead-center on target. A second campaign
against North Vietnam, still four years in the
future, would be vastly more successful than
ROLLING THUNDER largely because of LGBs.

IGLOO WHITE

On 31 May 1968, a little-known program
called Muscle Shoals was re-named Igloo
White. This was to become an ambitious

The 'Pukin Dogs' of VF–143 had taken the F–4B
Phantom into combat during the initial Gulf of
Tonkin air strikes and soon, whilst embarked
aboard USS *Enterprise* (CVAN–65), the squadron
also flew the F–4J Phantom in combat. The F–4J
variant had improved systems but still was not
equipped with a gun. (USN VIA M. J. KASIUBA)

effort to plant mines along the Ho Chi Minh
Trail infiltration network, mines equipped
with sensors which could detect the presence
of men and machines moving south.

Some of the sensors, dropped by tactical
aircraft like the F–4 and F–105, could 'smell'
human beings moving down the trail; others
detected sound and movement. Spikebuoy
sensors dropped and planted by A–1E Skyraiders automatically radioed signals triggered by the vibrations of passing traffic. Air
Delivered Seismic Intruder Devices (ASID),
dropped by US Navy OP–2E and SP–2H
Neptunes, also transmitted signals from traffic vibrations.

The job of relaying sensor signals to a
ground command post (which could then

order strikes against the infiltrators) fell to the large and vulnerable EC–121R Super Constellations, known as Batcats and operating from Nakhom Phanom, alias 'Naked Fanny'. Later, in March 1969, the relay job was attempted with five YQU–22A modified Beechcrafts, designed for operation either piloted or as unmanned drones. These were unsuccessful and not much improvement was offered with the five QU–22B aircraft which came later, in June 1970. As it turned out, the EC–121R served in this role until the end of the conflict.

With North Vietnam mostly off limits, some of the Igloo White effort was directed towards supply trails running through Laos on their snake-line excursion into South Vietnam.

There were, of course, other ways of keeping tabs on North Vietnam. The US made it no secret that reconnaissance flights were continuing and would continue. In addition, drones were employed. The Teledyne-Ryan AQM–34L remotely piloted vehicle (RPV) carried a 2,000-exposure camera and a TV system which transmitted real-time reconnaissance pictures to an airborne receiving station. These could be relayed at ranges up to 150 miles (240 km). Photographic runs over the target were made at 1,500 ft (450 m); the RPV climbed to above 50,000 ft (15 250 m) for the flight home. Control was by preprogrammed on-board navigation system or by remote control from an airborne or ground-control station. C–130 Hercules aircraft were sometimes employed to carry the AQM–34L drones on their missions.

KENNEDY SLAIN

The candidate opposed to the US role in Vietnam with the greatest chance of winning was snuffed out on 5 June 1968 in Los Angeles when a gunman shot and killed Robert F. Kennedy. It now appeared that Vice President Hubert Humphrey would be nominated to run against a former holder of the same office, Richard M. Nixon. Humphrey was in favor of a US withdrawal, but was slow in distancing himself from the policies of the administration where he still served.

NAVY RESCUE

On 18 June 1968, another classic operation began when North Vietnam's defenses claimed an F–4J Phantom (155546) of the 'Tarsiers' of VF–33 aboard *America*. Part of a three-plane 'pouncer' night interdiction strike accompanying an A–6C Intruder equipped with night attack sensors, Com-

mander John Holtzclaw managed to evade two SAMs only to be hit by a third. He and his back-seater, Lt John Burns, ejected.

At sea aboard the destroyer USS *Preble* (DLG–15) Lt Clude E. Lassen was awakened just after midnight. The A–6C crew and Holtzclaw's wingman were in contact with the men on the ground. Lassen and crew launched in a UH–2A Seasprite and were given vectors toward the spot where Holtzclaw and Burns were evading the North Vietnamese in heavy foliage.

Lassen brought his Seasprite in at low level in sheer darkness with small-arms fire whipping around him. Holtzclaw and Burns were about 200 feet (61 m) apart; the Phantom pilot was guiding the helicopter with a flare when the device suddenly sputtered out, leaving the pilot in deepening shadows. Lassen grazed a tree with the helicopter, heard the impact, and quickly regained control. He fought for control while his crewmen used their machine-guns to fire on the North Vietnamese closing in on Holtzclaw and Burns.

Though Burns was badly injured, the two survivors trekked to a new pick-up point in a more open area. Lassen made a second attempt to set down and found himself engaged in a furious gun battle with the North Vietnamese. Again unsuccessful, Lassen took the UH–2A aloft only to be missed by a SAM that passed within feet of his helicopter.

Lassen was low on fuel. He had been hit. He refused to give up. Under heavy fire, he made a third pickup attempt, and this time he snatched the F–4J crew up from what was almost certain capture. The UH–2A Seasprite pilot from squadron HC–7 struggled back to another destroyer, not the one he had started from. The helicopter was literally out of fuel, flying on fumes, when it touched down on the pitching deck. Lassen had become the second of only two naval aviators to win the highest American award, the Medal of Honor.

Two Navy F–8H Crusader pilots had shot down MiGs in June and July and now it was time for the new F–4J Phantom to score its first MiG kill. Lt Roy Cash, Jr, of the 'Tarsiers' was aloft on 10 July 1968 in an F–4J Phantom (155553) with Lt Joseph E. Kain, Jr, in the back seat. Using the callsign Rootbeer, the two-man F–4J crew became engaged in a fight with a MiG–21. They picked it off with an AIM–9 Sidewinder heatseeking missile, scoring the first kill for the F–4J and the 115th of the war.

Unfortunately, two more F–4J Phantoms were lost on *America*'s first combat cruise with the new type. VF–33 lost 155554 on 4 June 1968, and VF–102 lost 155548 on 16 June 1968, both victims of conventional antiaircraft fire.

The Crusader was doing better than the Phantom but its time was approaching an end. Navy Phantoms, denied good targets because of the Johnson bombing halt, were to be given a re-match against the MiG before the conflict was over.

COMMAND CHANGES

On 10 June 1968 in Saigon, General Creighton Abrams replaced General Westmoreland as the field commander of US forces on the ground. Abrams was a tough, respected armor officer. Westmoreland was bound to become Army chief of staff.

On 23 July 1968, Major General Robert F. Worley, who had replaced Major General Gordon M. Graham in Saigon as deputy commander of Seventh Air Force, was killed in an RF–4C Phantom crash. Worley was flying an RF–4C Phantom (65-895) of the 460 TRW at Tan Son Nhut and his backseater, Major Robert F. Brodman also perished after the aircraft took ground fire near the DMZ and was lost in a landing attempt. At the time, Worley's loss provoked a storm of criticism about generals flying combat aircraft, but in retrospect there seems to have been no other way to lead men in battle. Graham, who has also flown repeated combat missions in the RF–4C, puts it this way:

'When Bob Worley came over as my replacement, I had two weeks overlap. I flew with him several times to thoroughly indoctrinate him in what needed to be done, and what to expect to encounter, and what *not* to be done as well. He did everything right until the last mission he flew. He and I were the only Air Force general officers who flew combat missions in fighters. Momyer knew of it and forbade it. In fact, he threatened to court-martial me if I didn't stop. I did it and Bob did it because we believed that someone in the upper levels of command needed to know the straight story. Intelligence officers, wing commanders and buck pilots were fine to listen to, but much of the time were either biased, self-serving, plain wrong or misguided. When Bob was killed all hell broke loose and a witch hunt of gigantic proportions occurred. Momyer handled it rather well, but no Air Force general officer ever flew a fighter mission again.'[48]

On 31 July 1968 in Honolulu, General John D. Ryan departed the PACAF commander's slot to be replaced by General Joseph J. Nazzaro. Ryan later became Air Force vice chief of staff. Nazzaro, like Ryan, was a 'SAC weenie', a Curtis LeMay protege who had made his career in bombers while the Vietnam war was being fought with fighters.

On 31 July 1968 in Saigon, General Wil-

'One could feel the confidence of the MiG pilots,' wrote General William W. Momyer at the end of his tour in July 1968. The men in MiG cockpits were trained in the Soviet Union but were driven by an indigenous zeal. Here, a North Vietnamese pilot looks at an unidentified item while standing in front of a MiG-17. (VIA PHILIP D. CHINNERY)

liam W. Momyer was about to depart his posting as commander of Seventh Air Force, to be replaced by General George Brown. Momyer collected some of his thoughts.

MOMYER ON MiGS

The departing commander set down some thoughts on the North Vietnamese air opposition. It was a kind of succinct history of the MiG threat.

'MiG strength in mid-July 1966 [had been] about sixty-five aircraft. There were about ten to fifteen MiG-21s and the remain-

der were MiG-17s. There was a decided reluctance on the part of the MiGs to engage during those months. Our MiG kill rate was running at that time about four to one.

'Most of the engagements were in formation. MiGs didn't attempt to split the attack formation. They hung out to the side and jumped stragglers or someone who was shot up. Their operations were characterized by a lack of precise GCI control. This was evident by the hit and miss nature of the engagements. Most of the flights would take a position over Thud Ridge, southeast of Hanoi and near Thai Nguyen. Usually, a MiG combat air patrol (CAP) was kept over Phuc Yen and Kep [airfields]. Those were [North] Korean pilots who did the airfield CAP.

'Since my main objective was to destroy the transportation system, I didn't consider the MiG threat of sufficient gravity to divert any forces to this task. I, therefore, buried the F-4s in the strike force in the role of a fighter-bomber. They carried six 750 pound [340 kg]

bombs, the same as the F-105. There was a standing instruction that if a MiG threatened the strike force it would try to evade and hold its bombs. As the campaign developed, it became a favorite tactic of the MiG to feint an attack in order to force us to jettison the bombs. If attacks by MiGs became determined, the F-4s were first to jettison ordnance and go on the offense. As a last resort the F-105s would jettison and engage.

'During this time, I tried to use the F-104 [Starfighter] as a MiG screen. Because of its limited range there was insufficient time in the target area, nor was RHAWS gear available for the F-104s. Lack of a doppler or INS for the F-104 made navigation too loose for the environment where a border violation was always hanging over our head. All of these factors coupled with the loss of an F-104 to a SAM forced the withdrawal of this unit from Route Package Six.

'By early November of 1966, the air defense proficiency of the North Vietnamese had improved rapidly. The control of fighters was much more precise and they were starting to drive a wedge into the formation of the strike forces. One could feel the confidence of the MiG pilots going up with each fight. Since we couldn't hit the airfields, they had no problem of recovery. With the heavy defenses over and surrounding the airfields, we couldn't put a flight into the area at low altitude to try and pick them off.

'As the battle wore on I was pressured by the wing commanders to put nothing but missiles on the F-4s and F-105s and let them go after the MiGs. I stood these commanders off with the assertion that killing MiGs contributed little to the destruction of the enemy's ability to support his forces in South Vietnam. It was necessary, however, to run a few limited F-4 sweeps. These produced some kills but not in great numbers.

'In late December [1966], I laid down the elements of a fighter sweep. I proposed to send in a force of F-105s and F-4s configured for air-to-air fighting. This force would follow the same route and fly the same type of formation as a normal strike force [which was] augmented. The timing was set to follow the Christmas and New Year standdown. Based on previous experience the MiGs should come up in force after a period of bad weather. I figured this would happen after the holidays. The North Vietnamese reacted as we had hoped they would. The force was taken as an F-105 strike. The MiGs jumped it with real vigor. As a result the F-4s were able to catch them by surprise and we knocked down seven MiGs. It was the largest number of MiGs shot down in one engagement, and was the only tactical surprise of note we were able to pull off during my tour.'

[Momyer may not have had as much a role in Operation *Bolo* as this narrative suggests.]

'After February 1967, the MiGs started to operate more in pairs. High speed attacks were becoming common. The MiG–21 for the first time appeared with the *Atoll* heat-seeking missile. This was the beginning of a fundamental change in tactics. Up until this time there had been some of the dogfighting which characterized World War II. This was to the distinct disadvantage of the MiG–21 since the F–4 had a superiority of performance under 10,000 feet [3 048 m]. The MiG–17 could out-turn both the F–4 and the F–105. Under 10,000 feet [3 048 m], the F–105, after bomb release, was the fastest aircraft in the sky. Above fifteen thousand [4 572 m], the MiG–21 was the best performing aircraft both in speed and acceleration.

'Because of the good early warning, the MiGs were held until the last minute before being scrambled. This gave more time to the controller to determine the main thrust of the strike. Because of the small area in which targets were located we were never successful in feinting the MiGs out of position. We tried many variations in routes of penetration, but the amount of area for maneuver didn't provide the needed deception. At one point on the northeast railroad between the twenty mile buffer zone and the thirty mile circle, we had about twenty miles to maneuver in. Obviously there can't be much flexibility in approach to targets with these restraints.

'When weather permitted, we brought the strike forces in from the east and west simultaneously. The object was to split the MiGs or to force them to concentrate on one strike force while the other went in free. Rarely did they split their forces. The GCI control was so extensive they held the fighters in a central area and committed them when they had the advantage of a tail attack.

'By March 1967 the air battles began to pick up in intensity. The MiGs showed a very decided increase in aggressiveness. The MiG–17s began to move away from the airfields and hit us from below. The MiG–21s continued to stay and fight still depending upon the cannon for their kills. Apparently there were problems with the *Atoll* for there were very few firings of this air-to-air missile.

'We had the biggest month of the war [so far] against the MiGs in May [1967]. We shot down twenty-eight. For all practical purposes the MiGs were temporarily driven out of the battle. The enemy went back to review his tactics. Most of the aircraft were moved out of North Vietnam to China. We were cleared for attacks against Kep and Hoa Loc airfields. This further aggravated the enemy's problem. Phuc Yen was the only airfield still restricted from attack.

'In August [1967], the enemy began to challenge our strike forces in depth. The number of MiGs based in North Vietnam never reached the previous levels. There were about thirty-five to forty MiGs, fifteen to eighteen of which were MiG–21s. As the intensity of the air campaign increased with the opening of targets within the ten-mile circle, the North Vietnamese had to challenge this effort with everything they had.

'I could no longer afford to let the F–4s function in a dual role as a fighter-bomber. I was now compelled to configure four F–4s with Sparrows and Sidewinders for a CAP. The CAP covered the tail of each section of 16 strike aircraft and stayed with the force. When this didn't stop the attack, the CAP was given authority to float in the strike force stream. Traveling at speeds above five hundred knots [780 km/h] as they approached the target did not permit much real freedom of movement for the CAP. The CAP left the strike force at the target and picked them up on the other side as it egressed the area.

'The MiG–21s changed their tactics abruptly in October of 1967. For the first time I felt their aircraft was being employed the way it should have been to exploit its high speed and zoom characteristics. The GCI controllers had reached a very high state of training. I felt the Russians had probably put their best air defense officers in the Bac Mai, Phuc Yen and Gia Lam GCI control facilities. At least the Bac Mai facility which acted as the main coordinating center was probably directed by a very capable Russian tactician. I have no evidence to support this, but the dramatic change in tactics exemplified a very knowledgeable person running the intercepts.

'The MiG–21s were held at a point to the north and northwest of Phuc Yen to hit the strike forces on ingress. Normally the strike forces were flying at about sixteen thousand feet [4 876 m] increasing speed to five forty [820 km/h] for the bombing run. The MiG–21s would be swung to the west then a turn to the south sliding in behind the strike forces as they passed the Black River. Usually the MiGs were at 21,000 feet [6 400 km] and made their attack at Mach 1.2 to 1.4. All of these attacks were made with *Atoll* missiles. The attack was followed by a high speed climb. Controllers would position them for another attack but usually one pass was all that was made.

'When these attacks started to develop, I increased the CAP to eight F–4s per sixteen strike aircraft. One CAP of four remained with the strike force to beat off an attack which broke through the other CAP of four. The lead CAP of four could freelance to locate itself for best defensive engagements. We tried to integrate the formation from

Commando Apple, Commando Lance, Rivet Top and College Eye [all surveillance aircraft] so the freelance CAP could take the initiative from the MiGs.

'Our MiG kill ratio declined throughout this time. We ended up with a one-to-one ratio and more of our effort being devoted to the MiG threat. It seems to be there are some significant lessons we should draw from this experience in view of the great emphasis being put on an air-to-air fighter.

'Air superiority can only be gained by destroying the enemy air force on the ground and keeping it destroyed. We couldn't do this in North Vietnam because of the restraints on hitting the airfields. When we were given the authority, we couldn't sustain the attack against the airfields because of the sanctuary in China. He could pull his aircraft out as we started in, let them engage, and then recover in China. Thus, our only hope of knocking out the aircraft on the ground was denied and properly so.

'We turned to hitting the airfields in an attempt to deny their use. The idea being to force the MiGs to operate from China thereby limiting the time they could engage in the air battle. To keep the airfields knocked out and hit the other targets were beyond the capacity of the force. The large number of workers available for airfield repair meant these fields had to be hit every day if they were to be denied. This was not feasible. Consequently, we could never keep the airfields knocked out. The lesson to be learned is that it requires a larger force to destroy enemy air when he can flush to nearby sanctuaries during bombing attacks on his airfields. It is completely fallacious to conclude from this experience that knocking out the enemy air on the ground is not sound.

'When a fighter force such as the one we had was penetrating a sophisticated defense system like that in North Vietnam, the advantage will be [sic] with the defense system insofar as air-to-air engagements are concerned. Our air strike forces at the best will lack the real time that the defense forces posses. We were confronted with this time after time. Our fighters in spite of sophisticated missiles couldn't fire without visual identification. By the time a visual contact was made, the enemy was already in his attack. To a degree this will always prevail when we have large numbers of attacking forces in the area. One cannot afford to go guns free since we become a greater threat to ourselves than to the enemy. On the other hand, the enemy having every precise control doesn't have to go guns free since the controller is putting him onto a target that he knows is hostile.

'We again demonstrated that fighters cannot escort a strike force in the jet age. We

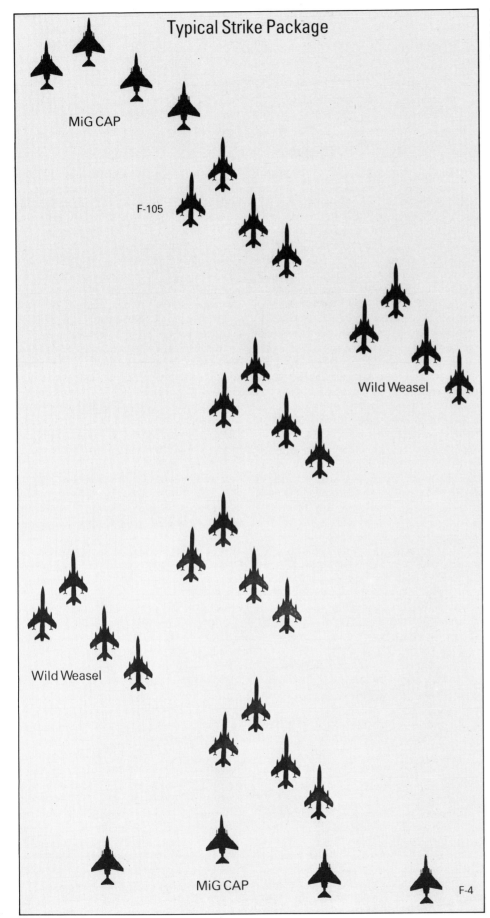

Typical Strike Package

MiG CAP

F-105

Wild Weasel

Wild Weasel

MiG CAP

F-4

Typical Air Force strike force on a mission into North Vietnam during the ROLLING THUNDER period, 1965–68. Composition of US Navy Alpha Strikes was similar.

found this in Korea. I think the air fighting in this war again confirmed this lesson. Having greater performance than the MiG–21 would not have stopped the attacks on the strike forces, which was what they were after since it was the strike forces which were doing the damage and not the CAPs. The MiGs would have broken through any screen we put up around the force as they did time after time. If they didn't have the advantage, the controller held them until the advantage turned to their favor and then committed.

'Any aircraft we have to take into battle should make a direct contribution to the battle. An air superiority fighter or CAP is a parasite in that it contributes only if it permits the striking aircraft to put their bombs on the target. If the F–105s [had not had] the performance to evade combat, we would have been in serious trouble. There was no amount of F–4 escort which could have protected them even if the F–4 had been given the performance of the MiG–21. What payed was the ability of the F–105 to live in the environment and fight its way out realizing that if it got trapped, the MiG would have the superior position, if for no other reason than fuel considerations, which would force the F–105 out of afterburner in order to get to the tanker.'

Not all of Momyer's views were shared by all concerned. Within weeks, Lt Col. Edward Hillding, building up the first F–4E squadron at Eglin AFB, Florida and preparing to take it into combat, would feel that Momyer—in his new role as TAC chief—was too concerned about the shark's teeth Hillding's men painted on their aircraft. The general's views of the MiG situation are controversial, but his is an excellent and succinct summary of the ROLLING THUNDER MiG effort.

SANDY MISSION

On 1 September 1968, Lt Col. William A. Jones III, commander of the 602nd Special Operations Squadron at Nakhon Phanom, launched in an A–1H Skyraider on a Rescap, or combat rescue, mission. It has already been noted that the Navy had retired the Skyraider from combat service the previous April (although a few EA–1F Skyraiders operated from carrier decks in the electronics role with squadron VAW–33 until December), but the USAF continued to employ the prop-driven machine for the Sandy mission, the perilous job of escorting helicopters on combat rescue missions. Today, with the callsign Sandy 1, Bill Jones was flight leader and on-scene commander of an attempt to rescue the crew of an F-4D Phantom (66-8688) of the 389 TFS/432 TFW, downed by AAA fire the previous day. Bill's wingman was Captain Paul A. Meeks in Sandy 2.

Entering North Vietnam from Laos, Lt Col. Jones heard Phantoms talking to the downed pilot. The second crew member had apparently already been captured. Though the downed pilot remained in voice contact, his exact location was not clear. Bill Jones took his Skyraiders beneath clinging overcast with rugged hills all around him, some with their peaks lost in the gray murk. It was the most dangerous kind of flying, but Jones persisted, trying to obtain visual references to match the survivor's voice description of his location.

A ghastly misunderstanding ensued, eating up precious fuel and valuable time needed to save the downed airmen. The Phantom flight marked a spot that was actually eight miles away from the downed pilot. More than an hour was wasted in the wrong location before another fighter established contact with the downed airman. As Jones and Meeks turned toward the scene, the fighter pilot warned of a heavy concentration of 37 mm and smaller caliber AAA guns in the area.

Lt Col. Jones had barely gotten this warning when an explosion shook his A–1H, the aircraft shuddered uncertainly, and the cockpit began to fill with smoke. He had been hit but the tough, durable Skyraider was not ready to go down yet. The smoke cleared and Jones flew a zigzag pattern that kept him ahead of criss-crossing AAA fire.

Bill Jones' Rescap mission now depended upon the two items which were running out—fuel and time. Again, Jones in the injured Sandy 1 led Meeks in Sandy 2 beneath the overcast, provoking enemy fire, still trying to pinpoint the survivor's position. Finally, the downed pilot reported on voice radio that two Skyraiders were directly overhead. While trolling for fire and taking damage, Lt Col. Jones had pinpointed the survivor. Jones was so low that an AAA gun was actually firing *down* at him from a slope.

The AAA emplacement was perilously close to the downed airman. Jones ordered another aircraft in the region to remain in orbit, feeling that he had the gun pinpointed closely enough for accuracy. He brought the A–1H Skyraider around in a turn so tight that its wings were vertical to the ground. He opened up with 20 mm cannon fire and dropped CBU–58 cluster bombs. Almost simultaneously, more gunfire ripped into his Skyraider and pierced its thin metal skin.

Jones now had a life-threatening problem. The rocket motor for the Skyraider's ejection system, located behind Jones' head, had been ignited by the AAA fire. Fire rushed back from the canopy. This time when smoke crept up around Jones' clothing and obscured the instrument panel, it did not hesitate. The heat seared Jones' face and hands as flames began to consume the Skyraider. He decided that there was no choice but to bail out. He climbed, levelled off over a clear area, and blew his canopy.

The ejection seat didn't work! Bill Jones was stunned with disbelief. He reached for the secondary release and nothing happened! Thoughts of home and family rushed through his mind as air rushing into his open cockpit fanned the flames. His oxygen mask literally melted off, baring his full face to the heat. Jones was being burned very badly while trying to radio his position and that of the downed airman—and hearing the screech in his earphones as the airwaves were overloaded, other pilots screaming at him to *bail out, now!*

Bill Jones continued maneuvering in a Skyraider which, by any standard, should have disintegrated in a flaming fireball in mid-air. The North Vietnamese continued to stalk him with criss-crossing AAA fire, while their troops pressed relentlessly closer to the survivor. Few examples of greater persistence or downright bravery emerge from the entire American effort against North Vietnam. Jones' A–1H was engulfed in a dazzling

halo of flames and was trailing a thick, acrid stream of smoke that swept back over the confined valley, a tell-tale lure for the AAA gunners. The aircraft was already mortally damaged, yet for long moments no further AAA fire struck it.

In excruciating pain, choking, but with a functioning radio, Lt Col. Jones struggled to transmit the location of the downed flier and the AAA batteries. The familiar screech, which occurs when a radio frequency is overloaded, racked his ears while pilots in the area shouted at Bill to get out of his burning Skyraider. Just when he thought he had broken through to pass the vital information to the rescue force, his transmitter gave off electrical smoke and died.

Somehow, with Meeks helping on his wing (Jones could still receive), Lt Col. Jones coaxed the A–1H back towards Nakhon Phanom. His eyes were rapidly swelling shut from the burns when he set up a bad-weather approach to Nakhon Phanom. He landed his aircraft but it was 100 'totalled'. From an ambulance stretcher, Jones gave information which led to a later, successful 'save' of the

The F-8 Crusader reached its peak in Navy and Marine Corps operations toward the end of the ROLLING THUNDER campaign. Losses of F-8 fighters were remarkably low, even though four *Essex*-class carriers and two Marine squadrons sent them into battle in 1968. On 19 September 1968, the final Crusader MiG kill of the war was scored. (VOUGHT)

survivor. Bill Jones had won the Medal of Honor. He also survived 98 combat missions only to die in a private plane crash in 1969.

CRUSADER KILLS

The final months of ROLLING THUNDER also brought the finest hour for the Crusader. From the beginning of 1968 through the total bombing halt which finally clamped down on 30 October 1968, no fewer than four of the relatively small *Essex*-class carriers were working in the Gulf of Tonkin, these being the familiar *Bon Homme Richard, Hancock, Oriskany* and *Ticonderoga* each with two Crusader squadrons on board. In addition, *Intrepid* carried a small detachment of Crusaders to provide fighter protection for the anti-submarine carrier. Further, most carriers, including the larger vessels like *America*, had a detachment of recce Crusaders.

The recce pilots who flew pre-strike and post-strike photo missions in the RF–8G Crusader continued to face high risk and were not necessarily bound by President Johnson's edict which limited strike missions

to the lower part of North Vietnam between April and October. Two RF–8Gs from detachments of squadron VFP–63 were lost during the final months of ROLLING THUNDER, 144616 from *Ticonderoga* on 28 March (while over Laos) and 146886 from *Bonnie Dick* on 22 May. Navy RF–8G pilots were among the privileged few who could still fly over Hanoi and Haiphong, and it happened more than once that a recce Crusader sped out of Route Package Six with a MiG on its tail. There is no record of a MiG ever shooting down a recce Crusader, however, and in the entire war combat losses totalled only ten RF–8As and seven RF–8Gs, a very respectable figure.

Losses for the 'fighter' Crusader were also comfortingly low. Marine Corps pilots who operated the type with the 'Red Devils' of VMF–232 and the 'Lancers' of VMF–235 at Da Nang had a particularly good record with the aircraft. The Marines flew into the southerly Route Packages fairly frequently, but in the entire war lost only two Crusaders in North Vietnam. Their excellent combat record could not prevent the occasional accident, however. Traffic was exceedingly crowded at Southeast Asia airbases and mid-

Though it would soon be overshadowed by the Phantom, the single-seat Crusader remained a participant in the struggle against North Vietnam through to the end. One of the last variants of the Crusader to see action is typified by this F–8J aircraft (150347), seen on landing approach to NAS Atsugi, Japan, while embarked aboard USS *Oriskany* (CVA–34). (MASUMI WADA)

air collisions happened all too often. On 23 February 1968, a Marine F–8E Crusader (150857) of VMF–235 collided in flight with a Marine A–6A Intruder (152631) of VMA–533 in the pattern at Da Nang. All three crewmen were killed.

For the Navy, the end of ROLLING THUNDER brought low losses of 'fighter' Crusaders and some very satisfying MiG kills. F–8C 146989 of the 'Sundowners' of VF–111 on *Oriskany* was lost on 2 January 1968; F–8E 150909 of VF–194 on *Ticonderoga* on 14 February 1968; and F–8H 148648 from *Hancock* on 17 September 1968. None of these was claimed by a MiG and a total of only four combat losses over a prolonged period of sustained operations was a respectable figure indeed.

So, too, were the successes of Crusader

pilots who took their single-seat, cannon-armed steeds into the fray against Colonel Tomb and Hanoi's other MiG pilots. To those who flew it, the Crusader was the only *real* fighter of the war. To Commander Lowell R. (Moose) Meyers, skipper of VF-51 on *Bonnie Dick*, the Crusader was the warplane in which he had logged more than 1,000 hours whilst awaiting the chance for the ultimate test. It came on 26 June 1968 when Meyers was on a MiGCAP mission in an F-8H (148710). Meyers was returning from North Vietnam when he got into a scrape with MiG-21s and shot one of them down, using an AIM-9 Sidewinder missile. Meyer's 'Screaming Eagles' had been in the conflict since the Gulf of Tonkin air strikes; the squadron's one-time skipper Jim Stockdale was a POW in Hanoi and the MiG-17 victory, the 113th of the war, was welcomed by all of VF-51's people.

On 9 July 1968, Lcdr John B. Nichols III from VF-191 on *Hancock* was flying escort for a reconnaissance flight, a circumstance which permitted him to be north of the 19th Parallel bombline. Nichols' fighter with the callsign Feedbag 101 had become enmired in a protracted conflict with a MiG-17, a battle in which Nichols' adversary stubbornly refused to go down. Nichols scored a hit with an AIM-9 Sidewinder, drawing clots of smoke. The MiG continued to try to turn inside him, sputtering but fighting tenaciously. Nichols maneuvered into position to unleash 20 mm cannon fire, saw his shells impacting against the MiG, and still could not bring it down. He closed in and fired again from pointblank range. Finally, the MiG-17 disintegrated and fell in flames.

The war's next MiG kill in chronological order was the first aerial victory for the F-4J Phantom on 10 July 1968, and has already been described. All carriers larger than the *Essex* class, *America* again being an example, were now Phantom-equipped, but the F-4J interlude was the only 'break' in a consistent series of Crusader achievements.

On 24 July 1968, Commander Guy Cane of VF-53 flying an F-8E Crusader (150349) from *Bonnie Dick* shot down a MiG-17 with an AIM-9 Sidewinder. A week later, the penultimate MiG kill of ROLLING THUNDER also was credited to a Crusader. It happened on 1 August 1968. Lt Norman K. McCoy, another 'Screaming Eagle' from VF-51 on *Bonnie Dick*, was flying an F-8H Crusader (147716) when he, too, employed a Sidewinder to prevail over an opponent, this time a MiG-21. Cane and McCoy were also very experienced Crusader pilots who had waited over the full years of a career for the chance to claim an enemy aircraft.

As the presidential campaign narrowed to a contest between Hubert Humphrey and Richard M. Nixon, a Crusader pilot scored the final kill of 1968, the final kill of the ROLLING THUNDER campaign, and the last until 1970.

These distinctions went to Lt Anthony J. Nargi on 19 September 1968. It was the 118th MiG kill of the war and the 18th and last MiG kill credited to a Crusader. Nargi was aboard the anti-submarine carrier *Intrepid* with the VF-111 detachment on the ship. He and his wingman were informed of MiGs aloft within the vicinity of the vessel and were catapulted upward to intercept. The MiG-21 pilots apparently sighted the Crusader and took evasive action. Nargi went into a tight turn and wracked his F-8C Crusader (146961) behind one of the MiGs. He got the tone in his earphones telling him to fire an AIM-9 Sidewinder. The missile went off its rail cleanly, tracked perfectly, went up the MiG's tailpipe, and blew the North Vietnamese fighter to pieces. The MiG pilot ejected and a characteristic red-orange North Vietnamese parachute furled back into the slipstream.

The remaining MiG-21 pilot, undaunted, proved exceedingly aggressive in duelling with the two Crusaders. Nargi and his wingman maneuvered with the MiG and fired missiles at it but without result. *The air-to-air war was over.*

THE KILL TO LOSS RATIO

From August 1964 to October 1968, air-to-air combat resulted in 118 MiGs shot down, a figure which, thanks to steady re-supply, was higher than the total number of MiGs in the North Vietnamese air force at any given time, so far. During the same period, 56 US aircrafts were lost in air-to-air action. The 2 : 1 kill ratio marked the poorest performance by American fighters in any conflict and was a sharp contrast to the Korean War where the kill ratio, once touted as being as much as 15 : 1, really *was* 7 : 1.

Pilot experience did not seem to be a factor. Most US pilots during ROLLING THUNDER were highly experienced. The Red Baron study conducted by the Air Force after the war showed that before 1966 more than half of all fighter pilots had 2,000 flying hours and the average pilot had logged 510 hours in the aircraft type he flew in combat; at this juncture the kill ratio was a slightly more favorable 3 : 1. By the end of ROLLING THUNDER in October 1968, the average fighter pilot had only 240 hours in his aircraft type and the score had fallen to an absolute .85 : 1. The study showed that total flying hours had no direct correlation to a pilot's chances of being shot down by a MiG. On the other hand—witness the case of Colonel Robin Olds—a seasoned pilot with more flight time in his logbook stood the best chance of shooting down a MiG.

The Navy felt that training in air combat maneuvering (ACM) was the key to improving the air-to-air combat skills of its pilots. An analysis of air-to-air combat over North Vietnam was completed in 1968 by Captain Frank W. Ault, and this led to the Navy instituting an ACM program with three goals: to improve air combat capabilities among all US Navy fighter squadrons, to improve the reliability of air-to-air missiles, and to create an elite cadre of high-capability combat instructors. It was almost as if Ault and others were prescient, as if they knew another day might come to fight over North Vietnam.

Ault was right, of course, and in retrospect the Navy's decision not to mount an internal cannon on its F-4 Phantoms proved to be less significant than it seemed at the time. The US Navy Postgraduate Course in Fighter Weapons, Tactics and Doctrine, soon to be re-named Top Gun, was launched by squadron VF-121 at NAS Miramar, California. The program involved three weeks and about 35 flight hours of realistic, if simulated, air combat against actual adversaries flying 'dissimilar' aircraft, these being A-4F Skyhawks and T-38A Talons, the latter being an excellent stand-in for the MiG-21. Top Gun created superb Phantom pilots like Commander Ronald (Mugs) McKeown and Commander Randall (Randy) Cunningham who would be very well prepared if, indeed, a second round of fighting *did* erupt over North Vietnam. In fact, because of Top Gun and the similar 'Aggressor' ACM training introduced by the Air Force only later, the findings about flying experience would be reversed and the greatest successes in the future would be achieved by younger pilots with fewer flight hours but with realistic combat training under their belts. The Air Force, which in 1968 still had not acquired its own ACM syllabus, was still talking about the gun-armed Phantom as the means of attaining a better kill ratio and had sent Lt Col. Edward Hillding to Eglin AFB, Florida to 'work up' the 40 TFS, the squadron that would take the cannon-armed F-4E into combat.

ROLLING THUNDER ANALYZED

A week before Americans were to cast ballots for the next occupant of the White House, the bombline was brought down to the 17th Parallel and Lyndon Johnson's bombing halt

became a total bombing halt for all of North Vietnam. For now, except for reconnaissance, all combat operations against North Vietnam came to an end. ROLLING THUNDER had ended. The campaign had lasted for three years and seven months.

Raphael Iungerich arrived in Saigon as a junior Air Force officer in 1966 and departed Vietnam almost ten years later as a CIA analyst. Until leaving the intelligence agency in recent years, Iungerich was an authority on both the ROLLING THUNDER campaign and the Vietnamese situation in general.

'I took part in the war and followed it carefully for more than a decade. I read all the reports, talked to pilots, reviewed the photography, debriefed prisoners and defectors, and went through my own metamorphosis of thought and opinion. [At first] I believed in the course charted by Kennedy, then Johnson. As the years grew long and the results were few, [my] doubt changed into bitterness and anger until I became convinced that not only was the war unwinnable but it was not worth winning in the manner it was being conducted.

'It will be argued that aerial warfare is but one component of military success, that without clear political goals and battlefield gains no amount of ordnance dropped on targets can achieve the ultimate victory. It is stated that at the height of the war over Nazi Ger-

Boeing KC–135 Stratotanker aircraft of the Strategic Air Command, used from the beginning of the war until its end. (USAF)

many, German industrial production increased; or similarly that US aerial interdiction of troops and supplies in North Korea did not stop the Chinese from intervening en masse. This is true. Yet bombardment of Germany did weaken the morale of the Nazis and the German people, and did lead to a perception that the war could not be won. The aerial destruction of Japan was so great that even without the use of atomic bombs in 1945, Japan would soon have lost its capacity to continue the war. During the Korean conflict the US enjoyed absolute aerial supremacy over the North and, if permission had been granted early on to destroy the bridges over the Yalu River and perhaps to destroy adjacent staging areas on the Manchurian side, there would be no North Korean communist state today.

'[During the 1965–68 ROLLING THUNDER campaign] Secretary McNamara's policy of granduated response punctuated with frequent "good will" bombing pauses was not unlike an arm-wrestling match between an NFL offensive lineman and a scrawny high school-age troublemaker wherein the [National Football League] behemoth would like to punish the kid but because of a guilty conscience over the physical dissimilarity, cannot bring himself to inflict "disproportionate" damage or to cause humiliation by actually defeating the boy. The outcome of this tale is dreary enough: our football hero salvages his conscience and turns to leave ("a pitiful, helpless giant," as Richard Nixon would say) just as the mean little punk with no such qualms seized upon this weakness and promptly despatches his adversary by shooting him in the back. Who says that crime doesn't pay?

'Not only was the [ROLLING THUNDER] policy flawed in concept, it was never fully implemented even under the tight restrictions imposed. Air operations over the Hanoi-Haiphong area and throughout the northeast corridor of the country were simply not permitted during the early years of ROLLING THUNDER. [At first] military barracks were the chief target, although it is doubtful if many troops were caught inside their barracks. The southern panhandle of North Vietnam took a severe beating, but this theater of operations had little bearing on the conflict in the South or on North Vietnam's will to resist. It was as if Johnson and McNamara wanted to prove that the US could destroy an insignificant area as a signal of what could be done to more important targets.

'[As early as the end of 1965] it was apparent to all that ROLLING THUNDER was not doing the job. Infiltration into the South was up, and popular support for the North's leadership solidified. Admiral Sharp had recommended from the outset that all railroads, overland and water routes from China be interdicted. Secretary of State Dean Rusk and Ambassador Henry Cabot Lodge agreed with Sharp but were overruled by McNamara. The gradualists carried the day again and another bombing halt, this time for six weeks, was declared at Christmastime [1965]. Ten years later at a Maryland conference, former Chairman of the Joint Chiefs of Staff Admiral Thomas Moorer referred to Secretary McNamara as "the line equivalent of twelve Soviet divisions."

'Within a year from the start of ROLLING THUNDER, the pattern was clear. The North Vietnamese leaders knew that Washington did not have the will nor the goal of achieving victory, largely out of fear of stirring up the public's distaste for bombing and concern over possible Chinese and Soviet countermoves. Meantime, the North Vietnamese took advantage of the extended bombing pause to build up their air defense (almost nonexistent in early 1965) and to rush more troops to the southern front. At the same time they hurried to offload from Soviet ships as much weaponry, POL (petroleum, oil, lubricants), supplies and foodstuffs as they could.

'The story of North Vietnamese POL supplies is bizarre. Most of the North's POL came by sea from the Soviet Union, and throughout 1965 it was stored in large storage tank farms vulnerable to air attack. Because a country and its armed forces cannot long exist without a sufficient and continuing supply of POL, US military officials requested authority to strike these storage centers at the beginning of the ROLLING THUNDER campaign. The White House felt such attacks would be unnecessarily provocative (as if war itself is not provocative) and denied permission.

'One can only surmise how surprised Hanoi was when no bombs fell on these POL tanks. But taking no chances, the North began to quickly disperse its POL supplies, placing them in submerged or bunkered sites concealed throughout the countryside, or in thousands of 50-gallon barrels located in urban areas, taking advantage of America's well-known aversion to bombing civilian population centers.

'When President Johnson reluctantly authorized the bombing of POL supplies in mid-1966, it was too little and too late. The rules of engagement were so restrictive that each sortie required prior White House approval on crew composition, flight pattern and defensive measures to be used. Even finding the dispersed and hidden POL sites was no small task. Thus, what could have been a lethal strike against North Vietnam's POL capacity a year earlier had now become a lost cause. With the major port of Haiphong off limits, Soviet ships were able to offload POL modules onto waiting trucks with impunity.

'Bombing of North Vietnam and infiltration routes in Laos continued to be about the same until the spring of 1967. All of a sudden President Johnson, impatient with the meager results of two years of bombing, gave authority to the Air Force and Navy to strike an extended list of targets, many located in the strategic northeast corridor. Populated centers were still proscribed, but with the exception of Haiphong and two other deep-water ports, all river mouths were mined. Throughout the summer months of 1967, North Vietnam was hammered hard, and the results became evident as North Vietnamese morale began to sag.

'But just as quickly, President Johnson [again] changed course and reapplied the earlier bombing restrictions. No doubt the President was influenced by mounting dissent at home, by Secretary McNamara's change of heart (the Defense Secretary may have grown weary of hearing the conflict called "McNamara's War"), and by a new Joint Chiefs of Staff request for 200,000 additional troops to fight in South Vietnam.' [As noted elsewhere, CIA analyst Iungerich is under a misapprehension here: about *half* of the 200,000 troops being requested were for Vietnam duty.]

'In effect 1967 was the last year ROLLING THUNDER ever had a chance of success because in 1968, following the Tet offensive and violent demonstrations in the US, bombing attacks on northern targets were sharply curtailed and ended altogether just before the November elections.

'When the bombing commenced, North Vietnam did not have jet interceptors or SAMs. Only a few airfields were operational. There were less than two dozen radar sets and only a few obsolete AAA guns. By 1967, US fliers had to confront aerial defenses more formidable than those ever encountered over Germany during World War II. The number of jets, SAMs and AAA [increased] even more dramatically in the years to follow.'

The preceding analysis of the ROLLING THUNDER campaign is repetitive of other words which appear in this narrative—but for good reason. Iungerich is not just another frustrated pilot. Over time, he became one of the most respected CIA officers working on the Vietnam 'problem,' to use his agency's parlance. His expertise covers a range of subjects from air combat tactics to the Vietnamese language. Anyone seeking to understand the hundreds of thousands of sorties flown by American pilots against North Vietnam from March 1965 to October 1968 *must* be attentive to Raphael Iungerich. For this reason, the following remarks by this CIA expert are italicized here:

'ROLLING THUNDER *must go down in the history of aerial warfare as the most ambitious, wasteful and ineffective campaign ever mounted. And President Johnson may receive history's judgment as one of the most indecisive and paralyzed war leaders to ever exist. While damage was done to many targets in the North, no last-*

ing objective was achieved, even the limited goals earlier mentioned. Hanoi emerged as the winner of ROLLING THUNDER.'

ROLLING THUNDER had satisfied almost no one.

The military officer quoted earlier, who felt that his hands were tied behind his back, summed up the feeling of Air Force, Navy and Marine officers and pilots who felt that the prolonged air campaign had violated a basic principle: when you fight a war, you must fight to win. Men in Thuds and Crusaders, Skyhawks and Phantoms believed that they had been sent against formidable defenses, to attack questionable targets, under too many restrictions, with no realistic chance of waging the war in a manner that would make it *possible* to win. At the very time when anti-war opponents back home criticized them for bombing raids which the

uninformed regarded as atrocious, military men felt impotent.

Despite all the restrictions, the on-again, off-again mood of the campaign, and the general confusion, these pilots had, in fact, done more damage to North Vietnam than is generally recognized. In the years since the conflict, a few North Vietnamese officials, speaking with uncharacteristic candor, have acknowledged that at various points in 1967 and 1968 the bombing was hurting badly. The diversion of resources to repair, maintain and expand bridges, roads and railways—to say nothing of infiltration routes— was a drain on an already overburdened society. Prior to the Tet offensive, when Hanoi did not fully control the Viet Cong anyway, a more vigorous bombing campaign might have caused North Vietnam's leaders to sue for a settlement. But each time that North

For all of its confusion and contradictions, the 1965-68 ROLLING THUNDER campaign *did* inflict serious damage on North Vietnam. In a 27 April 1967 strike by warplanes from USS *Kitty Hawk* (CVA–63), the Haiphong cement plant was left in ruins, releasing torrents of black smoke that were visible for miles. (USN)

Vietnam started to hurt, the US relaxed the pressure.

By the end of ROLLING THUNDER on 30 October 1968, preliminary peace talks were taking shape in Paris. The talks had not progressed beyond such issues as the shape of the table to be used at meetings. The Saigon authorities refused to talk to any representative from Hanoi. The North Vietnamese wanted to talk directly with the US and were not prepared to negotiate with the South Vietnamese. The weak start of the talks seemed to have no relation to the air battles that had been fought in Route Package Six. The talks were going nowhere.

With the benefit of hindsight, it is clear that ROLLING THUNDER could have been successful only if the civilian leaders in Washington had made a policy decision to use military power effectively. Most professional airmen believed then, and still believe now, that North Vietnam could have been taken out of the war in a matter of weeks with the men and machines already located in Southeast Asia, and with no additional resources. What was missing was a plan, a policy, a coherent decision to use airmen and aircraft as they were intended to be used. Because men in mufti were seeking to turn warplanes into weapons of policy rather than to employ them correctly as weapons of war, ROLLING THUNDER failed. Although the Communist side never won a major victory in battle, not on land, sea

or air, ROLLING THUNDER failed because the policymakers gave the war away by default. It happened just as Lt Col. Edward Hillding's men were working up to participate in a conflict which now seemed to have come to an end.

ENTER THE F–4E

As Hillding points out, the F–4E was a very different Phantom—longer, heavier, with different fuel capacity, different radar. 'Everybody wanted to jump into one and go shoot down a MiG.' Based on Vietnam experience and first flown on 30 June the previous year, 1967, the F–4E carried an internally-mounted General Electric M61A1 Vulcan, or Gatling, rotary cannon with provision for 640 rounds while retaining the Sidewinder / Sparrow capability. The F–4E also had an additional (seventh) fuel cell in the fuselage which counter-balanced the weight of the gun. Installed in the redesigned nose was a smaller, Westinghouse APQ-120 solid-state radar fire control system with a reduced, elliptical dish. Power was provided by two 17,900 lb (8 120 kg) thrust General Electric J79-GE-17 engines with afterburners.

Hillding took the new fighter to Eglin

where Captain Steve Stephens designed a colorful patch for the 40 TFS and painted shark's teeth on the Phantoms. General Momyer, now Tactical Air Command chief following his stint in Saigon, did not *want* shark's teeth—throughout the Vietnam conflict, leaders failed to grasp the morale-building benefit of such insignia—but was persuaded to remember those which had been painted on his own P–40 Warhawk in World War Two. Captain Thomas McInerney, encountered in this narrative when he introduced the F–4D to combat, joined Hillding's squadron to do the same with the F–4E.

'Working up' in the F–4E at Eglin was an exciting time for the men who believed wrongly that the bombing halt was only for a short duration. Many were seasoned combat veterans. Tom McInerney had the job of Weapons Officer and was tasked to bring the squadron up to par with the new Phantom's cannon and its other systems, including the very unpopular Bullpup-B missile. Captain Jack Isham was given the job of preparing the men for ground survival, in advance of the usual survival exercises carried out in the Philippines en route to the battle zone. Isham's strongest memory from those days at Eglin—the largest airbase in the world, on

The F–4E variant of the Phantom arrived in combat, replete with Lt Col. Edward Hillding's much-prized shark's teeth, just as a cessation of bombing of North Vietnam left F–4E crews with only Laos to fly in. Captain John E. Ford III of the 469 TFS/388 TFW at Korat took this photograph of a toothed F–4E going into battle on 30 November 1968. (USAF)

swampland in the Florida panhandle, near Fort Walton Beach with its summer hotels, tourist bars and ski-ball joints—is a curious one. His thoughts were devoted not so much to the new F-4E airframe but to the survival tools which could have been mentioned at any juncture in this narrative.

Every airman carried 'Device 9H12A', which looked like a deck of playing cards. In fact, the deck contained 'Survival plant recognition cards'—a color photograph of a sample of foliage on one side, a description of its properties on the other. The purpose was simple: if you were down on the ground in North Vietnam, you needed to know which items of vegetation were edible.

Also memorable to Isham, and perhaps a

The operational effectiveness of tanker aircraft as "force multipliers" was beginning to be realized in practice over Vietnam, yet the key role of the KC-135 is rarely mentioned.

bit silly, was a tiny pocket handbook known technically as an 'Item 711' but graphically entitled *Southeast Asia Pointee Talkee*. The handbook was intended as a guide to communication where a language barrier existed. It contained comical stick drawings of a downed pilot trying to tell a rice paddy farmer that he wanted to be escorted to the south. 'Talkee Pointee' was a foolish and, yes, racist American perception of how Asian peasants spoke English; it was based on a popular notion about the Chinese language when in fact the tongues which mattered—Vietnamese, Lao, and later Khmer—had almost nothing in common with Chinese. *Southeast Asia Pointee Talkee*, based on good intentions, was a waste of the taxpayer's dollar.

As Hillding's men broke in the new F-4E Phantom above the Florida swamp and over the gulf of Mexico, Captain Isham gawked at another survival item, a beautiful silk scarf with an American flag at the top and a mes-

sage in no fewer than thirteen languages. The 'survival scarf' actually pre-dated the conflict against North Vietnam, having been devised in April 1961, but it remained in use throughout the conflict. The message beneath the American flag read:

'I am a citizen of the U.S.A. I do not speak your language. Misfortune forces me to seek your assistance in obtaining food, shelter and protection. Please take me to someone who will provide for my safety and see that I am returned to my people. My government will reward you.'

The message was repeated in (no less than) Burmese, Thai, Laotian, Khmer (Cambodian), Vietnamese, Malay, Chinese, Modern Chinese, Tagalog, Visayan, French and Dutch. In most of those cultures, the word 'citizen' was incomprehensible. The idea that a government would reward some rice farmer, especially if he happened to be a North Vietnamese rice farmer, did not seem to fit

with any of the other things being done by the government at the time: How the hell, Isham wondered, was Washington going to 'reward' some rural peon for aiding a downed pilot when Washington could not even figure out which targets to drop bombs on? As for the part about being 'returned to my people', Isham imagined himself humping over a ridgeline in North Vietnam being pursued by enemy soldiers with bullets flying around his head. Whoever had designed the 'survival scarf' had had noble intentions. A similar scarf had helped P–40 pilots of the Flying Tigers in World War Two. But the idea was a bummer in 1968.

Hillding, Stephens, McInerney, Isham and the other men of the F–4E sqadron at Eglin spent more than a year 'working up' and, as Isham puts it, were *damned* if they were going to allow *anybody* to prevent them from shooting down MiGs. They had everything: the tactics, the cannon, the aggressive fighter-pilot spirit which, in the end, matters most. They were going to become aces, some of them, a feat even the exalted Robin Olds had been unable to achieve. When they learned that they were going to Southeast Asia in *November*, and that combat missions over North Vietnam had *halted at the end of October*, some of the men were impossible to be around. One F–4E pilot (not among those named) threw a training manual at his wife. Another just stared at the teeth Hillding had painted on the aircraft and shook his head. How could a government reward a god-damned peasant when a government could not even arrange the proper timing for the guys who had worked so hard to become MiG killers?

Upon receiving the news, Isham ignored the Fort Walton Beach side of Eglin AFB, which looks out on an azure gulf, and went instead to the other side of the base, inland, to a motel in the town with the unlikely name of Niceville, Florida. Here, he convened with a handful of fellow pilots, raised a glass or two, and lamented the end of ROLLING THUNDER as much as any man alive. 'I wanted a crack at a MiG. I wanted a MiG. What else is there?'

Despite the adverse reaction to the bombing halt, morale in the squadron was generally high—especially when orders were cut for Southeast Asia and it became absolutely clear that they were going to war in the F–4E, MiG or no MiG. Even if they could not fly 'up North'—and many thought the prohibition would quickly be lifted—there was a job to be done. Hillding will never forget a chief master sergeant who begged, pleaded, to accompany the squadron into combat. The man was typical of the senior NCOs, or non-commissioned officers, who are the backbone of any fighting organization. Hillding just

looked at him. 'Sarge, you're already done two tours in Vietnam. You've been wounded. Your wife is having open-heart surgery. We're going to have to fight this next part of the war without you.' When Hillding's 40 TFS prepared to become the first squadron *ever* to deploy to Vietnam *en masse*, the senior NCO watched the men readying their aircraft—and wept.

The night before departure, shark's teeth were added to the few F–4E Phantoms in Hillding's squadron which did not already have the individualistic markings. The actual departure from Eglin—the first time a fighter squadron deployed as a cohesive unit—was a ceremony with several TAC generals (but not Momyer) in attendance. Twenty F–4E Phantoms took off in formation, winged over the base and the surrounding communities, veered away from the Gulf, climbed over the Florida panhandle, and headed to war. While pausing en route at Hickam AFB, Hawaii, Hillding's F–4E squadron attracted some unwanted attention from a 'PACAF weenie' who objected strongly to the teeth painted on the aircraft and, in weeks ahead, would complain about it. The aviation artist Keith Ferris joined the squadron for a back-seat ride on the leg from Hickam to Andersen AB, Guam—again, as earlier, accomplished with KC–135 refueling. A pause at Guam enabled some of the aircrews to see a performance by the well-known stripper, Gypsy Rose Lee. While some men were observing Gypsy's G-strings, Hillding held an unusual meeting with the commander of the KC–135 tanker force that would take them the rest of the way.

His plan was that the lead F–4E would take more fuel in order to fly slower, while following elements in the Phantom formation would manage their fuel differently, the purpose being to arrive over their destination—Korat AB, Thailand—all at the same time. At Korat of course was Colonel Paul Douglas, usually called P. P. Douglas, who would be Hillding's boss and was one of the best fighter wing commanders in the business. In World War Two, Douglas had had a P–47D Thunderbolt named *Arkansas Traveler*. During ROLLING THUNDER, he'd applied the same nickname to a Thud. He would eventually turn one of Hillding's F–4Es into yet another *Arkansas Traveler*. P. P. Douglas, like Ed Hillding, had one primary skill: leading men in battle. Hillding wanted to arrive over Korat with perfect timing, in a superb display of flight discipline, with a few rolls and banks which would make Korat's Thud people see the Phantom as the wave of the future. He did. He made a spectacular arrival. And the instant the tires screeched on Korat's runway, Hillding's squadron became the 469

TFS—formerly, and proudly, one of the Thud elements of Douglas' 388 TFW. The squadron commander stepped out of his aircraft (67-303, he recalls) to find numerous people, including a couple of generals, welcoming the arrival of the F–4E. There was much good cheer, camaraderie and talk about carrying the war to the enemy. There was also a message from Hickam, drafted by the 'PACAF weenie,' commanding Hillding to remove the teeth from his aircraft. Hillding, a man with an easy grasp for priorities, was more concerned with the morale of his men than the message. He devised an excuse to delay removing the unique marking which gave the 469 TFS its identity, its spirit, its aggressiveness. The teeth stayed.

The first combat missions in the F–4E Phantom were flown on 26 November 1968, nineteen days after the arrival at Korat. There was, at this time, no combat in the country which is the subject of this narrative—North Vietnam. Hillding's men went into Laos.

In December, the vice commander of PACAF, Lt Gen. Edmundson, visited Korat. Edmundson was not merely a PACAF weenie, he was also a SAC weenie, having spent most of his time in the bomber community. Edmundson, Mike Carnes, P. P. Douglas, Hillding and possibly McInerney were all present when Edmundson announced that those teeth had damned well better come off the F–4Es, or else. At the same time, the 469 TFS was obtaining superb BDA (battle damage assessments) and scoring more hits with ordnance than any previous squadron. The outfit's clergyman, full name no longer remembered but known to all in the squadron as Chaplain Joe the Baptist, personally graced each aircraft, and sometimes mentioned serial numbers in his prayers, one possible explanation for the good BDA. Isham said that morale was the highest he had seen in any unit. The men were up. Edmundson's edict was followed, sort of. Hillding removed the teeth from 67-303 but discovered an administrative reason why there was not enough paint remover to cover the other airframes. Colonel Allen K. McDonald, who replaced Douglas as wing commander, not only did not remove the teeth: he named his F–4E *Betty Lou*. Soon other nicknames appeared. General Edmundson went back to Hawaii to focus on other problems, unaware that Chaplain Joe was praying for him. Hillding eventually located the paper needed to instruct painters (USAF Form 781) and scribbled a message something like 'de-paint these aircraft when resources permit'—which meant sooner or later, sort of.

General Nazzaro, PACAF chief, arrived at

Korat. With the E-model Phantom now in service, there were signs saying, 'We do the job with Es' and there were shark's teeth on Hillding's *Jeep*. A conversation ensued:

Nazzaro: 'You may have been told to remove those shark's teeth from your aircraft.'

Hillding: 'I, uh, think we were, uh, told that, sir.'

Nazzaro: 'Well, you can forget what you were told.'

Hillding: 'You mean we can *keep* the teeth, general?'

Nazzaro (quietly): 'I didn't say *that*.' (Winking).

Nazzaro had been a SAC weenie, too, but for some reason he seemed to be able to communicate with fighter pilots.

Soon after the F–4E Phantom went into combat, Hillding, McInerney and others discovered that the Air Force was planning to put a new breed of animal in the back seat. Until now, all Air Force Phantoms of all var-iants had been flown by *two pilots*. Now the 469 TFS was to receive a new animal called a weapons systems officer (WSO), a term no one ever used. The term actually employed was, simply, navigator. Not long after the first combat missions of the E model in November 1968, Chaplain Joe blessed the first missions in which the back-seater was not a pilot.

It appears that the first F–4E lost in combat was 67-286 of Hillding's 469 TFS/388 TFS, downed over Laos on 1 January 1969. No record exists of whether *Pointee Talkee* or the scarf helped the crew.

In Saigon, following Momyer as chief of Seventh Air Force, General George Brown settled into the job and the war. Brown, too, had spent much of his career in SAC. He felt overburdened with a war in Laos which was not publicly acknowledged, and for which his men received no credit, and he was not pleased with the decision to cease bombing North Vietnam.

General Brown wanted to get the next squadron of F–4Es, and the next, into the fight. Losses of Thuds had been so heavy that the F–105 could no longer be the primary strike aircraft. Ahead lay the time of the Phantom.

YEAR-END WRAPUP

If a history of the air war against North Vietnam has been compiled at the end of 1969, it

---

Its days of dominance were almost over, but up until the end of the ROLLING THUNDER campaign on 31 October 1968, the F–105 Thunderchief had been the primary weapon of war against North Vietnam. 'Daisy Mae,' an F–105D (58-1172), camouflaged, coded RU, and belonging to the Takhli-based 357 TFS/355 TFW, is seen hauling fuel and bombs in the general direction of Hanoi. (REPUBLIC, VIA JERRY C. SCUTTS)

would have been said that the war was over and that the result was, at best, ambiguous.

On 5 November 1968, Richard M. Nixon narrowly defeated Vice President Hubert M. Humphrey in the presidential election. Despite press reports that Nixon had a 'secret plan' to end the Southeast Asia war, Nixon himself had never said he did. Humphrey lost because he was too late in distancing himself from the war policy of the Johnson administration.

Fighting over Laos, not strictly a part of this history, was a continuing challenge for American airmen. On 15 November 1968, a series of interdiction campaigns known as Commando Hunt began in Laotian airspace. That same week saw the arrival of the F–4E Phantom, and, on 19 November, the departure of the F–111A detachment, which pulled out of Southeast Asia to return to Nellis AFB, Nevada. It could not be known, now, that the F–111A would return to fight over North Vietnamese skies again.

On 22 December 1968, the first of the newly-arrived AC–119G gunships went into service at Nha Trang AB. Other terms, including Gunship III and Combat Hornet, were used to describe this gunship derived from the ageing C–119G Flying Boxcar transport, but if the AC–47 was known as Spooky and the AC–130 known as Spectre, the AC–119G quickly acquired the name Shadow. (A later variant, the AC–119K, became the Stinger.) General George Brown, the commander of Seventh Air Force in Saigon who had replaced Momyer, was especially enthusiastic about the big, twin-boomed craft, which was painted an ominous black. The Air Force had selected the 'One Nineteen' as its third gunship type, in addition to the AC–47 and AC–130, because of the availability of airframes, sturdiness and loitering times. The Shadow was to become an important weapons system in South Vietnam and an incidental part of the fighting in Laos and 'up North'.

Like other gunships, the AC–119G was a sort of flying tank. Equipment specified for the aircraft included Southeast Asia communications gear, the GAU–2B/A six-barrel 7.62 mm machine-gun, no fewer than 50,000 rounds of ammunition for day flights and 35,000 rounds plus 60 flares for night missions. The later AC–119K had 20 mm cannons added.

The AC–119G aircraft had been late arriving in South Vietnam because of program delays and equipment problems. A function as simple as venting gun smoke from the fuselage interior required weeks or months of evaluations, changes and further tests. Eventually, 26 airframes were converted by the Fairchild-Hiller plant in St Augustine, Florida. The aircraft were assigned to the 71st Special Operations Squadron of the 14th Special Operations (formerly Air Commando) Wing at Nha Trang. Some were later assigned to Phan Rang AB and Tan Son Nhut AB. Shadow joined Spectre in the continuing conflict but, in late 1969, was not supposed to be flown into North Vietnam.

At the end of 1968, the number of US combat troops in South Vietnam had reached 536,100, a figure very close to the final peak of about 550,000 which would be reached before the Nixon administration began slow and phased withdrawals. In the ground war in South Vietnam, the communist side continued to exhibit an almost limitless capacity for absorbing casualties, enduring suffering and pressing the fight. On the Americans' home front, the opposition to the war continued to gather strength, making Americans less willing to sacrifice than their enemy. New problems were becoming firmly rooted among the US forces: racial conflict, in an army where the number of blacks was double the black share of the US population; narcotics problems in a combat zone where hash, morphine, opium and heroin were regularly available. Thus, at the height of its commitment to the war, the US had stopped bombing North Vietnam and was watching its own forces move in the direction of disarray while the communist enemy—who, to be sure, had problems of his own—fought on.

In 1968, losses of US Navy and Marine Corps aircraft had continued at about the same rate as the previous year, even though bad weather at the beginning of the year and a bombing halt at the end reduced the total number of sorties. Despite its much-envied all-weather capability, the A–6A Intruder remained somewhat loss-prone and very controversial.

A total of 392 USAF aircraft were lost in all of Southeast Asia (not merely North Vietnam) during 1968. The majority, 257, fell to AAA fire. Of the total, 304 were combat losses while 88 were operational. A desk-bound statistics expert decided that the value of the aircraft lost was $441 million. Viet Cong attacks on airbases in South Vietnam had resulted in 35 aircraft being destroyed on the ground. SAMs and MiGs claimed only 12 aircraft, compared to 40 in 1967. Again, the F–105 Thunderchief bore a heavy share of the losses, with the F–4 Phantom close behind. But the day of the Thud was ending.

US Air Force munitions expended in 1968, according to the same mentality which created exact numbers for things that could not be measured, totalled 1,092,000 American tons, a 60 per cent increase over 1967 expenditures. The USAF flew 1,034,839 combat sorties.

But, except for the occasional reconnaissance flight, not a single American aircraft flew in the skies of North Vietnam.

1969 INTERLUDE

1 January 1969 began a year in which no American warplanes were to fly combat missions into North Vietnam. American prisoners, of course, remained in the North, scattered in a half-dozen camps where treatment varied from poor to execrable. The only other Americans who spent much time 'up North' were the intrepid fliers of reconnaissance aircraft. A heavy portion of the recce job was carried out by the RF–101C Voodoo, which possessed the range, durability and staying power to cope with Hanoi's ever-improving defenses.

With a new president about to take office

and with emphasis being placed on reducing US casualties, aircraft previously committed to operations against North Vietnam were diverted to interdiction efforts in Laos (Commando Hunt) and to increased support of friendly ground forces in the South.

Peace talks, a curious term for a situation where killing was routine, groped slowly in Paris. A US Congress Armed Services Committee report stated that since the 31 October 1968 bombing halt, the increase in North Vietnamese logistics operations toward Laos and the DMZ were of such volume that it appeared the North Vietnamese were establishing a massive logistics system as a foundation for future expanded operations. The report concluded with the obvious: if peace talks failed, the bombing halt would have provided Hanoi with a new lease on life, and the war would drag on.

On 20 January 1969, Richard M. Nixon took office as President and his administration began working on the Vietnam enigma.

To replace Clark Clifford, Nixon's Secretary of Defense was Melvin R. Laird, a former congressman and a pragmatic leader and manager. The only Secretary of Defense interviewed at length by the author of this narrative, Laird was thoroughly familiar with the Vietnam situation from the start and was soon to become a key figure in pushing for 'Vietnamization'. To steer foreign policy, the new administration's Secretary of State was William P. Rogers, a respected lawyer and former attorney general who often said, himself, that Southeast Asia was not his *forte*. In the end, running foreign policy was not Rogers' strong suit either, not with a new figure on the scene as the President's national security advisor: Henry Kissinger, nominally far less important than Rogers, quickly acquired 'clout' in the administration that Rogers never possessed.

It seems clear that Nixon was uncomfortable with the absence of American aircraft in North Vietnam's skies and concerned that Hanoi was recovering and rebuilding. Nixon knew that any solution to the war would require a stronger South Vietnam, serious action against Hanoi's infiltration routes, and a withdrawal of at least some American troops as a visible sign of progress. The little-publicized air campaign over Laos was continuing in fits and starts, and much of that campaign was directed against the segments of the Ho Chi Minh Trail which circled through Laos en route to South Vietnam. But the pressure to withdraw American troops brought with it pressure to show that the enemy was being harmed. To bring the boys home, Nixon might have to go North again.

MARITIME PATROL

Some operations continued to impinge directly on North Vietnam's war-fighting capacity, even when aircraft did not overfly the country's sovereign space. The US Navy's use of the venerable P–2 Neptune patrol aircraft is an example of a modest but cost-effective effort which was not limited to any single geographic sector in Southeast Asia.

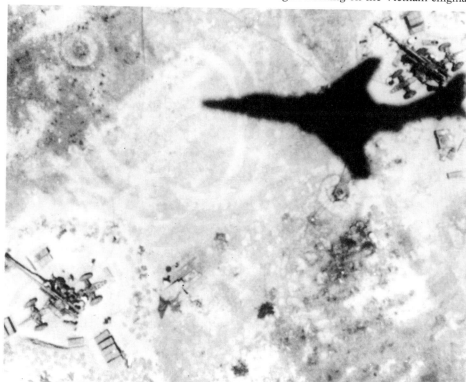

With no bombs falling on North Vietnam, much of the burden of air reconnaissance fell on the RF–101C Voodoo. Remarkably, however, not a single RF–101C was lost in combat or to operational causes anywhere in Southeast Asia in 1969. This photograph taken by a Voodoo's cameras shows the shadow of the aircraft passing over a North Vietnamese SAM site. (USAF)

US warplanes could not bomb North Vietnam but pressure was still being applied in 1969 to the infiltration routes which snaked through Laos. US Navy squadron VAH–21 operated four AP–2H Neptunes painted in mottled gray camouflage, specially armed and designed to seed the Ho Chi Minh Trail with sensors. Experience with the TRIM Neptune helped later with the TRIM A–6C Intruder. (LOCKHEED)

VO–67, the first 'observation' squadron on the US Navy inventory in two decades, had earlier enjoyed a brief life (from November 1967 to July 1968) employing the OP–2E variant of the Neptune against the Ho Chi Minh Trail. Painted in a unique jungle green over light gray, the OP–2E had had the Neptune's traditional belly-mounted ASP–20 radar removed and a smaller radar unit installed on the chin just beneath the observer's glazed nose. The Neptune's anti-submarine sensors were removed and provisions were made for window-mounted machine-gun

stations. A camera installation was positioned in a bulge beneath the fuselage under the tail. The Navy's contribution to the already-described *Igloo White* program, the OP–2E was used to drop Spikebuoy and Adsid acoustical sensors along the North Vietnamese infiltration routes. This was to prove a vain attempt to build an electronic 'shroud' around North Vietnam. The OP–2E part of the story, with the green Neptunes flying from Nakhon Phanom, quickly became history. But even during the 1969 interlude in air operations over North Vietnam, other Navy patrol craft continued to apply the pressure.

A fancier Neptune was the AP–2H operated by VAH–21 at Cam Ranh Bay. Equipped with cannons, grenade launchers, forward-looking infra-red (FLIR) and low-light level television (LLLTV), the AP–2H Neptune was in essence the Navy's version of the fixed-wing gunship, employed against trucks hauling war materiel down the Ho Chi Minh Trail. The squadron was an outgrowth

of the NAS Patuxent, Maryland, Project TRIM (Trails and Roads Interdiction, Multi-Sensor). TRIM was an electro-optical sensing system which, it was hoped, would detect night and bad-weather movements of North Vietnamese supplies. Again, during the 1969 interlude, VAH–21 (which had begun operations in September 1968) could not operate in North Vietnamese airspace, but the Neptune crews could attack truck convoys and other LUCTARs (lucrative targets) on the infiltration routes running through Laos.

Four AP–2H aircraft were employed for a brief period until these operations ended in the middle of the year. These aircraft, such as the AP–2H (148337) nicknamed *Napalm Nellie*, were painted in a new multi-shade, mottled gray paint scheme with reduced-size national insignia. The LLLTV unit was mounted in the chin beneath the nose and required extra windows in that area. In the end, the VAH–21 Neptunes were themselves

an interlude of sorts. It is of interest to note that no detailed analysis of their operations against North Vietnamese truck movements has ever been published.

The more traditional Neptune, the SP-2H, served with patrol squadrons like VP-1 as part of the attempt to interdict supplies coming to South Vietnam by sea.

Neptunes may have skirted the periphery of the North Vietnamese state, but recce pilots continued to fly over it with regularity. In Pentagon discussions, Secretary Laird and others pondered what to do if Hanoi's SAMs or AAA shot down a recce aircraft. Should a combat mission be mounted to attempt a rescue? Would that violate the terms of the bombing halt? Should warplanes be despatched with full loads of ordnance, solely to engage AAA batteries that were firing on recce aircraft? In a curious twist of reasoning, Laird and others said that Hanoi would be guilty of aggression if it fired at RF-101Cs, RF-4Cs or RF-8Gs flying over its own territory!

The role of the recce pilot and his crew has been remarked upon frequently in this nar-

rative. By 1969, some RF-4C Phantoms were carrying a weapon systems officer (WSO) in the back seat instead of a pilot and were introducing new types of ECM pods and other accutrements. Flying the RF-4C remained a risky, unforgiving challenge. Bombing halt or no bombing halt, Paris peace talks or no Paris peace talks, Hanoi's gunners did not hesitate to shoot. Many an RF-4C returned with battle damage. Early in the year, when the weather was excruciatingly poor, every step of a mission was fraught with peril. Once hit by AAA fire, with navigation systems damaged, a pilot faced a difficult job relocating a KC-135 tanker or coaxing his craft to its home base.

North Vietnam, of course, continued to hold that reconnaissance missions were 'provocative' and 'warlike.'

SR-71 BLACKBIRD

If a single reconnaissance aircraft annoyed the North Vietnamese more than any other, and fueled their argument that recce flights

Supplied by Michael France, a leading analyst of air combat over North Vietnam, this photograph shows RF-4C Phantom 69-350 of the 14 TRS/432 TRW, stationed at Udorn, Thailand, forming on a KC-135 tanker prior to a reconnaissance mission. Although actually taken at a later date, the photograph illustrates the sort of action which accompanied a recce mission during the 1969 bombing hiatus. (MICHAEL A. FRANCE)

were 'provocative,' it was the SR-71 Blackbird. There had always been a strategic reconnaissance job to be performed 'up North,' the role of the RC-135 having already been described, but the SR-71 was more than an American reconnaissance asset: it was, very arguably, the most spectacular aircraft in the world. While RF-101C, RF-8G and RF-4C aircraft came home with the on-site tactical intelligence needed by battlefield commanders, the SR-71 joined the RC-135 in obtaining photographs and other intelligence materials needed at the national policy level. A significant part of the strategic intelligence portfolio had belonged to the Central Intelligence Agency, which had developed the

The SR–71 strategic reconnaissance aircraft, operated by SAC, had an important role in gathering intelligence about happenings in North Vietnam. Because the SR–71 used a special fuel called JP–7, a specially-equipped variant of the Stratotanker, designated KC–135Q, was needed to refuel the recce platform. Although this view shows a refueling over the continental US, this 'team' paired up often during the fight against Hanoi. (USAF)

U–2 and the SR–71 Blackbird's predecessor, the A–12. It is understood that under the new Nixon administration, a 1969 decision took the CIA out of the strategic reconnaissance business and made the Strategic Air Command—which, of course, possessed the RC–135 and SR–71—solely responsible. A 'turf fight' must have preceded this decision. In any event, once the CIA withdrew, strategic recce assets belonged to SAC. Like the B–52 bombers and KC–135 tankers which played such an important role in the way, these assets never came under command of Seventh Air Force in Saigon.

The sleek SR–71 Blackbird was not merely spectacular. It was unique. A follow-up to the U–2, it was probably designed to be capable of overflying the Soviet Union, although incursions into Soviet territory were presumably banned since the undertaking given by President Eisenhower in 1960 following the shooting down of Francis Gary Powers' U–2 over Sverdlovsk. The new aircraft was originally developed with CIA funding in civilian form as the A–12, which is reported to have first flown in 1962; the military SR–71 first took to the air on 23 December 1964 and even its existence remained a secret for several years.

The SR–71 is powered by two 30,000 lb (13 610 kg) thrust Pratt & Whitney J58 engines which are simply monstrous in size and power. The air intake inlet cone on each engine is controlled by computer and the engines are radical in design: the engine shifts into another cycle at 2,000 mph (3 220 km/h), bypassing the conventional compressor to function as a ramjet.

Looking in dull black finish almost as if it should carry a cloak and dagger, this 'spook plane' entered Air Force inventory on 7 January 1966 with the delivery of an SR–71 (64-17956) to the 4200 Strategic Reconnaissance Wing at Beale Air Force Base, near Marysville in northern California. This wing later became the 9 SRW and has since been responsible for SR–71 operations including those carried out in North Vietnamese airspace by a detachment based at Kadena AB, Okinawa. Paul Crickmore, an authority on early development of the aircraft, says that the CIA's civilian A–12 variant also operated over North Vietnam until an incident on 5 June 1968 in which aircraft 932 and CIA pilot Jack Weeks were lost—*not*, it should be emphasized, as a result of North Vietnamese action. Indeed, no one in North Vietnam or anywhere else has ever succeeded in shooting down an A–12 or an SR–71.

Crickmore notes that the first mission of the military SR–71 in the combat theater was flown on 10 April 1968 by a 9 SRW pilot,

Major Jerome F. O'Malley. Almost nothing has been disclosed about sensors employed on these missions or about the targets covered, but it is assumed that cameras and ELINT (electronic intelligence) devices cut a wide swath across Hanoi's homeland. O'Malley, who had figured prominently in SR–71 development, later served in the Southeast Asia conflict with the 432 TRW at Udorn and ultimately became a four-star general, commanding Tactical Air Command, before his untimely death in the crash of a small transport in 1985. Other SR–71 pilots operating against North Vietnam became a kind of exclusive clique, identifying themselves by a shoulder patch with a picture of, and the word 'Habu'—a pit viper snake indigenous to Okinawa where the SR–71s were based at Kadena. It should be noted that collectors of military patches will approach these men in vain: the 'Habu' shoulder patch is never given out to anyone who has not actually flown the SR–71

Crickmore says that SR–71 recce missions over North Vietnam were reduced during the early months of the Nixon administration so as not to elicit protective reaction missions by ordnance-laden warplanes at a time when Nixon and Kissinger had hopes for negotiations. Later in 1969, SR–71 missions were apparently increased again.[51]

'UNDERSTANDING' ON RECONNAISSANCE

With the cessation of bombing of North Vietnam, there was supposed to be an understanding that the US would continue unarmed photo reconnaissance—primarily with tactical aircraft like the RF–101C rather than strategic platforms like the SR–71—to observe efforts by the North Vietnamese to move men and material into the South. It may have been, unfortunately, a one-sided 'understanding'. Still, the first reconnaissance missions were unarmed and flown without escort aircraft.

Once recce planes started falling victim to North Vietnam's formidable defenses, directives were issued to escort the photo planes with armed fighter-bombers. Colonel Ed Hillding's 469 TFS at Korat with its shark-teethed F–4E Phantoms drew this job more than once. US Navy F–4J Phantoms also appeared in the company of photo planes, heavily laden with ordnance. Normally, there were two to four fighter-bomber escorts for the recce plane, depending on the threat, the environment and anticipated hostile action.

The rules of engagement, or the specific instructions prescribing the conditions under which the fighter-bombers were authorized

to attack enemy targets, prohibited counter-action except when they, or the reconnaissance aircraft being escorted, were fired upon. Pursuant to these rules of engagement, the escort aircraft were required to have evidence that they or the reconnaissance aircraft were fired upon before they could attack the missile or anti-aircraft sites. This authority came to be known as 'protective reaction,' a term which the press attributed to Defense Secretary Laird.

The rules of engagement changed often. Over an extended period of time it was necessary continually to update and modify the rules depending upon the situation at a given time. For example, when the North Vietnamese attempted to move their MiG force farther south and position fighters at jet-capable fields near the DMZ in the Route Package One area, the rules of engagement were modified to 'loosen' the terms under which MiGs could be engaged. In addition to the escort aircraft protecting the recce plane from ground fire, it now became necessary to provide high-altitude MiGCAP cover as well. Likewise, the rules of engagement had to be revised when Hanoi introduced improved weaponry, such as a coordinated net of SAM and AAA sites centrally controlled from long range by a sophisticated version of the already familiar *Fan Song* radar. Thus, even during the bombing 'interlude', it was necessary to employ a standoff anti-radiation missile such as the Shrike of Standard ARM—carried by the F–105G, which had replaced the F–105F in the Wild Weasel role. The rules were changed to permit attacking the *Fan Song* radar/missile sites when they were 'activated against' the reconnaissance or escort aircraft. The US might not have been bombing the North, but all that changed the moment the North Vietnamese began tracking its aircraft on radar!

Despite repeated changes in the rules of engagement, the basic concept of 'protective reaction' remained constant from the start of the total bombing halt until a much later time, March 1972. The rationale for protective reaction strikes was gradually broadened, however, so that it encompassed action deemed necessary to protect the incremental US troop withdrawal from South Vietnam. President Nixon repeatedly threatened to increase the level of fighter-bomber activity over North Vietnam, although his pronouncements fell short of a warning that full-scale bombing might be resumed.

Three types of 'protective reaction' strikes were officially recognized within the rules of engagement during the bombing halt. Research by Brigadier General Gordon A. Ginsburg, used here with permission, defines these three categories of air action:

'"Type I" described the somewhat routine immediate protective reaction strikes which provided protection for the reconnaissance aircraft during their missions over North Vietnam. These were the strikes conducted by the two to four fighter-bomber aircraft assigned to escort a reconnaissance plane.

'"Type II" protective reaction strikes were also immediate strikes at enemy forces in North Vietnam, but conducted in support of US aircraft performing missions in Laos or South Vietnam. Admiral [Thomas] Moorer [Chairman of the Joint Chiefs of Staff] testified that this category of strikes was necessary to protect US aircraft from being fired upon by anti-aircraft or missiles just inside the North Vietnamese border because " . . . the enmey was not allowed to have a sanctuary where they.[sic] could sit across the line and fire away as they [sic] chose without getting a reaction from our planes."' [The internal quote is from subsequent House of Representatives hearings.]

'"Type III" strikes encompassed massive attacks and were described as "limited duration" or "reinforced" protective reaction strikes. Strikes of this type were pre-planned, pre-brief, specifically defined missions, authorized by higher authority on a one-time basis and were exceptions to the standing rules of engagement. Therefore, Type III strikes, although called "protective reaction", were not authorized within the rules of engagement for normal protective reaction strikes, but rather were conducted under a temporary suspension of the day-to-day rules.'[52]

Subsequent congressional hearings made it clear that Type III strikes were authorized at the highest level in Washington where President Nixon, adviser Kissinger and Secretary Laird played key roles in the decision-making process.

The existence of these strikes seemed to fly in the face of the official policy that North Vietnam was not being bombed. The situation aroused the ire of Senator Harold E. Hughes, who thought that his fellow congressmen and perhaps the American people were being fooled about what was going on. In hearings which took place much later than the 1969 time-frame—on 23 November 1971 —and refer to a later period, 1970–71, Senator Hughes spoke on the floor of the Senate:

'Although there has been a great deal of discussion about the air campaigns in Laos and Cambodia, I have noticed very little talk about the continued [since the bombing halt] air war against North Vietnam . . .

'Compared with the costs and severity of the air campaign in neighboring areas, the continued attacks on North Vietnam are not very significant.

'Type III limited duration, protective reaction air strike,' or something like that. The press and public wondered why it was not simply called bombing. F–4E Phantom II 67-309 of Colonel Edward Hilding's 469 TFS, based at Korat, Thailand, seems to be carrying everything but the kitchen sink as it heads into North Vietnam at a time when the US was not bombing North Vietnam. At least, not much. (USAF)

'But at a time when we are being told that the air war is winding down, the fact is that the air war in North Vietnam is being increased.

'So far this year [1971], there have been 82 so-called protective reaction strikes against North Vietnam. This figure is more than four times the 20 such strikes reported for all of 1970.

'In November [1971] alone, there have already been 13 such attacks. Admittedly, November is a month when infiltration normally increases and US attacks along the [Ho Chi Minh] trail can be expected to increase . . .

'No one can question the right of pilots who are attacked to defend themselves. But not all of these strikes have been in response to direct attacks, since the current rules of engagement give pilots the right to retaliate whenever [*Fan Song*] anti-aircraft radar "locks on" to their own planes.'

There was no doubt about it. Some US air action was taking place over North Vietnam. In the near future, it would emerge that not all of it was fully authorized!

NIXON POLICY

While reconnaissance crews shouldered the burden of missions over North Vietnam in mid-1969, the Nixon administration continued to seek what it called an honorable way out of a war which was unpopular at home and which obstructed White House foreign policy goals. Nixon and his increasingly dominant foreign policy advisor, Henry Kissinger, wanted to achieve detente with the Soviet Union and hoped to defrost the long cold winter of absolutely no contact with China. 'Vietnamization' might help to palliate protestors at home but only a negotiated

end to the war would help Nixon's plans for closer ties with Moscow and Peking.

On the domestic front, the good news was that Nixon seemed serious about reducing the US role in the war, thus undercutting some of the protest; the bad news was journalist Seymour Hersh's discovery of the 1969 My Lai massacre during which American soldiers wantonly murdered innocent civilians in a South Vietnamese village.

On the foreign front, Nixon's desire to ease tensions with the USSR and China seemed hampered by the absence of any progress in the stagnated Paris peace talks. My Lai, at least, was an isolated occurrence (and a minor

Principal concern of most Americans when Nixon took office was to 'bring home' men like this 1st Cavalry Division trooper, photographed using an M60 machine-gun in South Vietnam. Reconnaissance missions and peace talks continued, but Americans wanted to see visible results and Nixon met this need by announcing periodic troop reductions which brought the number of US servicemen in South Vietnam below 500,000. (US ARMY)

one, compared to Viet Cong atrocities) and homefront opinion was shored by Nixon's commitment to turn over a larger share of the fighting to South Vietnamese troops whilst gradually withdrawing Americans. (During 1969, Nixon announced troop cutbacks of 25,000 on 8 June, 25,000 more on 16 September, and 50,000 on 15 December, getting the total well below the 500,000 mark).

The Phantom had become the dominant tactical aircraft in the battle zone, the Navy and Marine Corps operating the F–4B and F–4J, the Air Force flying the F–4C, RF–4C, F–4D and F–4E. News releases from the period showed Phantoms carrying heavy bomb-loads on missions 'in Southeast Asia' —the closest anyone came to publicly admitting that, in addition to the continuing struggle in South Vietnam, American fliers were operating in Laos.

On 6 March 1969, the first F–4C Phantom to be processed through the Pacer Wave potting compound replacement program was readied at Yokota AB, Japan. The program had been undertaken the previous year when it was discovered that the original potting compound used in Phantom cannon plugs and aircraft electrical systems had such a low melting point that high ambient temperatures at the Southeast Asia bases caused it to liquefy and drain, thus causing electrical short-circuiting.

Also in March 1969, PACAF's first F–4C Wild Weasel aircraft arrived at Yokota AB and was assigned to the 347 TFW. Within two months, Wild Weasel Phantoms were in place in Japan at Yokota and Misawa and had undergone the Pacer Wave treatment. Thirty-six F–4Cs were modified for the Wild Weasel electronic warfare role, rendering them able to carry Shrike missiles for action against SAM sites. They could be distinguished externally by a small antenna 'bump' on the fuselage side above the wing root. It was not yet time, but the Phantom Wild Weasels of the 67 TFS / 18 TFW located at Kadena AB, Okinawa, would eventually fight over North Vietnam, performing the same anti-SAM mission as the F–100F, F–105F and F–105G.

The AGM–12E Bullpup, a modified version of the earlier AGM–12B with a cluster warhead, was introduced into Southeast Asia combat, almost certainly in action in Laos, on 9 April 1969. The new missile was employed by the F–4 Phantom wings at Da Nang and Udorn.

AC–130 HERCULES GUNSHIP

In early 1969, an additional AC–130A Hercules was ferried to Wright-Patterson AFB,

Ohio for the next step in the continuing development of the fixed-wing gunship which was now nicknamed Spectre. Under Project Surprise Package, this AC–130A was modified with two 40 mm Bofors cannon in place of the previously-used aft pack of 20 mm guns. Miniguns previously mounted in the gunship were now deleted. Among new sensors added for night missions over the Ho Chi Minh Trail was the General Electric ASQ–145 Low-Light Level Television (LLLTV), to complement the forward-looking infra-red (FLIR) already employed. FLIR and LLL-TV would literally turn night into day for Spectre crews, while a new target computer enabled the AC–130A to 'lock on' and maintain a fix on the moving enemy. The AC–130A could orbit above North Vietnamese convoys and pour down a continuous barrage of firepower with devastating accuracy.

The AC–130 gunship worked effectively as part of a 'hunter killer' team when operating in conjunction with F–4D Phantoms from the 497 TFS / 8 TFW at Ubon or B–26K Invaders from the SOS at Nakhon Phanom. Said Hercules pilot Curt Messex: 'We just loved working over the trail with the B–26Ks from Naked Fanny. They moved at about the same speed as us, carried an inexhaustible amount of ordnance, and could roam over the Trail with us all night long. They were professionals, every one of them, and they were always ready to take on the other guys in a fight.' It is thought that the B–26Ks, which were eventually withdrawn from action later in 1969, simply wore out from accumulating too many airframe hours. When working with Phantoms, the AC–130 gunships used lasers to illuminate targets for F–4Ds carrying precision-guided munitions (PGM)— 'smart' bombs. AC–130s attacking North Vietnamese truck convoys were often engaged by anti-aircraft or SAM batteries which, in turn, came under attack from the escorting F–4Ds.

One of the original batch of AC–130A gunships (54-1629) was hit over Laos on 24 May 1969 and crashed at Ubon, killing two crewmen. Introduction of the more advanced AC–130E would have to wait for the following year, but there was no doubt that the gunarmed Hercules had proven a potent weapon against North Vietnamese infiltration.

RETURN TO NORTH VIETNAM

On 5 June 1969, North Vietnamese AAA batteries hit an RF–4C Phantom (66-0388) from the 11 TRS / 432 TRW at Udorn. The reconnaissance aircraft limped out of North Vietnam and crashed at sea. In retaliation,

the Nixon administration ordered the first air strikes into North Vietnam since the end of ROLLING THUNDER under a different President eight months earlier. Apparently, a limited number of strikes by Air Force and Navy aircraft were carried out against AAA, SAM and radar sites associated with the shootdown of the recce Phantom. Carrier-based Navy aircraft continued to handle a major part of the reconnaissance commitment over North Vietnam; the production line for the RA–5C Vigilante was re-opened and a number of RF–8A Crusaders were brought up to RF–8G standard. But the Air Force's ageing and corrosion-prone RF–101C Voodoo remained the principal tactical recce asset 'up North', the RF–4C Phantom only gradually replacing it. Strategic reconnaissance by RC–135s, SR–71s and other platforms continued at a reduced level, the aircraft following flight paths tailored to avoid any accusation by Hanoi that it was being provoked.

On 8 June 1969, President Nixon met with South Vietnam's President Thieu at Midway Island to discuss the conflict. General Abrams, the US field commander in South Vietnam, was also present. It can be assumed that the American side at these discussions pushed hard for further progress in 'Vietnamization', while the Thieu party asked for further military aid to make it possible for the South Vietnamese to assume more of the burden in the conflict. It was at this meeting that Nixon made one of his periodic announcements of a US troop withdrawal, 25,000 men in this instance.

A speech at Guam on 25 July 1969 by President Nixon formalized the Vietnamization concept and was touted as a landmark shift in US policy. The Nixon Doctrine, enunciated for the first time, held that while the US would continue to honor its defense commitments, it would look to its Asian allies to provide the bulk of the manpower for their own defense. This was to have important consequences for other Asian countries, including Korea, but in Vietnam it meant the firmest emphasis on 'Vietnamization' so that improved capability by South Vietnamese forces would permit a gradual withdrawal of US troops.

The eventual result would be a South Vietnam fully capable of defending itself, the US presence being reduced to token air cover and ultimately withdrawn altogether. South Vietnam would survive as an independent state—the original purpose of the US involvement—and Americans would no longer be dying far from home.

Bureaucrats in Washington set forth to make the Nixon Doctrine work. Progress in Vietnamization had to be reported regularly at all levels in the military and civilian departments of the administration. Vietnamization was the ideal solution, for it would solve the American dilemma no matter what the North Vietnamese chose to do.

To a critic, the Nixon Doctrine amounted to recognition of a simple truth—that demonstrations and protests at home had finally turned the bulk of the population, that more Americans now opposed the war than supported it. A way out had to be found and Vietnamization was a way out. At last, the US would solve its problem as Senator George Aiken of Vermont had proposed years earlier—by announcing that it had won and getting out; but Vietnamization was a gradual process, unlikely to satisfy protestor and average citizen alike who could not wait. Opponents of the US presence in Vietnam had reduced their demand to two words: 'Out now!' Nixon was in fact not merely surrendering to the war's opponents, nor was he seeking to create a fiction that would permit a withdrawal. He genuinely expected, wanted and intended to bring South Vietnam up to the point where it could defend itself.

On 15 August 1969, Secretary of Defense Melvin R. Laird issued new mission statements for US forces in South Vietnam. The new missions, formalizing the Nixon Doctrine, were to assist the South Vietnamese armed forces to take over an increasing share of combat operations. The stated objective sounded familiar—to permit the people of South Vietnam to determine their future without outside interference. To men in Washington, making decisions about a country thousands of miles away, it was North Vietnam, not the US, which constituted the 'outside interference'. The real purpose was to permit a withdrawal of US troops and the initial pullout of a small increment of American soldiers, Operation Keystone Eagle, was quickly completed by 29 August. The second phase of withdrawals ordered by Nixon on 16 September, Operation Keystone Cardinal, called for removing 35,000 troops. A third round would cover 50,000 more.

In August 1969, the North Vietnamese prematurely released three prisoners of war. This was to happen on three occasions, a total of nine men gaining their freedom early. With one exception (a 19-year-old enlisted sailor who had fallen overboard from a US Navy warship and floated ashore in North Vietnam), the premature releases did not have the approval of the POW wing commander, Colonel John Flynn. Other POWs have accused the remaining eight men of failing to resist their captors as staunchly as they might. Nevertheless, the men who were released confirmed American fears that the remaining POWs were being subjected to brutal and inhumane treatment.

HO CHI MINH DIES

On 4 September 1969, North Vietnam announced the death of Ho Chi Minh at age 79. Ho had been the moving force behind the struggle by the Vietnamese communists for so long that it seemed difficult to imagine events continuing without him. In fact, Ho had been ill for some time. Leadership in North Vietnam passed to party head Le Duan and Prime Minister Pham Van Dong.

One measure of the continuing intensity of the conflict was the fact that 37 F-4D Phantoms were lost in combat in 1969, only six less than in the previous year when they had been flying against the North. On 20 September 1969, an F-4D Phantom of the 366 TFW collided with a DC-4 of Air Vietnam near Da Nang AB. The airliner crashed, killing all 75 persons on board and two on the ground, but the F-4D pilot landed successfully after his back-seater had ejected.

On 8 October 1969, Souvanna Phouma, the neutralist premier of Laos, requested increased American aid to meet pressure from North Vietnamese forces operating in his country. The request drew almost no public notice, like the continued bombing missions being flown in that country.

Also in October 1969, the Canberra bomber absented itself from the war scene. The 8 TBS inactivated and its B-57s were ferried to the continental US for storage. B-57s had been among the first US aircraft to deploy to Vietnam and the departure of these airframes left no American Canberras in the war zone, although Tropic Moon B-57G aircraft would return a year later on 15 September 1970.

On 21 October 1969, the first six jet-assisted AC-119K gunships of the 18 SOS began arriving in Southeast Asia. The AC-119K was intended to be an improvement over the AC-119G aircraft already in operation. The AC-119G, or Shadow, employed 7.62 mm miniguns while the AC-119K, or Stinger, mounted 20 mm cannons. The latter was to prove effective against North Vietnamese truck convoys and sampans. Both were considered highly vulnerable to ground fire and were usually escorted during missions into the Laotian infiltration routes by F-4D Phantoms.

In another October move, the 44 TFS moved from Korat to Takhli, thus ending the presence of the F-105 at the former base and concentrating all Southeast Asia F-105 assets at the latter.

Among other Air Force changes in 1969: The 37 TFW at Phu Cat AB was inactivated on 31 March 1969, while the 12 TFW wing designator was moved from Cam Ranh Bay AB to Phu Cat, signalling the latter airfield's shift from F-100D Super Sabre to F-4D Phantom aircraft. The 41 TEWS at Udorn

was inactivated on 31 October 1969 and its EB-66 aircraft were redistributed to other units or returned to the US. During November, detachments of F-102A Delta Dagger aircraft at Udorn and Da Nang—never really significant participants in the conflict—were withdrawn. The 609 SOS operating the B-26K Invader at Nakhon Phanom was inactivated in November and its aircraft returned to the US the following month. Finally, the US presence at Nha Trang AB, where the 'Green Hornet' Huey helicopters of the 20 SOS had operated, was ended entirely—another step towards Vietnamization, the airfield being employed solely by South Vietnamese units.

On 15 November 1969, massive anti-war demonstrations were held in the US. Opponents of the war made it clear that Vietnamization was not enough; they would settle for nothing less than a complete American withdrawal. On 15 December, President Nixon announced that an additional 50,000 Americans would be withdrawn from South Vietnam over a four-month period.

YEAR-END WRAPUP

As a measure of the low level of operations directed against the North during the long bombing halt, figures showed that during 1969 only 779 combat sorties were flown over North Vietnam by USAF aircraft, as compared with 966,949 in all of Southeast Asia. (The larger figure included 19,498 Arc Light strikes flown by B-52s in Laos and South Vietnam.) Ever adept with numbers, PACAF headquarters also had figures to show that the South Vietnamese were shouldering more of the burden of their own defense. During the final six months of calendar 1969, USAF strength in Southeast Asia was reduced from 96,372 to 92,086, which some handy sliderule expert calculated was a personnel reduction of 4.4 per cent. Wrapping up the year, it was noted that USAF losses for the year were 294, 97 fewer than in 1968, though it was not stated how many of these occurred over North Vietnam. Total USAF losses in Southeast Asia were now 1,783. Given the 'body count' mentality which caused Americans to be mesmerized by numbers—none of the figures just cited can be precisely accurate—it was unavoidable that some master of precision would decide that the value of the lost aircraft was not a penny more or less than $2,254,948,000.

One number which really meant something: For the first time, figures proved that the war was winding down. By 31 December 1969, the number of US troops in South Vietnam had been reduced to 474,000.

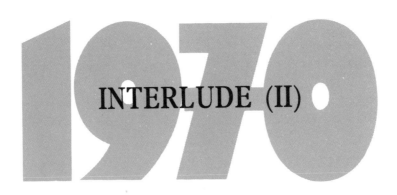

1970 INTERLUDE (II)

It was a long slow torment for the men held prisoner by Hanoi. Another year began in which no US warplanes flew over North Vietnam—well, almost none. The war continued. Neither side appeared to be making dramatic progress.

An F–105G Thunderchief (63-8329) of the 44 TFS/355 TFW at Takhli was on a 'protective reaction' mission into North Vietnam when it was shot down on 28 January 1969. An HH–53C helicopter orbiting over Laos and awaiting clearance to enter North Vietnam to pick up the downed crew suddenly came to quick and unexpected grief. In the first encounter with a MiG since the bombing halt and perhaps the first MiG incursion into Laos, a MiG–21 shot down the HH–53C with an air-to-air missile. This is believed to

be the only instance of a helicopter being downed by a fighter in this manner.

On 1 February 1970, it was noted that a more fortunate Thud, F–105D Thunderchief (61-0159) of the 354 TFS/355 TFW at Takhli had more than 4,000 airframe hours and 600 combat missions to its credit—more than any other F–105 in the USAF. It was nicknamed *Have Gun Will Travel*, the name appearing on the fuselage below the cockpit, and was credited with a MiG kill.

On 18 March 1970, Cambodia's Prince Norodom Sihanouk was ousted by his premier, General Lon Nol. The Department of Defense revealed that prior to March 1970, the USAF had secretly carried out 3,630 B–52 strikes in Cambodia. Sihanouk's ouster apparently did little to reduce North Vietnamese influence in Cambodia. Behind the scenes, Nixon administration officials debated the idea of a move into Cambodia to 'clean out' Hanoi's sanctuaries in that country.

The first MiG kill in nearly two years occurred when USS *Constellation* (CVA–64) launched another round of 'protective reaction' strikes into North Vietnam on 28 March 1970. Lt Jerome E. Beaulier of the 'Ghostriders' of squadron VF-142 was at the con-

trols of an F–4J Phantom (155875) with Lt Stephen J. Barkley in the back seat. Beaulier used an AIM–9 Sidewinder missile to despatch a MiG–21.

The 12 TFW at Phu Cat AB in South Vietnam was now fully operational in the F–4D Phantom and was eventually to have the peculiar distinction of operating in all four countries of Indochina—South Vietnam, North Vietnam, Laos and Cambodia. Like the other Phantom units scattered around the region and on board carriers at sea, its pilots kept hoping that something would change to give them a crack at a MiG. It did not, during 1970, but the 12 TFW became especially effective in the air-to-ground 'mud-moving' part of the war.

On 4 April, 50,000 people gathered in Washington to protest President Nixon's conduct of the war. Their numbers would have been higher had they known what was coming next. The talk of 'flushing out' North Vietnamese bastions in Cambodia turned to action on 29 April when 12,000 South Vietnamese troops and their American advisors attacked Cambodia at the region known as the Parrot's Beak. By 1 May 1970, the Cambodia 'incursion' had become, in fact, a full-scale invasion. On 2 May 1970, the USAF lost its first aircraft in Cambodia, this being an F–4D Phantom (65-0607) of the 480 TFS/ 12 TFW at Phu Cat. The action in Cambodia seemed to strike a raw nerve in the American body politic: soon, massive anti-war demonstrations were taking place all over the United States, these being by far the largest protests since Nixon had taken office.

On 9 May 1970, an estimated 75,000 to 100,000 demonstrators gathered in Washington to oppose the Cambodia involvement. The protests were exacerbated by the fatal shooting of four Kent State University students by members of the Ohio National Guard during a campus demonstration against the war. Demonstrations soon spread to some 400 campuses. The Nixon administration stayed with its public position that it was necessary to eradicate North Vietnamese sanctuaries along the Cambodian-South Vietnam border and the operations continued.

In 1970, the 12 TFW at Phu Cat AB, South Vietnam, became another user of the F–4D Phantom. Here, F–4D 66-7591 of the 389 TFS/12 TFW sits in the arming area at Phu Cat loaded with six 500 lb (227 kg) high-drag bombs and three napalm tanks. This was a typical payload for operations in South Vietnam, but a time would come when Phantoms would have to return to the North. (NORMAN TAYLOR)

ENTER THE A-7E

The A-7E variant of the Navy's Corsair II attack aircraft, powered by a 14,250 lb (6465 kg) thrust TF41-A-2 turbofan and equipped with improved throttles and armed with an M61A1 Vulcan 20 mm cannon, offered something no other aircraft had yet been able to provide: the pilot knew his exact longitude and latitude on Earth, precisely to the foot. The navigation and weapons delivery system (NWDS) on the A-7E was the most advanced of its time, and the A-7E also seemed to be a Corsair with enough power, free of the steam-ingestion problems encountered by the underpowered A-7A and A-7B variants. The first squadrons to employ the A-7E variant on an operational basis were the 'Blue Diamonds' of VA-146 and the 'Argonauts' of VA-147 under Commander Wayne L. Stephens and Commander Robert N. Livingston. They took the new aircraft aboard USS *America* (CVA-66), an east coast/Atlantic Fleet carrier which was about to handle its share of the burden in the combat theater.

America transited the Panama Canal and made the Pacific crossing to Dixie Station, off the coast of South Vietnam. On 26 May 1970, LtJg Dave Lichtermann of VA-146 was catapulted from *America*'s deck in the first A-7E to be launched in combat. The Diamonds' skipper followed and led a strafing attack against a Viet Cong emplacement. An hour later, Livingston and Lcdr Thomas

Gravely of the Argonauts rolled in on an enemy supply route to deliver the first bombs dropped in anger by the A-7E. There would be no action 'up North' for these squadrons at this juncture but the A-7E would eventually have its day over North Vietnam, too.

On 5 June 1970, another new aircraft type reached the Southeast Asia battle zone. The Military Airlift Command's first mission with the C-5A Galaxy transport ended with the aircraft's safe arrival at Cam Ranh Bay. Two months later, a C-5A Air Transportable Loading Dock was placed in operation at Cam Ranh Bay. Though it would never fight 'up North,' the C-5A played a vital role in ferrying supplies to the men who did.

On 15 June 1970, the final Blind Bat flaredrop mission by a C-130A Hercules was flown in Laos. The C-130A aircraft assigned to this mission were transferred to Naha AB, Okinawa, ending another of the many roles performed by the Hercules type during the conflict.

On 29 June 1970, US ground troops were withdrawn from Cambodia, the Nixon administration insisting that the men's job was finished and that it was not bowing to protest. Operations over Cambodia by Air Force and Navy aircraft would continue. On that same date, almost unnoticed with Cambodia on the front-pages of newspapers, the Joint Chiefs of Staff put in writing a summary of the rules of engagement which indicated when, and

whether, US aircraft could attack targets in North Vietnam. Secretary Laird's 'limited duration, protective reaction' air strike could be carried out only if reconnaissance flights were engaged or were about to be engaged by SAM sites. The language may not have seemed important at the time but it was to be crucial to events surrounding a future Seventh Air Force commander two years hence:

'JCS in their message of 29 June 1970 restated the authority [of field commanders] as fighter aircraft, including Iron Hand, were authorized to strike any SAM anti-aircraft artillery site in North Vietnam below 20 degrees north which fired at *or was activated against* US aircraft continuing missions over Laos or North Vietnam. This authority was limited to immediate protective reaction. No subsequent retaliation was authorized.' [53]

On 1 September 1970, at Seventh Air Force headquarters in Saigon, General George Brown was replaced as the ranking airman in by General Lucius D. Clay, Jr. One

---

On 13 July 1970, a pilot of the 'Blue Diamonds' of attack squadron VA-146 catches the wire with its tailhook aboard the carrier USS *America* (CVA-66) at Dixie Station off South Vietnam. *America* took into battle the first two squadrons to employ the A-7E Corsair II, which had improved engine, navigation system and armament as compared with earlier A-7A and A-7B models. (LTV)

It would never fly in North Vietnam, but it helped those who did. The C–5A Galaxy was the United States' largest transport aircraft and could carry enormous amounts of materiel into the war zone. Introduced to Southeast Asia on 5 June 1970, the aircraft type is exemplified by this C–5A transport (68-0222) of the 437 MAW, which flew numerous support missions into Saigon. (LOCKHEED)

With the A–7E Corsair and A–6A Intruder aboard its carriers in Vietnamese waters, the US Navy had a formidable attack force capable of operating at long range, in all weather. Taken two years after the initial combat deployment of this squadron, this photograph shows an A–7E Corsair (156833) of the 'Argonauts' of VA–147 keeping up the pace with an accompanying Intruder. (USN)

of Clay's first duties was to welcome the crews of two helicopters who had gotten to the fighting the hard way.

A week earlier, on 24 August 1970, the first trans-Pacific helicopter flight was completed by two HH–53C helicopters of the 37 ARRS. The two aircraft were ferried from Eglin AFB, Florida, to Da Nang. Two HC–130N Hercules accompanied the helicopters, providing no fewer than *thirteen* aerial refuellings during the 9,000 mile (14 485 km) flight. It was a slow way to get two helicopters to war, but it was also a unique accomplishment.

As the combat cruise of USS *America* (CVA–66) continued in mid-1970, pilots gained experience with the A–6C Intruder, a new variant of the all-weather attack craft which had already proven so successful. The A–6C incorporated the TRIM feature (Trails, Roads, Interdiction Multi-Sensor) with large wing-mounted pods containing electro-optical sensors. A video display available to the second crewman on the A–6C, the bombardier-navigator (B/N), assisted in the detection and identification of targets along infiltration routes. Also on board *America* was the KA–6D Intruder tanker aircraft which has already been cited as one of the unsung achievements of the war.

The USAF's 13 TBD returned to Southeast Asia on 15 September 1970 with Tropic Moon B–57Gs for night and all-weather interdiction. The squadron was based at Ubon and immediately began flying against North Vietnamese supply routes.

The earlier consolidation of F–105 assets at Takhli was 'undone' in September 1970 when Detachment 1, 12 TFS moved to Korat from Takhli with six F–105G Wild Weasel aircraft. The unit was given a new provisional designation as the 6010th Wild Weasel Squadron two months later on 1 November 1970. In the meanwhile, all F–4C Phantom Wild Weasel aircraft were temporarily consolidated in the 80 TFW at Yokota AB, Japan.

IGLOO WHITE PROGRESS

The *Igloo White* program aimed at seeding the Ho Chi Minh Trail with sensors remained an exceedingly important effort. The second attempt to introduce a Beech aircraft as a signals relay craft proved less than fully successful, however. Five improved Beech QU–22B aircraft arrived at Nakhon Phanom and began operations with Detachment 1, 533 TRW, flying in relay orbit on 1 October 1970. Engine problems temporarily grounded the QU–22B fleet almost immediately. Recovery efforts were begun to get the aircraft back on flying status and to use them to replace the ageing EC–121R Super Constellation relay aircraft, but it was not to be.

It soon developed that the 27 QU–22B aircraft (69-7693/7705; 70-1535/1548) were not

effective as unmanned drones, which was the way the Air Force planned to use them to relay signals from sensors on the Trail. The Beech aircraft required a pilot and systems operator and, still, results were so disappointing that the EC–121Rs were retained.

In yet another shift of the Thud population, on 10 December 1970, the 355 TFW and its associated units inactivated at Takhli. This brought an end to combat operations by the following squadrons, with their respective tailcodes: 41 TEWS (RC); 44 TFS (RE); 333 TFS (RK); 364 TFS (RM); and 357 TFS (RU). All had become familiar in the war waged by the F–105 Thunderchief, and it all ended with a flyover by twelve aircraft, with most of the wing's airframes being sent back to McConnell AFB, Kansas. The only Thuds remaining in the combat zone were the F–105G Wild Weasels of the 12 TFS at Korat.

The Voodoo was next to leave Southeast Asia. The 45 TRS, which had first brought its RF–101Cs to Vietnam as long ago as November 1961 and which now had an AH tailcode, departed Tan Son Nhut on 16 November 1970. The RF–101C airframes went to the Air National Guard unit at Meridian, Mississippi. It had been a long time in coming, but the RF–4C Phantom II was now to become the principal USAF tactical recce platform.

SON TAY RAID

Just before midnight, 20 November 1970, secretive new arrivals at Udorn clambered aboard two C–130E Combat Talon transports, five HH–53C helicopters and a sole HH–3E. They took off and flew through heavy darkness on a course for the Son Tay prison 28 miles (40 km) northwest of Hanoi.

The C–130 Hercules performed so many jobs in Southeast Asia that the end of the Blind Bat flare-drop commitment on 15 June 1970 was but one of many milestones. C–130A Hercules 56-543, nicknamed *Ashiya Queen* of the 374 TAW, is seen arriving at NAS Atsugi, Japan, in January 1970. This particular 'Herk' had an unusual history: turned over to the South Vietnamese Air Force in November 1972, it later reverted to USAF inventory—apparently as a result of being flown out at the end. (VIA JERRY GEER)

RF-101C Voodoo 56-0096 of the 45 TRS/460 TRW stationed at Tan Son Nhut but seen at Da Nang in 1967. Some time after this photograph was taken, the squadron's Voodoos began to wear an 'AH' tail-code. Withdrawal of the 45 TRS on 16 November 1970 left the RF-4C Phantom as the natural replacement for the Voodoo in the tactical reconnaissance role. (VIA JERRY GEER)

A massive operation was under way, refuelled by KC–135s and other Hercules, escorted by Skyraiders, Phantoms and Thuds, and helped out by a finely-orchestrated and wholly diversionary Alpha Strike by Navy Skyhawks, Intruders and Phantoms on targets around Haiphong.

The night strikes around Haiphong were aggressive and furious but they were solely to distract. At Son Tay, the elite helicopter-borne assault force intended to pull off a dramatic rescue of more than 100 Americans being held as prisoners of war. It was a remarkable undertaking and a measure of a nation's commitment to its prisoners.

Under Brigadier General Leroy J. Manor, the Son Tay raid was launched by men pulled from Army and Air Force assignments around the world and trained in utmost secrecy in the remote swamp ranges at Eglin AFB, Florida. For the actual mission, among other aircraft types, they would need just one HH–3E—no more, no less. The type was scheduled to be phased out of Southeast Asia at year's end, so providing one with a second as a backup, was no simple matter. When he flew with the 37 ARRS crew that ferried an HH–3E from Da Nang to Udorn for undisclosed purpose, MSgt James Muelchi had not the slightest clue what the helicopter would be used for. Nor was any clue given as to the reason for sudden tent cities at Udorn as newcomers streamed into the base. They were coming from *somewhere*, but—well, no one was allowed to know it was Eglin.

The secrecy around Udorn was all-consuming. For months, the members of the raiding force had trained under such a cloak of confidentiality that no radio transmissions or written communications were allowed. Unable to use the Pentagon's worldwide communications network, Manor selected his on-the-scene strike force commander, Army Ranger Colonel Arthur (Bull) Simons, by traveling to Fort Bragg, North Carolina to see him personally.

Reconnaissance coverage of the Son Tay camp, apparently including SR–71 photography, had indicated continuing activity. No one could know that because of flooding which had ruined the camp's water supply and as part of a relocation effort ironically aimed at improving prisoner treatment, North Vietnam had in fact closed down the Son Tay camp. As much as four months ago, on 14 July 1970, the POWs at Son Tay had been packed up and moved to other prisons. A cadre of guards remained, some North Vietnamese troops were billeted at the camp and the absence of Americans was not a fact that lent itself to easy detection by the photographic interpreters. More than 115 aircraft and a thousand men were covering a night penetration of North Vietnam in utmost secrecy to assault an ex-prison camp for the purpose of rescuing prisoners who were not there.

One of the HH–53C Super Jolly Green helicopters went slightly off course when pilot Major Frederick M. Donohue made a courageous decision to ignore a warning light telling him (inaccurately, as he gambled) of a transmission failure. Donohue's gunners opened up on guard towers when he discovered that he had overshot the camp and was approaching the adjacent North Vietnamese sapper school. The sole HH–3E, intended to crash-land in the center of the POW camp while the HH–53Cs surrounded

it on the outside, began by landing in the wrong place. The HH–3E lifted up again but another HH–53C set down and disgorged some of Bull Simons' assault troops in the wrong place. The result was a fire fight at the sapper school which, according to some participants, killed Russian advisors as well as North Vietnamese troops.

Finally, the attack force got to the right place. Donohue flew his HH–53C across the camp raking its guard towers with his 7.62 mm GAU–2A/B miniguns. The HH–3E dropped into the camp's center courtyard, wrecked beyond repair as had been expected. Assault troops fanned from the HH–3E to seize the initial advantage inside the camp. An officer used a bullhorn to shout, 'Keep down! We're Americans!' No POWs were present to hear him.

While the fire fight was unfolding—the only time American troops fought on the ground deep inside North Vietnam—the Navy diversions were wreaking havoc with Hanoi's defense net. A–4F Skyhawks of the 'Warhorses' of VA–55 from USS *Hancock* (CVA–19) were tearing up vehicles and truck parks near Cape Mui Ron. Other carrier-based aircraft ranged over Haiphong, their crews unaware that they were drawing attention away from the raid. In fact, one naval aviator recalls knowing that 'something was going on' on the far side of Hanoi 'but none of us had been briefed on what it was all about'.

Inside the prison, two-man assault teams systematically cleared each cell block.

Two of the key participants in the Son Tay night raid aimed at freeing US prisoners were the HC–130 Hercules and the HH–3E Jolly Green helicopter. Only one HH–3E was employed on the rescue attempt, and was deliberately crashed in the courtyard of the prison to enable assault troops to immediately reach cell blocks. (LOCKHEED)

A-4F Skyhawk 154205 (foreground) of the 'War-horses' of squadron VA-55 from *Hancock*, is typical of the aircraft which attacked targets around Haiphong on the night of 20 November 1970. While only *Hancock*'s carrier battle group skipper knew it at the time, the men were creating a diversion for the dramatic attempt to rescue prisoners of war at Son Tay, near Hanoi. (USN)

Simons' men broke in on the camp commander and killed him in his bed. Less than a half hour from the beginning of the raid, the assault troops blew up what remained of the HH-3E and withdrew in the HH-53C helicopters. Belatedly, SAMs flew through the night around the covering force. Two Thuds took near misses from SAM explosions. One limped out of the combat zone and recovered at Udorn. The other F-105G Wild Weasel (62-4436) from the Korat-based 12 TFS/388 TFW could not make it back. The crew ejected over Laos.

A night-fighter, apparently a MiG-21, stalked the HH-53C piloted by Lt Col. Royal H. Brown, fired a heat-seeking *Atoll* missile at the helicopter, and missed. Brown's and another HH-53C were delayed on the way home by a complex and ultimately successful effort to recover the crew of the F-105G.

Eventually, Manor's entire force came home. Had the POWs been at Son Tay, they would have been rescued. The assault force pulled off an incredibly tricky mission deep inside North Vietnam at night, inflicted

heavy casualties and suffered no serious wounds and no one killed. The raid forced the North Vietnamese to concentrate the POWs in three central locations, a move said to have improved prisoner morale. So although the POWs were not there to be rescued, the raid was in many respects a success.

It is widely written that when American POWs learned of the Son Tay raid, they were heartened and their morale shot up. This does not seem to be true. Major Kenneth W. Cordier, already a prisoner for nearly four years, was thrown into the depths of despair. Cordier viewed the Son Tay raid as evidence of American desperation. 'The raid convinced me that there was no hope we would ever get out of North Vietnam. They would only attempt such a rescue mission if there was no other way—and, of course, it wouldn't work twice.' Cordier and his fellow POWs continued to suffer. No such ambitious attempt was mounted again.

AC-130E GUNSHIP

To continue developments with the AC-130A Hercules gunship, nine further AC-130A aircraft, converted by E-Systems under a program nicknamed Pave Pronto, introduced the 'Black Crow' sensor, which could detect radiation emissions from a truck's ignition system. The Pave Pronto AC-130A aircraft began to arrive in Southeast Asia

during December 1970. Their new 'gadget' was only the latest in the seemingly endless attempts to use technology as a means of targeting North Vietnamese infiltration convoys. Meanwhile, the original batch of AC-130A airframes, fatigued by nightly missions into North Vietnam and later Laos, were returned to the United States.

Also during December 1970, six EB-66 aircraft deployed to Korat to augment the 42 TEWS/388 TFW and more F-105G Wild Weasels were added to the squadron which had originally been the 12 TFS but was now the 6010 WWS. A total of twelve F-105G aircraft were now stationed at Korat. An official history makes it clear that the additional EB-66 and F-105G assets were needed to support B-52 Arc Light operations in Cambodia. Flying and fighting over Cambodia would continue—indeed, it would continue beyond the end of this story of the war against North Vietnam—but little was said about it publicly.

YEAR-END WRAPUP

US Navy carrier-based aircraft logged a total of 86,000 missions during the calendar year 1970, the overwhelming majority of which were in South Vietnam. Figures were not kept for land-based US Marine aircraft at Da Nang, Chu Lai and elsewhere, but the Marines continued to play an important role in the overall conflict—if not in operations 'up North'. Marine A-4E Skyhawks, A-6A Intruders and F-4B Phantoms, the last-named soon to be replaced by the F-4J, were maintained and operated under some of the most difficult conditions in Southeast Asia, yet their loss figures were no higher than those of the other services. The Marines lost only four F-4B Phantoms in combat during the year, one of which collided with a Vietnamese air force O-1 Bird Dog. The First Marine Aircraft Wing, headquartered at MCAS Iwakuni, Japan, had overseen the operations of Marine Air Group Twelve since the beginning of the conflict. Major General Frank C. Lang, one of the commanders of the 1st MAW during this period, notes that his men had to 'make do' when supplies were needed or equipment was not available. 'We did not have the same enormous support system that was available to the other services. We had a higher proportion of [people who were] fighters and a lower proportion of administrative types. We sometimes had to do a fair amount of improvisation to keep our Phantoms flying.'[54]

The US Air Force in 1970 flew a total of 711,440 combat sorties throughout Southeast Asia, a significant reduction from the

previous year's aggregate of 966,949. Nearly 30,000 sorties were flown in Cambodia. B–52 Arc Light sorties added up to 15,103, of which 1,292 were in Cambodia. Those who keep the numbers noted that 774.2 thousand tons of air munitions were expended. During 1970, total US Air Force resources in the Pacific region, namely those which fell under PACAF headquarters, had been reduced by 19 tactical squadrons, 500 aircraft and 32,000 personnel, the bulk of this reflecting the Nixon administration's clear intent to whittle down the US presence in South Vietnam.

During 1970, 171 USAF aircraft were lost in Southeast Asia, 127 in combat and 44 to operational causes. The number-keepers had

it that 1,950 USAF aircraft had now been lost in the conflict altogether, representing a cost of $2.5 billion. Hanoi's figures for US aircraft destroyed were far, far higher and were even less credible than some of the American statistics which, so often, invited debate.

Significant progress had been made in 1970 towards getting the South Vietnamese air force to handle more of the burden of the fighting in the South. By 31 December 1970, the Vietnamese air force had 728 aircraft in 30 squadrons. Saigon's air arm would never be able to operate against the high-density defenses of the North, however, and the feeling was growing that another round of fighting awaited in the North. 'You have this year

By 1970, the EF–10B Skyknight had been replaced by the EA–6A Intruder as the principal Marine Corps electronic warfare aircraft in Southeast Asia. This EA–6A Intruder (156989) and all others in the combat theater were operated by Marine Composite Reconnaissance Squadron One (VMCJ–1), under the First Marine Aircraft Wing, headquartered at MCAS Iwakuni, Japan. (USMC)

to do as you like,' ran a line from Hemingway. 'But the year after that, or the year after that, they will fight.'

On 31 December, Congress repealed the Gulf of Tonkin resolution which had made it all possible to begin with. US troop strength in South Vietnam stood at 335,800.

PROTECTIVE REACTION

Still, the skies above the 17th Parallel were devoid of US warplanes except for the reconnaissance aircraft which continued to tweak Hanoi's defenses; still, the American prisoners of war in North Vietnam waited, many of them now in despair that their seemingly interminable captivity would ever end; still, the publicly-acknowledged negotiations in Paris were producing no visible result.

In 1971, there were to be more of Secretary Laird's Type III 'protective reaction' strikes. There were also to be more protests in the United States, some of them violent, and for the first time it would be evident that even large numbers of *veterans* of the conflict now opposed it. The only clear, consistent measure of progress was the Nixon administration's effort to 'Vietnamize' and to bring out American personnel—a policy which continued relentlessly.

A brief campaign, apparently in response to SAM sites tracking a US recce aircraft, took place in the Ban Korai Pass area in February 1971 and was given the evocative name Louisville Slugger. This brief venture into North Vietnam involved Air Force aircraft only, and totalled 67 sorties. A number of SAM transporters were reported destroyed.

North Vietnamese forces continued to buildup in the panhandle where the country was divided and in Laos. A major move, perhaps even more significant than the Cambodian incursion of the previous year, seemed necessary to blunt the enemy's operations in Laos. Jointly planned in Washington and Saigon, the new operation was nicknamed Lam Son 719, commemorating a Vietnamese victory over the Chinese in the fifteenth century.

On 8 February 1971, South Vietnam's President Nguyen Van Thieu made the announcement of Lam Son 719, stating that South Vietnamese troops supported by US aircraft and artillery had crossed the border into Laos to cut off the Ho Chi Minh Trail and interdict the flow of supplies from the North. *Hancock*'s battle group was already sending the A–4F Skyhawks of squadrons VA–55 and VA–164 into Laotian fray. Three South Vietnamese infantry divisions were involved in

the ground fighting. It quickly became apparent that the South Vietnamese forces were overextended and outnumbered, and the amount of US air support needed to prevent a disaster became far more than originally anticipated. In the US, domestic critics argued that the conflict was being expanded.

Some 16,000 South Vietnamese troops aided not merely by US tactical airpower but also by massive heli-lifts found themselves in conflict with North Vietnamese forces at least twice as numerous as they. The American portion of the operation, nicknamed Dewey Canyon II, quickly proved essential. Lam Son 719 eventually would involve 8,000 US tactical air strikes and the loss of six USAF, one Navy and one Marine aircraft as well as no fewer than 107 US Army helicopters. Communications foul-ups were common as South Vietnamese army, US Army, US Air Force and US Navy people discovered that their methods of talking with each other were not always compatible. On one instance, faulty information from a forward air controller (FAC) caused a flight of USAF Phantoms to release their ordnance on friendly forces.

Lam Son 719 was filled with images which were confusing and contradictory. On 6 March 1971, B–52 Stratofortresses began to bomb the Tchepone area where North Vietnamese troops were concentrated; while military damage was unquestionably inflicted, the US news media focused on reports of civilians killed in the bombing. Pictures of seemingly panicked South Vietnamese troops hanging from helicopter skids contributed to the perception that the operation was a fiasco. Poor coordination between FACs, Army helicopters and *Hancock*'s A–4F Skyhawks has been documented—one confusing incident resulting in downed helicopter crews being captured while faulty communication forced a flight of Skyhawks to ditch its ordnance.

Most analysts now believe that in spite of the difficulties and the individual tragedies, Lam Son 719 was a successful operation which dealt a serious setback to the North Vietnamese. A Nixon administration official opined that the success of the operation

would make it possible to speed up the Vietnamization process and to withdraw US troops from South Vietnam even more rapidly. Much of the American public had by now lost interest in whether the North Vietnamese were set back. To many Americans, the only objectives to be achieved were to get out, and to secure the release of prisoners of war. To their credit, even the staunchest anti-war critics insisted that the POWs would have to come home in any settlement.

More mundane problems continued to plague air war planners. In March 1971, two QU–22B Beech drone aircraft crashed, bringing to four the total number of these aircraft lost. It had already been determined that these drones, known under the program name Pave Eagle, would not be able to replace the EC–121R Super Constellation as a relay aircraft for signals from *Igloo White* sensors. Now, it was realized that the fallback plan of 'keeping on' the EC–121R was not going to work either. As an alternative made necessary by the severe ageing of the EC–121Rs, the sensor gear from a QU–22B was installed aboard a C–130 Hercules airborne battlefield command and control center (ABCCC) for testing. The success of this project led to the conversion of additional ABCCC Hercules airframes to perform relay functions and allowed the number of EC–121Rs to be reduced to six.

Another round of 'protective reaction' airstrikes occurred on 21–22 March 1971, apparently in retaliation for attempted action against a US reconnaissance aircraft. Known as Operation Fracture Cross Alpha, the strikes involved both Air Force and Navy aircraft. Twenty armed reconnaissance strikes were accompanied by 234 attack missions. An official PACAF history stated that the first US aircraft to be lost to a SAM since February 1968 was claimed on 22 March 1971 when an F–4D Phantom flying escort was shot down near Dong Hoi, North Vietnam. However, the official listing of fixed-wing aircraft lost in the conflict does not support the SAM casualty.

The brief skirmishes in the North did nothing to placate those who opposed the war

and wanted the US out. On 24 April 1971, up to 500,000 anti-war protestors converged on Washington, D.C. At least 150,000 convened at a similar demonstration in San Francisco.

The first US aircraft lost to a SAM over Laos was an O-2A Skymaster (67-21388) of the Nakhon Phanom-based 56 SOW, shot down on 26 April 1971. The aircraft had been flying northwest of the Ban Karai Pass.

LAST O-1; LAST F-100

In June 1971, the last O-1 Bird Dog in USAF service was transferred to the South Vietnamese air force. Those who wallow in numbers would have it that during their Southeast Asia service the O-1s had flown 471,186 combat sorties and had suffered 119 losses. It has already been noted that the 'slow movers' occasionally flew in the lower reaches of North Vietnam during the period when combat operations were conducted up North.

The last F-100 Super Sabre wing in Southeast Asia, the 35 TFW at Phan Rang AB, ceased operations on 26 June 1971. The wing's squadrons and their tailcodes were the 352 TFS (VM), 614 TFS (VP), 612 TFS (VS) and 615 TFS (VE). The last of the F-100s departed South Vietnam for the continental US on 30 July 1971, ending a combat deployment which, according to the keepers

'Phantoms were to be seen more regularly ...' This illustration of F-4C Phantoms at Da Nang AB makes the point that the Phantom was becoming the best-known fighter of the war. By 1971, the F-4C had been to a large extent replaced by the F-4D Phantom. (USAF)

of the numbers, had encompassed 360,283 combat sorties and the loss of 243 aircraft. Though it had never been a significant player north of the 17th Parallel, the F-100 or 'Hun' was a bona fide veteran of the fight against Hanoi and would be much-missed, even if Phantoms were to be seen more regularly.

Bird Dog and Super Sabre were thus 'out-

By the time the Phan Rang-based 35 TFW ceased operations on 26 June 1971, the F-100 Super Sabre was a battle-scarred veteran of combat throughout the region, including limited exposure to the heavy defenses up North. Camouflaged F-100D aircraft like this 56-3093 found their way to Air National Guard units in the US. (VIA M. J. KASIUBA)

lasted' by the oldest airframe in US Air Force inventory, the venerable C-47 Gooney Bird, which carried out a variety of missions throughout the conflict. Flown on rare instance north of the 17th Parallel, the Gooney Bird was also an important asset in gathering intelligence on enemy operations. The EC-47P airframes of the 361 TEWS at Phu Cat frequently ventured into Laos and apparently Cambodia as well, their crews taking enormous risk.

The domestic view of the Southeast Asia conflict took a new turn on 13 June 1971 when the pretigious *New York Times* published the 'Pentagon papers,' a highly-classified study of US involvement in the war which had originally been prepared for Secretary McNamara. Released to the press by a former analyst, Daniel Ellsberg, the 'papers' appeared to catch US officials in a number of misleading statements, if not outright lies, about the American role in the conflict. Nixon administration figures, who had had nothing to do with creating the 'papers' and even less with releasing them to the *Times*, were infuriated at the publicity which followed. Again, questions were raised as to whether the long struggle was being waged with a clear sense of purpose and whether the high cost in American lives was producing a desirable result. Advocates of

almost any position could find something in the 'Pentagon papers' to support their point of view but it was the opposition to the war which gained the most from publication of the documents.

1 August 1971 saw Air Force command changes which did not attract much attention at the time but would later. General Lucius D. Clay, Jr, who had held the post as chief of the Seventh Air Force in Saigon, moved to Hawaii to assume duties as PACAF commander in chief, replacing General Joseph J. Nazzaro. It was the first time that the man in charge was not a 'SAC weenie', a sign of changes that were taking place within an Air Force no longer dominated solely by bomber men—although Chief of Staff General John Ryan obviously was just such a SAC veteran.

To replace Clay in Saigon, General John D. Lavelle, formerly PACAF vice commander in chief, received a fourth star and was assigned to head Seventh Air Force.

Lavelle's was an honored name in the Air Force. In the course of time, however, he would be remembered almost exclusively because of charges that he permitted unauthorized air strikes into North Vietnam.

END OF BULLPUP

All AGM-12 Bullpup air-to-ground missiles not used in combat during August 1971 were shipped back to the United States for disposition. An official history, remarking upon the never-popular Bullpup, concludes: 'This action reduced the USAF's AGM-12 capability to zero.' Recalling how Bullpups had bounced off North Vietnamese bridges during ROLLING THUNDER, there were those who felt the capability had been zero all along.

On 8 September 1971, the final AC-119G Shadow gunship was turned over to the Vietnamese Air Force. The USAF continued to operate the jet-augmented AC-119K Stinger.

Another 'protective reaction' move on 21 September 1971 saw USAF and US Navy aircraft striking the Dong Hoi POL storage facilities and destroying 350,000 gallons of fuel.

The Phu Cat-based 12 TFW with its F-4D Phantoms reached a turning point when the F-4Ds from the 389 TFS/12 TFW—reassigned without personnel to the United States—were flown to the US for IRAN (inspect and repair as necessary) on 8 October 1971. In November, the F-4D Phantoms of Phu Cat's other squadron, the inactivated 480 TFS/12 TFW, were flown to Taiwan for

Flown on rare instance north of the 17th Parallel, the venerable Gooney Bird soldiered through to the end of the conflict. This EC-47P (44-76668) of the 371st Tactical Electronic Warfare Squadron at Phu Cat AB, South Vietnam is seen intercepting enemy communications over Laos on 3 April 1971. (NORMAN TAYLOR)

IRAN prior to assignment to RAF Lakenheath, England. In their move to a European clime, the F–4Ds would again replace F–100s. The move left Phu Cat without Phantoms.

AC–130 GUNSHIP PROGRESS

Further development of the AC–130 Hercules gunship continued as eleven examples of a new model, the AC–130E, were introduced—these having greater capacity for fuel and ammunition. The AC–130E began combat operations on 25 October 1971.

Flying the Hercules gunship, better known as Spectre, was no easy experience. The pilot of an AC–130E at times felt like 'an occupant in a spam can', as one officer put it. The aircraft commander's visibility from his left-hand front seat was not as good as that of his sensor operator. His flying skills as a pilot were largely slaved to the dictates of the computer. A target such as a North Vietnamese infiltration convoy moving through the Laotian segment of the Ho Chi Minh Trail could, in fact, be attacked without the pilot ever

seeing it at all. But if anything went wrong or the aircraft took hits, the pilot suddenly had the world on his shoulders.

Perhaps the crew member with the 'hairiest' job was the illuminator operator (IO). In the AC–130A, the IO lay exposed on the open rear loading ramp door, his head over the lip of the ramp, connected to the aircraft by a tether. Part of his job was to call out sightings of intense anti-aircraft fire or SAM missile launch to enable the pilot to take evasive action, knowing that an abrupt maneuver might, as it often did, send him hurling into space, dangling. On the improved AC–130E, a Plexiglas canopy was mounted over the cargo door enabling the IO to do his job with the door closed, a situation which also markedly enhanced crew comfort.

RETURN TO NORTH VIETNAM

On 7–8 November 1971, yet another major foray into North Vietnam caused critics of the war to ask if, perhaps, the US was doing a little more than merely 'reacting'. Appar

F–4D Phantom 65-798 of the 389 TFS/12 TFW at Phu Cat airbase in South Vietnam on 17 April 1971, loaded with six 500 lb (227 kg) high drag bombs and four napalm tanks. These Phantoms will probably be striking Viet Cong guerrillas in the South, but by 1971 the Phantom was also the principal aircraft employed in 'protective reaction' strikes up North. (NORMAN TAYLOR)

ently in reaction to another 'lock-on' by a SAM site against a recce aircraft, Air Force and Navy fighter-bombers struck airfields at Dong Hoi, Vinh and Quang Lang. The very new, MiG-capable strip at Quang Lang was to remain a principal cause of concern. Farther south than other North Vietnamese airfields, Quang Lang existed solely because Hanoi wanted to shoot down one of the B–52 Stratofortresses operating in South Vietnam, Laos and Cambodia.

Although no one knew it yet, this was the time period when Seventh Air Force commander, General John D. Lavelle, allegedly made false reports about North Vietnamese reaction to US recce flights, precisely for the purpose of being able to retaliate:

'The first false report, if it can be traced to a

F-4J Phantom of the 'Fighting Falcons' of VF-96 from USS *Constellation* (CVA-64), flown by Lieutenant Randall Cunningham and Lieutenant (j. g.) William Driscoll just after their carrier's arrival in Southeast Asia in October 1971. At the time, except for 'protective reaction', no missions were being flown up North and it seemed unlikely Cunningham and Driscoll would ever see a MiG. (USN)

specific incident, arose out of an attempt to intercept a MiG in late November 1971 which had fired three missiles at a flight of B–52s. Subsequently, there were MiG attacks on B–52s and two attempted attacks on RC–135s. General Lavelle was vitally concerned and developed a plan called "Quick Check Recce," which directed that the MiG be destroyed "under the guise of protective reaction reconnaissance." The plan was ordered executed against an airfield [Quang Lang] where the MiG was based. General Lavelle

was in the Operations Center at Seventh Air Force and was personally directing the operation. The strike was successful and the lead pilot reported by radio that the target had been hit without enemy reaction. General Lavelle [later] testified: "At that point I said we cannot report 'no reaction.' Our authority was protective reaction, so we had to report some enemy action."'[55]

General Lavelle would later argue that he did not knowingly encourage falsehood and that the existing tensions at the time led to his remark. It was too late. The seeds had been sown for a minor scandal in which the general would later be accused of 'reacting' in North Vietnam when there was no enemy action to 'react' against. This would happen later; at this point, no one outside Seventh Air Force knew of any allegation of false reporting.

Later, it became apparent that the charge of false reporting applied to the 7–8 November action and that 'late November' was not

the first such instance. Somewhere between 20 and 30 instances of unauthorized bombing of North Vietnam, one Air Force figure being 24, would be attributed to General Lavelle between 7 November 1971 and 9 March 1972. These numbers refer to *missions*, not *sorties*. Whatever his reason, and the reasons seemed eminently justified, General Lavelle was indisputably doing something that had not seriously been attempted by any general officer since Douglas MacArthur—going against the basic American principle of civilian control of the military.

WINDDOWN

On 12 November 1971, President Nixon announced that an additional 45,000 American troops would leave South Vietnam during the following two months.

Henry Kissinger had begun probing for

some means of conducting secret peace talks with the North Vietnamese, separately and apart from the talks taking place in public view in Paris where William J. Porter, one of the key US diplomats participating in the talks, kept staring into the face of his North Vietnamese counterpart and seeing a man who had no intention of offering a settlement. The film actress Jane Fonda had been to Hanoi to commiserate with the North Vietnamese and, indeed, to be photographed visiting one of their Triple-A sites. In the State Department in Washington, Marshall Green, Assistant Secretary of State for East Asian Affairs, expressed the opinion that any agreement with the North Vietnamese was far ahead in a distant future. After years of bombing and not bombing, after invading Cambodia and then Laos, after returning to North Vietnam in a limited way to achieve limited results, the US in its struggle with Hanoi appeared to be getting nowhere.

As Christmas approached, USS *Constellation* (CVA–64) was one of the US warships in action in Vietnamese waters. One of the F–4J Phantom pilots in Commander Lowell F. (Gus) Eggert's carrier air wing, Lieutenant Randall Cunningham, was a veteran of 'Top Gun' dissimilar air combat training and felt he could win if he ever got the chance to fight a MiG—something which seemed unlikely so long as US combat missions were limited to 'protective reaction'. Also aboard *Connie*

was an A–7E Corsair pilot, who shall go unnamed, who felt that he could deliver ordnance to any target they might assign him—if only they would assign a target. 'We have been trained to do a job,' he wrote home, 'and they won't let us do it up North, where it really matters.'

The approach of the Christmas holidays was also noted in Arizona where Air Force pilots trained in the F–4D Phantom and talked, as all Phantom pilots did, of their prospects of coming up against the MiG. Colonel Andrew Baird, the wing commander, had been out there before and felt he would be going back. When a young wife asked to see him, asked Baird what risks awaited her young captain who was flying Phantoms, the colonel had a premonition that a new round of fighting lay ahead above the 17th Parallel. Baird spoke to Mary Ackerman as truthfully as he could:

'Maybe I'm wrong. Maybe our diplomats in Paris will wrap it up before I have to take these men back to Hanoi. But my sense of history tells me that some of these men will bleed and die before we put this one away. It has always been so . . .'[56]

There exist convincing reports that North Vietnam's MiG fighter pilots also sensed, in late 1971, that the fight was not over yet. And why should they object? In the ROLLING THUNDER campaign, they had acquitted themselves very well against the Americans.

If the Americans came to fight them again, would they not win once more?

On 10 December 1971, President Nixon announced that North Vietnam would be bombed if it increased the level of fighting as US troops were withdrawn from South Vietnam. Meanwhile, progress with the South Vietnamese Air Force was one measure of Nixon's Vietnamization effort: by the end of 1971, Saigon's air arm had 1,202 aircraft and, according to the numbers experts, had flown a total of 524,152 sorties, 59,805 of which were combat sorties. And what were all the others? And did anyone know that the correct figure was not 524,151 or 524,153? One accurate number: 57 South Vietnamese air force aircraft were lost to combat and operational causes in 1971.

Christmas Day turned out to be the eve of the largest 'protective reaction' campaign yet. Over 26–30 December 1971, in response to a North Vietnamese buildup, and in particular an increase in the number of SAM sites in the lower part of the country, Air Force and Navy aircraft flew 1,025 sorties. All of this action took place south of the 20th Parallel. The campaign was given the name Proud Deep Alpha, and represented the most extensive air operations up North since the November 1968 bombing halt. The North Vietnamese could be forgiven for wondering if the new year would hold further problems for them. It would.

THE FINAL FIGHT

The new year began with the American air presence in Southeast Asia, especially the Air Force's, caught in a paradox. The US was simultaneously carrying out a full-scale air campaign and carrying out reductions in force. The continuing reductions, the visible result of the Nixon Doctrine and Vietnamization, provided some assurance to the American public, if not to that significant segment

The A–37B Dragonfly arrived late in the war and was used by South Vietnamese and US air forces, this example being operated by the 8 SOS at Bien Hoa AB. Although it was very effective when dropping retarded bombs on Viet Cong guerrillas in the jungle, as shown here, the A–37B like other aircraft turned over to Saigon's air arm was not equipped to survive against the defenses north of the 17th Parallel. (USAF)

of the public which could be satisfied only by immediate withdrawal. At the same time, Hanoi must have seen the reductions as an invitation to achieve the final victory and overwhelm South Vietnam. For months, intelligence reports had hinted at a North Vietnamese plan for a dramatic final effort, perhaps around Easter.

The previous year's Proud Deep Alpha strikes had proven that whenever there were obvious and threatening buildups in the North, the US was prepared to fly interdiction strikes, but the reduced number of aircraft available to cope with vastly improved North Vietnamese air defenses meant that each new trip above the 17th Parallel was frought with peril. In the South, a surge of B–52 Stratofortress activity at the start of 1972 rendered more difficult Hanoi's pros-

pects for a coming offensive but restraints against operations up North enabled most preparations for the offensive to continue unabated.

The Vietnamization effort continued and the South Vietnamese Air Force appeared to be making good progress toward self-sufficiency as 1972 began. A sense of an increasing North Vietnamese threat prompted the US to review and accelerate the buildup of Saigon's air arm. Eventually, this would mean robbing American allies in order to pay President Thieu: F–5E Tigers showed up in Saigon still painted in the desert camouflage employed by Iran. Eventually, Iran, Taiwan and South Korea were repaid for allowing their A–37, F–5E and other aircraft to be diverted into South Vietnamese hands. Meanwhile, Project Enhance and Project En-

hance Plus, as the reinforcement efforts were named, placed an additional 619 aircraft into South Vietnamese hands. No one made much notice of the simple truth that none of these aircraft was well-equipped to do battle up North. The conventional wisdom was that Saigon's air arm was now almost completely self-sufficient. It is understood that when Henry Kissinger embarked upon secret negotiations with Hanoi's Le Duc Tho, Kissinger did so in the belief that US air cover would no longer be required to assure the survival of South Vietnam.

The history of the South Vietnamese Air Force is really outside the scope of this work but it should be noted in passing that some US advisors doubted the air force would ever be self-sustaining. Although some of its senior and middle-grade officers were top caliber, many of its pilots and maintenance people were not. Even a relatively simple aircraft like the A-37 Dragonfly was not always 'kept flying' on the intended schedule.

On 13 January 1972, President Nixon announced that further troop reductions would bring American troop strength in South Vietnam down to 69,000 by 1 May. As he spoke, Nixon knew of secret talks between Kissinger and Le Duc Tho. He also knew of increasing intelligence reports of a planned final offensive by Hanoi.

CUNNINGHAM'S FIRST KILL

Concern over the North Vietnamese buildup at Quang Lang was heightened when a naval recce flight brought back photography of ground crews pushing MiG-21s into a cave. A major MiG force at this base in a southerly part of North Vietnam would be a new development and would threaten B-52s operating in Laos. Clearly, more photographic coverage was called for. Secretary Laird's rules for the Type III 'protective reaction' strike, described earlier, specified that when the North Vietnamese fired upon a recce flight, only warplanes already in the air could 'react' in support of the unarmed photographic aircraft. A proper escort of heavily-armed F-4J Phantoms was thus planned for the new recce mission to Quang Lang, code-named Bluetree.

F-4J Phantom pilot Lieutenant Randall H. (Duke) Cunningham of *Constellation's* 'Fighting Falcons' of VF-96 was scheduled to lead a two-plane section in the Bluetree effort. The mission kept getting postponed by poor weather, which was always at its worst in North Vietnam in the first months of the year, and for a time it looked like the job might be shifted to *Coral Sea* (CVA-43), the

second carrier accompanying *Connie* at Yankee Station. At one point, Commander David Moss, skipper of the A-7E Corsair 'Mighty Shrikes' of VA-94, was briefed for the mission although in the end, Dave's ship did not get the nod. Crews on both carriers brief the mission and manned their aircraft repeatedly only to have it scrubbed at the last minute.

On 19 January 1972, a 'break' in the monsoon's murk enabled *Connie* to launch a photo-recon RA-5C Vigilante escorted by Intruders, Corsairs and Phantoms. Cunningham flew an F-4J Phantom (157267) with RIO LtJg William P. Driscoll in the back seat. The Viggie and its companions made an end run to position themselves for an eastward run-in over Quang Lang, cutting across South Vietnam near Hue, backtracking over Laos, and descending towards the North Vietnamese airfield.

The RA-5C was immediately engaged by 37 mm and 57 mm fire and SAMs began to fly. The Intruders and Corsairs fell upon the AAA batteries. Cunningham's section, which included the Phantom crew of Lieutenants Brian Grant and Jerry Sullivan, positioned themselves between Quang Lang and the MiG field at Bai Thiong, so as to intercept any MiGs coming down from the latter base to threaten the strike group. It was a big moment for Cunningham, who had had months to convince himself that he might not ever see a MiG. In the meanwhile, however, he realized that he had set himself up as SAM bait! He saw the sharp red burn of a sustainer rocket engine against the green jungle at ten o'clock low and knew that a SAM was rush-

ing up at him. He broke into the onrushing missile but Grant did not and the SAM passed within 100 feet (30 m) of Grant's Phantom—sparing Grant, it appeared, only because its proximity fuse malfunctioned.

Almost immediately, Randy Cunningham saw a second SAM, closing fast. He broke hard into it. The missile continued harmlessly outside the radius of his turn.

Cunningham was plunging downward from 15,000 feet (4570 m), considerable energy having been expended by his outmaneuvering the SAMs, when he spotted what he first thought to be a pair of A-7E Corsairs following their own shadows northeast over the jungle treetops. Cunningham spotted twin plumes of flame as the two aircraft went into afterburner—and reminded himself that the Corsair was not equipped with burner! He reversed, still nose low, and began to collect energy, accelerating through 600 knots (740 km/h) and closing on what turned out to be two Bai Thiong-based MiG-21s. Cunningham's RIO shouted at him to engage from a distance with Sparrows but the pilot distrusted the radar-guided missile and

Constellation arrived in Vietnamese waters in October 1971 and remained in the battle zone for the next five months. For the first half of that period, the only action up North was by RA-5C Vigilantes like this one (156614) which always had their 'protective reaction' escort like this F-4J Phantom (155799) of the 'Silver Kites' of VF-92. This November 1971 reconnaissance mission was similar to the 19 January 1972 mission to Quang Lang which produced a MiG kill for *Connie* pilots Cunningham and Driscoll. (VIA JIM SULLIVAN)

wanted to get close enough for heat-seeking Sidewinders.

Once close enough, Cunningham selected Sidewinder, got a good tone in his earphones, and fired. As the AIM–9 went off its launch rail, the MiG–21 broke hard into the attacking Phantom, throwing off the missile. Cunningham maneuvered furiously, taking advantage of the 'Top Gun' training that had exposed him to more than 150 realistic ACM engagements. He was again closing on the hard-turning MiG–21, reversing momentarily to catch sight of the second MiG which, to his relief, was high-tailing it to the northeast. Able to concentrate fully on the first MiG, Cunningham pulled his Phantom's nose toward the adversary.

Incredibly, the MiG–21 pilot seemed to lose sight of the Phantom. Now, the MiG reversed its flight path directly in front of the VF–96 fighter. Cunningham fired a second AIM–9 which tracked straight and exploded in a blinding flash, tearing off the MiGs empennage and sending it augering to the ground. Cunningham was ready for more, but the second MiG had quit the fray entirely. Cunningham and Driscoll were close to bingo fuel and now turned back toward Laos for the prolonged journey back to *Connie*'s deck. The Bluetree photo mission, which had cost no US losses, was a complete success. The MiG kill was the 122nd of the war and the first in nearly two years. Cunningham and Driscoll would be heard from again.

At Udorn, Major Robert Lodge was talking up the current state of the war with F–4D Phantom pilots of the 'Triple Nickel' 555 TFS/432 TRW. Lodge seemed to know that a new round of fighting waited up North. He wanted to lead, when the time came. He wanted to lead a tough and aggressive band of fighter pilots. Although still relatively junior, Lodge was probably the best fighter tactician in Air Force uniform. One thing about Lodge everyone knew: if any man could become an ace in this war, he would.

Meanwhile, USS *Kitty Hawk* (CVA–64) was en route to join *Connie* and *Coral Sea* in the Gulf of Tonkin. Whatever might happen in secret negotiations, a balloon effect was under way with respect to the reports of a North Vietnamese buildup. The evidence that the enemy planned his final offensive to win the war was now overpowering. *Kitty Hawk*'s airmen, too, felt that they would probably get a crack at some MiGs. When Captain O. H. Oberg passed the helm of *Hawk* to Captain M. W. Townsend, he also presented a small plaque which read: BOMB THE NE RAIL LINE EQUALLY—DAY AND NIGHT. Night missions would be part of the struggle ahead.

It is almost impossible to describe the awe

felt by younger fighter pilots toward Major Robert A. Lodge. A graduate of the Colorado Springs academy, Lodge had made it clear that he intended not merely to kill MiGs but to lead others in killing MiGs. Minor inconveniences, such as the fact that there was no fighting in North Vietnam at the time, could not stand in the way. Lodge is understood to be the first Air Force pilot to shoot down a MiG in Laos. On 21 February 1972, he took his F–4D Phantom (65-784) up a narrow valley, at night, with 1Lt Roger C. Locher in the back seat.

At the time of the previous Air Force MiG kill four years ago, USAF Phantoms had been flown by two pilots. As noted earlier, that had changed now. Locher was a weapon systems officer (WSO), although in ordinary conversation he was more likely to be called a navigator. No one had ever gone after a MiG at night before and, while the effort is a measure of Bob Lodge's indomitable fighting spirit, back-seater Locher must take credit for much of the success of the low-level, after-dark mission.

The AIM–7 Sparrow radar-guided missile was Lodge's weapon that night and it is thought that the MiG pilot never knew what hit him. Lodge was initially given vectors to pursue a MiG–21, then advised to break away when friendly radar showed the MiG and his Phantom blending with the ground in an area where jagged ridgelines waited to catch the Phantom's wingtip and flip the aircraft to its doom. Lodge ignored the advice.

At breathtakingly low level, Lodge claimed the MiG–21. It was probably the single most difficult MiG kill of the war, and Lodge and Locher returned to Udorn secure

in the knowledge that they had achieved something very special. Like the Navy's Cunningham and Driscoll, they would be heard from again.

In March, even though full-scale operations over North Vietnam were still only the subject of speculation, two more MiG fighters were shot down in air-to-air engagements. One of these fell to Lt Col Joseph W. Kittinger, Jr of the 555 TFS/432 TRW, a colorful Air Force figure best remembered as the man who had once parachuted from a balloon at an altitude of over 100,000 feet. Joe Kittinger's 1 March 1972 MiG kill was the first for F–4D Phantom 66-7463 which would become the top-scoring MiG killer airframe of the conflict. Lt Garry L. Weigand was pilot of F–4B Phantom 153019 of the 'Sundowners' of VF–111 which scored the other victory, a 6 March 1972 success against a MiG–17.

On 28 March 1972, perhaps in connection with the ultimate move about to be launched by Hanoi, an AC–130A Hercules (55-0044) of the 16 SOS/8 TFW was hit by a SAM over Laos and lost with its crew. The Hercules or Spectre gunships had been operating for some time as a part of the 8 TFW's Wolfpack at Ubon, now commanded by Colonel Carl S. Miller. An official history indicates that this

'*Kitty Hawk* was en route to join *Connie* ...'
As reports kept coming to confirm Hanoi's plans for a major offensive, the decision was taken to put as many as four carriers at Yankee Station in the Gulf of Tonkin. This view of *Kitty Hawk*'s deck on its 1972 combat cruise shows A–7E Corsairs of VA–192 and VA–195, and F–4J Phantoms of VF–114 and VF–213. (LTV)

Superb study of F-4D Phantom 65-0720 of the Udorn-based 555 TFS/432 TRW visiting Phu Cat on 19 September 1970, appearing before the lens of Norman Taylor whose photography has assisted historians over the years. This F-4D Phantom is from the same squadron as Major Robert A. Lodge and Lt Col. Joseph W. Kittinger, who scored MiG kills early in 1972 while North Vietnam was still 'off limits'. (NORMAN TAYLOR)

was the first Hercules gunship lost over Laos, but in fact it was probably simply the first lost to a SAM. Records show that AC–130A Hercules (54-1625) had been lost in Laos two years earlier on 21 April 1970. Further tribulations awaited gunship crews.

EASTER INVASION

The long-awaited final offensive by Hanoi began on the night of 29/30 March 1972 when 12 divisions, supported by armor and artillery, invaded South Vietnam. In Hawaii, CINCPAC, Admiral John S. McCain, Jr. moved to assure that no fewer than *four* carriers would be on station in the Gulf of Tonkin as a wholly new war began to swarm down on the South. Over 120,000 troops were sent into South Vietnam during that long Easter weekend, the border city of An Loc was taken under seige and the North began to employ tanks on a large scale for the first time in the war. In Saigon, General Lavelle committed virtually all of Seventh Air Force's assets to responding to the invasion and made it known that he would need reinforcement from outside.

At Udorn, F–4D Phantom pilot Captain Sid Curtis, one of Major Bob Lodge's charges, sat in his hooch on Good Friday evening 31 March 1972, not yet aware of what was going on. He was trying to compose a letter to his girlfriend. A sergeant with the

Triple Nickel poked his head into Curtis's quarters to announce that tomorrow's routine mission had been cancelled.

'What's this, cancelled? How come?'

'Something going on up North. A major offensive—'

'I heard something—'

'It's true. The bastards are coming down the pike.'

'Which bastards, Sarge? You don't mean those rag-tag guerrillas we've been dropping bombs on?'

'Oh, lord no, Captain. NVA. North Vietnamese regulars. The reserve divisions that have stayed up north until now. With tanks. Would you believe, tanks?'

'But the negotiations—'

'I don't know shit about no negotiations, sir. All I know is the bastards are coming down with everything they've got.'

Curtis had to tell somebody. He bounded outdoors and came upon another 555 TFS pilot. In measured tones, Sid Curtis informed Captain Richard S. (Steve) Ritchie that Lodge, Curtis, Ritchie and a good many other folks were going to get a crack at the MiGs, after all.

Reinforcements were going to be needed, fast. On 31 March 1972, F–4D Phantoms of the 3 TFW at Kunsan AB, Korea, deployed to Da Nang and Ubon to augment existing fighter forces. This was just the beginning of what was to be a major buildup of tactical air assets in the face of the invasion.

Everybody—Air Force, Navy, Marines— began flying around the clock. Captain Frederick S. Olmsted, Jr, another Udorn-based F–4D Phantom pilot, was doing some 'protective reacting' up North when he was given vectors to engage a flight of MiG–21s. Olmsted's Phantom (66-230) closed in and the captain used a Sparrow to shoot down a MiG–21.

On 2 April 1972, the invading North Vietnamese forces captured the provincial capital of Quang Tri. 6 April 1972 marked a major White House decision to return to North Vietnam—the beginning of an air campaign up North known as FREEDOM TRAIN. The old restraints of the Johnson years were off and targets were opened up. FREEDOM TRAIN was not going to be a repetition of ROLLING THUNDER, everyone said. With US warplanes going north again on a sustained basis for the first time in nearly four years, it was a new war . . .

6 April 1972 also marked, in response to the Easter invasion, the rapid deployment of

On 9 April 1972, in the wake of North Vietnam's massive Easter invasion, strikes against targets in North Vietnam by B–52 Stratofortresses were resumed. These were mounted from U-Tapao in Thailand and from Andersen AFB, Guam, where this B–52D is seen lifting off from the runway. (USAF)

Tactical Air Command squadrons to Southeast Asia, under the nickname Constant Guard, to augment the depleted residual air units remaining after the withdrawals of the Nixon era. Constant Guard I marked a move of F–105Gs from McConnell AFB, Kansas, to Korat and F–4E Phantoms from Seymour Johnson AFB, N.C., to Ubon.

Bombing strikes against targets in North Vietnam by B–52s were resumed on 9 April 1972. On 11 April 1972, the first strikes against the interior of the country were launched against Vinh. Four days later, POL storage areas near Haiphong were hit.

There had been, of course, a total breakdown of the publicly-known peace talks in Paris and the private contacts between Henry Kissinger and Le Duc Tho. North Vietnam had shown bad faith with its full-scale invasion, meant as the final master stroke to end the war. The US was in no mood to talk when it had made the decision to fight. Now that American warplanes were going North again, no less a personage than President Nixon had made it clear that he wanted any restrictions on their use to be minimal and sensible. If Hanoi thought the invasion was going to lead to conquest of South Vietnam, American airmen believed that FREEDOM TRAIN was going to win the war for the good guys and bring the POWs home.

INVASION AND GUNSHIPS

While Hanoi had been plotting to take over the South at a time when Nixon Doctrine troop withdrawals seemed to make a takeover possible, work had been underway to improve the AC–130 Hercules gunship. Tests at Wright-Patterson AFB, Ohio, had tried a number of weapons including 57 mm and 106 mm recoilless rifles. These tests led to the installation of a 105 mm howitzer, possibly the largest weapon ever carried by a warplane. The long-barrel howitzer was fitted with a flash suppressor and mounted on the Hercules' port door. When the Easter invasion committed US aircraft against North Vietnamese armor for the first time, this howitzer-armed AC–130E Spectre was subjected to its baptism of fire.

On the first day of the invasion, 30 March 1972, over Laos Captain Waylon O. Fulk and the crew of his AC–130E Spectre (69-6571) attacked a convoy and touched off a blaze of secondary fires and explosions. Moments later, AAA fire found Fulk's aircraft. A 57 mm round slammed into the starboard wing and another gouged open the right side of the fuselage. A leaking pylon fuel tank erupted in flames, wrapping the right wing in a billowing fireball. A geyser of burning fuel had also drenched the side of the fuselage, igniting a new fire there.

Captain Fulk directed his 14 crew members to be ready to bail out. He brought the AC–130E away from the battle scene whilst alerting rescue forces and nearby aircraft. Another aircraft arrived and its pilot advised Fulk on the extent of the damage. Steadying the crippled AC–130E as best he could, the pilot called for the crew to bail out and radioed

The howitzer-equipped AC–130E Spectre gunship was introduced to battle just in time for the 30 March 1972 Easter invasion by North Vietnam. On that date, Captain Waylon O. Fulk received the Air Force Cross for heroism during an AC–130E combat mission against truck convoys in Laos. (USAF)

Seen at Misawa AB, Japan on 16 July 1974 following the end of the Vietnam conflict, A–4E Skyhawk 149658 of the 'Greyhounds' of attack squadron VMA–211 is typical of the Marine Corps aircraft which were re-introduced to Southeast Asia at the time of the Easter invasion in 1972. Marine assets fell under the 1st Marine Aircraft Wing, head-quartered at MCAS Iwakuni, Japan. (NORMAN TAYLOR)

position information. Fulk and the illuminator operator were last to leave the stricken aircraft. Moments after they jumped into the night, the fires and ammunition explosions transformed the AC–130E into a plummeting fireball. The following day, all 15 crewmen were picked up in what one historian calls the largest and most successful mass crew rescue ever recorded. Captain Fulk received the Air Force Cross.

L'AFFAIRE LAVELLE

With the invasion on and the war 'hotting up,' the last thing anybody in Saigon needed was a mini-scandal. But on 11 April 1972, when General John W. Vogt, Jr, suddenly and unexpectedly took over Seventh Air Force, it became clear that his predecessor, General John D. Lavelle, was being relieved for falsifying reports of unauthorized air strikes against North Vietnam—*before* the invasion had caused US aircraft to return North in force.

A full report on the Lavelle case fills a volume but it should be noted once more that the general was charged with ordering about two dozen unauthorized bombings of military targets in North Vietnam between 7 November 1971 and 9 March 1972. On the

latter date, the Inspector General of the Air Force went to Vietnam to look into allegations and on 23 March 1972, the inspector reported to Chief of Staff General John D. Ryan. Three days later, Lavelle was summoned to Washington, relieved of his assignment, and permitted to retire.

The whole time that Lavelle had ordered 'protective reaction' strikes in violation of the rules given him, the US had been bombing Cambodia in secret. The difference, of course, was that the latter bombing had been authorized by the President. Lavelle's error was not in attacking a few AAA and SAM sites but rather, as has been stated earlier in this narrative, usurping civilian authority.

With all of North Vietnam's invasion forces across the line and moving down, the battle for An Loc in South Vietnam began in earnest on 13 April 1972 and two strong attacks were repulsed with the aid of continued

air strikes. The town was besieged by NVA forces and a massive airlift effort was begun to supply the defenders. From 15 April 1972 until the ground resupply routes were re-opened on 23 July, a total of 763 airdrop sorties would provide 10,081 tons of supplies. Heavy B–52 Stratofortress bombings took place around An Loc, as did strikes by carrier-based aircraft.

The Easter invasion brought a dramatic increase in the number of US Marines in South Vietnam, which had fallen below 500

F–4J Phantom 155801 of the 'Red Devils' of VMFA–232, at about the time this squadron deployed to Nam Phong, Thailand in response to the North Vietnamese invasion. The A–4F Skyhawks in this photograph belong to an Okinawa-based US Navy unit, but the March 1972 buildup of forces in Southeast Asia also included two Marine Skyhawk squadrons. (VIS ROBERT F. DORR)

RF–4C Phantom 68–609 of the Udorn-based 14 TRS/432 TRW was the airframe being piloted by Captain Donald S. Pickard when he sought to assist in the rescue of downed squadron mate Captain Woody Clark. The RF–4C Phantom played a major role in FREEDOM TRAIN and LINEBACKER operations throughout 1972. (USAF)

the previous year. Marine Corps A–4 Skyhawks, which had been withdrawn from theater, returned to Bien Hoa AB with the 'Greyhounds' of VMA–211 and the 'Tomcats' of VMA–311, operating the A–4E variant. The Marines also had one A–6A Intruder squadron, VMA(AW)–224, embarked on *Coral Sea*. As the magnitude and extent of the invasion was understood, two Marine Corps F–4J Phantom squadrons were added to the fighting force, the 'Silver Eagles' of VMFA–115 and the 'Red Devils' of VMFA–232. The skipper of the latter squadron had a Phantom colorfully adorned *HEAD DEVIL*. The Phantoms went into the new base at

HH–53C Super Jolly Green carrying the rescued RF–4C Phantom back-seater, Captain Ernest (Woody) Clark lands at Udorn on 22 April 1972 following Clark's rescue after 50 hours in North Vietnam. Now a lieutenant colonel, Clark remains on active duty in the Air Force. (DONALD S. PICKARD)

Nam Phong, Thailand, where a 10,000 foot (3 000 m) runway was carved out of grit by Navy Construction Battalions. Nam Phong was a place of fierce crosswinds and choking red dust. 'I never promised you a rose garden,' went a Marine Corps recruiting song of the era, and precisely because it was not one, Marines named the airfield the Rose Garden. The two Phantom squadrons there were to be joined soon by A–6A Intruders of VMA(AW)–533.

The sudden intensity of the new war was highlighted on 16 April 1972 when three MiG–21s were shot down in one day by Phantom crews of the Udorn-based 432 TRW. One pilot, Captain Frederick S. Olmsted, Jr, achieved the distinction of getting his own second MiG kill while also chalking up the second kill for the airframe he was flying, F–4D Phantom 66–7463 which had previously scored with Kittinger at the controls. Another Udorn crew credited with a MiG–21 on that day was Major Edward D. Cherry and Captain Jeffrey S. Feinstein. Major Robert A. Lodge did not score on that day but like Lodge, Feinstein was not yet finished with his war . . .

At the very time when Hanoi had unleashed all of its forces to conquer the South and friendly air units in the South had been reinforced, President Nixon made it clear

that the Nixon Doctrine was still in force. On 20 April 1972, in the midst of the NVA invasion, Nixon announced a further cut of 20,000 US personnel.

COMBAT RESCUE

Among the more difficult jobs in the FREEDOM TRAIN operation was the reconnaissance mission in the Route Package One panhandle of North Vietnam, where the enemy was thought to be installing SAM sites. The continuing threat of SAMs and MiGs getting closer to aircraft operating in the South and in Laos was on everyone's mind. An RF–4C Phantom recce crew from Udorn's 14 TRS/432 TRW received two distinguished flying crosses for the 'hairy' job of trying to ferret out those SAMs. When RF–4C Phantom 68–598 embarked on the same mission on 20 April 1972, it was hit by AAA fire and shot down near Vinh. NVA troops almost immediately overwhelmed and captured the pilot of the RF–4C, Major Edward Elias. (Elias was subsequently a member of the third and final trio of prisoners of war to be released prematurely by Hanoi.) The back-seater of the aircraft, Captain Ernest (Woody) Clark became the subject of an unusually prolonged rescue effort.

Clark was luckier than the pilot, if a man could be called lucky when his parachute was ripped to shreds by tree branches and he struck the ground hard enough to break several ribs. He heard North Vietnamese troops moving toward him from the next valley, a scant 2,000 feet (610 m) away.

Jolted and hurt, Woody Clark retained the use of his AN/ARC–64 survival radio which gave him beeper and voice contact with friendly aircraft overhead. One of those friendlies was another RF–4C Phantom (68–609), piloted by squadron mate Captain Donald S. Pickard.

It remained true that an airman shot down in North Vietnam could expect mistreatment, denial of medical treatment, even torture. World opinion had forced Hanoi to treat the POWs somewhat better than in earlier days, but this was little comfort to Woody Clark as he began an unusual marathon which would last two days and nights, an astonishing 50-plus hours, in densely-populated hill country with NVA troops stalking him.

While Clark clawed and fought his way through jungle, up hillsides, across streams—sleeping infrequently and once coming within a few meters of a North Vietnamese soldier, RF–4C pilots Pickard and Greg Bailey criss-crossed the area, getting D/F fixes on Woody's hand-held radio. Cap-

MiG-21 in flight over the terraced paddy fields of North Vietnam. North Vietnam's reputed top ace, Colonel Tomb, flew the MiG-21 but was reported to favor the earlier MiG-17 because of its maneuverability. Hanoi has never revealed details about the names or scores of its aces. (VIA MIKE O'CONNOR)

tain Pickard even devised an elaborate scheme to drop Woody an RF-4C wingtank filled with food and medical supplies, though the plan was not carried out. Dozens of airmen, including Sandy escorts in A-1H Skyraiders were looking for Clark.

In the end, he was one of the lucky ones. After two days and nights, an HH-53C Super Jolly Green settled down and a pararescueman lifted him aboard. Clark had successfully evaded capture for what was, so far, the longest period of all—although Major Bob Lodge's back-seater, Captain Roger Locher, would eventually surpass his two-day record a dozen times over.

On 26 April 1972, Constant Guard II, the latest reinforcement move, brought squadrons of F-4E Phantoms from Eglin AFB, Florida and Homestead AFB, also in Florida, to Udorn. The base already occupied by Lodge, Locher, Curtis, Ritchie, Olmsted, Feinstein, Bailey, Clark and Pickard was becoming very, very crowded.

And Colonel Tomb? The legend that North Vietnam had fielded the greatest fighter wing commander of them all refused to die. Sometimes Colonel Tomb, sometimes Comrade Toon (neither is a surname in the Vietnamese language), he was said to be more experienced, more able, than the best of the American fighter pilots. He had defeated an older generation led by Robbie Risner and Robin Olds. Now he would prevail over the newer breed of American fighter pilot typified by Major Bob Lodge and Lieutenant Randy Cunningham.

Constant Guard III brought four squadrons of F-4D Phantoms from the 49 TFW at Holloman AFB, New Mexico, to new billets at Takhli. The squadrons and over eight million pounds of cargo were airlifted in less than a week, beginning 6 May 1972. Constant Guard IV was the deployment of two squadrons of C-130E Hercules from the US to a nearby base on Taiwan.

6 May 1972 also brought no fewer than three MiG kills as the 'Screaming Eagles' of VF-51 on *Coral Sea* and the 'Aardvarks' of VF-114 on *Kitty Hawk* pitted their Phantoms against Colonel Tomb's air force. A VF-51 crew flying an F-4B Phantom (150456) bagged a MiG-17, reportedly the favorite mount of the erstwhile Tomb, while two VF-114 F-4J Phantoms (157245; 157249) shot down a pair of MiG-21s—all using Sidewinders. Unlike their performance during the ROLLING THUNDER period, the communists were not extracting similar casualties from the Americans.

FREEDOM TRAIN, begun a month earlier, did not seem to be the total answer. An even wider air war up North was now being planned.

The new campaign had been under consideration for some time. Kissinger had advised Nixon that it might force North Vietnam to negotiate seriously, but that it could also threaten a summit meeting with Soviet President Breshnev, now in the final planning stages. The JCS had recommended that the best way to deliver a telling blow to North Vietnam was to mine Haiphong harbor. Nixon ignored the risk to US-Soviet relations, accepted the howl of protest that would come from the anti-war protest lobby,

MiG-21 4326 has been widely reported in some periodicals as one of the mounts used by North Vietnam's super ace, Colonel Tomb. The legendary Hanoi fighter wing commander actually was known to prefer the MiG-17 and was flying the latter aircraft when shot down. (VIA MIKE O'CONNOR)

and ordered the go-ahead. The President was an avid football fan and some of his advisors might have discussed calling the campaign TOUCHDOWN, FORWARD PASS or TIGHT END. If so, they did not use these names. FREEDOM TRAIN was replaced by LINEBACKER.

On 8 May 1972, A-6A Intruders from the three carriers now at Yankee Station seeded Haiphong harbor and surrounding areas with airdropped anti-shipping mines. A-7E Cor-

The F-4J Phantom flown by Randy Cunningham and Willie Driscoll for their first two MiG kills, 19 January and 8 May 1972, survived the war and has continued in service without ever receiving any special markings. 157267, now converted to F-4S standard and assigned to the 'Crusaders' of Marine squadron VMFA-122, is seen at Andrews AFB, Maryland on 11 June 1983. (JOSEPH G. HANDELMAN)

sairs supported the mining operation. Commander David Moss, skipper of the A–7E-equipped 'Mighty Shrikes' of VA–94 on *Coral Sea*, survived being hit by a SAM. Parachuting into waters just off Haiphong, he was rescued while under fire from shore batteries. F–4B and F–4J Phantoms flew top cover for the mine-scattering mission and in the process VF–96's Randy Cunningham and his back-seater Willie Driscoll racked up their second MiG kill. The pair were flying the same F–4J Phantom (157267) they had used to get their first MiG. At about the same time, a curious incident occurred where a Navy surface ship downed a MiG with a Talos surface-to-air missile—one of the few times when one of Colonel Tomb's fighters threatened the Fleet.

LINEBACKER

As the Intruder mining missions bottled-up no fewer than 27 merchant vessels in Haiphong—and virtually sealed off North Vietnam's supply of AAA shells and SAM missiles—the Udorn-based crowd in the 432 TRW was also in the air for LINEBACKER's first day. A MiG kill scored by Major Barton P. Crews and back-seater Captain Keith W. Jones, Jr, a MiG–17 downed by a Sparrow, proved to be the third of the war for F–4D Phantom airframe 66-7463 which had previously drawn blood at the hands of Kittinger and Olmsted. 463 would probably become the best-known Phantom of the war, but it was another F–4D aircraft (65-784) which was taken into battle on 8 May 1972 by the war's best pilot, Major Robert A. Lodge. Lodge and back-seater Roger C. Locher, who had been promoted to captain since their previous kill on 21 February, engaged a MiG–21.

Major Lodge was leading Oyster flight, a four-ship of F–4Ds charged with providing MiGCAP for Air Force and Navy strike aircraft carrying out LINEBACKER missions in the Hanoi area. Oyster one and three had improved radar sets that enabled them to detect MiGs at extended range. The Navy's radar picket ship, known by its callsign Red Crown, was also available to them. When Lodge put himself on a due north heading, his intention was to go to the aid of Crews and Jones who, as it turned out, did not need it. Red Crown advised Lodge that he was about to be pounced by MiGs to his right. Lodge brought his flight into a hard right turn to an easterly heading.

Captain Locher picked up the MiGs on the Phantom's radar at a distance of 40 miles (64 km). They were at twelve o'clock, high. Lodge maneuvered aggressively to get with-

in missile range but the MiGs, apparently under ground control, turned away. Lodge then found himself chasing the MiGs, but not yet within range to fire at them. To be certain that he did not fire on a friendly aircraft, Lodge went into afterburner and drew close enough to make visual confirmation of a brace of MiG–21s. He closed to within about a mile (1.6 km) and unleashed a Sparrow. The MiG went down. It was the second kill for Lodge and Locher who celebrated by painting a second red star on the splitter vane of 65-784. Nobody at Udorn had the slightest doubt who the first ace of the war was going to be.

THE TENTH OF MAY

10 May 1972, third day of the LINEBACKER campaign against North Vietnam, will be remembered for the largest air-to-air score of the war, eleven MiGs shot down. It was the day LtJg Curtis R. Dose of the 'Silver Kings' of VF–92 redeemed a family's investment over two generations by joining the ranks of MiG killers; the day the Navy's Cunningham and Driscoll became aces; and the day Major Robert A. Lodge collided with destiny. To many, including Hanoi's Colonel Tomb, it was the biggest day of the war . . .

Curt Dose was the son of Bob Dose, skipper of a World War Two fighter squadron, later commanding officer of *Midway*, and a renowned test pilot of the 1950s. Curt had gone through the Naval Academy at Annapolis and ACM training at 'Top Gun'; he was a seasoned veteran of a previous cruise with VF–92, with 160 missions under his belt.

At 0830 hours, Curt Dose and Lieutenant Austin Hawkins launched in a two-aircraft

F–4J Phantom division from USS *Constellation* (CVA–64). In the back seat of Dose's F–4J (157269) was radar intercept officer Lcdr James McDevitt. En route to the busy and threatening airfield at Kep, already alerted that MiG–21s were preparing to launch, Dose was about to stir up a hornet's nest.

Air Force strikes were being mounted by Colonel Carl S. Miller's 8 TFW, the Ubon-based Wolfpack, and by Colonel Charles Gabriel's 432 TRW ay Udorn. The latter also put up a two aircraft RF–4C recce mission from the 14 TRS/432 TRW, which went aloft at 0830 hours. Major Sidney S. Rogers and Captain Donald S. Pickard took their RF–4Cs up toward the Yen Bai airfield complex and the Paul Doumer Bridge. Pickard was about to have his day ruined by his Phantom's wingtanks.

Also from Udorn, four F–4D Phantoms

Following the 10 May 1972 action in which he shot down Colonel Tomb and became an ace, Lt Randy Cunningham describes the fighting to VF–96 squadron mates aboard NSS *Constellation* (CVA–64). During the action, Cunningham and LtJg Willie Driscoll shot down their third, fourth and fifth MiGs and were themselves downed by a SAM. The F–4J Phantom crew became the first American air aces since the Korean War.

under Major Robert A. Lodge, again using the callsign Oyster flight, headed up towards Hanoi on another MiGCAP flight. The fiery, aggressive Lodge, remembered as a hard-charging leader from his days at the Colorado Springs academy, was gunning for Colonel Tomb again. Lodge pushed his men hard, himself harder. When another F–4D flight was delayed in approaching the hard-fought Hanoi-Haiphong area, Lodge took the assigned areas of both flights for himself.

Curt Dose and Austin Hawkins' pair of *Connie* F–4Js from VF–92 stirred up enemy defenses first and almost certainly provoked MiG action against the later strikes of the day. The two Phantom pilots went in at low level and 'beat up' Kep airfield, obtaining a spectacular view of two MiG–21s running up their engines in clouds of dust at runway's end. Dose was pondering a shot at them when his back-seater reported that they were rolling. Dose and Hawkins abruptly found themselves engaging two MiG–21s at perilously low level in the Kep pattern.

The North Vietnamese pilots were fully aware of the Phantoms; they pickled off their centerline tanks and went into some fancy

maneuvering to try to improve their situation. Dose did some fancier maneuvering. At 0905 hours, the VF–92 pilot unleashed a pair of AIM–9 Sidewinders in quick succession at one of the MiGs. It was possibly the first time a Navy aviator had fired Sidewinders while at supersonic speed and treetop level. Another Sidewinder from Hawkins, like Dose's two, missed. Dose got off his third Sidewinder and watched it rush up the MiGs tailpipe and explode.

Dose's Silver Kites had a sister squadron on *Constellation*, the 'Fighting Falcons' of

VF–96. While Dose and Hawkins worked over Kep, VF–96 fliers Randy Cunningham and Willie Driscoll were still 'mounting up'. The pair's two previous MiG kills had been achieved in the same F–4J Phantom (157267) but today they were flying another, the squadron's CAG aircraft (155800). Cunningham and Driscoll were part of the Navy's second strike of the day, an Alpha Strike of 27 Phantoms, Intruders and Corsairs from *Connie* heading to attack the marshalling yards at Hai Duong, a crucial supply bottleneck between Hanoi and Haiphong. This force launched at 1130 hours. The men were refueling on the tankers by 1145 hours.

The Air Force's Wolfpack, the 8 TFW, arrived over its target carrying laser-guided and electro-optical guided bombs.

They got a little place down south of the ridge
Name of the place is the Doumer Bridge

began a fighter pilot's song about the 5,532 ft (1 686 m) Paul Doumer Bridge, the 19-span rail and highway trestle at Hanoi. Captain Thomas P. Messett was one of the pilots in

This could be Randy Cunningham's flight heading into battle on 10 May 1972. Not quite distinguishable to the naked eye is a tiny MiG symbol painted inside the black triangle at the base of the vertical tail of all of these 'Fighting Falcon' VF–96 Phantoms, representing Cunningham's first MiG kill on 19 January 1972. This photograph was taken in the interim over the Philippines on 8 March 1972, and no one could have known that the aircraft in the tail-end slot (155800) would be flown by Cunningham when he became an ace, killed Colonel Tomb, and was downed by a SAM. (ROBERT L. LAWSON)

the initial strike force. Messett's Phantoms drew within sight of the long bridge basking beneath clear sky—the pilots' view broken only by bursting AAA shells.

Messett and his wingmen in F–4D Phantoms had to maintain rigid flight discipline while rolling in on the bridge so that their 1,000 lb (454 kg) Mark 84 bombs could enter the laser 'basket'—a cone of airspace, created by the Paveway laser designator carried by their flight leader, within which the bombs would guide. These 'smart' bombs had not been used up North before and they were going to change everything. Criss-crossing tracers joined bursting 57 mm and 85 mm shells over the bridge as Messett's force went in, but the AAA threat was less serious than previously: With the F–4D's automated bombing system, it was possible to release ordnance at 14,000 ft (4270 m), well out of range of the smaller-caliber AAA.

Pulling off, Messett was certain that some of his Mark 84s broke the trestle's span.

Recce pilots were not having an easy day. In their RF–4C Phantoms, Sid Rogers and Don Pickard headed deep into Route Package Six to position themselves for immediate post-strike photography, to see how well Messett and mates had done against the Doumer Bridge. For a sustained time of struggle and discomfort, they eluded SAMs and MiGs that seemed to be everywhere around them, and Pickard later brought home a grainy photograph of a MiG–17 stalking him from below and behind. Rogers and Pickard both made their photo run successfully. Moments later, Pickard's Phantom (68-606) was severely damaged, not by North Vietnam's ground-to-air arsenal but by his own starboard wingtank: as soon as he jettisoned his tanks, one of them damaged the wing, causing a fuel leak.

This happened at about 1215 hours and marked the beginning of a long and difficult fight for survival. Unable to team up with a tanker, Pickard coaxed and prodded his way home, at one point steering towards the Marine airstrip at Nam Phong when Udorn's pattern was cluttered with battle-damaged aircraft. Pickard egressed, crossed Laos near Vientiane, and in the end decided to land at Udorn after all. Flying on one engine, hardly approved procedure in the Phantom, Captain Pickard was limping on a straight-in approach when a malfunction of the cockpit de-fog system filled the inside of his canopy with ice. 'Blind', Pickard was talked-in by his wingman. He set down at Udorn with barely enough fuel to taxi off the runway.

Randy Cunningham and his usual wingman Lt Brian Grant began their mission by hurtling downward through 37 mm and 57 mm AAA at Hai Duong to deliver Mark 20 Rockeye CBU–58 cluster bombs. In his earphones, Cunningham heard warnings that MiGs were in the air approaching the strike group.

Cunningham was first to spot the incoming enemy. He called, 'MiG–17! MiG–17! Brian, he's on my tail. I'm dragging him! Get him, baby!' This high-risk attempt to set up a kill for Grant, a measure of Cunningham's value as a team player, proved unsuccessful. Moments later, reversing and turning into the MiG, Cunningham fired a Sidewinder. The missile accelerated off the rail and tracked straight towards the camouflaged MiG, causing a quick, brittle blast that blew the North Vietnamese craft to bits. Cunningham and his RIO Willie Driscoll, at about 1400 hours, had just scored their third kill.

They had only begun.

A swirling dogfight raged over Hai Duong with Phantoms and Corsairs seeking to outmaneuver MiG–17s and MiG–19s. The North Vietnamese pilots were as threatened as the Americans by the SAMs that flew around them.

Cunningham's squadron mate Lieutenant Michael J. Connelly, flying a VF–96 Phantom (155769) with RIO Lt Thomas J. J. Blonski in the back seat, shot down two MiG–17s in quick succession. Yet another Phantom crew from the same squadron, Lt Stephen C. Shoemaker and LtJg Keith V. Crenshaw, despatched another MiG–17 with a Sidewinder fired from their Phantom (155749).

Cunningham and Driscoll rescued a wingman by using another Sidewinder to bag a

It took US Navy fighter ace Randy Cunningham 12 years to get this close to his nemesis. On 20 January 1984, long after the battles in which his F–4J Phantom prevailed over the Soviet-built fighter, Commander Randall H. Cunningham examines a MiG–17 donated to the Fighter Aces Museum, Mesa, Arizona, by the King of Morocco. (DOUGLAS E. SLOWIAK)

MiG–17—their second kill of the day and fourth of the war.

But they were not finished yet . . .

With Air Force and Navy aircraft operating all over Route Package Six, North Vietnam's defenses must have been 'lit up like a Christmas tree,' as one pilot put it. Major Bob Lodge led his Oyster flight of four F–4D Phantoms from the Udorn-based 555 TFS/432 TRW northwest from Hanoi at low altitude and high speed toward Yen Bai airfield. No US aircraft were north of Lodge, meaning that he could fire radar-guided Sparrows head-on without visual confirmation of the MiGs. Warnings from Disco and Red Crown, and further warnings from Bob Lodge's back-seater, Captain Roger Locher, pressed home the message that there were plenty of MiGs aloft in the region, itching for a fight.

Lodge's Oyster flight engaged a formation of MiG–21s and fired Sparrows from almost the limits of visual range. Oyster two, the F–4D Phantom (66-8734) piloted by 1Lt John Markle with Captain Stephen Eaves in the back seat, quickly brought down a MiG–21 using Sparrow. The MiGs lacked comparable head-on fighting capability—outside

FLOATING CRANE

REPLACED SPANS ←

Named for the former French Governor-General of Indochina, the Paul Doumer Bridge crossing the Red River near Hanoi remained a target for US airmen throughout the conflict. This 27 May 1968 view shows that partial damage was inflicted by a ROLLING THUNDER strike. On 10 May 1972, the damage inflicted by 'smart' bombs was far greater. (USAF)

gun range, that is—but they continued boring straight at Lodge's flight. One pilot who had a clear view of the incoming MiGs was the pilot in the Oyster three slot, Captain Steve Ritchie. He was a very experienced Phantom pilot, having done an earlier tour as a 'Stormy FAC', but he had not been in direct conflict with MiGs before. Today, he was flying the celebrated 66-7463 which had already accounted for three MiGs.

Bob Lodge's purpose was to prevent MiGs from reaching the strike forces in the Hanoi-Haiphong region. He succeeded, but Oyster flight was suddenly engulfed in MiGs.

Ritchie's back-seater, Captain Charles B. DeBellevue, attained a radar lock-on enabling Ritchie to fire Sparrows. Their first missile departed its launch well, shot away, armed itself, closed on a MiG–21—and missed. The second Sparrow hit the MiG where its wing roots joined the fuselage. A brilliant explosion consumed the MiG although the pilot managed to escape and his parachute furled back into the slipstream.

Bob Lodge had blasted one MiG–21 out of the sky at the onset of the fight, the third

aerial kill for the man who seemed certain to achieve acedom, and he missed a crack at another only because he was too close—and lacked a gun. Now, four MiG–19s dropped out of the clouds and worked into Bob Lodge's six o'clock position. Lodge was still chasing a MiG–21 and may not have heard Markle's voice when the captain yelled at him that he was being tailed. Bob Lodge's F–4D Phantom (65-784) was now an inviting target for the MiG–19s as they closed to within

1,500 ft (460 m) and opened fire with their cannons. 'Break right!' boomed Markle's voice in Lodge's ears. 'Break right, now! They are firing at you!'

Cannon shells pierced the Phantom's thin metal skin, rupturing its hydraulic and electrical lines, exploding with a furious noise and setting the F–4D afire. Lodge's back-seater, Locher, ejected. The Oyster flight leader's Phantom was mortally damaged.

There are those who believe, to this day, that Bob Lodge did not eject because he still wanted a few more seconds to bag the MiG–21 in front of him. Given Lodge's hairtrigger senses and fighting abilities, that seems unlikely. Far more credible is the story told by Captain Greg Bailey—that Lodge had been exposed to very sensitive classified information on a previous tour of duty and had made a personal decision that he would not fall into North Vietnamese hands with that information. Major Robert A. Lodge did not eject. The fire consumed his Phantom. Lodge was listed for a time as MIA (missing in action) before his death was confirmed. With three MiGs to his credit, with a legend as an aggressive fighter leader who almost certainly would have become the top scoring MiG killer of the war, Lodge should have received

While others fought MiGs on 10 May 1972, Captain Donald S. Pickard fought to save an RF–4C Phantom crippled by damage from its own wingtank. It later turned out that Pickard's wingman had had a camera failure, so his 'save' of his aircraft brought back the only reconnaissance film of the strike on the Doumer Bridge. Today, Colonel Pickard is serving with the Tactical Air Warfare Center, Eglin AFB, Florida. (USAF)

Accompanying Major Bob Lodge with Oyster flight on 10 May 1972 was a very experienced Captain Richard S. (Steve) Ritchie, who was already on his second tour in Southeast Asia. Ritchie was flying the war's top-killing F-4D Phantom (66-7463) when he shot down a MiG-21 and received credit for his first kill. (USAF)

dering movement which brought the F-4J beneath the belly of the MiG.

Just this maneuver had been used in a novel, *The Last Tally-ho*, but in real life it was an incredible way for Cunningham to out-guess Colonel Tomb. The MiG, now just on the edge of slow-speed control, pitched back toward the ground and attempted to escape straight down. But the Phantom was now in perfect position. Cunningham had a good tone and the seeker head of his third Sidewinder was engaged. The AIM-9 missile went straight at the MiG. Long seconds ticked past and Cunningham and Driscoll were certain they had missed. Then, a flash of flame and black smoke erupted from the MiG-17. The MiG flew straight into the ground. There was no parachute.

Cunningham was heading for egress near Nam Dinh when he heard warning calls that more SAMs were flying through the air. A SAM detonated within feet of the Phantom. At first, the aircraft continued flying normally but it quickly became evident to Cunningham that he was losing hydraulics and lateral control. It now became a battle to

reach the coast—chances of survival being much greater if he could go 'feet wet'. Using a combination of manual rudder, afterburner and downright imagination, Cunningham somehow got to the water. He and Driscoll ejected and were scooped out of the drink. They had achieved their third, fourth and fifth MiG kills, had apparently taken out North Vietnam's best pilot, and had *become aces*—the first of the long and difficult conflict.

With *Connie*'s successes receiving so much attention, it might have gone unnoticed that *Coral Sea* and *Kitty Hawk* also had Phantom squadrons in the air. An F-4B Phantom (151398) flown by Lieutenant Kenneth L. Cannon of the 'Screaming Eagles' of VF-51, with Lt Roy A. Morris, Jr, in the back seat, scored the eleventh and final MiG kill of the day, shooting down a MiG-17 near Hanoi.

USS *Constellation* (CVA-64) arrived off the Vietnamese coast in late 1971, when it seemed unlikely that there would be major action against Hanoi. A few months later, *Connie*'s pilots became the first aces of the war and inflicted heavy damage to the communists' infrastructure. (USN)

the Medal of Honor. He did not, and his dogfight is usually remembered not for his valor but because it marked wingman Steve Ritchie's first kill.

In his Navy F-4J Phantom, Randy Cunningham saw another hostile aircraft rushing at him, this time a MiG-17. Positioning his F-4J to pass the MiG close aboard so often as he had done during 'Top Gun' training, Cunningham almost forgot that *these guys* had guns—23 mm and 37 mm nose cannons on the MiG-17. The MiG pilot fired quick careful bursts at him while Cunningham pulled abruptly into a vertical climb. He looked back to see that the MiG was in the climb with him—a difficult maneuver that could have been accomplished only by one of the most aggressive and experienced of North Vietnamese pilots. Later, he was told that the MiG-17 was piloted by Colonel Tomb.

There ensued a furious dogfight in which each pilot tested the other's skills to the limit and neither was able to prevail. After some minutes of parrying with the MiG and keeping watch on his fuel state, Cunningham went into a vertical climb again. Again, the MiG-17 stayed with him.

This time, Cunningham did the unexpected. He retarded both throttles to idle and put out the speed brakes. In the same motion, while heading straight up, he applied hard rudder to force the Phantom into a shud-

Perhaps even less noticed were the courageous actions of men who flew Intruders, Corsairs and other types in the massive 10 May 1972 air battles. *Coral Sea* sent Commander David Moss and other A–7E Corsair pilots of the 'Mighty Shrikes' of VA–94 to suppress SAM installations around the Haiphong region. *Kitty Hawk* mounted several strikes by its A–7E Corsair squadrons, the 'Golden Dragons' of VA–192 under Commander D. R. Taylor and the 'Dam Busters' of VA–195 under Commander Mason L. Gilfry.

One of the Dam Busters, Lieutenant Michael A. Ruth, began that day the way most combat pilots did. 'You feel a concern. It's not fear, because the people who experience fear can't do this. But you're concerned and you're very quiet. You know that you'll talk wildly when it's all over, but beforehand you're just quiet and serious.'

Ruth was part of a 37-ship Intruder and

A–7E Corsair 157523 of the 'Dam Busters' of VA–195 returns from 10 May 1972 combat operations against North Vietnam with ordnance expended. The nickname comes from attacks with aerial torpedoes on the Hwachon Dam during the Korean War. Lieutenant Michael A. Ruth, A–7E Corsair pilot of the 'Dam Busters' of VA–195 from *Kitty Hawk*, was decorated for his courage in assaulting the Hai Duong Bridge during the massive air battles of 10 May 1972. (USN, VIA M. J. KASIUBA)

Corsair strike force from *Kitty Hawk* aimed at the bridge that *was not* named after Paul Doumer, the strategic rail and highway span at Hai Duong. A document put out by Vice Admiral William P. Mack, commander of the Seventh Fleet, said that 'the destruction of this vital bridge [will] cut the east-west flow of military supplies and limit the enemy's freedom of logistical movement in support of their (sic) forces in the south.'[57]

A massive Alpha Strike swarmed down on the area around the Hai Duong Bridge. Executive officer of the Dam Busters, Lcdr Norman D. Campbell, flew an A–7E Corsair (156858), leading an Iron Hand flight and carrying four AGM–45 Shrike anti-radiation missiles. To attack the bridge's center span came VA–195's Lt Charlie Brewer and Lt Mike Ruth. Their two Corsairs were carrying Mark 83 1,000 lb (454 kg) and Mark 84 2,000 lb (908 kg) bombs configured to combine minimal drag with heavy punch.

SAMs and AAA fire were everywhere as Mike Ruth lined up behind Brewer and began his run-in. Tracers criss-crossed the air in front of him but, because of the earlier efforts by Phantom crews, there was no threat from MiGs. This was small comfort. Ruth was under exceedingly heavy fire. His citation for the Distinguished Service Cross says that he 'continually maintained close section integrity ... despite intense enemy

opposition. Positioning his aircraft at an optimum roll-in point, Lt Ruth commenced a devastating attack and despite a wall of intensive anti-aircraft artillery fire placed all ordnance directly on target.' Other strike pilots delivered similarly telling blows to North Vietnamese targets during the 10 May 1972 LINEBACKER strikes.

An incredible sidelight of the 10 May 1972 fighting is the story of Captain Roger Locher, who ejected from Bob Lodge's F–4D Phantom. Locher remained on the ground, very deep in North Vietnam, for *twenty-three days* while hundreds of sorties were mounted in an attempt to rescue him. Unlike Captain Woody Clark, whose survival has been related earlier, Locher was in very heavily populated territory, very far from the coast and from Laotian ingress routes, and no more than a few kilometers from a MiG airfield. Incredibly, Locher used his survival radio to remain in contact intermittently with rescue forces and he was eventually plucked to safety by an HH–53C Super Jolly Green. No other flier of the conflict was 'down' for so long without being captured.

The furious level of fighting on 10 May 1972 was many things to many people: In the US, it sparked new protests about a perceived escalation in the conflict. In Hanoi, it was a stunning blow—perhaps the first time the

A happy man: Captain Roger Locher emerges from HH–53C rescue helicopter after spending *twenty-three* days evading capture deep in North Vietnam. Locher and his F–4D Phantom pilot, Major Bob Lodge, were credited with three MiG kills and were shot down by a MiG–19 on 10 May 1972. (TONY MARSHALL)

North Vietnamese had experienced the potential of unfettered American air power. The loss of eleven MiGs in air-to-air combat, even when measured against the loss of a valued combat leader like Major Bob Lodge, had to be a serious blow to the North Vietnamese air force. The bottling-up of Haiphong harbor and the severing of the country's major bridge spans—none of which had been accomplished during the 1965–68 ROLLING THUNDER effort—was *felt* in Hanoi. Captured documents showed that key officials in the communist government felt that their invasion of the South had bogged down and that the infra-structure of their own nation in the North was being ripped asunder. No one knew it at the time, least of all the anti-war demonstrators back home, but a remarkable thing was happening. The United States was winning the war.

Along with his hawk's claws, President Nixon had also extended a laurel wreath: in public statements connected with the heavy fighting on 10 May 1972, Nixon said that the

US would stop all acts of force if the enemy agreed to return all American POWs and an internationally supervised cease-fire were agreed upon. The POWs remained all-important (Major Ken Cordier had eluded guards and fought his way to a high, small window to look up into Hanoi's skies and see Phantoms overhead, the first American warplanes seen by the POWs in four years). Not exactly stated in explicit terms but clearly implied was that the Nixon administration would settle for a simple end to the fighting: Give us our POWs, leave South Vietnam in existence, and we'll go home.

Nixon's people were talking and fighting tough, but were willing to accept a settlement on reasonable terms. Indeed, the withdrawal of US forces and the Vietnamization of the war continued. During May, the Tropic Moon B–57G Canberras of the 13 TBS were returned to the United States. The combat career of the B–57 had finally ended. The venerable Thud was also finally phased out of the Pacific region with the sole exception of the F–105G Wild Weasel aircraft of the 17 WWS operating at Korat.

LINEBACKER PROGRESS

On 11 May 1972, an analysis presented to General Vogt at Seventh Air Force in Saigon

and also made available to Admiral Mack at Seventh Fleet seemed to confirm the general impression that the new LINEBACKER campaign was having an impact on Hanoi. The air operations seemed to be stopping the flow of supplies entering North Vietnam by land and was disrupting the enemy's entire transportation system. It was noted that the use of precision guided weapons, 'smart' bombs, was a significant factor in the campaign's effectiveness.

Deprived of Colonel Tomb's leadership, the North Vietnamese MiG force continued to suffer losses. On 11 May 1972, a MiG–21 was downed in a fray with F–4D Phantoms but the action was so furious and confusing that no credit was awarded to any individual crew for the kill. On 12 May 1972, Lt Col. Wayne T. Frye and Lt Col. James P. Cooney of the 'Triple Nickel' 555 TFS / 432 TRW at Udorn, the pilot and back-seater of an F–4D Phantom (66-8756) shot down a MiG–19 using a radar-guided Sparrow. Frye and Cooney believed that they deserved 'a world's record for the total age of a Phantom aircrew for a MiG kill'. Between the two, they had lived 85 years on this planet. They were also the first and only pair of lieutenant colonels in the same aircraft to get a MiG.

Phantom crews at this juncture commanded the skies. The tactics that had been developed for the Vietnam conflict had finally reached the point where they worked. Almost forgotten was the emphasis on speed which had been so important in fighter combat in previous wars, for both the Phantom and MiG–21 could fly much faster than they could fight. American pilots used a 'fluid four' formation which enabled each set of two aircraft in a four-ship flight to be ready to move when MiGs were spotted. Barrel roll and vertical scissors attacks, trading speed for position, were used effectively against the MiGs despite the latter's advantage in maneuverability over the Phantom. All reference to 'up' and 'down' was discarded as air combat became a matter of energy maneuvering, irrespective of an aircraft's location relative to the ground.

Two MiGs fell to Navy crews on 18 May 1972, one of these being the first use of the more advanced AIM–9G variant of the Sidewinder missile. Air Force and Navy crews claimed no fewer than four MiGs on 23 May 1972, one of these being the first downed by an F–4E Phantom, although the internal 20 mm cannon used in the F–4E model was not used for the kill.

Addition of the Grumman E–2A Hawkeye AWACS aircraft to the Fleet off the North Vietnamese coast greatly enhanced the potential of carrier-based squadrons to inflict harm on Hanoi's homeland. Operating in

unison with Disco and Red Crown, the
Hawkeye did more than merely guard Yankee Station's carrier forces from attack. The
early-warning aircraft provided radar and
electronic information about SAM and MiG
operations, giving American crews 'one up'
on the enemy. The improved E–2B variant of
the Hawkeye soon followed and was in action
with squadron VAW–116 on *Coral Sea* during the hectic fighting of May and June 1972.

On 31 May 1972, USAF fighters claimed
two MiG–21s in air battles. Captain Steve
Ritchie got one of these while flying an F–
4D Phantom (65-801) of the 555 TFS/432
TRW, his back-seater being Captain Lawrence H. Pettit. While the two men of a
Navy crew always flew together, Air Force
crews did not. This was Ritchie's second
MiG victory, but with a different GIB (guy in
back) than on the first.

The internally-mounted cannon on the F–
4E model Phantom finally claimed a MiG on
2 June 1972, when Major Philip W. Handley
and 1Lt John J. Smallwood claimed a MiG–
19 while flying F–4E (67-210). Their unit, the
58 TFS/432 TRW, was one of a number of
squadrons that had been brought into Southeast Asia to reinforce units already there.

2 May 1972 was also the day USS *Saratoga*
(CV–60), an east coast/Atlantic Fleet carrier,
arrived at Yankee Station. She was the first
Navy carrier to drop the CVA (attack carrier)
in favor of the CV (carrier), a decision which
resulted from *Sara* carrying her own ASW
(anti-submarine warfare) elements. *Sara* had
not originally been scheduled for a WestPac
cruise, but the sudden intensity of fighting
occasioned by the Easter invasion and the
LINEBACKER campaign meant that the ship
was needed urgently. Commander Lewis
Dunton, an A–7A Corsair pilot of the 'Bulls'
of VA–37, recalls the ship being literally uprooted on hours' notice for her very first-ever
combat deployment.

Several more MiGs fell in air action in
June, without the communists achieving significant success in return. On 21 June 1972, it
was *Saratoga*'s turn. Cdr Samuel C. Flynn,
Jr, executive officer of the 'Tomcatters' of

VF–31, launched from *Sara* at the controls of
an F–4J Phantom (157293) with Lt William
H. John attending the back-seat radar position. Flynn and John, using the callsign
Bandwagon, were given vectors to lead a division towards a flight of MiG–21s. A relatively
close-quarters battle ensued and Flynn employed a heat-seeking Sidewinder to bring
down his quarry. An interesting sidelight is
that Flynn later returned to serve as skipper
of VF–31 and one of the aircraft in the squadron, which currently operates F–14A Tom-

cats, is always painted in markings to repre-
sent the MiG kill.

Operations by *Saratoga*'s air wing, especially her Corsairs, coupled with Air Force
missions to break the siege of An Loc and
thus bring to an end any prospect that
Hanoi's invasion would achieve its intended
purpose. The obvious bears repeating: Hanoi
had intended that the invasion would achieve
the final victory over the South. It did not.

On 29 June 1972, General Frederick C.

Key figure behind the LINEBACKER campaign, which responded to Hanoi's Easter invasion, was President Richard M. Nixon. Perhaps the most knowledgeable recent US president on foreign affairs, Nixon sought to contain the Watergate scandal, achieve detente with the Soviet Union, defeat Senator McGovern in the 1972 campaign, and bring North Vietnam to a settlement. Many civilian policymakers in Washington never realized that US aircraft in Route Package Six were winning the war. (USAF)

Weyand replaced General Creighton Abrams as the American field commander in Saigon. Behind the scenes, the administration was looking for some way to end the conflict which had tortured Americans and Vietnamese alike for so long. Henry Kissinger made it known to Le Duc Tho that a solution could be reached if Hanoi would merely fulfil two requirements: South Vietnam would survive as a separate state and American POWs would be returned. There was some talk inside the administration of pressuring President Thieu into accepting some form of Viet Cong 'participation' in a Saigon government, but this was exceedingly unrealistic.

It seems unique to the American character to behave like a loser while winning, and vice-versa. Since the mining of Haiphong, North Vietnam was having the greatest difficulty merely surviving, let alone fighting, and the relentless LINEBACKER effort was wearing the enemy down. Yet Washington was willing to accept terms which made it seem the US was losing instead of winning. It was another election year. The incumbent Nixon was in many respects at the peak of his popularity. There had been a break-in at Democratic party headquarters in the Watergate Hotel in Washington, and the Democrats were about to nominate a staunch anti-war campaigner (and former B-24 Liberator pilot), Senator George McGovern, to stand against Nixon. Nixon's supporters were playing 'dirty

tricks' with the Democrats when they were so far ahead, they did not need to; the Washington policymakers were willing to make concessions to Hanoi when they were winning by so much, they had no need to concede anything at all.

RITCHIE'S THIRD AND FOURTH

The Navy had an ace. The Air Force had none. On 8 July 1972, for the first time, it began to look like the USAF might catch up. Captain Steve Ritchie went aloft from Udorn in an F-4E Phantom (67-362), still wearing an ED tailcode indicating its home at Eglin AFB, Florida—one of the Constant Guard aircraft that had reinforced the 555 TFS/432 TRW. Ritchie was accompanied by Captain Charles B. DeBellevue.

Ritchie's Paula flight was assigned the MiGCAP role for a LINEBACKER strike, flying at low altitude west of Phu Tho and south of Yen Bai—the latter a 'sore thumb' that the

Americans yearned to cut off. Disco and Red Crown advised Ritchie of 'blue bandits', the term for MiG-21s, southeast of his position at a distance of about 40 miles (62 km). Ritchie took Paula flight toward the hostile aircraft in patrol formation and crossed the Black River on a southerly course. Red Crown informed him that his own radar image had just merged with that of the MiGs.

Ritchie turned north. He spotted two MiG-21s at his ten o'clock position. He ordered the flight to punch off its external fuel tanks and executed a hard left turn as the MiGs swung to the right. Ritchie was able to get off a radar-guided Sparrow missile which struck a MiG dead-center causing it to explode and disintegrate in mid-flight.

Ritchie then turned hard right, rebuilding lost energy, and pursued the lead MiG-21, which was now in a rear-quarter attack on one of his wingmen. Again, he was able to 'acquire' the target for the radar-guided Sparrow. He fired one Sparrow which hit the MiG-21 and caused a brilliant yellow fireball. The aircraft went into the ground. Steve Ritchie had now matched Robin Olds' remarkable feat of achieving four air-to-air victories over North Vietnam and his backseater, Chuck DeBellevue, had credit for three.

The next two Udorn MiG kills were scored by the team of Lt Col. Carl G. Baily and Captain Jeffrey S. Feinstein. This left Feinstein with three MiG kills, Baily with two.

Captain Steve Ritchie scored his third and fourth MiG kills on 8 July 1972 flying an ED-coded Constant Guard F-4E Phantom rather than the F-4D model with which his 'Triple Nickel' 555 TFS was equipped. F-4E Phantom 68-374, here taking off from its home base at Eglin AFB, Florida, is one of those which deployed to Southeast Asia for the LINEBACKER buildup. (USAF)

'Ace fever' was rampant at Udorn. Somebody, it seemed, was going to match the feat of the Navy's Cunningham and Driscoll by downing five North Vietnamese aircraft.

ENTER THE PROWLER

July 1972 saw the introduction to battle of the Grumman EA–6B Prowler, a modified electronic warfare version of the A–6 Intruder with a 40 in (103 cm) extension of its fuselage to make room for its third and fourth crew members, and with a variety of 'black box' devices designed to make life difficult for the enemy's sensors. The first EA–6B had made its maiden flight four years earlier on 25 May 1968, powered by two 9,300 lb (4 128 kg) thrust Pratt & Whitney J52–P–8A engines. Later, a switch was made to the 11,200 lb (5 080 kg) thrust J52–P–408. The

Prowler was configured to carry jamming pods which covered eight frequency bands. Possibly ahead of its time, the Prowler was the premier electronic warfare aircraft in the world at the time it was introduced to combat by a crew of VAQ–132 aboard USS *America* (CVA–66), another east coast/Atlantic Fleet carrier which had returned to the conflict. *America* was also of interest for another reason. One of its two F–4J Phantom squadrons was a Marine Corps unit, the 'Shamrocks' of VMFA–333, one of the very few Marine units to fight North Vietnam from shipboard.

There were now no fewer than *six* American carriers operating off the enemy coast, virtually half of the carrier force available to the entire US Navy—*America, Hancock, Kitty Hawk, Midway, Oriskany* and *Saratoga*. The weather, which was supposed to get better by July, didn't. Every mission being flown up North, from bombing to reconnais-

The Grumman EA–6B Prowler electronic warfare aircraft was the last new aircraft type to be introduced to the conflict against North Vietnam. This crew from squadron VAQ–132 flew the first combat mission in the EA–6B from the carrier USS *America* (CVA–66) in July 1972. (VIA PETER B. MERSKY)

sance, was impeded by the poor weather conditions. For the crew of *Oriskany*, things were made worse when the ageing World War Two carrier bumped up against an ammunition ship in a collision which wrecked one of its aircraft elevators. The carrier completed its cruise, but with severe difficulty.

Vietnamization continued. President Nixon continued to maintain that he would bring home all of the Americans from Southeast Asia, and made this a campaign promise in his electoral race against Senator McGovern.

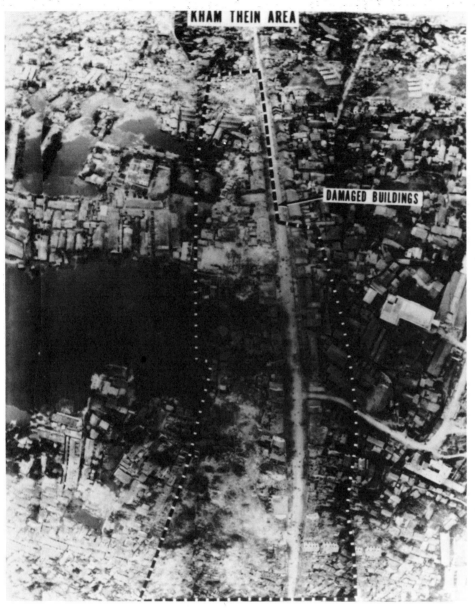

KHAM THEIN AREA

DAMAGED BUILDINGS

A Navy / Marine crew flying an Air Force Phantom scored a MiG kill on 12 August 1972. Captain Lawrence G. Richard, USMC, was the pilot of the F–4E Phantom (67–239) of the 58 TFS / 432 TRW, another 'temporary duty' unit brought in as part of the Constant Guard reinforcements. His back-seater was Lcdr Michael J. Ettel, USN. The pair were escorting a weather reconnaissance flight when aggressive MiG–21s engaged them. They used an AIM–7 Sparrow to knock down a MiG–21.

US COMBAT TROOPS OUT

The ultimate aim of President Nixon's Vietnamization program was announced to have been achieved on 12 August 1972: *all* United States combat troops had departed South Vietnam. Some 43,500 American servicemen

remained in what was called advisory and administrative roles. To the Air Force, Navy and Marine fliers pitted in the fight of their lives deep in North Vietnam, it seemed that what *they* were doing was 'combat'. To Americans soon to decide at the polling place whether to return Nixon to office, the announcement was good news.

The fighting up North was fast and furious. Among participants were the US Marine fliers of the 'Red Devils' of VMFA–232, fighting from the dust-strewn Rose Garden at Nam Phong. On 26 August 1972, a Marine F–4J Phantom was lost in air-to-air combat for the first time in the war. The details of the incident are believed to be presented here for the first time. The language is not evocative, but the event must have been:

'**Aircraft:**
'Section of [two] Marine F–4Js each configured with two AIM–7E Sparrows, two

AIM–9D Sidewinder, external wing tanks and a centerline tank.
'**Engagement Description:**
'Approaching BARCAP [barrier combat air patrol] orbit point, Red Crown called, "Bandits 030° for 42 miles, heading 190°." F–4s turned 030° to intercept.

'Wingman was having difficulty reading Red Crown and was unsure about lead's tactical plan. As the wingman RIO recalls, "We were at 20,000 feet, 360 [knots air speed], and no afterburner. We asked lead to relay calls from Red Crown but got no reply. Then we heard Red Crown say, '28 miles.' We couldn't figure out what the lead was doing. We were still straight and level, 360 KCAS, no burner, and had all three tanks. We blew off tanks at 18 miles. Lead still had his. At about 12 miles, we went completely visual. The last call we got from Red Crown was at eight miles. We were still not in afterburner and had less than 400 KCAS."

'Lead picks up the account. "The next call I heard was, 'Hold your plots merged.' We started a descending left turn from about 24,000 feet. Wingman was on the right about 1,000 feet back in a good supporting position."

'**Engagement results:**
'While in the turn, lead saw what he thought were two afterburner ignition puffs in his seven to eight o'clock high position which seemed to be pointed toward his four o'clock. At this time he eased his left turn to check his three o'clock and his RIO saw the wingman's aircraft explode.

'Pulling hard right toward the fireball, lead observed a MiG–21 passing his three o'clock in a left turn. As the angles-off increased, the MiG dove away for separation and disappeared.

'Observing two good chutes, lead began an orbit of the area and initiated the SAR [search and rescue] effort. The RIO was recovered. The pilot, First Lieutenant Sam Cordova, was not.' [58]

This loss of an F–4J Phantom (155811) was attributed, with the benefit of hindsight, to 'unsound tactics utilized by military lead.' The RIO who was rescued after the shootdown was quoted, 'All through the intercept ... I just wanted to get the hell out! It was obvious that if we were engaged we would be extremely lucky to get out, let alone bag a MiG.' [59] Later he added, 'Our flight failed to do basics: didn't punch tanks, no afterburner, poor communications, lack

It was the fate of the Nam Phong-based 'Red Devils' of VMFA–232 to lose the first Marine Corps Phantom shot down by a MiG, on 26 August 1972. By the time this F–4J (153859) was seen at Misawa AB, Japan, on 15 July 1974, the war was over and the Marines had finally ended their long presence in Southeast Asia. (NORMAN TAYLOR)

of aggressiveness. We entered the fight defensive!'[60]

Notwithstanding greatly improved training, there were bound to be times when this sort of thing happened. In this instance, the loss of a Phantom in air-to-air combat was attributed to poor airmanship on the part of the section lead. On other occasions, simple failure in communication was often a problem.

FIRST USAF ACE

It was inevitable. As the fighting continued, the Air Force finally achieved what the Navy had accomplished already. As an official his-

Captain Charles DeBellevue got his fourth kill on the day Ritchie got number five, but eventually wound up with six MiG victories to become the ranking American ace of the war. Here, DeBellevue poses with his F–4D Phantom (66-7463) at Udorn. (USAF)

tory puts it, 'Captain Richard S. Ritchie, 555 TFS, Udorn, shot down his fifth MiG–21 over NVN on 28 August 1972 to become the first USAF ace of the conflict.'[61]

Ritchie's back-seater, Captain Charles B. DeBellevue, who was not yet an ace himself but would be, was an honest advocate for the aircraft they were flying:

'Well, not having flown anything but an F–4 and, of course, the various models each handle a little differently, I'd say the F–4 is very honest. It talks to you. If you're doing something it doesn't want to do, it will let you know. Now, you can press the issue and keep going with it—in which case the airplane will pretty much take over, go out of control or whatever. But before you lose control, it will talk to you. The wings will start rocking or, in the D model, which is what we flew in SEA, once you reach a regime approaching the limits of maximum performance, you can't see the instrument panel because the airplane is vibrating and shuddering so much. It's talking to you. If you know how to fly it, you'll ease off a little bit—no big deal.'[62]

DeBellevue, of course, later became a front-seat pilot in the Phantom and remains on active duty as an F–4 flier today.

Ritchie performed a victory roll when he returned to Udorn. Upon landing, he was met by fire engines, high-pressure water and champagne. Some say Ritchie was steered to his fifth kill, set up for it, as part of a team effort. In fact, Ritchie was in a somewhat unfavorable position relative to the MiG–21, fired two Sparrow missiles to get himself into better shape, and finally fired two *more* Sparrows to achieve the MiG kill. It was the crowning achievement of Ritchie's second combat tour in Southeast Asia and he fully deserved credit for a major achievement.

Intelligence reports make it clear that Hanoi really *was* 'hurting' under the burden of the LINEBACKER campaign and that leaders of the communist regime were having second thoughts, for the first time in more than a generation, about their prospects of taking over South Vietnam. LINEBACKER still imposed *some* restrictions on US aircrews, and a few inviting targets still escaped American attention, but there was no doubt that

Washington's strategy, for once, was working. Not that protest against the US role in the war slackened, but some Americans felt that they could finally see the end in sight— an end with South Vietnam intact. On 29 August 1972, President Nixon felt able to announce withdrawals that would reduce US strength in South Vietnam to 27,000 from 1 December. The President had come a long way since the time when the figure was well over half a million!

On 1 September 1972, Admiral Noel Gayler became CINCPAC. The new chief of US forces in the Pacific was a representative of a new generation of naval officer, partly a fighter, partly a technocrat. Gayler left considerable authority in the hands of the Seventh Fleet and Task Force 77 commanders, as well as the skippers and CAGs aboard his carriers.

On 9 September 1972, the team of Captain John A. Madden, Jr, and Captain Charles B. DeBellevue, aboard an F–4D Phantom (66-267) of the 555 TFS / 432 TRW, shot down two MiG–19s in a single fight. For De-Bellevue, the kills were his fifth and sixth, making him the ranking American ace of the war. Madden would eventually claim three MiGs and would have a claim for a fourth denied by the Seventh Air Force Enemy Aircraft Claims Evaluation Board because of 'insufficient evidence'.

There were, of course, continuing losses and an increasing population of 'new guy' POWs. Men who had been in captivity for as much as eight years considered the 'new guy' captives to be junior to them in every respect.

Steven Ritchie and Chuck DeBellevue stand in front of F–4D Phantom (66-7463) at Udorn. Later, the airframe had to be repainted to record its sixth kill. Ritchie shot down three MiGs in this aircraft and two in another for his total of five. (USAF)

After the end of the Southeast Asia conflict, the F-4D Phantom (66-7463) associated with Captain Steve Ritchie was transferred to the 8 TFW, or Wolfpack—hence the WP tailcode—which had moved to Kunsan AB, Korea by the time this 30 March 1974 photograph was taken. (DAVID W. MENARD)

At the time, of course, none knew if they would ever get out of North Vietnam, but the state of despondency attributed to Major Ken Cordier earlier had been replaced by simple joy at the knowledge that American warplanes were operating in Hanoi's skies again. An A-7B Corsair pilot of the 'Marauders' of VA-82 from USS *America* (CVA-66) became the latest 'new guy' POW on 10 September 1972 and the communists went to unusual lengths to photograph the remains of his Corsair in a pond.

On 11 September 1972, *America* with a Marine Phantom squadron embarked achieved a wholly different kind of distinction. For the first time in the war, a Marine

The F-4D Phantom (66-7463) associated with Captain Steve Ritchie and responsible for six MiG kills has remained in US Air Force inventory virtually up to the present day. Here, with postwar 'Europe One' wraparound camouflage and black tailcodes, the Phantom is seen with the 309 TFS/31 TTW, tailcode ZF, stationed at Homestead AFB, Florida but visiting Shaw AFB, S. C. on 15 February 1984. (NORMAN TAYLOR)

Corps aircraft flown by a Marine crew shot down a MiG-21. It was not an entirely happy day, even for the successful MiG killers.

Aboard the 60,100-ton USS *America* (CVA-66) where the 'Shamrocks' of VMFA-333 were flying F-4J Phantoms, Major Lee Thomas (Bear) Lasseter's MiG kill mission of 11 September 1972 was a kind of landmark. In one sense, it was a piece of history—another score in the air-to-air war. In another, it was merely the latest of a continuing series of strikes which were often so frequent that the men ate, slept, flew, and sometimes flew again—this routine broken by a mad rush to get on and off the dangerous flight deck, by sweltering in cramped billets beneath the thundering steam catapults, and by snatching quick precious moments under stress to write a letter home. Aboard a carrier, events were too cluttered, life too intense, for convenient division into beginning, middle and end.

Bear Lasseter was a Marine. The Shamrocks were the first Marine squadron to deploy to the battle zone with a carrier air wing. Lasseter was also, in the parlance of a shipmate, 'a fine fighter pilot and a tremendous human being'. So far, no Marine at the controls of a Marine aircraft had succeeded in shooting down a MiG. But they said that if anybody could do it, Lasseter could.

It wasn't for lack of trying. Broad, burly, mustachioed Bear had been waging the

Captain Richard S. (Steve) Ritchie became the first Air Force ace of the Vietnam conflict, and third American ace in all, when he downed his fifth MiG-21 on 28 August 1972. In this view taken much later at Udorn, Thailand on 5 February 1973, Ritchie stands in front of the F-4D Phantom (66-7463) which accounted for one more MiG than he did. Two of Ritchie's victories were achieved in another aircraft, an F-4E. (USAF)

Marines' war from the front seat of a Phantom since flying F-4Bs from Chu Lai with VMFA-542 in 1965. A major then, too, in a service slow on rank, he had been in this war off and on for a very long time indeed.

By this stage in the war, Navy and Marine aviators were good enough that MiG pilots did not tangle with them readily. Lasseter's usual back-seat radar intercept officer (RIO), Captain John D. (L'il John) Cummings, another veteran of combat in Phantoms, put it this way: 'Remember that [by] September 1972 the Navy fighter program was in good shape, thanks to Top Gun. Cunningham and the other Navy MiG killers had proven themselves and the North Vietnamese seldom challenged Navy aircraft. Most of our MiGCAP missions were fairly routine except for the constant SAM and AAA threat.'[63]

On 10 September, the day before their fateful MiG mission, Bear Lasseter and John Cummings flew MiGCAP in Route Package Six, 20 miles (32 km) south-southwest of Hanoi. It was their second mission that day. Their aircraft was F-4J Phantom bureau number 153904, side number AJ-211, callsign SHAMROCK. The AJ tailcode was a

A–7B Corsair (156798) of the 'Marauders' of VA–82 aboard USS *America* (CVA–66) was shot down over North Vietnam on 10 September 1972 and the pilot captured to become a 'new guy' POW. This view of the A–7B in a pond appears to have been 'set up' for North Vietnamese photographers. (VIA PHIL CHINNERY)

vestige of *America*'s traditional role as an *east* coast / Atlantic Fleet carrier, even though the ship had been on the line in the Western Pacific since July. Says Cummings:

'We got a call that MiGs were airborne north of us. Bear snapped the plane in a northerly direction and I buried myself in the radar trying to find them. A few seconds later our wingman called that he was receiving SAM indications and both Bear and I looked behind our wingman for SAMs, but none were on the way. We received another call from the PIRAZ ship [Red Crown] that MiGs were at our eight o'clock at 4 miles [10.4 km]. Bear called for an in-place turn to the left (wingman was on the right) and then called to drop tanks while we were both in the turn. (We were over Hanoi when we dropped tanks). As we came out of the turn I had radar contact on the MiGs about 20 miles [32.3 km] southwest of us and at about 20,000 ft [6 096 m]. We were at about 3,000 ft [851 m]. I locked one up and we took a heading to intercept. Shortly thereafter my radar died. Our wingman, who did not have radar contact, was low on fuel so we had to head back to the ship. This was the first time that MiGs had come up [against VMFA–333].' [64]

Radar failure was a mishap to which the Phantom was prone, sometimes at critical moments when an air-to-air engagement was about to unfold. That did not offer any comfort to Bear Lasseter who, at this late stage in the LINEBACKER campaign, sensed that more of the air war lay behind than ahead. The Navy and Air Force had already produced Phantom aces and, by now, had established clear superiority over the MiG–21. Out there in the thin upper air above the karst ridgelines and rice paddies of Route Package Six, there simply wasn't time for a mechanical mishap or a mistake. While *America* prowled the rough seas off the enemy coast, the men in VMFA–333's radar shop were put to work checking the status of each aircraft in the squadron.

The next day, 11 September 1972, Lasseter's back-seater flew two hops. The first

Rare view of a North Vietnamese airfield being bombed during the 1965–68 ROLLING THUNDER campaign. This happens to be Kep, being struck by F–105s in November 1965. During the LINEBACKER period, such scenes were more commonplace. (USAF)

was with a newer pilot, Lieutenant Eric Denkewalter, on his very first trip into Route Package Six. On this mission, their aircraft was F–4J Phantom bureau number 155516, side number AJ–202. Apparently, there was some MiG and SAM activity, but not close to where the Marines were operating. 'This was an uneventful flight—if you can ever call flying into RP–6 uneventful.' Cummings learned that in the afternoon he was on the schedule to fly with Bear Lasseter providing MiGCAP for a strike force hitting a 'fairly

In this 1965 photograph, Colonel Thomas H. Miller (at left) has just taken command of Marine aviation in South Vietnam and stands in front of an F–4B Phantom of the 'Gray Ghosts' of VMFA–531 at Da Nang with radar intercept officer W/O John Cummings. Seven years later, Captain Cummings was back-seater in an F–4J Phantom (155526) when he and Major Lee (Bear) Lasseter shot down a MiG. (MILLER)

easy' target near the coast, north of Haiphong.

Because it *was* an easy target, Major Lasseter chose as wingmen Captain Scotty Dudley and his RIO, Captain Diamond Jim Brady. Lasseter and Cummings would be aboard aircraft 155526, side number AJ–201, while Dudley and Brady were flying 154784, or AJ–206. Dudley and Brady were also making their first trip into Route Package Six. The mission was briefed by the strike leader for a radio-silent rendezvous and Bear Lasseter briefed the tanker crew of the Grumman KA–6D Intruder fuel ship on the refuel-

Although US Marine Corps fighter squadrons were supposed to be able to operate from carriers, they rarely did so, One exception was the 'Shamrocks' of VMFA–333, who operated the F–4J Phantom from USS *America* (CVA–66) in the final days of the LINEBACKER campaign. F–4J Phantom (153855) from the squadron carries a bombload and Sidewinders as it heads toward North Vietnam. (USMC)

ling point for the MiGCAP. SHAMROCK flight would take on fuel, then precede the strike force over the target. The two F–4J Phantom crews were also assigned the weather recce job.

As always, when getting into the F–4J for

This F–4J Phantom (154784) was lost in combat on 11 September 1972. When photographed here, the aircraft was assigned to the Navy's 'Black Aces' of VF–41. When lost in action, it belonged to the *America*-based 'Shamrocks' of VMFA–333 and was piloted by Captain Scotty Dudley with RIO Captain Jim Brady in the back seat. (JIM SULLIVAN)

the mission, Lasseter was a big man trying to fit into a big aircraft. Dominating the front part of the aircraft were the huge air intakes with their hydraulically-operated splitter ramps, designed to limit airflow at speeds above Mach 1.6 to prevent the General Electric J79 turbojets from choking on supersonic airflow into their turbines. Access to the front cockpit was obtained through a ladder which went over the forward engine intake and the pilot simply swung into the aircraft and dropped in. After climbing in, he had to strap the Phantom on. Lasseter was attached to his craft by two hoses, three wires, lap belt, shoulder harness and two calf garters to keep his legs from flailing about in a high-speed bailout. His G-suit, survival vest and parachute harness were far from comfortable, but they meant life or death. Not everything in the big, roomy cockpit was designed for comfort—controls and indicators for air-to-

ground delivery systems, not being used that day, seemed to have been squeezed in wherever there was room. But at least it was simple enough to start the Phantom. One switch and one button fired up each of the J79 engines.

Lasseter taxied out and moved the aircraft into position on *America*'s steam catapult. Deck crews attached the catapult harness to the Phantom's forward gear. Lasseter exchanged hand signals with a weightboard man, determining the proper weight setting of the aircraft for the catapult. Then came that instant when time seemed to stop as thousands of pounds of steam pressure slammed the Phantom from 0 to 150 mph (240 km/h) in a split second. Cummings, who was in the back seat, describes what happened next:

'At about 0700 we launched, joined with our wingman, and proceeded to meet the KA–6D tanker to top off our fuel before going over the beach. It was at this time that we encountered the first of several glitches. The KA–6D wasn't there! We looked for it for what seemed to be a long time before I broke radio silence to ask his position. The KA–6D was about 20 miles [32.1 km] from us.'

Cummings adds a bitter note on the sort of confusion inevitable in a combat situation:

'After the mission I asked the pilot why he was not at the briefed rendezvous point and he said that he was told by the PIRAZ ship to orbit at a different point. Since the controller was on another ship and not at our briefing, the fallacy of blindly complying with radio instructions without letting us know of a change in plans should have been obvious.'

Bear Lasseter hooked up the Phantom to refuel and wingman Scotty Dudley was refueling when Cummings picked up the strike force on his radar. More confusion: 'The strike force had rendezvoused and was heading for the target in order to make their target time. We had to stop Scotty's refueling in order to be in MiGCAP position before the bombers got to the target.'[65] Major Lasseter concluded that Dudley had had time to get enough fuel for the mission. After all, the target, a suspected SAM assembly area, was close to the coast and the assigned MiGCAP station was just a little further inland.

It is exactly this kind of thinking which can be regretted, later, when a battle is joined and there is no going back to change any part of what happened.

Lasseter's SHAMROCK flight crossed the North Vietnam coast near Isle De Cac Bah just northeast of Haiphong. Lasseter turned on a westerly heading and passed abeam the primary and secondary targets. Lasseter broadcast a code word to inform the strike force that the weather was good. Then, en

Possibly the only surviving photograph of Major Lee (Bear) Lasseter (third from right) was taken when he served with F–4B Phantom squadron VMFA–542 in South Vietnam in 1965. Lasseter on 11 September 1972 became the only Marine pilot to shoot down a MiG while flying a Marine aircraft. He died in 1980; the Lasseter Theater at MCAS Beaufort, SC, is named in his honor. (JOHN D. CUMMINGS)

route to MiGCAP station, he received a message from the controller aboard the PIRAZ ship, a Navy Chief named Dutch Schultz. The message was brief and simple: Lasseter's SHAMROCK flight was being vectored to intercept bandits 61 miles (98 km) to the west.

A man more philosophical than the hulking Bear Lasseter might have concluded that this was a perfect illustration of 'the fallacy of blindly complying with radio instructions.' Dutch Schultz, sitting aboard a destroyer in the Tonkin Gulf, might think it wise to vector SHAMROCK flight's Phantoms toward MiGs so far removed from the strike force. But was it wise? It became more important to wonder whether Dudley had acquired enough fuel before his *coitus interruptus* with the KA–6D. It was not standard practice to engage MiGs located so far from the strike force they were supposed to protect. Furthermore, though Lasseter had no way to know it, controller Schultz—credited with a good job—was steering the Phantom force because more senior officers, who should have been running the battle, were in the PIRAZ destroyer's wardroom, having dinner!

MiG ENGAGEMENT

The MiGs were circling Phuc Yen airfield about 10 miles (16 km) north-northeast of Hanoi and the PIRAZ controller kept giving Lasseter information which confirmed this. On the way to the engagement, Bear and his back-seater discussed Scotty Dudley's fuel situation again. Cummings remarked that he was apprehensive about being sucked off CAP station and about the possibility that other MiGs might come at the strike force from one of the airfields to the north, such as Kep. There was another section of Phantoms on MiGCAP using another radio frequency and Cummings assumed that they would be kept close to the strike force since Lasseter's section was being vectored to the intercept. This kind of caution, which would seem very important when looking back at the event later, was mixed with some enthusiasm: Bear Lasseter and John Cummings had been flying fighters a long time. They really wanted to have a go at the MiGs.

RIO Cummings always carried a Canon SLR camera with a 100 mm lens and had a cassette tape recorder strapped to his harness. The aircraft also had a working scope camera. 'The fact that I was able to turn all this crap on as well as use the camera during the ensuing fight is something of a minor miracle.' The camera would not survive the battle ahead but the tape of the conversation with the PIRAZ ship, callsign OSWALD, did survive. The text is remarkably succinct:

OSWALD: 'Okay, RED ONE and TWO, we have bandits west of you at 61 miles. Take a vector of 3 . . . correction . . . 290.'
CUMMINGS: 'Rog. I'm steady up. Okay, Bear, coming up Hot Mike.'
LASSETER: 'Hot Mike now.'
OSWALD: '277 62.'
CUMMINGS: 'Roger. DECM gear is all on.'
OSWALD: '276 at 60 now.'
CUMMINGS: 'Rog.'

The 'Shamrocks' of VMFA–333 had some of the most colorful markings of any squadron which participated in the long slog against North Vietnam. A 16 April 1975 postwar shot depicts the squadron's F–4J Phantom 154786, one of the survivors of the conflict. (JIM SULLIVAN)

With a MiG at 276 degrees at 60 miles, with microphones open so pilot and RIO could talk while communicating with the PIRAZ ship, and with the Phantom's defensive electronic countermeasures equipment on, SHAMROCK flight headed into the fray. The PIRAZ controller, Chief Schultz aboard the destroyer, continued passing instructions. Cummings picked up the MiGs on the Phantom's scope at 19 miles. Lasseter was holding SHAMROCK flight at an ingress altitude of about 3,000 feet. Though Lasseter and Cummings had not figured it out yet, the MiGs had been at about 20,000 feet when the Phantoms were first vectored in, but had rapidly spiraled down to about 1,000 feet, which is where they were when they appeared on the Phantom's scope. Because of their low altitude, Cummings was having a hard time maintaining radar contact and the PIRAZ controller was no longer holding them on *his* scope, either. Lasseter, Cummings, Dudley and Brady were all looking straight into the sun, which made visual contact all the more difficult.

The MiG–21s were in a modified trail formation with the trailer about three miles (4.8 km) behind and to the right. Cummings still had intermittent radar contact until about 6 or 7 miles (11 km). At this point, Scotty Dudley's voice was on the airwaves: 'Tally-ho! Tally-ho! Twelve o'clock. Keep going, straight.' Lasseter barked an order to his RIO: 'Okay, John, go boresight.'

This lengthy buildup to the actual engagement, based on research by Wausau, Wisconsin, historian Mike O'Connor as well as interviews by the author,[66] is meant to give the reader more of the 'flavor' of an actual combat mission than space would permit for every action that took place over North Vietnam. In the end, what happened was simple enough. Lasseter fired two Sparrows. Cummings looked ahead to see that both had missed and that the MiG was gaining angles on the Phantom.

For four and a half minutes, the fight went on—a furious, fuel-gasping duel. Throughout the engagement, AAA and SAM warnings were continuous. Cummings had never seen flak so heavy before or since. During the melee, Cummings fired two more Sparrows and two Sidewinders, but the MiG stayed low and played his turn so that he was on the edge of the missile envelopes.

Just as Dudley announced bingo fuel, the MiG–21 reversed and Bear Lasseter got a clean shot with a Sidewinder. Cummings recalled that 'the growl of the Sidewinder tone was loud enough to drive you from the cockpit'. The missile struck the MiG very solidly and blew apart everything aft of the cockpit—the 177th MiG kill of the war.

Another MiG evaded a Sidewinder fired by the Marines by *popping a flare* which lured away the heat-seeking missile—an incident not reported in any other encounter in the conflict. Low on fuel, frustrated, heading home, Lasseter and Dudley ran into communications problems while SAM warnings boomed in their earphones. More MiGs pursued the Phantoms. Too many people on the radio airwaves resulted in Lasseter missing a critical SAM warning. A missile exploded only feet from the Phantom. The instrument panel and all the fire lights lit up and both wings were riddled with holes. Dudley informed Lasseter that he was burning badly.

The Phantom pitched forward into a nose-down inverted spiral with increasing negative G forces. Lasseter and Cummings knew they had to get out, now. Lasseter reached behind his helmet and, against the G forces, began threading his face curtain out an inch at a time. Cummings got his face curtain handle past his helmet and pulled upward and forward along the canopy, hard enough to crack the cartilege in his rib doing it. Neither man was certain who actually triggered the ejec-

F-4J Phantom 153904 of VMFA-333 during the squadron's *America* cruise in the combat zone. (ROBERT L. LAWSON)

tion but they were delighted to be pulled out of the Gulf of Tonkin by a 'Big Mother' rescue helicopter.

Only later did the crew learn that Dudley's Phantom hadn't made it home either. Dudley's crew, out of fuel and short of the tanker, had also ejected and been rescued. In retrospect, it appears that the North Vietnamese tried to 'sucker' the Marines into

John D. Cummings was the back-seat radar intercept officer on the 11 September 1972 MiG kill by an F-4J Phantom. Cummings went on to become the first Marine to log 4,000 hours in the Phantom type. A warrant officer in this early portrait taken at Da Nang in May 1965, Cummings is now a lieutenant colonel serving at the Pentagon. (CUMMINGS)

exposing themselves to SAM fire and succeeded in doing so, but at the unexpected cost of one MiG-21 and very nearly at the cost of a second. Bear Lasseter later assumed command of VMFA-333 for the latter part of its combat cruise and the squadron racked up a superb record in the continuing LINEBACKER operations against North Vietnam. Throughout the carrier cruise, not a single aircraft was ever forced to divert to land and the only accident was a hard landing by the Navy CAG flying one of the Marines' aircraft. They may or may not have been suckered, but the Marines had acquitted themselves well.

Throughout September 1972, officials like Kissinger, Laird and Rogers looked for some opening in Le Duc Tho's bargaining position, strikes against targets in North Vietnam continued and air-to-air action raged. Air Force crews of the 35 TFS/388 TFW flying F-4E Phantoms shot down two MiGs on 12 September 1972. Four days later, another MiG fell, Captain Calvin B. Tibbett of the Triple Nickel becoming one of the few men to get credit for two MiG kills.

RETURN OF THE ONE-ELEVEN

On 28 September 1972, two F-111A squadrons from Nellis AFB, Nevada, 428 and 430 TFS, arrived at Takhli to relieve the F-4D Phantom squadrons of the 49 TFW which had deployed temporarily under Constant Guard III. The return of the F-111A to Southeast Asia was long overdue and most important. Although the earlier deployment

of the aircraft in 1968 had been star-crossed and had ended with the type being withdrawn, the F-111A now proved itself to be a well-designed and thoroughly able fighting machine. Its superb navigation system and all-weather capability, coupled with ordnance-carrying capacity, made it the only Air Force craft capable of the kind of 'lone wolf' night/bad-weather operation which had been routine for the Navy's A-6A Intruder.

With all the fighting that was going on, opponents of the US posture in Vietnam felt that their protests were leading towards an end to the long, long conflict. At the same time, policymakers and military men believed that the battering of North Vietnam was going to produce just such an end to the fighting, but on terms acceptable to the US. Saigon's President Thieu opposed any US settlement with Hanoi, fearing that a negotiated end to the fighting would put him at risk (correctly, as it turned out) while officials in the administration looked at Henry Kissinger's secret talks with Le Duc Tho with real hope.

Incredibly, at the very point when it had won the war, the US backed off. Henry Kissinger announced that, as a result of his talks with Le, 'Peace is at hand.' On 23 October 1972, LINEBACKER operations against North Vietnam were halted and all bombing north of the 20th Parallel was curtailed. Once again, the skies over Hanoi and Haiphong were free

The F-111A Aardvark returned to Southeast Asia on 28 September 1972 when two squadrons arrived at Takhli. A couple of F-111A crew members later attained the dubious distinction of becoming 'new guy' POWs, but losses of the type were not inordinately high and the F-111A proved itself during LINEBACKER operations to be a potent fighting machine. (USAF)

Captain Jeffrey S. Feinstein, weapons systems officer on an F-4D Phantom of the Udorn-based 13 TRS/432 TRW, was credited with his fifth MiG on 13 October 1972 to become the fifth American ace of the Southeast Asia War. (USAF)

Captain Jeffrey Feinstein, the fifth USAF ace of the war, standing in front of the best-known F-4D Phantom, 66-7463. (USAF)

of US warplanes. An official history says simply: 'Termination of LINEBACKER was the result of perceived progress in the ongoing peace negotiations. Unfortunately, the desired effect was not realized.'[67]

Very quietly, with very little notice, the 186th MiG kill of the war had been achieved two weeks earlier by an F-4D Phantom (66-7501) of the 13 TFS/432 TRW with Lt Col. Curtis D. Westphal in the front seat and Captain Jeffrey S. Feinstein in the back. The crew had used a Sparrow to blast a MiG-21 out of the sky. Feinstein, who flew more often in the company of Lt Col. Carl G. (Griff) Baily, rarely did anything to call attention to himself but he had just achieved a kind of immortality. Feinstein was the fifth and last American ace of the war and the second man to attain this status who sat in the back seat of a Phantom and who was not a pilot.

Were Feinstein and his mates winning the war? By October 1972, the skies over North Vietnam were much as they had been over Nazi Germany in 1945: American warplanes roamed at will, unchallenged, uncontested. The North Vietnamese had virtually no AAA ammunition or SAMs left. They had squandered their principal national force of 12 army divisions (leaving only one division in reserve at home) on an invasion that had failed. By every possible measure, North Vietnam in October 1972 had lost its war against the United States. As one official put it, perhaps with a premonition: 'The only thing we haven't done is to fly B-52s over their heads around the clock.'

Why, then, did the US let up?

Why was the LINEBACKER campaign ended and bombing north of the 20th Parallel brought to a halt?

Those are questions not for airmen but for policymakers. In a week's time, the American people were going to re-elect Richard Nixon as President, Watergate or no Watergate, and everybody knew it. Nixon, then, needed no

face-saving gesture toward opponents of the war. He appears to have halted the bombing because he genuinely believed that Hanoi was now ready to settle the conflict at last.

He was almost right. *Some* in Hanoi were ready. Some were going to need more persuasion.

ENTER THE A-7D

Just as LINEBACKER was coming to an end, the 354 TFW at Myrtle Beach AFB, South Carolina, under Colonel Thomas M. Knoles III deployed with three squadrons, arriving at Korat with a new addition to the USAF

combat inventory, the A-7D attack aircraft. Technically not given the name Corsair II like its US Navy counterpart, the A-7D was in most respects virtually identical to the A-7E which had already been flying in combat from carrier decks for two years. Knoles' wing was soon joined by a locally-activated PACAF squadron, the 3 TFS, under Lt Col. Edward R. (Moose) Skowron, also operating

At the end of the LINEBACKER campaign, 23 October 1972, US warplanes were able to roam the skies of North Vietnam virtually at will. Here, Marine Corps F-4B Phantom 153062 of the 'Silver Eagles' of VMFA-115 operates in conjunction with Air Force F-4D and F-4E Phantom fighters. (VIA PETER B. MERSKY)

Preflighting a mission, 13 TRS/432 TRW, Udorn. From left to right are SSgt Salvador Herrera, a maintenance crewman, Captain Jeffrey Feinstein, a Phantom back-seater, and Lt Col. Carl G. (Griff) Baily, Phantom pilot. When this photograph was taken on 11 August 1972, it could not have been predicted that Feinstein would gain credit for five MiG kills and become the fifth and final American ace of the Vietnam war. (USAF)

Shark-toothed A–7D attack aircraft, not really called a Corsair in USAF service, belongs to the 3 TFS under Lt Col. Edward (Moose) Skowron. The unit, with its JH tailcode, began combat operations just as the LINEBACKER campaign came to an end. (USAF)

the A–7D. The SLUF ('short little ugly fella') was more popular with pilots than many realized and the aircraft acquitted itself well during bombing missions in the final week of LINEBACKER.

Almost immediately, a new role was assigned to the A–7D. As part of the Vietnamization effort, A–1 Skyraiders were desperately needed for turnover to the South Vietnamese air force. To relieve the Skyraiders in the 'Sandy' role, escorting armed helicopters into enemy territory on combat rescue missions, the Air Force chose the A–7D. Tactics had to be changed, for the A–7D could not 'slow down' enough to keep pace with an HH–53C Super Jolly Green helicopter. Instead of directly escorting the chopper, A–7D pilots flew slow lazy circles while maintaining a kind of formation and leading rescue forces to the scene where downed airmen needed help.

In November 1972, a two-man F–105G Wild Weasel crew was downed south of the 20th Parallel in the heavily-defended Vinh

region. Captain Colin A. (Arnie) Clarke of the Korat-based 354 TFW spent nearly *twelve hours* in his A–7D cockpit, with four refuelings from KC–135 tankers, fighting poor weather, faulty communications and heavy ground fire to guide HH–53Cs to the rescue. Clarke was hit by a 57 mm shell, and was tracked by a SAM site which, for reasons unknown, chose not to fire. He waged a running battle with AAA batteries, repeatedly risking getting below fuel minimums while taking damage. Clarke's was a marathon effort which resulted in the rescue of the crew of the last F–105 shot down in Southeast Asia. For his perseverance, Clarke was decorated with the second highest American award, the Air Force Cross.

LINEBACKER INTERLUDE

Americans who re-elected Nixon that first week in November genuinely believed, as did Kissinger, that peace was coming. But these hopes were abruptly dashed. Once Nixon ended LINEBACKER and kept US warplanes south of the 20th Parallel, the communists simply followed past form and began rebuilding. As a kind of symbolic display of their real intentions, on 22 November 1972 the North Vietnamese succeeded at last—

after seven years of trying—in shooting down a B–52. B–52D Stratofortress (55-110) of the 307 Strategic Wing from U-Tapao, itself operating south of the 20th Parallel in keeping with Nixon's show of restraint, was hit by a SAM. The Stratofortress made it to Thailand where the crew ejected and was recovered. In finally claiming a 'Fifty-two', Hanoi may have committed a serious error: this juncture in history was not the right moment to get people thinking about B–52s. Nor did the North Vietnamese assist matters by stomping out of the peace talks on 13 December 1972.

If there was a breakdown in the peace process, no one could have been happier than South Vietnam's President Thieu. He was resisting becoming a signatory to a Kissinger-Tho agreement that would end the conflict at the very time when the North Vietnamese seemed unlikely to sign the settlement themselves. As one State Department official says it; 'Everything was becoming unraveled.'

There was, in the end, no choice for the American President. Nixon was determined not to give the mixed signals or the indications of weakness which had been transmitted by his predecessor. Secure in his election victory, convinced that force would end the war, Nixon prepared for the first time

Vought A–7D attack aircraft of the 354 TFW, from
Myrtle Beach AFB, S. C. (MB tailcode), which
deployed to Korat in October 1972 and participated in the final week of LINEBACKER operations
against North Vietnam, which ended on 23 October
1972. Later, the A–7D participated in combat
operations in Cambodia. (USAF)

The B–52 Stratofortress was vital to the war
against North Vietnam in the final days and, in
the end, more than half of the entire Strategic Air
Command B–52 force was committed to the
'Eleven Day War'. Here, B–52D Stratofortress 55-
0087 of the 307 Strategic Wing taxies at U-Tapao,
the Thai base from which many bomber strikes
were launched. (USAF)

The first B–52 Stratofortress tail-gunner to shoot down a MiG, SSgt Samuel O. Turner, is awarded the Silver Star for gallantry by General John C. Meyer, SAC commander-in-chief. Turner (since deceased) got his MiG–21 on the night of 18 December 1972, on one of the first missions of 'the Eleven-Day War'. (USAF)

to authorize a maximum, round-the-clock bombing effort against the urban centers of Hanoi and Haiphong. Steps were taken to strip the Strategic Air Command's force of about 450 B–52 Stratofortresses around the world and to commit fully one-half of that force to the new bombing effort. Folksinger Joan Baez, visiting Hanoi, would call it the 'Christmas bombing' (although, in truth, a respite would come on that holiday). SAC people would call it 'the Eleven-Day War'. But the official name was inevitable. The final campaign of the American war against North Vietnam was to be known as LINEBACKER II.

LINEBACKER II

The final campaign was fought over the eleven-day stretch from 18 to 29 December 1972 (with, as noted, a break in the fighting on Christmas day). It brought the population at Anderson AFB, Guam, up to some 12,000, or nearly three times the number of people the base was intended to accommodate— meaning that B–52 people ate, slept and moved around the base in improvised fashion. Even the base gymnasium was pressed into service to accommodate the overflow, this quickly taking on the appearance of a huge dormitory which provided little privacy or respite from the demands of a 72-hour work week. The LINEBACKER II campaign was to cost no fewer than 15 B–52s shot down by Hanoi's surface-to-air missiles (although none by MiGs, despite enemy claims). It was to demand an unusual measure of commitment from everyone involved.

On 18 December 1972—the first day of the campaign, and also the day when Captain John Madden claimed an F–4D Phantom MiG kill which was disallowed—waves of B–52 Stratofortresses swarmed over the Hanoi-Haiphong region. SSgt Samuel O. Turner, the fire control operator or tail-gunner of an U-Tapao-based B–52D Stratofortress (56-0676) flying in a three-ship cell called Brown flight, became the first enlisted man and the first gunner to shoot down a MiG–21. Another B–52 tail-gunner that night claimed a MiG kill which was disallowed for lack of sufficient evidence.

There has been much debate about the B–52 tactics employed in LINEBACKER II. The

The final American campaign against North Vietnam had to be fought with an aircraft that had been designed in the 1940s as a nuclear bomber. Boeing B–52D Stratofortress is readied on Guam for a mission to the Hanoi-Haiphong region in December 1972. (USAF)

River port areas of Hanoi destroyed by heavy bombing, apparently by B–52 Stratofortresses, during the LINEBACKER II campaign. (USN)

faults lay not with the bomber crews who for years had requested changes in their tactics, pointing out that straight-line approaches were adequate in the South but that 'jinking' and 'dodging' techniques were needed up North. Dana K. Drenkowski, a B–52 pilot, argues that SAC crews indoctrinated for lone-wolf nuclear missions simply never had the training for mass formation flying and

HANOI PORT (AREAS A,C,E)

16 BUILDINGS DAMAGED

DESTROYED BUILDING

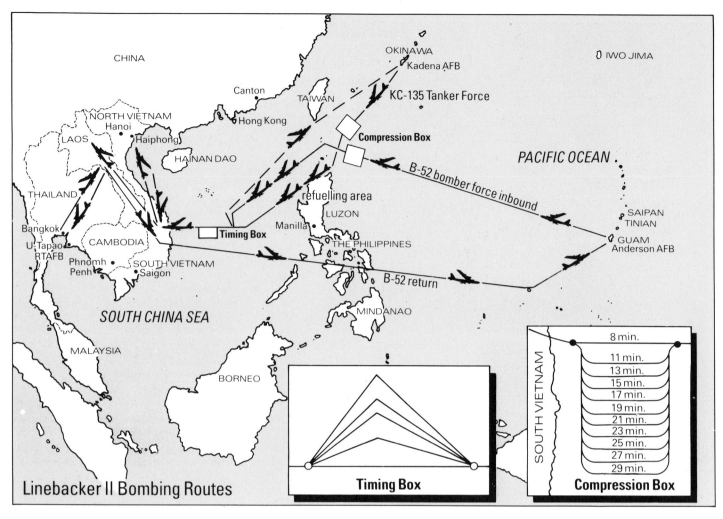

Linebacker II Bombing Routes

Timing Box

Compression Box

Routes followed by B–52 Stratofortress bombers during the December 1972 LINEBACKER II operations. The B–52s operated from Andersen AFB, Guam and U-Tapao, Thailand.

were in constant danger of repeating the tragic collision that had marred the first Arc Light mission back in 1965.

Careless actions, like the turning on and testing of ECM a certain number of minutes prior to bomb release and the repeated use of the same approach to a target, increased the chance that a B–52 would be shot down before it could inflict any harm on North Vietnam. Against the thousands of SAMs in the Hanoi-Haiphong region (most brought in after the 23 October cessation of bombing in that very region), masses of B–52 Stratofortresses flew in a straight line, taking no evasive action, the intervals between three-ship cells of B–52s being known and anticipated by North Vietnamese gunners.

The simple fact that crews kept flying while exhausted made their job difficult. Morale was lowest at U-Tapao, where weary men flew at least one mission per day, while crews from Guam, coming longer distances,

flew only once every second or third day. Drenkowski and others faulted the Air Force for piecemeal attacks, lack of surprise, lack of flexibility, a poor sense of priorities and a lack of internal communication—so that the men flying the missions were often the last to know what was happening.

Of course, B–52s were not the only aircraft in North Vietnam's skies. Air Force F–4s, F–105Gs, A–7Ds and F–111As carried bombs against carefully-picked targets while Navy carrier-based F–4s, A–6s and A–7s carried their share of the load, but LINEBACKER II will best be remembered as a B–52 operation, and perhaps it can be understood better from the viewpoint of the crew of one participant.

Approaching Hanoi on the night of 27 December 1972 as pilot of a B–52D Stratofortress (56-0599) from the 307 Strategic Wing at U-Tapao, Captain John D. Mize looked out to see five or six SAMs hurtling through the sky in front of him. Mize's tail-gunner, TSgt Peter E. Whalen, peered from his lonely perch in the rear of the B–52D. Whalen later described it. 'When the SAMs come up through the clouds, you see a bright glow as the rocket fire reflects on the cloud. The clouds magnify the light and make the SAM

look bigger than it really is. When the sky is clear, you can see the initial flash when the SAM is launched.' Captain Mize had learned that the SAM you could see coming wasn't the one that would kill you.

By this ninth day of the 'Eleven-Day War', North Vietnam's defenses were badly battered and SAMs were 'unguided missiles', being fired in salvoes as if sheer numbers alone would do the job. As his B–52D approached its target (one of the SAM sites ringing Hanoi), John Mize now saw *fifteen* SAMs airborne at once. Ten seconds after releasing its load of 84 500 lb bombs, the B–52D was shaken by a tremendous concussion on its left side. Shrapnel from the exploding SAM wounded Mize in the left thigh and lower left leg. His right hand, still on the control column, was gashed by flying steel.

Tail-gunner Whalen was hit by shrapnel. Radar navigator Captain Bill North, off from the crew where there were no windows, knew the aircraft was hit when his lights and electrical systems went out. Navigator Lt Bill Robinson, in the same location, felt shards of metal tear into his leg.

The B–52D lurched left, then right. Mize was hurled forward against his harness. En-

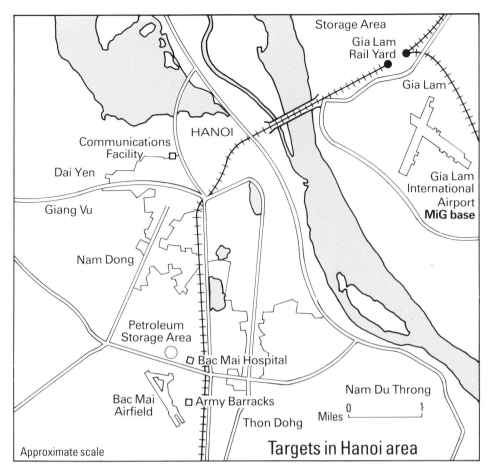

Targets in and around Hanoi during the 'Eleven Day War' or LINEBACKER II operations of December 1972.

gine fire warning lights flashed in front of his face. The abrupt loss of three of its eight engines sent the bomber plummeting several thousand feet.

Hurt, Mize struggled to regain control. With sheer physical effort, he brought the B–52D into level flight. He called each man in the crew of six to determine how badly they were injured and to check damage. Navigator Robinson gave Mize a heading to leave the target area. Mize felt there was a remote chance of reaching Nakhon Phanom, the nearest Thai airbase, but his first concern was to reach a safer place to eject. Busy with these emergency reactions, he also struggled with a fourth engine on the left side of the aircraft.

Later, the B–52D pilot would make his struggle for life sound almost routine. 'I'm not the first guy to fly a B–52 on four engines,' Captain Mize later told a group at his home unit, the 7th Bombardment Squadron at Ellsworth AFB, SD. 'I had not previously done any real needle, ball and airspeed flying or what is referred to as "flying by the seat of your pants," but the B–52 can be flown that way.' In fact, the situation was critical. *All*

four lost engines were on the port side, giving Mize power on starboard only. The B–52 was burning and shaking. It could become a torch, Mize knew.

With all of his automatic navigation equipment gone or shut down, Robinson used airspeed and distance traveled in minutes along with estimated headings to try to get the burning Stratofortress to Thailand. His difficulty was compounded by the airspeed indicator being unreliable because of damage. Captain Mize had fallen away from his three-ship cell of B–52s, so no other bombers were nearby to help with the navigating.

Rescue forces were alerted. A rescue HC–130 Hercules command ship joined Mize near the border of North Vietnam and Laos, just as his crew made a last-minute check of their ejection seats. They were at 12,000 feet over mountainous terrain with sheer cliff-sides. Robinson's calculations were that by going another 30 miles they could have flat terrain.

Altitude was of critical importance, with only four of the bomber's eight engines working and only enough electrical system for cockpit lights and a radio. Mize flew the aircraft with a brute-force method which consisted of descending about 1,500 feet to pick up airspeed, then climbing 1,000 feet. More than an hour after 'bombs away' on Hanoi, he

finally reached more hospitable terrain in Thailand.

The situation rapidly deteriorated. The bomb bay doors fell open, one landing gear started cycling maddeningly up and down, and other electrical systems went amuck. Mize knew, now, that there was no hope of coaxing the B–52D to a crash landing at Nakhon Phanom. When he could hold it no longer and feared loss of the intercom, he ordered the crew to bail out.

Four men blew themselves out into the night sky, including co-pilot Captain Terrance Gauthers. The navigator pulled his 'eject' handle and nothing happened. Bill Robinson's downward ejection seat would not function.

'Climb out!' Mize barked. He wanted Robinson to jump through the hole opened up where Bill North had ejected. Robinson got up to do this and the two men could no longer communicate. Still, Mize delayed his own ejection, wanting to be satisfied that the navigator had gotten out.

There was now underway a perilous waiting game in which, no longer able to talk to Robinson, Mize could only attempt to retain control of the B–52D long enough for the navigator to jump. By now, the only lighting in the B–52D was in the forward cabin. Flames were spreading from the wing. Captain Mize continued to struggle with the controls but the bomber was falling now, relentlessly. *Wait*, he thought, mentally going through his own ejection procedure but worried about Robinson. *Wait ... wait ...*

Though Mize had no way to know, Robinson jumped successfully. Captain Mize did not know either that rescue forces had set up a string of covering aircraft and helicopters which followed the crippled B–52's path, setting up the largest mass pickup of the war.

Time ran out. The electrical system died. Mize ejected.

In the night and the cold in the Thai jungle, helicopters homed in on the URC–64 beeper radios carried by each crewman and all six from the bomber were rescued within 15 minutes of Captain Mize's bailout. Though Mize himself soft-pedals it, it was apparent later that only a superhuman effort by the Stratofortress pilot enabled the B–52D to reach a location where rescue was possible. The final moments in the life of 56-0599, when Mize 'held on' to get the navigator out, punctuated Mize's award of the Air Force Cross, the second highest American decoration for valor. The medal was presented by General John C. Meyer, commander in chief of the Strategic Air Command, Mize being the only SAC member to win this honor in the conflict.

A second B–52D tail-gunner, A1C Albert

183

B–52D tail-gunner TSgt Peter E. Whalen (left) stands with Captain John D. Mize, pilot of a B–52D Stratofortress (56-0599) of the 307th Strategic Wing at U-Tapao, Thailand, Mize was the first SAC officer to be awarded the Air Force Cross, for heroism as a B–52D pilot during the 'Eleven-Day War'. (USAF)

E. Moore, was also credited with a MiG kill.

Over the eleven-day period of LINEBACKER II, 714 B–52 Stratofortress sorties, 830 USAF tactical sorties and 386 US Navy / US Marine Corps tactical sorties were flown. The North Vietnamese, say those who record such figures, fired no fewer than 1,293 SAMs during the battle. Two F–4 Phantoms and two F–111As were among other US casualties.

There was an uproar in the US; Joan Baez wrote a song about it; people protested; not a few supported Nixon; and while all the debate raged, North Vietnam was devastated. After many years of conflict, it had taken only eleven days to prove what airpower could do. For all practical purposes, North Vietnam had been taken out of the conflict.

Meanwhile, Vietnamization moved ahead. The rapid expansion of the South Vietnamese air force under Project Enhance and Enhance Plus resulted in a year-end strength of 1,817 assigned aircraft. Major aircraft types included 246 A–37B Dragonflies, 135 F–5 fighters and 540 UH–1 Huey helicopters. It was acknowledged that the Saigon air arm had more airframes than it could operate, but this was a planned, deliberate action by the US Government in case Congress cut off authority for future replacements of assets.

YEAR-END WRAPUP

US Air Force people in Saigon who kept the numbers decided that tactical forces in PACAF flew 254,895 combat sorties and expended 899.5 thousand tons of munitions in Southeast Asia during the year, suffering the loss of 194 aircraft. These figures include 115,298 attack sorties and 28,383 B–52 Arc Light sorties. KC–135 Stratotankers accomplished 111,770 aerial refuelings. The year ended with the 'Eleven-Day War' over, Le Duc Tho preparing to sign his name on the dotted line, and the long war finally in sight of a conclusion.

END OF A CONFLICT

Another bombing halt to commemorate a holiday, this time a 24-hour cessation to 2 January 1973, was followed by resumption of strikes into North Vietnam. During the first two weeks of the new year, B–52 Stratofor-

F–4B Phantom (150407) of the 'Chargers' of *Midway*-based VF–161 with parabrake deployed at NAF Atsugi, Japan, in April 1975. In another F–4B Phantom (153045) virtually identical to this one, Lt Victor T. Kovaleski and LtJg James A. Wise shot down a MiG–17 on 12 January 1973, the final kill of the war. Thus, the carrier *Midway* was credited with the first and last MiGs downed in the conflict. (VIA JIM SULLIVAN)

tress operations continued at a reduced pace. By the time operations halted, the Stratofor-tresses had flown a further 535 sorties, while Phantoms and other tactical aircraft flew an additional 716 sorties against North Vietnam. It was only when peace negotiations genuinely began to make progress for the first time that all air strikes against North Vietnam were halted, on 15 January 1973. Reconnaissance flights over the North continued until the halt of all United States combat operations in North *and* South Vietnam on 27 January 1973, the final day of the war, although fighting in Laos and Cambodia would continue.

The 197th and last MiG kill of the war took place on 12 January 1973 when Lt Victor T. Kovaleski of the 'Chargers' of VF–161 operating from USS *Midway* (CVA–41) used a Sidewinder to take down a MiG–17. Kovaleski's back-seat RIO on this mission was LtJg James A. Wise. It should be noted that the carrier *Midway* scored the first and last MiG kills of the war and that Lt Kovaleski also had the peculiar distinction of piloting the last aircraft to be shot down over North Vietnam, a Phantom downed on 14 January 1973. He and his RIO were rescued.

When the air-to-air statistics were tallied

and ready for study, it appeared that the US had ended up with about a two-to-one advantage over the North Vietnamese MiG—not nearly as well as American pilots had done in previous wars and not nearly good enough. One of the most significant results of the air-to-air conflict over the North was the creation of the US Navy's 'Top Gun' and the USAF's 'Aggressors'—the mock enemy which gave truly *realistic* air-to-air combat training.

With the benefit of dissimilar air combat (DAC) maneuvering as a part of their development syllabus, American pilots could hope never again to be bested by anyone like Colonel Tomb.

On 28 January 1973, 'The Agreement on Ending the War and Restoring the Peace in Vietnam' was signed in Paris. According to the agreement, by 60 days thereafter all US military personnel were to be withdrawn

from South Vietnam. All American prisoners would be released and returned. Residual responsibilities of Seventh Air Force headquarters in Saigon were quickly moved to Nakhon Phanom, Thailand, and US Navy vessels in the Gulf of Tonkin prepared themselves for a new responsibility—clearing the mines that had been seeded around Haiphong. The long battle was over.

POSTSCRIPT

United States combat operations against North Vietnam, which had begun on 5 August 1964, ended on 27 January 1973 when Commander Dennis Weichman, skipper of the 'Blue Tail Flies' of attack squadron VA–153 brought his A–7B Corsair back to USS *Oriskany* (CVA–34) after completing the final combat mission of the war. The prisoners of war were released soon afterward and men like Major Ken Cordier came home at last. The FREEDOM TRAIN, LINEBACKER and LINEBACKER II campaigns of 1972 had achieved what earlier efforts could not: US air operations had forced Hanoi to a settle-

ment on terms acceptable to Washington. South Vietnam was intact as an independent state.

It might be argued that the story should not end there, that it should include air operations in Cambodia which continued until 15 August 1973; the final collapse which resulted in the evacuation of Saigon on 30 April 1975; and perhaps even the *Mayaguez* incident of 12 May 1975. But the author would like to submit that whatever happened after Commander Weichman landed on *Oriskany* is not legitimately a part of this history. This narrative describes a war from its beginning

to its end, and any reader will agree that the warriors in that conflict carried out their difficult job with courage and honor. What happened afterward was not caused by young men like Dennis Weichman who fight our battles for us but, rather, by old men like me who make policy. Every man who flew against North Vietnam knew from the beginning that the battle could have ended with South Vietnam surviving, not merely for a decent interval, but permanently. It is the diplomat, not the warrior, who must be held to account if the air war was won in vain.

END NOTES

CHAPTER TWO. 1965

1. Titus, Colonel Robert F. (later Brigadier General) 'Air to Air Experience in Southeast Asia' (SECRET/NOFORN), paper prepared for AIAA Missile Conference, 10–12 January 1969 (declassified 31 December 1977).
2. Personal correspondence with author.
3. Sharp, Admiral U. S. G., 'Report on the War in Vietnam (As of 30 June 1968)' paper prepared in 1968 (UNCLASSIFIED).
4. Ibidem.
5. Correspondence.
6. Correspondence.
7. Hopkins, Charles K., *SAC Tanker Operations in the Southeast Asia War*, Omaha: Headquarters, Strategic Air Command, Office of History, 1979, p. 47.
8. Graham, Major General Gordon M. (later Lieutenant General), 'End of Tour Report' (SECRET), paper prepared 1 August 1967 (declassified 31 December 1977).
9. Correspondence.
10. Titus, Colonel Robert F., op. cit.
11. Titus, Colonel Robert F., op. cit.
12. Graham, Major General Gordon M. (later Lieutenant General), personal correspondence with author.

CHAPTER THREE. 1966

13. Momyer, General William W. 'End of Tour Report' (SECRET), paper prepared 1968 [declassified 31 December 1977].
14. Momyer, General William W., op. cit.
15. Graham, Lt/Gen. Gordon M., op. cit.
16. O'Neil, Captain Edward W. Jr 'Flying 'In the Barrel' Summer 1966' (SECRET) written summer 1966 (declassified 31 December 1974).
17. Correspondence.
18. Titus, Colonel Robert F., op. cit.
19. Correspondence.
20. Bowers, Ray L. *The United States Air Force in Southeast Asia: Tactical Airlift*, Washington: Headquarters, United States Air Force, 1983, p. 429.
21. Interview with author, 20 January 1986.
22. Interview with author, 20 January 1986.
23. Bowers, Ray L., op. cit., p. 430.
24. Interview with author, 20 January 1986.
25. Interview with author, 10 December 1985. This interview, arranged by the US Air Force Office of Public Affairs, included a round-table discussion with veterans of the 20th squadron, Lt Col. Edward Glass, Lt Col. Philip D. Stinson,

Major Frank A. Gray, Major Joseph L. Viviano and public affairs representative TSGT Thaddeus Hosley.
26. Bowers, Ray L, op. cit., p. 430.
27. Momyer, General William W. *Air Power in Three Wars (World War II, Korea, Vietnam.* Washington; Headquarters, United States Air Force, 1978, p. 220.
28. Correspondence.
29. Interview with author, 22 January 1986.
30. Correspondence. Letter from Major Myron L. Donald, 30 November 1977.
31. 'Memo for Gen. Graham, SLAR/IR' (SECRET), 15 November 1966 (declassified 31 December 1977).
32. Correspondence. Letter from Brig. Gen. Robert F. Titus, 1 January 1986.
33. Correspondence. Letter from Lt Gen. Gordon M. Graham, 20 December 1985.
34. Karnow, Stanley. *Vietnam: A History.* New York: Viking Press, 1983.

CHAPTER FOUR. 1967

35. Correspondence. Letter from Michael A. France, 1 January 1984.
36. Momyer, Gen. William W. op. cit.
37. Memorandum. Broughton, Colonel Jacksel. 'Application for Correction of Military Records,' 22 December 1967.
38. Cable from Momyer to Ryan, 000327 May 1967 (SECRET) (declassified 31 December 1975).
39. Correspondence. Letter from Colonel Omni L. Bailes, 3 November 1985.
40. Titus, Brigadier General Robert F, op. cit. Many years after the conflict, General Titus was interested to look back at what he had written and was delighted to obtain a copy of his paper on air-to-air missiles and fighter combat from the author.
41. Graham, Major General Gordon M., op. cit.
42. Interview with Major General Thomas G. McInerney, 14 February 1986.
43. Momyer, General William W., op. cit., pp. 8–10.
44. Ibidem
45. *Historical Highlights of the First Twenty-Five Years of PACAF: Pacific Air Forces, 1957–1981.* Hawaii, 1982: US Air Force.

CHAPTER FIVE. 1968

46. Correspondence.
47. Momyer, General William W., op. cit., p. 10.

48. Correspondence.
49. Momyer, General William W., op. cit., pp. 10–14.
50. Iungerich, Raphael. *From the Jaws of Victory.* Unpublished essay, quoted with permission.

CHAPTER SIX. 1969

51. Interview with Paul Crickmore, 21 March 1986.
52. Ginsburg, Colonel Gordon A. (later Brigadier General) *The Lavelle Case: Crisis in Integrity.* Professional Study no. 5255, Air War College, Maxwell AFB, Alabama (UNCLASSIFIED). Used with General Ginsburg's kind permission.
53. Ibidem.
54. Interview with Major General Frank C. Lang, 7 August 1973.

CHAPTER EIGHT. 1971

55. Ginsburg, Colonel Gordon A., op. cit., p. 49.
56. Interview with Colonel Andrew Baird, 6 June 1982. Also, correspondence.

CHAPTER NINE. 1972

57. Interviews with Commander Michael A. Ruth, 11 October 1983 and 2 January 1985.
58. Cross, Captain Jerry, USMC. *F-4 Training Optimization.* US Marine Corps report (UNCLASSIFIED), October 1984, provided courtesy Mike Spick.
59. Ibidem.
60. Ibidem.
61. PACAF, op. cit.
62. 'An Interview With Lt Col. Chuck DeBellevue' *The Navigator* (AFRP 50-3, Volume XXX, Number 3, Winter 1983) (UNCLASSIFIED). Used with permission.
63. Interview with Lt Col. John D. Cummings, 18 August 1985. Also research notes prepared on interview with Cummings by Mike O'Connor, provided courtesy Mike O'Connor and used with permission.
64. Ibidem.
65. Ibidem.
66. Correspondence.
67. PACAF, op. cit.

INDEX